History
of
France

History of France

Revised and Enlarged Edition

G. de Bertier de Sauvigny
Catholic Institute of Paris

David H. Pinkney
University of Washington

French text translated by James Friguglietti
Eastern Montana College

Forum Press, Inc.
Arlington Heights, Illinois 60004

English translation and revision
Copyright © 1983
The Forum Press, Inc.
All Rights Reserved

This book, or parts thereof, must not be used or reproduced in
any manner without written permission. For information,
address the publisher, Forum Press, Inc., 3110 North Arlington
Heights Road, Arlington Heights, Illinois 60004-1592.

Histoire de France copyright © 1977 by Flammarion.

Library of Congress Cataloging in Publication Data

Bertier de Sauvigny, Guillaume de, 1912–
    History of France.

    Bibliography: p.
    Includes index.

    1. France—History.   I. Pinkney, David H.   II. Title.
DC38.B4713   1983   944   82-20978
ISBN 0-88273-425-3 (pbk.)
ISBN 0-88273-426-1

Cover illustrations: Front cover, Chartres Cathedral (Photo by
George Kufrin/Free Lance Photographers Guild, Inc.); back cover, Pompidou Center (Photo by G. Clyde/Alpha Photo Associates, Inc.).

Manufactured in the United States of America
95 94 93   MG   5

Contents

Graph

Maps

Genealogical Charts

Tables

Preface

The larger part of this book is the work of the French author, G. de Bertier de Sauvigny. It grew out of a course on the history of France that he offered at the American College in Paris from 1970 to 1976 and from his conviction that a need existed for a brief, basic history of France especially adapted to the requirements of readers who came to the subject with little previous knowledge of it. Such a volume should provide, he believed, the framework of dates, events, and names indispensable to an understanding of French history, literature, and art, and around which additional knowledge could be systematically organized. His *Histoire de France*, published by Flammarion in 1977, he intended, would fill this prescription. That it achieved his goal is abundantly demonstrated by its large and continuing sales and its early translation and publication in German.

Professor de Bertier's book was devoted largely to political history and personalities. The director of The Forum Press believed that the American market required a somewhat fuller book, including more social, economic, and cultural history. For this new edition, the American author, David H. Pinkney, wrote most of the sections dealing with those areas of history and combined them with Professor de Bertier's text. He has also made minor changes in that text to adapt it to use by Americans—university students and others—and to incorporate recent scholarship that is significant to such a basic book.

Both authors are grateful to James Friguglietti for his careful translation into English of Professor de Bertier's French text and to Barbara Salazar for her meticulous editing of the entire manuscript.

G. de Bertier de Sauvigny
David H. Pinkney

Introduction

At dawn on August 15, 1944, an American soldier stood at the rail of a ship in the vast invasion armada that lay off the coast of southern France and watched the lush and beautiful land emerging in the morning light. "Man!" he exclaimed. "Is this ever a place for an invasion!"[1] That American soldier on that lovely dawn in 1944 expressed, probably unknowingly, a sentiment more than two thousand years old. Preceding him to France's colorful shores, fertile valleys, rich fields, and in time lively cities had come the Celts, the Phoenicians, the Greeks, the Romans, the Huns, the Goths, the Burgundians, the Franks, the Muslims, the Normans, the English, the Italians, and the Germans. Not all came as invaders and conquerors. The Valois and Bourbon kings attracted artists, architects, and craftsmen. English, German, and Russian aristocrats on the grand tour in the eighteenth century were the first in a long line of tourists. In the nineteenth century Americans came to study medicine, art, and architecture, and the English established a veritable colony on the French Riviera. In the 1920s came the American

---

1. We are indebted for this story to David Schoenburn, *As France Goes* (New York, 1968), p. 3.

literary expatriates—Ernest Hemingway, F. Scott Fitzgerald, Archibald Macleish, and many others.

Over the centuries many who came stayed on. Thousands of Roman soldiers never went home when their duty in France was completed. The Franks, come from across the Rhine, settled down and took over the country. Many who could not stay carried away with them a rich and sustaining memory of life in France and especially in Paris. Ernest Hemingway wrote, "If you are lucky enough to have lived in Paris as a young man, then wherever you go for the rest of your life, it stays with you, for Paris is a moveable feast."

French history is a moveable feast, too. It waits to be tasted and consumed by all who wish to enjoy its pleasures and rewards. It can be nourishing and entertaining, exciting and instructive. To hope to understand France and the French without a knowledge of French history is to entertain an illusion, because for the French their history is very much a part of their present. One cannot know how they see themselves and their role in the world, including their relation to the United States, without knowing their history. It is a very long history, in contrast with our three or four centuries. It goes back almost three millennia, to pre-Roman times, and the more one knows of this long story, the more likely one is to understand and to appreciate. And a good knowledge of French history has another use—it is an essential introduction to all European history. "Since the Frankish invasion of Clovis [fifth century of the Christian era]," an English author recently declared, "the history of Europe is more the history of France than that of any other country."

For four and a half centuries, moreover—since the sixteenth century, when the French began to explore and settle in North America— the histories of France and the United States have been intertwined, and each has profoundly influenced the other. It is widely known that French ideas contributed to the American Revolution and influenced the shaping of the new American republic, but how many Americans know that the first American political parties were an outgrowth of the French Revolution, that the United States Navy was created in reaction to decisions made by Frenchmen in Paris, or that the United States Military Academy was modeled on a French military school? Well known, too, is the United States' role in the liberation of France from German occupation in 1944, but how many Americans know that American financial and technical aid and example launched an industrial revolution that transformed France in the 1950s and 1960s?

French history illuminates American history and the American present. For the past two and a half centuries the French and the Americans have discerned the great problems of government, of social and economic organization, and of human change and progress in similar ways, and the French past is a rich treasury of experience in efforts to solve those problems.

This book offers the American reader a quick tour of French history from the Celts and the Gauls to the presidency of François Mitterrand. It touches on the great events, calls attention to the great sights, introduces the leading personalities, and underscores the most important developments in politics and government, in the economy, in society, and in cultural life. The reader will complete the book, we hope, with a sense of the long course of French history, a clear conception of the sequence of major events and developments, and some understanding of how France came to be what it is today.

SUGGESTIONS FOR FURTHER READING

Blumenthal, Henry. *American and French Culture, 1800–1900: Interchanges in Art, Science, Literature, and Society.* Baton Rouge, 1975.

Brinton, Crane. *The Americans and the French.* Cambridge, 1968.

Duroselle, Jean-Baptiste. *France and the United States from the Beginnings to the Present Day.* Chicago, 1978.

Echeverria, Durand. *Mirage in the West: A History of the French Image of American Society to 1815.* Princeton, 1957.

Jones, Howard Mumford. *America and French Culture, 1750–1848.* Chapel Hill, N.C., 1927.

Rémond, René. *Les Etats-Unis devant l'opinion française, 1815–1852.* 2 vols. Paris, 1962.

I
The Origins

The country that is today called France emerged into history during the age of the Roman Empire, when it was called Gaul (Gallia), the land of the Gauls. Only much later did it come to be known as Francia, the country of the Franks, the German tribe that in the meantime had established its dominion over most of Roman Gaul.

The history of the country we know as France began only in 843, after the division of the empire of Charlemagne, greatest of the Frankish rulers. But if before that date France did not exist as a state, the country was there, and so was its population, marked by the material and intellectual cultures of successive waves of earlier peoples. Thus any study of the history of France must begin with a brief outline of those ancient cultures that have become part of the body and soul of the French people.

I. THE EARLY PEOPLES

The Prehistoric Period. The valleys of southern France provided a favorable environment for the primitive cave dwellers who lived by hunting and gathering. It was in this region that the most impressive traces of

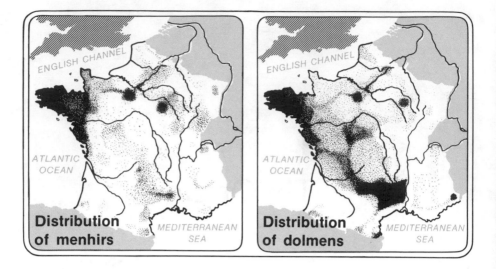

Distribution of menhirs

Distribution of dolmens

human prehistory have been found, such as the famous cave paintings at Lascaux, which go back to about 20,000 B.C.

Between 2,000 and 1,500 B.C. there spread across all of Western Europe, including the British Isles, a culture that has been called megalithic (from the Greek *megas*, great, and *lithos*, stone), because of the giant monuments of unfinished stone that these people erected. In France these megaliths are most numerous and visible in Brittany; the formations at Carnac are composed of no fewer than 2,000 menhirs (long stones) arranged in seven regular rows. But such menhirs, or dolmens, are also found in other French provinces. Megaliths that have today disappeared have left traces in such place names as Pierrefitte (raised stone) and Pierrelatte (wide stone).

Greek Colonization. The most advanced peoples of the eastern Mediterranean appeared on the coasts of France and Spain about 1,000 B.C. First came the Phoenicians, who established trading posts or ports on such present-day sites as Monaco and Port Vendres. What interested them most were copper and tin, the elements needed to make bronze, which were extracted from mines in Spain, the Pyrenees, and even remote Cornwall, and then transported to Mediterranean ports by sea or even by overland routes.

The Greeks soon followed in the Phoenicians' footsteps, but they were not satisfied with ports alone. Around the year 600 B.C. they established a true city named Massilia, or Massalia, near the mouth of the great Rhône Valley. The mother city of this colony was Phocaea, on the coast of Asia Minor in what is now Turkey. When the Persian invaders besieged and captured Phocaea, a large part of its population took refuge in Massalia, which soon became a prosperous metropolis and spawned a chain of other Greek settlements along the coasts of France and Spain. The names of several modern cities recall those of ancient Greek colonies: for example, Nice (Nike, victory), Antibes (Antipolis, meaning "the town across [the bay]"), and Agde (Agathe, from *agathos*, good). Even today the inhabitants of Marseilles like to call themselves Phocaeans. Recent construction in the city's center has unearthed interesting remains of the ancient Greek town.

The Greeks did not venture to settle in the interior of the country, but their trade routes extended far to the north. A remarkable testimony to the importance of this trade is the great bronze krater (vase) discovered in 1953 at Vix, about 310 miles north of Marseilles. The use of money and writing was introduced along with trade goods.

The Arrival of the Celts. About the same time that the Greeks settled at Marseilles, the interior of the country was being invaded by the Celts or Kelts, a people who came from the mountainous region of central Europe. Possession of iron weapons, horses, and chariots enabled these warrior tribes to subdue the original inhabitants, who soon assimilated their conquerors. The Celts also spread into Italy, and the Romans fought a hard struggle before they managed to drive the invaders back beyond the Alps. As we have seen, the land of the Celts soon became known as Gallia.

II. INDEPENDENT GAUL

What contemporary French culture owes to the Celtic or Gallic period (600–50 B.C.) seems almost negligible compared to the rich heritage from the period of Roman domination. An introduction to French history and literature, however, cannot ignore the mythic image of the ancient Gauls as it was revived by the historians and poets of the early nineteenth century, notably Chateaubriand in his epic novel *The Martyrs*. Myth and history received a new impulse after France's defeat in the Franco-Prussian War of 1870–71, when the French projected into the distant past their hatred of everything German and glorified the Gauls' resistance to their conquerors, whether Roman or German. A form of popular imagery, instilled in generations of schoolchildren, thus became a part of the French national tradition.

The People and the Government. An estimated 15 million people lived in Gaul before the Roman conquest. It was divided into some sixty tribal states. Many factors explain this lack of unity, the most important no doubt being the great size of a country where dense forests, vast swamps, and wide rivers isolated one settled area from another. The names of a good number of these tribes, as the Romans recorded them, are still recognizable in the names of modern French towns and provinces (see Table 1).

Table 1. French towns and provinces named for Gallic tribes

TRIBE	TOWN	PROVINCE
Ambiani	Amiens	
Andegavi	Angers	Anjou
Atrebates	Arras	
Bituriges	Bourges	Berry
Carnutes	Chartres	
Cenomani	Le Mans	Maine
Lemovicences	Limoges	Limousin
Namnetes	Nantes	
Pictavi	Poitiers	Poitou
Senones	Sens	
Tricasses	Troyes	
Turones	Tours	Touraine
Veneti	Vannes	

In most of these primitive states power had been torn from the families of kings or chieftains by the warrior aristocrats, who governed through elected officials and more or less regular assemblies. Often the lower classes rebelled against the ruling minority and sought protection in a restoration of monarchy. As a result of these upheavals and continuing rivalries among the ruling families, the tribes and towns lived in an almost permanent state of unrest and insecurity.

Social Conditions. While government took many forms, social structure, customs, and religion remained virtually the same throughout Gaul. Two privileged classes dominated the rest of the population—the priests, or druids, and the nobles, or *equites*, as the Romans called them.

The druids were trained for their position by years of study that concentrated not only on secret rituals but on astronomy, medicine, and philosophy as well. They comprised a highly respected and privileged class, exempt from military service and taxes. They served as judges and teachers. Each year druids from all over the country came together in the land of the Carnutes to elect a supreme leader. Associated with the druids and enjoying some of their privileges were the bards, who were, so to speak, the living memory of the people. The long poems that they sang during festivities recalled the legends of the gods and the great deeds of ancient heroes.

The nobles were rich men who owned land and horses. Their political power and social influence depended on the number of men they could raise for war: slaves, clients who served them in return for protection, and warriors who (like the Japanese samurai) followed their masters even into death.

The freemen among the common people subsisted on an economy based on farming, herding, and hunting. All adult men took up arms when the need arose and fought alongside the cavalry of the nobility.

Some of these features of Gallic society may perhaps be seen in medieval society: a clergy that benefited from the same privileges as the druids, and a weaker class that customarily received the protection of a strong man in exchange for dues and services.

Life and Customs. Dwellings were circular huts made of timber, branches, and clay, covered with straw or reeds, with an opening at the top to allow smoke to escape from the central hearth. The towns, which the Romans called *oppida* (the plural of *oppidum*), were sometimes extensive, but they in no way resembled the Greek and Roman cities. They were only enclosed spaces in which the surrounding population might find refuge in times of danger. Their walls were rudimentary constructions of unfinished stones or tree trunks. Consequently, today nothing remains of these fortifications.

The Gauls wore a long loose shirt, bound at the waist by a belt; long trousers (*braies* in Old French, from the Latin *braca*); and over that a kind of shawl or poncho (*saie* in Old French, from the Latin *saga*). Their woolen cloth was roughly woven and dyed in bright colors, often with stripes and squares like the Scottish plaids. Men liked to wear heavy collars and bracelets of precious worked metal. These objects have been unearthed in their tombs; together with arms and coins, they provide the principal source of our knowledge of the Gallic artists' skill.

Roman authors provided a rather flattering picture of the Gauls' national character; they saw them as brave, lively, gifted at speaking, and sociable, but also headstrong, vain, unstable, quarrelsome, and altogether allergic to discipline. It is not difficult to recognize here some of the traits that foreign observers have attributed to the French in all ages.

Religion. Little is known about the Gauls' religious beliefs, for the druids strictly forbade them to put religious matters in writing, and until they were Romanized, the Gauls never made pictorial representations of their divinities. Their gods were largely personifications of such natural forces as light, night, storms, trees, and water.

The name of the god Borbo, who was believed to be present in springs, can today be found in the names of such thermal spas as Bourbon-Lancy, Bourbonne, and La Bourboule; and even, by way of a place name, the name of the last ruling family of France—the Bourbons.

The ritual gathering of mistletoe on certain days by druids wielding sickles with golden blades was connected with the worship of forests. A more repellent aspect of this primitive religion was human sacrifice; the victim was sometimes burned alive in a wicker frame. As late as the beginning of the seventeenth century, sacrifices of this kind took place at the solstice, with animals replacing humans. This is only one of numerous obscure survivals of Celtic culture in popular folklore; others include tombs of legendary saints, miraculous springs, sites of pilgrimages, and seasonal festivals, which were simply adopted by the first Christian missionaries.

III. ROMAN GAUL

The Conquest. The Romans began their conquest of Gaul about 120 B.C. They had been summoned by the people of Marseilles, who were being threatened by the Gallic tribes of the area. Soon the entire Mediterranean coast fell under Roman domination. This addition to the territory of the Roman Republic was called Provincia, *the* province par excellence; from Provincia came the present name, Provence. As many features of the landscape and language suggest, this province became more deeply imprinted by Latin culture than other parts of the country.

Between 58 and 50 B.C. Julius Caesar conquered all of the rest of Gaul. He accomplished this task with relative ease, for the undisciplined Gallic hordes were no match for the well-armed and well-trained Roman legions. But even more effective was the skill with which Caesar played on the rivalries among the various peoples and their chieftains. All the same, there were difficult battles. At one point the brave young chief of the Arvernes, Vercingetorix, succeeded in allying the majority of tribes and inflicted severe losses on Caesar's troops. But finally he was encircled and besieged with his army in the fortress at Alesia (the modern Alise-Sainte-Reine, in upper Burgundy) and was forced to surrender. The heroic figure of Vercingetorix was glorified in the nineteenth century as the symbol of national resistance to foreign invasion.

Roman domination was accepted fairly readily by the conquered. The conquerors had the wisdom to respect local customs and institutions. To the ruling aristocracy the Romans gave titles and official functions; to the warriors they opened the ranks of the army. In a short time a good number of the best generals and administrators of the Empire were of Gallic origin. The process of assimilation was virtually completed when the emperor Caracalla conferred Roman citizenship on all Gauls in A.D. 215.

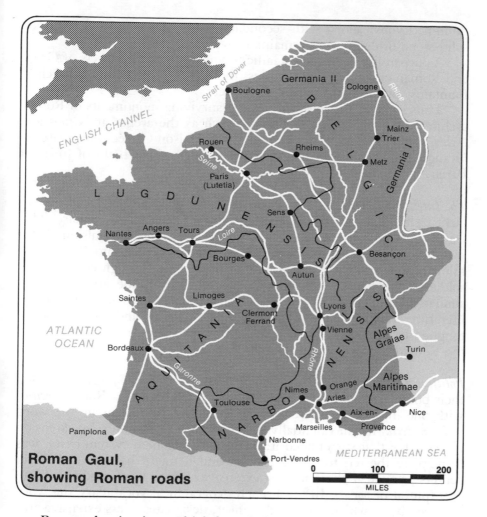

Roman Gaul, showing Roman roads

Roman domination, which lasted almost five centuries, had a deep and permanent impact on all aspects of French culture.

Material Progress. The Romans introduced into Gaul plants and fruit trees of Mediterranean stock along with techniques of agriculture and cattle breeding. The most remarkable of these acquisitions was the grapevine. Its eventual extension northward into climates where grapes could barely ripen can be explained by the fact that the church needed wine for the mass. Industry also benefited from the introduction of Roman technology, especially in textiles and arms.

The most visible accomplishment was a comprehensive network of roads. Five principal routes—real, paved roads—radiated out from Lugdunum (Lyons), along with secondary roads. They crossed rivers on solid stone bridges, some remains of which are still visible.

As urban life developed, Gallic towns imitated all aspects of Greek and Roman cities: forums, temples, theaters, arenas, triumphal arches, fountains, public baths fed by aqueducts.

Thus some of the most interesting surviving monuments of Roman architecture can be seen in France, such as the arenas at Nîmes and Arles, the temple at Nîmes known as the Maison Carrée, the theater at Orange, the bridge-aqueduct over the Gard, and the baths of Julian at Paris.

The Intellectual Heritage. The Latin language gradually replaced the ancient Celtic dialects; only in Brittany did a Celtic tongue persist. This transformation took place very naturally, under no compulsion. Latin was first adopted by the upper class, eager to enter into Roman administration, and then spread among the people through contact with soldiers, merchants, and settlers. Nonetheless, if the aristocracy assimilated Latin culture—and so well that some famous authors of Latin literature were of Gallic origin, such as Petronius and Ausonius—the tongue that the people learned was a corrupt Latin, from which sprang the Romanic language, the source of modern French.

Political Organization. The original Gallic states generally preserved their boundaries and local governments. Each became a Roman *civitas*, with one important difference: in Greek and Roman usage the word *polis* or *civitas* meant essentially the urban center and only by extension the country that surrounded it; in the Gallo-Roman system *civitas* was principally the territory of a people, and it might have several urban centers or none at all. The most extensive *civitates* were subdivided into *pagi* (plural of *pagus*). In the French geographical vocabulary the word *pays* (country), which is derived from it, designates a less extensive area than a province, sometimes the successor to a *civitas*. The administration of the Gallo-Roman *civitas* was gradually adapted to the Roman model, with a senate or curia elected by a popular assembly, and with officials chosen each year.

The symbol of unity was the worship of the emperor and of Rome. A colossal altar dedicated to Rome and to Augustus was erected at Lyons, the center of Roman administration. Delegations from the *civitates* assembled annually at the base of the altar to renew their pledge of loyalty by offering a solemn sacrifice. This gathering also gave them the opportunity to consider questions of common interest, so that it was in fact a kind of consultative assembly, which might eventually appeal directly to the emperor.

Christianity. As they did elsewhere, the Romans attempted to assimilate the local deities by identifying them with the gods of the Greco-Roman pantheon.

About the end of the first century the Christian religion was introduced into several of the major towns, notably Lyons, celebrated for its bishop Ireneus and the young martyr Blandina. Not until the end of the third century was an effort made to Christianize the people of the *pagi*, the *pagani* (pagans). When the emperor Constantine officially recognized the Christian religion in 313, the church was organized readily within the Roman administrative framework, with each *civitas* becoming a diocese governed by a bishop.

Soon the bishop became the most important figure in the town. Elected by the local body of Christians, he held a permanent position, unlike other elected dignitaries. This fact, combined with the religious character of his office, invested him with superior moral authority. The emperors themselves added to the bishops' privileges by exempting them, and all other clergy as well, from taxes and military service, and from the jurisdictions of the civil courts. The bishops served as judges over their subordinates and generally in cases that involved religion. Finally, with the accumulation of gifts, legacies, and taxes paid by the people, the bishop found himself possessed of a fortune, mostly in land, which he administered to support the charitable and educational work assumed by the church.

Under the impact of barbarian invasions, the Roman administration disintegrated; imperial officials lost their power for want of military and financial resources, and local authorities fled. In these circumstances the bishops were often the only ones to whom the people could turn. Organizing town defenses and negotiating with the invaders, they helped to preserve some of the benefits of the Roman Empire in Gaul.

Thus circumstances gave the clergy a political role that it was to exercise throughout the long history of France, sometimes to the detriment of its spiritual mission.

SUGGESTIONS FOR FURTHER READING

Brogan, Olwen. *Roman Gaul.* London, 1953.

Daniel, Glyn. *The Megalithic Builders of Western Europe.* London, 1958.

Powell, T. G. E. *The Celts.* London, 1958.

Sandars, Nancy K. *The Bronze Age Cultures in France: The Later Phases from the Thirteenth to the Ninth Centuries B.C.* Cambridge, Eng., 1957.

Duval, P. M. *La vie quotidienne en Gaule pendant la paix romaine.* Paris, 1953.

Lot, Ferdinand. *La Gaule: Les fondations ethniques, sociaux et politiques de la nation française.* New ed. Paris, 1967.

2
The Merovingian Era

During the fifth century, the political structure of Roman Gaul was destroyed by the eruption of barbarian peoples into the Empire. While their chieftains were carving out rather short-lived kingdoms, the wreckage accumulated and the general state of insecurity broke down social organization. The new masters, however, changed their ways of doing things as they came into contact with the Gallo-Roman population. The concept of the country's basic unity survived, as well as identification with a larger entity—the Empire. Eventually most of ancient Gaul fell under the rule of a Frankish dynasty, the Merovingians. Their domination, which lasted more than two centuries (the sixth and seventh), saw the birth of a new culture, the result of the fusion of German elements, Christianity, and remnants of the Roman order.

I. THE INVASIONS

Barbarians and Romans. To the Romans, all peoples who lived outside the limits of the Empire were barbarians. On the northwest border, beyond the Rhine, these tribes were basically Germanic. Seminomadic, more backward than the Gauls at the time of the Roman conquest, the Germans considered war to be the sole occupation worthy of adult males. Under the leadership of elected chiefs, they formed bands that went off to war on their own account or in the service of someone else.

To protect themselves from such incursions the Romans had created a border defense system in depth, made up of entrenched camps, fortified towns, and strategic roads. By the end of the fourth century this border zone, or *limes*, which had once crossed southern Germany, had been pulled back to the Rhine. A major army, based in the Paris basin, had to be able to move rapidly toward threatened points. As the central power weakened, the successive leaders of this army saw their authority grow to such a point that some of them sought to become independent monarchs.

The *limes*, however, did not constitute an impermeable barrier. During the latter half of the third century, a first wave of barbarians had flooded into Roman Gaul, leaving occasional islands of alien peoples. Eventually the Roman authorities, after restoring order, tended to favor a kind of peaceful penetration, first enlisting the barbarian warriors in their service as auxiliaries, then incorporating them as legionnaires. Barbarian chieftains received high military rank and civic honors. As civilian labor became scarcer, the barbarians were recruited as servants in the towns and as farm workers on the great estates. Communities of settlers, or *letes*, were established on uncultivated land. Some present-day place names recall these establishments: Allemagne (Germany) and Allemanche from the Alamanni; Gueux from the Gots; Marmagne from the Marcomani; Sermaize and Salmaise from the Sarmatians; Gandalou from the Vandals.

Thus the Germanic penetration was already well under way when, at the beginning of the fifth century, it suddenly took a catastrophic turn.

The Visigoths. The mass migration of the Germanic peoples had been provoked by the appearance on their eastern flanks of Asian invaders who were particularly fearsome—the Huns (of whom more later). The first to feel the blow were the Visigoths and the Ostrogoths in southern Russia. They took refuge first in the Balkan provinces of the Empire (378); then in 405, under the leadership of their king Alaric, they crossed into Italy and ravished it. Rome itself was captured and pillaged in 410. They went on to invade southern Gaul with the intention of crossing into Africa through Spain. But the emperor Honorius negotiated with their king and permitted them to settle permanently in the invaded provinces, all of Aquitaine from Bordeaux to Toulouse, in accordance with the so-called hospitality system. The barbarian soldiers were quartered with the residents, who had to support them, and their king exercised full military authority in the name of the emperor. The impotent and disarmed civil administration remained in theory in the hands of the imperial bureaucracy. Later, in the reign of King Euric (466–485), this first great barbarian state within the Empire spread over all of southern Gaul from the Atlantic to the Loire, to the Rhône, and beyond the Pyrenees till it covered most of Spain.

Alamanni, Burgundians, and Bretons. The shock waves that hurled the Goths into the Empire reached the Germanic tribes east of the Rhine by the end of the year 406. En masse they broke through the defenses of the *limes*, whose garrisons had been summoned home to Italy. Some of them swept like a torrent across the whole country: the Alans, Suevi, and Vandals ravaged the Gallic provinces for two years, then crossed into Spain to pillage and then to settle there.

Others, who roamed less widely, eventually established permanent settlements. The Alamanni settled in the Alsatian plain and in portions of Switzerland. Highly resistant to Roman culture, they created in these areas a linguistic zone that has lasted until our own time.

The Burgundians, who first settled in the Rhineland, later moved into what is now French-speaking Switzerland, around Geneva. From there they spread into the valleys of the Rhône and Saône rivers. At the beginning of the sixth century the Burgundian king Gondebaud ruled over a vast state between the Juras and the Alps to the east and the upper reaches of the Loire to the west, bounded on the north by the plateau of Langres and on the south by the Durance River. This state, destroyed by the Franks in 536, left such deep traces that it periodically revived and gave its name to the French province of Burgundy.

In a similar way the name of Brittany was imposed on the Roman province of Armorica. At the end of the fifth century, the Bretons, driven from Great Britain by the Saxon invasion, sought refuge there. They readily assimilated with the native population, since the latter had kept alive the basic features of Celtic culture.

The Franks. By the end of the third century the Franks, who had long been settled on the lower reaches of the Rhine, had reached accommodation with the Roman authorities. In exchange for military service, they were granted land west of the Rhine in what is now Belgium. Taking advantage of the disorganization that followed the cracking of the *limes* at the end of 406, they moved slowly toward the south. One group, the Riparian Franks, occupied the region of the lower Moselle and Meuse rivers; another group, the Salians, advanced as far as the Somme after taking Tournai and Cambrai. Merovaeus, king of one Salic tribe, the Sicambri, founded a dynasty of leaders who reunited Gaul in a great Frankish kingdom.

The Huns. The Huns, nomadic Mongol shepherds from the steppes of central Asia, had unleashed the mass movement of Germanic invaders. They inspired terror by the lightning speed of their raids, which were led by a handful of horsemen, and their ferocity, which spared no one. By the mid-fifth century their king, Attila, had carved out a vast empire, and the Romans sent him tribute. In 451 Attila crossed the Rhine with his hordes, devastated Belgium, and penetrated the Paris basin. Everyone fled before him. The Parisians prepared to abandon their city but were dissuaded from doing so by the pleas of a woman venerated as a prophetess—St. Geneviève. Attila did in fact turn from an attack on Paris to besiege Orléans.

The resistance by the town of Paris, organized by Bishop Anianus, allowed the Roman general Aetius to assemble an army composed of the Roman legions under his Gallic commander and contingents of barbarians who had settled in Gaul—Visigoths, Burgundians, and Franks. When this army arrived before Orléans, Attila retreated to the plains of Champagne, which were more suitable for maneuvers by his mounted warriors. In 451 a decisive battle took place between Sens and Troyes, at the site known as the Catalaunian Fields. The Huns, who were vanquished but not destroyed, retired beyond the Rhine with their plunder. Attila died shortly afterward, in 463, and his empire collapsed. The episode throws into relief the collaboration and the beginnings of the fusion of the Gallo-Roman peoples and the settled German invaders.

II. THE FRANKISH KINGDOM—CLOVIS

Clovis. Clovis, the grandson of Merovaeus and son of Childeric, one of the best of Aetius' commanders, became king of the Sicambri in 481. The last emperor of the West, Romulus Augustulus, had been deposed at Rome in 476. About the same time that Clovis became king of the Sicambri, the Roman general Syagrius, a successor to Aetius, proclaimed himself king of Rome. Clovis, declaring himself the avenger of imperial authority, still represented by the emperor of the East at Constantinople, attacked and deposed Syagrius in 486. What remained of the Roman army came under his orders, and the town officials rallied to him without difficulty. Paris opened its gates to him, and there Clovis established his main residence, in the ancient palace of the emperor Julian, thus marking the transition from the rule of a small barbarian king to that of a representative of imperial authority.

In this role Clovis undertook to defend the country against an attempted invasion by the Alamanni in 496. His victory at Tolbiac, near Cologne, consolidated his authority.

Shortly afterward, Clovis took a political action of decisive importance for the future of his dynasty and his country. The two other barbarian peoples settled in Gaul, the Visigoths and the Burgundians, had earlier adopted the Christian religion in its heretical form of Arianism, which was favored by the emperors at Constantinople. The Gallic bishops and people had remained faithful to Roman orthodoxy. This religious difference remained an obstacle between the Gallo-Roman population and its barbarian masters. Until now the Franks had retained their old Germanic religion. In other words, as pagans they had remained above the quarrel between the Arians and the Roman Catholics. In 496 Clovis married Clotilda, a Catholic princess and niece of the Burgundian kings. Under her influence he embraced Roman Catholicism, and with 3,000 of his warriors was baptized at Rheims by the bishop Remi. Thereafter the ruling class of Frankish warriors merged with the Gallo-Roman large landowners and officials. Throughout Gaul the orthodox bishops regarded Clovis as their champion.

In 500 Clovis attacked and defeated the king of the Burgundians but was satisfied to impose tribute on him. Then it was the Visigoths' turn. The war loosed against them in 507 was like a religious crusade. It was decided at Vouillé, near Poitiers, by the defeat and death of the Visigothic king, Alaric II. As a consequence, the entire country between the Loire and the Pyrenees recognized Clovis' authority.

Shortly afterward the Eastern emperor sent him the insignia of patrician and consul, thus formalizing his role as civil and military representative of the Empire. During these years, by murder or treachery, Clovis had succeeded in eliminating the other Frankish kings and securing recognition of his authority over all of these peoples. When he died in 511, his kingdom reached from the Pyrenees to well beyond the Rhine.

The First Merovingians. Clovis' four sons—Thierry, Clodomir, Childebert, and Clotaire I—divided their father's possessions in accordance with Frankish tradition, and each succeeding generation did likewise. As a result, no fewer than thirty members of this Merovingian dynasty bore the royal title simultaneously or successively. It is a confused and bloody story, shot through with conflicts, marriage alliances, murders, usurpations, fratricidal wars, and struggles for succession.

Although it was constantly brought into question, the idea of the fundamental unity of the Frankish kingdom persisted throughout these conflicts. Its subdivisions were composed of complementary parts divided among several regions of Gaul. The provinces that had previously been autonomous—Aquitaine, Burgundy, and Provence—were the most often divided, so that separatist tendencies were thwarted. The towns chosen as capitals by Clovis' four sons—Rheims, Orléans, Paris, and Soissons—were all located in the Paris basin, in the country that had been the center of gravity of the Frankish monarchy in Clovis' time. Paris was even considered to be joint property. And, it was at Paris that the

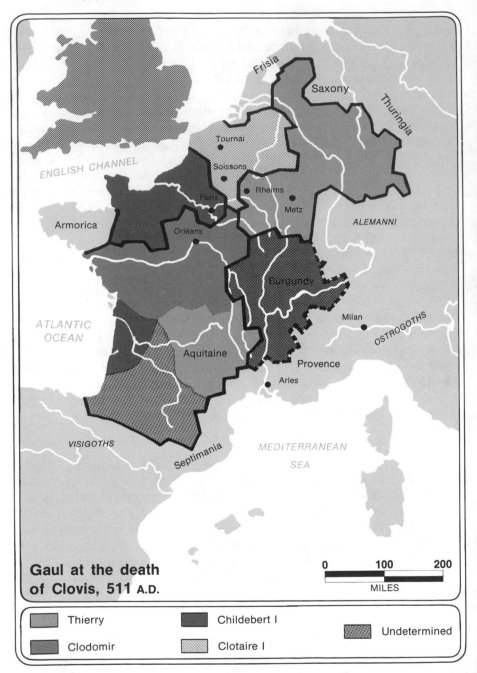

Gaul at the death
of Clovis, 511 A.D.

Thierry		Childebert I	
Clodomir		Clotaire I	Undetermined

seat of government was established at the various times when the whole country was reunified under a single ruler: Clotaire (558–561), Clotaire II (613–623), and his son Dagobert I (629–639).

Dagobert I. Dagobert I is the only Merovingian king who has kept a good reputation, thanks no doubt to the gratitude of the clergy, on whom he conferred many benefits. In particular, he founded the abbey of St. Denis, where he eventually was buried. The church advisers with whom Dagobert surrounded himself, among them the bishops Eloi and Ouen, infused his government with a concern for order, justice, and morality rarely found among the other Merovingian kings.

Frankish Expansion. Together or on their own, the first Merovingian kings sought to extend their boundaries. The conquest and division of the Burgundian kingdom in 536 eliminated the last of the other German kingdoms that remained in ancient Gaul. The annexation of Provence, ceded by the Ostrogothic kingdom of Italy, provided a convenient outlet to the Mediterranean. On the other hand, two repeated attempts failed to conquer Septimania (the modern Lower Languedoc and Roussillon), which remained in the hands of the Spanish Visigoths.

The Merovingians also extended their rule over most of southern Germany, either by outright annexation, as in the kingdom of Thuringia, or in the form of a protectorate, as in Bavaria. This expansionist activity did not continue beyond the end of the sixth century. After the death of Dagobert the Franks lost part of their German conquests, and on other borders they had a difficult time driving back incursions by neighboring peoples.

The Erosion of Royal Power. The power of the Merovingian king was based primarily on a close entourage of high officials charged with service at his court, on a chancellery that dispatched letters and edicts, and on a number of devoted warriors called *leudes* or *antrustions*. Within this rudimentary court the greatest power was naturally in the hands of *major-domus*, the mayor of the palace, who oversaw the vast domains from which the king drew most of his resources.

In the country the old Gallo-Roman jurisdictions, the *civitates* and *pagi*, were governed by counts (*comites*). Holding full power from the king, they were watched and sometimes superseded by the bishops. In some regions a duke (*dux*), the supreme military leader, was elevated over all the counts of a province.

Lacking money, the king offered these officials immunities and land to ensure their loyalty. By the end of the sixth century this land (or benefice), originally granted on a temporary basis, was held for life; finally it became hereditary. Thus the Merovingian monarchy was left without authority when it no longer had anything to give, and true power slipped into the hands of an aristocracy of large landowners who monopolized the offices and dignities of counts and bishops. The most powerful among them got their hands on royal power itself by becoming mayors of the palace.

The Disintegration of the Seventh Century. The idea of the unity of the kingdom was weakened by centrifugal tendencies and divisions more permanent than those established by the partition of the sixth century. The Bretons had always managed to keep their autonomy. Aquitaine under Dagobert became the seat of a duchy whose leaders made themselves virtually independent sovereigns. Later the same thing happened in Burgundy and Provence. Most important, the north of the kingdom, the seat of Frankish power, was divided into two great autonomous units: Austrasia to the east, between the Marne and the Rhine, and Neustria, including most of the Paris basin, between the Somme and the Loire. Austrasia retained a largely Germanic character through its contacts with Germany; Neustria remained more open to foreign influence because of its seacoast and direct contact with the Romanized populations south of the Loire.

After the death of Dagobert the history of Frankish Gaul was dominated by the antagonism between Austrasia and Neustria. The principals in this duel were no longer the Merovingian monarchs, now insignificant kinglets, but the mayors of the palace. At first the Neustrians seemed to have the upper hand, but after the decisive battle of Tertry, near St. Quentin, in 687, the Austrasian mayor of the palace, Pepin II of Herstal (or Héristal), reestablished the Frankish kingdom under a series of puppet kings, degenerate descendants of the Merovingian dynasty. Neustria, however, retained its distinct administration with a mayor of the palace who was none other than Pepin's son.

The Rise of a New Dynasty. During Dagobert's time a powerful family emerged in Austrasia, supported by a network of alliances and clients and with enormous domains in the Meuse and Moselle valleys. Its leader, Pepin of Landen, became mayor of the palace of the Austrasian kingdom. His son and successor, Grimaud, dethroned the Merovingian king and replaced him with his own heir. The attempt proved premature, for Ebroin, the Neustrian mayor of the palace, opposed the move vigorously and restored the representative of the legitimate dynasty to the throne. As we have seen, Pepin II of Herstal took his revenge in the following generation and became in fact, if not in law, the sole master of the Frankish kingdom.

Charles Martel. Pepin II's work seemed to crumble when, at his death in 714, he left as his only heir a six-year-old grandson. Neustrians and Aquitainians seized the opportunity to rebel, and Saxons and Frisians invaded the kingdom. As a result, the nobles of Austrasia chose as their leader a bastard son of Pepin II, Charles Martel. Their confidence was well placed, for through his energy and the amazing swiftness of his military campaigns, Charles soon restored the situation in Neustria and on the northern border. The opportunity for Charles to intervene in the south came in 732, when the Moslems of Spain, who had invaded Gascony, crossed the Garonne and the Dordogne, spreading fear and devastation. The Duke of Aquitaine, who had until now been Charles's enemy, called on him for help. The Franks and Moslems fought a great battle near Poitiers. The victory that Charles Martel won brought him the grateful submission of the Aquitainians, as well as incomparable influence throughout Christendom. The battle was also one of the most decisive for the history of Western Europe, because it stopped what had seemed to be the irresistible spread of Islam.

In succeeding years Charles again had to war against the Moslems, who had taken Arles and Avignon with the connivance of the nobles of Provence. He brought the province back to obedience and drove the Moslems from the Rhône Valley but did not succeed in dislodging them from Narbonne and Roussillon.

In exchange for the services he had thus rendered to Christendom, Charles Martel appropriated a considerable amount of church property and distributed it among his followers and warriors. He was thus far more successful in recruiting followers than his rivals, and did not have to give away his own property to do it, as the unhappy Merovingians had done. By 737 Charles Martel, duke and prince of the Franks, had become so powerful that he could neglect to replace the reigning Merovingian, Thierry IV, who had just died. But the hold of tradition was still so strong that Charles did not yet dare to proclaim himself king. It was left to his son to take this last step, reconciling law and fact and founding a new dynasty.

III. MEROVINGIAN SOCIETY

Towns and Villas. The Merovingian period saw the acceleration of a phenomenon already apparent by the end of the Roman Empire—the decline of urban life. Forced back into their central cities, hastily surrounded by walls that were often built with rubble from public monuments, the towns lost their administrative and even their commercial functions. The former dignitaries retired to their great estates, where they lived with their armed retainers, clients, slaves, and workers of all kinds. The barbarian invaders adapted to this way of life and became masters of the estates or *villas* of the Roman period. This transformation was marked, especially in the north, by the addition of the Latin suffix *court* (*curtis*) or *ville* to the name of a Germanic individual, producing such place names as Agincourt, Beaudricourt, Angerville, and Charleville.

Christianity. At the time of the invasions Christianity had been implanted only in the towns and their environs. Under the influx of barbarians, Christianity retreated in the northern part of the country. The reconquest and Christianization of the countryside began in the south. This task is still associated with the memory of Bishop Martin of Tours, whose name appears frequently on the map of Christian sanctuaries.

The spread of Christianity was marked by the founding of numerous monasteries. The monasticism of the Eastern variety, introduced by St. Honorat at Lerins and several other southern sites, was eclipsed by the monasticism that St. Colomban established in Ireland. His first monastery in France, established at Luxeuil in Burgundy in 590, soon gave birth to a dozen or so others. The rule of St. Benedict was introduced into France at the end of the seventh century, and eventually all but supplanted that of St. Colomban. These monasteries, richly endowed with land by the kings and nobles, became the active nuclei of a complete and self-sufficient economy, rivaling that of the large estates. But in their writing rooms and libraries, the monasteries also safeguarded a part of the cultural heritage of the ancient world, no the Arabs did that

Art and Literature. The Merovingian era contributed little to the architectural and artistic heritage of France. On the contrary, it saw the disappearance of numerous Roman structures, pillaged or demolished to provide material for new fortifications and churches. Today only a few traces of these new structures remain to show their rudimentary technique and small dimensions. The art of the time is best seen in tombs. The sarcophagi were decorated with sculptured motifs drawn from antiquity, and the magnificent jewelry found in them, fashioned with a technical skill superior even to that of the Romans, represented stylized animal forms inspired by the art of the distant peoples of Eastern Europe.

Literature, which was almost nonexistent, has left only one notable work, but one of great importance: the history of the Frankish kings (*Historia regum francorum*), written in Latin by Bishop Gregory of Tours (539–594). From it we draw most of our knowledge of Frankish Gaul.

Formation of the French Nation. The contributions of the Merovingian era to modern France would seem rather meager and even negative if it were not for one essential accomplishment: the fusion between what remained from Roman times and the Germanic contribution, a fusion considerably aided by the conversion of the Franks to Christianity. At the outset Gallo-Romans and barbarians were separated by the fact that in conquered Gaul the principle of personal law was applied: each ethnic group observed its own code of laws. The Franks followed the Salic law written in Clovis' time. But gradually the borrowing of customs that took place along with intermarriage tended to erase ethnic differences, beginning with the ruling aristocracy. This assimilation showed considerable variation from region to region: Germanic culture was more pronounced in the north of the country, while the Gallo-Roman heritage was better preserved in the south.

When one considers the fate of other fragments of the Roman Empire, the unique synthesis achieved in Frankish Gaul appears to be the nucleus of the social order of the medieval West.

SUGGESTIONS FOR FURTHER READING

Gregory of Tours. *The History of the Franks*. 2 vols. Oxford, 1927.

Lasko, Peter. *The Kingdom of the Franks: Northwest Europe before Charlemagne*. New York, 1971.

Latouche, Robert. *Caesar to Charlemagne: The Beginnings of France*. New York, 1968.

Musset, Lucien. *The Germanic Invasions: The Making of Europe, A.D. 400–600*. University Park, Pa., 1975.

Wallace-Hadrill, J. M. *The Long-Haired Kings and Other Studies in Frankish History*. New York, 1962.

Lot, Ferdinand. *Naissance de la France*. Paris, 1970.

3
The Carolingians

The three first monarchs of the new dynasty reunified the kingdom and enormously extended its boundaries by their conquests. This accomplishment was climaxed by the reestablishment of the Western Empire under Charlemagne. Thanks to his orderly and benevolent administration, which was strongly supported by the church, the Western world seemed to awaken for a time.

But this achievement proved to be fragile. The Empire disintegrated into three parts, then into a nebula of independent and rival principalities, while new barbarian invasions ravaged their territories. The ideas of state and monarchy inherited from the Romans disappeared almost entirely, giving way to the new order of feudalism.

I. THE EMPIRE OF CHARLEMAGNE

Pepin the Short (741–768). Before he died Charles Martel had disposed of his kingdom like a true Frankish king, dividing it between his two sons, Carloman and Pepin III, who was called the Short because of his small stature. The two brothers first had to put down the revolts that had broken out in the outlying territories of Aquitaine, Bavaria, Alemannia, and Saxony. To remove any pretext for conspiracies by the great families that rivaled their own, they restored to the throne a last Merovingian, Childeric III, but without actually sacrificing any of their real power. In 747 Carloman abdicated to become a monk at the abbey of Monte Cassino in Italy, and Pepin became the sole ruler.

Having restored order and internal peace, Pepin wrote in these terms to Pope Zachary: "Who deserves to be king, he who lives without worry and risk in his home or he who bears the weight of the entire kingdom?" Since he naturally received the correct answer to his question, Pepin had himself elected king by an assembly of nobles and bishops convened at Soissons in 751. Moreover, in a rite inspired by the Old Testament, he was anointed with sacramental oil by Bishop Boniface. Three years later a new pope, Stephen II, solemnly renewed this ceremony in the basilica of St. Denis, this time with the king's two sons participating. This new ceremony conferred on the new dynasty a strong religious sanction, superior to that of the Merovingians. To Germanic law, in which authority was conferred by election and transmitted by blood, was added divine right, which became an attribute of the French monarchy until its disappearance in the nineteenth century.

The new king repaid his debt of gratitude by warring against the Italian Lombards, who were enemies of the pope. After beating them twice, he detached the ancient Byzantine province of Ravenna and made it a gift to the papacy. The pope thereby became a temporal ruler, with land and subjects like other kings; this situation lasted until 1870. A special alliance was thus created between the papacy and the Carolingian dynasty.

Elsewhere, Pepin retook Septimania, the Mediterranean plain between the Rhône and the Pyrenees, from the Muslims, and in several military expeditions consolidated his authority over all Aquitaine.

The Accession of Charlemagne. At the death of Pepin in 768 the kingdom was once again divided between two sons, Carloman and Charles. And once more unity was accidentally restored by the elimination of one of the heirs, Carloman, who died in 771. Charles thus remained the sole ruler. He was then twenty-nine and had forty-three more years to live. Such longevity, exceptional for the time, was no doubt an essential factor in the greatness of his achievement. It also attests to the powerful vitality of a man whom contemporaries depicted as tall and strongly built, with a love of good food and women, swimming, and hunting. In addition, Charles received an excellent education, unlike the Frankish kings who preceded him. He called to court the Saxon monk Alcuin, considered to be the most knowledgeable man of his time. Charles read and spoke Latin as fluently as the Frankish language; he understood Greek and had some idea of mathematics and astronomy. He liked to have historical accounts or the Scriptures read aloud during his meals.

His Conquests. Each year the king led his army on some expedition, near or far, which resulted in the annexation of new territory or the establishment of an authority subordinated to his own supreme control. No systematic plan inspired his conquests, only a concern to safeguard his subjects against incursions by turbulent neighbors, or to establish the Christian order everywhere. To him, that was the supreme authority.

In Italy Charles seized the Lombard kingdom and adopted its crown. He further enlarged the Papal States and extended his own authority in one form or another over most of the peninsula. Only the southernmost areas of Calabria and Sicily remained under the sway of Byzantium.

He led seven expeditions beyond the Pyrenees into Spain and formed a frontier province, or "Spanish March," on his southern flank, with Barcelona as its capital. It was on the return from the first expedition that the Frankish rear guard, commanded by Count Roland, the king's nephew, was surprised and annihilated at the Pass of Roncevalles by Vascon (Basque) mountaineers, an episode immortalized in the *Song of Roland*, the first great medieval epic poem.

It was in Germany that Charlemagne extended the Frankish kingdom farthest, by incorporating virtually all the Germanic peoples who were still independent. The most stubborn were the Saxons; no fewer than eighteen expeditions, massive deportations, and a network of strategic roads and entrenched camps were needed to overcome them. The task was completed by the conversion of the Saxons to Christianity. In sum, the Frankish conquest in Germany had an importance similar to the Roman conquest of Gaul, and from it sprang modern Germany.

Through these conquests the Frankish state came into contact with other barbarians: Scandinavians in the north, Slavs in the east, and Avars, successors to the Huns, in the Danube plain. Three far-ranging campaigns were undertaken against the Avars; in the end their leader was converted to Christianity and paid homage to Charlemagne.

The Restored Empire. By about 800, Charlemagne had united under his authority most of the area of Western Europe that had been part of the Roman Empire. It seemed natural to restore the imperial dignity in his person, especially since Constantinople, then ruled by a woman, supported the Eastern bishops in their hostility toward the papacy.

Charlemagne went to Rome at the end of the year 800 to repress the aristocratic factions that threatened the security of Pope Leo III. The pope took the opportunity to do what all the Western bishops, and no doubt Charles himself, had hoped for. On Christmas night, in the Basilica of St. Peter, the pope placed a gold crown on Charlemagne's head while the crowd in attendance acclaimed him emperor. Thereafter

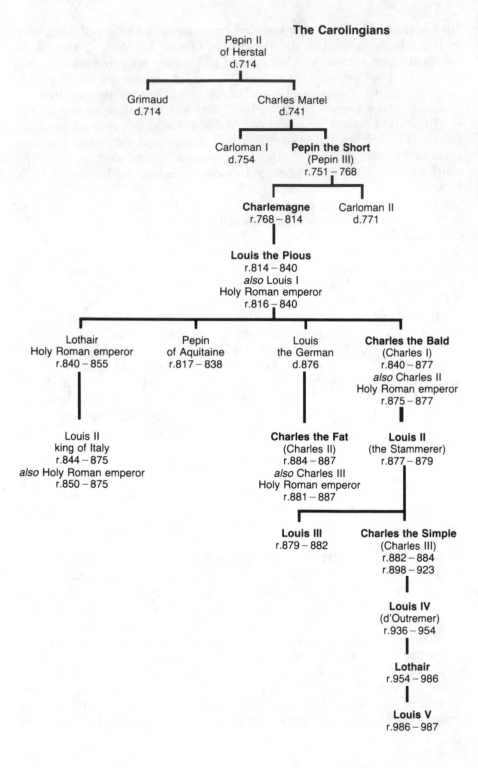

The Carolingians

Pepin II
of Herstal
d.714

Grimaud
d.714

Charles Martel
d.741

Carloman I
d.754

Pepin the Short
(Pepin III)
r.751 – 768

Charlemagne
r.768 – 814

Carloman II
d.771

Louis the Pious
r.814 – 840
also Louis I
Holy Roman emperor
r.816 – 840

Lothair
Holy Roman emperor
r.840 – 855

Pepin
of Aquitaine
r.817 – 838

Louis
the German
d.876

Charles the Bald
(Charles I)
r.840 – 877
also Charles II
Holy Roman emperor
r.875 – 877

Louis II
king of Italy
r.844 – 875
also Holy Roman emperor
r.850 – 875

Charles the Fat
(Charles II)
r.884 – 887
also Charles III
Holy Roman emperor
r.881 – 887

Louis II
(the Stammerer)
r.877 – 879

Louis III
r.879 – 882

Charles the Simple
(Charles III)
r.882 – 884
r.898 – 923

Louis IV
(d'Outremer)
r.936 – 954

Lothair
r.954 – 986

Louis V
r.986 – 987

Charlemagne's empire, 800 A.D.

DANES
Jutland
NORTH SEA
Mark of Brandenburg
FRISIANS
Saxony
Oder
SLAVS
Elbe
Flanders
Aix-la-Chapelle (Aachen)
ENGLISH CHANNEL
Austrasia
Soissons
Mainz
Rhine
St. Denis
Paris
Seine
ALEMANNI
Danube
Eastern Mark
Brittany
Auxerre
AVARS
Tours
BAVARIANS
Poitiers
Burgundy
Friuli
Neustria
Venice
ATLANTIC OCEAN
Acquitaine
Loire
Po
LOMBARDS
Rhône
Provence
ALPES
Ravenna
ADRIATIC SEA
Gascony
Garonne
Septimania
MEDITERRANEAN SEA
Roncesvalles
PYRENEES
Spanish March
Rome
Ebro
Barcelona

Tributary states   Territory restored to the Pope

—— Boundaries of the Holy Roman empire

his title in official documents was "Charles Augustus, crowned by God, great and peaceful emperor, ruler of the Roman Empire, and by the grace of God king of the Franks and the Lombards." After having protested at first against this "usurpation," the emperor at Constantinople eventually recognized Charlemagne as his "brother." The independent kings of Spain and Great Britain paid him homage. His fame extended beyond the Christian world. The powerful caliph of Baghdad, Harun al-Rashid, sent him an embassy and recognized him as the protector of the Christian shrines in Jerusalem.

The Government. Charlemagne sought to give both his conquests and his inherited states an orderly, uniform administration in accordance with Christian principles. In this system the emperor-king was charged by

God with the government of men on earth. To obey him was a religious duty, as was proclaimed by the oath of fealty that all holders of any authority were required to take.

When the king was not with the army, he traveled from one of his great domains to another with a few immediate retainers who formed his court. Only at the end of his reign did Charlemagne settle at Aix-la-Chapelle (Aachen), where he built a chapel, the most typical monument of Carolingian architecture that has survived.

Each year, before the great assembly of the army called the Champ de Mai (Field of May), the king convened a diet or *plaid* (*placitum*), an assembly of nobles and bishops. He consulted them about the affairs of the kingdom, and his decisions were then published in the form of documents called capitularies.

The task of applying them in each district of the Empire fell to the count (*grafio*) and to the bishops chosen by the king, usually from among the members of the Austrasian Frankish aristocracy. In some areas that were threatened by the enemy, a duke, a supreme military leader, was placed over the counts. The outlying defense zones called "marches" were headed by a *marchio* (marquis).

Charlemagne's most original innovation consisted of the *missi dominici*, deputies sent on a regular circuit in pairs—a layman and a bishop—to all the provinces to oversee the conduct of the counts and bishops and to see that the terms of the capitularies were carried out.

All freemen owed military service, but each year only the number deemed necessary were called to duty, and those were raised in the provinces nearest the site of the chosen operation. As the cavalry became increasingly important and equipment too expensive for everyone to afford, Charlemagne developed the practice of granting land in exchange for mounted service. The nobles were encouraged to do the same. This was one of the origins of feudalism (see p. 37).

The Church. Charlemagne also considered himself responsible for good order within the church. On several occasions he summoned councils or synods to secure their adoption of regulations governing education and the discipline of the clergy. It was in this way that each parish church came to be required in principle to possess a grant of land in order to ensure a living for the priest. In the towns the numerous clergy had to lead a communal life around the bishop. This is the origin of cathedral chapters, or canons (*canonici*). An effort was also made to bring more rigorous order to monastic life by imposing the Benedictine rule as reformed by St. Benedict of Aniane in all monasteries.

The Carolingian Renaissance. It was a similar concern for the instruction of the clergy that inspired Charlemagne to undertake two enterprises that contributed to what has been called, somewhat inaccurately, the "Carolingian Renaissance":

- The founding of schools in connection with all monasteries and cathedral churches. A model school attached to the imperial palace welcomed children of humble origin along with the sons of noblemen.

- A vast program to establish the original forms of sacred and profane texts and to transcribe them. Most of the ancient texts known today have been transmitted through fine Carolingian manuscripts copied in monastic writing rooms (*scriptoria*).

II. THE DISRUPTION OF THE EMPIRE

Louis the Pious. At the death of Charlemagne, on January 28, 814, his entire legacy fell to his sole surviving son, Louis the Pious, so called because of his zeal to strengthen the internal discipline of the church and increase the clergy's hold over civil society. His weakness of character also caused him to be called Louis the Débonnaire (Meek).

Under the influence of his ecclesiastical advisers, Louis sought primarily to exalt and consolidate the idea of empire. He dropped the title of king of the Franks and Lombards and had himself crowned emperor by the pope. In 817 he took measures to ensure the survival of a united empire. His eldest son, Lothair, was proclaimed associate emperor, and his two other sons, given kingdoms on the peripheries of the empire—Louis the German in Bavaria and Pepin in Aquitaine—were specifically made subordinate to their elder brother. So was the kingdom of Italy, which had been granted to Louis's nephew Bernard. When Bernard revolted, he was defeated and put to death. Italy then came under the direct control of Lothair, the associate emperor.

The Sons' Revolt. This balance was disturbed when a fourth son, Charles (later called the Bald), was born of Louis's second marriage. Charles's mother, the ambitious Judith, pressed the emperor to make a new territorial division that would ensure her young son a kingdom equal to those of his elder brothers. The latter joined together against their father. Louis was abandoned by the powerful church party, which was displeased to see the unity of the empire compromised. In 832 he was stripped of his powers and separated from his wife and son, who were sent to convents. Lothair was proclaimed sole emperor. Finally, in 833, Louis was forced to do public penance on his knees before the nobles and bishops at the church of St. Médard at Soissons.

This excessive humiliation shifted opinion in his favor. Louis the

German and Pepin of Aquitaine, unhappy with Lothair's pretensions, reconciled with their father. After driving Lothair from Italy, they restored all of Louis's powers in 835. A new division of territory gave the young Charles a kingdom between the Meuse and the Loire, to which Aquitaine was added shortly after Pepin's death.

The Treaty of Verdun (843). Louis the Pious died in June 840, as he was marching against his son Louis of Bavaria, who had again rebelled against the territorial settlement that favored Charles.

Claiming his imperial title, Lothair fomented revolts in his brothers' kingdoms in the hope of reducing them to subordinate roles. Louis and Charles joined forces against the emperor. A decisive battle took place at Fontenay, near Auxerre, on June 25, 841. Brutal, fratricidal, and savage, it cost 80,000 lives, according to one chronicler. The defeated Lothair fled to Italy. Louis and Charles consolidated their alliance by a solemn oath sworn at Strasbourg in the presence of their armies on February 14, 842. This document, drafted in both the Romanic and Germanic languages, is the first known example of the languages that have become modern French and German.

Lothair, finally accepting a triple partition in principle, entered into the negotiations that resulted in the Treaty of Verdun in August 843. Lothair's kingdom, between France to the west and Germany to the east—both of them relatively homogeneous—was made up of a string of very diverse countries stretching from north to south. For want of a better name, it was called Lotharingia. The name still survives in the modern Lorraine.

The Last Carolingians. After Lothair's death in 855, his artificial realm split into three kingdoms, each of which went to one of this three sons: Italy, Provence, and a Lotharingia that was reduced to the lands between the North Sea and the upper Rhône. These regions, especially the last, became the objects of a fierce struggle between the two great neighbors. A confused history began, composed of brief alliances and savage, poorly led wars between uncles and nephews. Eventually, Charles the Bald seized most of Lotharingia and even Italy after the death of Lothair's last surviving son, Louis II. Charles also saw to it that the imperial crown, which Louis II had acquired at his father's death, was bestowed upon him at Rome.

It was a brief moment of triumph, for Charles died during his return from Italy in 877. His feeble successors—Louis II (the Stammerer), Louis III, and Charles the Simple—proved incapable of ensuring the unity and defense of the western kingdom. Predominance soon passed to the descendants of Louis the German. One of them, Charles the Fat, had himself crowned emperor and in 885 was recognized as

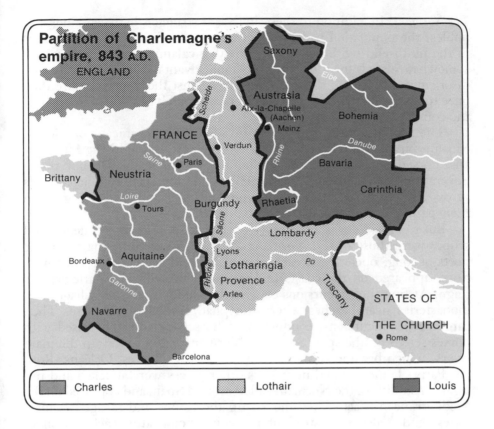

Partition of Charlemagne's empire, 843 A.D.

Charles — Lothair — Louis

king by the nobles of the kingdom of France, replacing Charles the Simple.

Henceforth the last Carolingians appeared to be only marionettes brought on stage or pushed into the wings at the whim of the nobles. In 888, since the emperor Charles the Fat proved incompetent and Charles the Simple was still too young, the nobles chose one of their own as king: Eudes, count of Paris. After Eudes's death in 898, Charles the Simple regained the throne and reigned for twenty-five years. But in 923 he was toppled by a band of rebels and replaced by Raoul, duke of Burgundy and Eudes's nephew by marriage. The son of Charles the Simple, Louis IV (called Louis d'Outremer "from across the sea"), was recalled in 936 and fought successfully to free himself from the stifling control of Hugh the Great (another nephew of Eudes), duke of France, Burgundy, and Aquitaine and regent of the kingdom. After the accidental death of Louis IV, his son Lothair (954–986) and his grandson Louis V (986–987) were mere kinglets; real power was exercised by the successor to Hugh the Great—Hugh Capet. Hugh finally had himself elected king in 987, thus founding the new Capetian dynasty.

The Normans. In addition to these incessant struggles between kings and nobles, the population had to suffer a new and final wave of invasions in the ninth and tenth centuries. The two calamities were in any case somewhat related, for if the invaders took advantage of the anarchy that disorganized defenses, the need to fight against them served more than once to justify usurpations of power or even paralyzed one or another of the competitors in the struggle.

The Mediterranean south was invaded by the Saracens or Moors, Muslim pirates from North Africa. In the east appeared the Hungarians, horsemen who a century earlier had settled in the Danube plain. Several times, notably in 926 and 937, the Hungarians conducted raids across Burgundy as far as Aquitaine, pillaging and massacring all in their path, as the Huns had done before them.

But the most devastating invasions, because of their frequency and scope, were those of the Normans (Northmen) of Scandinavia. Their fleets of long, open ships, each of which could carry about sixty warriors, appeared on the coasts of France by the end of Charlemagne's reign. At first their incursions consisted of sudden raids on villages and monasteries near beaches where they had landed by surprise. Then came deeper incursions, conducted on horseback and improvised with horses seized on the spot. Soon the Normans dared to sail up the main rivers, which became veritable invasion routes. Nantes, Orléans, Rouen, Paris, Toulouse, and numerous other places were attacked and pillaged. In addition, the Normans sailed around Spain and appeared on the Mediterranean coast. They moved up the Rhône and ravaged Nîmes, Arles, and Valence. Instead of returning home after each season of pillaging, as they used to do, they established permanent fortified bases close to the rivers' mouths.

On several occasions Charles the Bald tried to limit the destruction by paying enormous tributes. Then he entrusted the defense of the provinces between the Loire and the Seine to a single leader, Robert the Strong. The fame and power that Robert's exploits brought him were the source of the fortune that later raised his descendants to the throne of France. The first was his son Eudes, who successfully defended Paris when it was besieged by the Normans in 885.

The Nordic invaders began to enjoy the pleasures of sedentary life, however, and gradually they occupied all the country bordering the lower Seine. Charles the Simple offered to grant their leader, Rollo, all of this territory, along with the title of duke, if he would convert to Christianity and recognize the king of France as his sovereign. The bargain was sealed by the Treaty of St. Clair-sur-Epte in 911, putting an end to the invasions. It brought to this part of France, henceforth called Normandy, a very original human element, marked by a taste for distant expeditions inherited from the Vikings. Normans sailing from France later conquered England, Sicily, and southern Italy.

III. THE BIRTH OF FEUDALISM

The invasions as well as the internal struggles helped to being about the dissolution of the Frankish monarchy. Whether to assure themselves of followers in their quarrels or to fulfill the requirements for defense against the Normans, the Carolingian rulers had been led to cede to the nobility an increasingly important share of their domains and royal rights. This dissolution of the monarchy had a purely political or territorial aspect—the formation of large and virtually independent principalities—in addition to a social and judicial aspect that affected the very concept of state sovereignty.

Territorial Dismemberment. As a result of all these territorial readjustments, several regions that had once formed part of Roman and Frankish Gaul were permanently detached—the duchies of upper and lower Lorraine between the Rhine and the Meuse, the county of Burgundy, and Provence. For centuries thereafter all these countries belonged to the imperial German crown.

Within the kingdom of France itself a dozen or so virtually independent principalities had formed. Some, such as the duchies of Normandy, Brittany, and Gascony and the county of Toulouse, were formed on the basis of ethnic or cultural ties. Others sprang from the great territorial military districts created by the king or simply through the encroachments of a few enterprising and daring individuals, such as the counts of Flanders, Vermandois, and Champagne.

The Feudal Order. The eclipse of the idea of a monarchical state and its replacement by the new system of social and political relations called feudalism were the result of an inevitable process, carried out over several centuries.

A schematic picture of its development would include these stages: First, the encounter of two institutions that sprang from the state of insecurity resulting from the invasions and anarchy.

- Patronage or *commendatio*, in existence by the Merovingian era. The weaker placed themselves and their property under the protection of the stronger in exchange for certain services. Each man thus became the vassal of a lord, to whom he took an oath of fealty.

- The benefice, an institution developed systematically by Charles

Martel and his successors. The king or noble drew to himself warriors, knights, or local officials by granting them landed property. The oath that confirmed the grant created a bond of vassalage similar to that of the *commendatio*, with the difference that in this case the landed property or fief was granted by the superior to the inferior instead of being conferred by the inferior.

Second, the reversal of the relationship between fief and vassalage. While at the beginning protection and service were the reasons for the fief, now men entered vassalage solely to acquire a fief.

Third, the entry of aristocratic society into this network of relationships en masse. The small local lords, each master of a domain and fortress, recognized their own status as vassals of a superior lord, called a suzerain. The result was a kind of splintering of the idea of property and sovereignty. The fief was possessed both by the suzerain (who had eminent domain) and by the vassal (who had the use of it). The lord exercised over his vassals rights once reserved to the king, and the vassals knew no other authority than that of the lord to whom they had taken an oath of fealty or homage.

In this way political and social relations adapted themselves to a completely rural society. On estates isolated from each other by vast empty spaces lived men who were unable to grasp the abstract ideas of state and monarchy, and who could scarcely understand authority except in the person of a leader who was physically present.

The Carolingian achievement, which was inspired by the mirage of Rome, was almost certainly too ambitious to survive. Its disappearance exposed the foundations of basic and natural obligations that had slowly been built up from below. On them a new political order gradually developed.

SUGGESTIONS FOR FURTHER READING

Bates, David. *Normandy before 1066.* London, 1982.

Bloch, Marc. *Feudal Society.* Chicago, 1968.

Boussard, Jacques. *Civilization of Charlemagne.* New York, 1968.

Bullough, Donald A. *The Age of Charlemagne.* New York, 1966.

Duckett, Eleanor S. *Carolingian Portraits: A Study in the Ninth Century.* Ann Arbor, 1962.

Fichtenau, Heinrich. *The Carolingian Empire*. Toronto, 1979.

Ganshof, François. *The Carolingians and the Frankish Monarchy: Studies in Carolingian History*. Ithaca, 1971.

Riche, Pierre. *Daily Life in the World of Charlemagne*. Philadelphia, 1978.

Halphen, Louis. *Charlemagne et l'Empire carolingien*. Paris, 1968.

4
The Capetians: Kingdom

The contrast between the development of the Capetian monarchy and that of the two preceding dynasties is striking. Merovingians and Carolingians, powerful at first, gradually weakened and finished wretchedly. The Capetians, in contrast, began modestly and gradually strengthened themselves until they made their kingdom the main power of the Christian West. Chance played some part in this process, since for ten generations there was no conflict over the succession. But so did a spirit of continuity, realism, and caution, which enabled them to seize every opportunity to round out their domain bit by bit, successively absorbing the major fiefs and making use of feudal law to lay the groundwork for administrative unification of the kingdom.

I. THE RISE OF THE DYNASTY

A Century of Obscurity. Hugh Capet and his first successors really were masters of nothing beyond the collection of lands, châteaux, and towns called the royal domain, where vassals paid direct homage, without the intervention of another suzerain; and even here some local lords were powerful enough to resist them. Even though this royal domain was smaller than most other principalities of the kingdom, it included fertile plains and two points of commercial and strategic importance: Paris and Orléans. Most important, the sacred anointment had made the king the elect of God, the holder of a quasi-priestly power. The bishops and monasteries of the entire kingdom had to consider the king their natural protector, and the great princely families regarded him as their supreme arbiter.

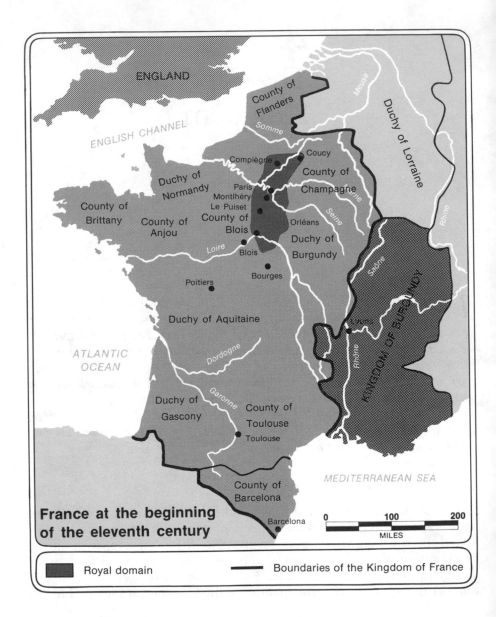

France at the beginning of the eleventh century

Royal domain — Boundaries of the Kingdom of France

These real assets were of little benefit to Hugh Capet's immediate successors—Robert II (the Pious) (996–1031), Henry I (1031–60), and Philip I (1060–1108). Their only merit was that they avoided any dismemberment of the royal domain and ensured each generation an uncontested succession by having their eldest sons crowned during their lifetimes and associated with the throne.

During the reign of Philip I events of enormous importance for the future of the kingdom took place. One was the conquest of England by the Duke of Normandy, William the Conqueror, in 1066. As a result the weak king of France found himself in the presence of a vassal who bore a royal title and was far more powerful than he. The other was the First Crusade, launched by Pope Urban II at a council held at Clermont, in Auvergne, in 1096. (see p. 68).

Louis VI (the Fat) (1108–37). After more than a century of stagnation and mediocrity, the Capetian monarchy came alive with Louis VI, called the Fat. A tireless warrior, he also had the good fortune to have as a friend and confidant a man renowned for virtue and wisdom— Suger, abbot of St. Denis. The king put an end to the brigandage of the lords of his royal domain and ensured order by imposing a rudimentary administration on the feudal framework. Provosts, placed in control of small districts, were charged with collecting the royal revenue, raising troops, and ensuring local justice.

Louis VI heightened the prestige of the crown by exercising his prerogatives throughout the kingdom: armed intervention and arbitration imposed in conflicts between great lords, the right of supervision exercised in episcopal elections, and charters of immunities granted to urban communes and monasteries.

Finally, Louis VI resisted the German emperor in his struggle with the papacy by giving asylum to two popes driven from Italy. When Emperor Henry V tried to invade the kingdom in 1124, Louis the Fat assembled contingents from all parts of the kingdom in an imposing army. The mobilization of that army alone forced the aggressor to withdraw.

The crowning of his work came in the same year as his death, when Louis VI married his son Louis to Eleanor of Aquitaine, heiress to the duchies of Guyenne and Gascony and to numerous fiefs in central France as well.

Louis VII (1137–80). Louis VII, very pious and honest but weak, wasted his opportunity. In 1146 he left to take part in the Second Crusade, preached by St. Bernard, placing the regency of the kingdom in Suger's hands. At his return in 1152 Louis VII had his marriage to Eleanor annulled, for in ten years of marriage the queen had failed to produce a male heir, and her misconduct during the crusade had been notorious. Two months later Eleanor married Henry Plantagenet, Count of Anjou and, since 1150, Duke of Normandy. With the Aquitainian domains brought by Eleanor, Plantagenet became master of an immense state that stretched from Picardy to the Pyrenees; even Brittany obeyed him. And in 1154 the crown of England fell to him. Enormously ambitious and energetic, the new sovereign, who took the title of Henry II, gave his states a strong administration and at the same time sought to extend his dominion still further, over the whole of the British Isles and on the Continent. The existence of an invading power ten to fifteen times greater in size and resources than the Capetian kingdom made a conflict inevitable. For almost a century the history of France was dominated by the struggle between the Capetians and the Plantagenets, a first Hundred Years' War.

In fact, the hostilities broke out as early as 1153. They continued intermittently until the death of Louis VII. Louis was frequently defeated in battle, but he still kept his possessions in the long run. He knew how to play on two circumstances: first, the ambitions of the sons of Henry II, whom he encouraged to intrigue and rebel; and second and most important, his alliance with the church and the papacy, then in conflict with the German emperor and the king of England. Thus in 1177 the papal legate compelled Henry II to make peace by threatening to impose an interdict on all his continental states.

II. PHILIP AUGUSTUS (1180–1223)

The King. Philip II, the only son of Louis VII and his third wife, Adele of Champagne, became king at age fifteen. The name Augustus, which his contemporaries bestowed upon him and which history has retained, signified Philip's success in augmenting (*augere*) his states and the royal power in the course of his forty-three-year reign.

If the personality of this great king is not well known, his acts indicate that he was a political realist, unscrupulous, patient, tenacious, and skillful in creating and taking advantage of all opportunities. Courageous in war but preferring to rely on ruse and diplomacy, and very jealous of his authority, Philip Augustus allowed the clergy not the slightest encroachment on the rights of the crown and obeyed the pope only so far as it suited his interests.

The Struggle against the Plantagenets. The young king began by flattering Henry II and using him to rid himself of the guardianship of his mother and his uncles in Champagne and then to put down a coalition of feudal nobles.

That accomplished, Philip turned against the Plantagenets. Richard

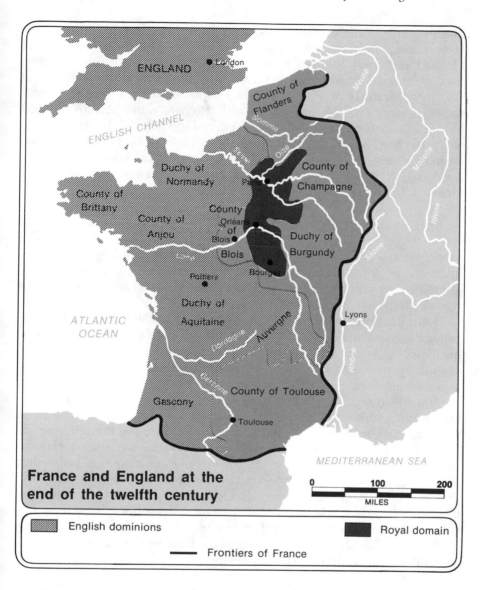

County of Flanders

ENGLAND · London

ENGLISH CHANNEL

Mense

Duchy of Normandy · Paris

County of Champagne

County of Brittany

Oise

County of Anjou

County of Orléans · Blois

Moselle

Blois

Duchy of Burgundy

Rhine

Poitiers

Bourges

Saône

Duchy of Aquitaine

Auvergne

Lyons

ATLANTIC OCEAN

Dordogne

Garonne

Rhône

County of Toulouse

Gascony

Toulouse

MEDITERRANEAN SEA

France and England at the end of the twelfth century

| 0 | 100 | 200 |

MILES

///// English dominions   ■ Royal domain

—— Frontiers of France

the Lionhearted, son of Henry II, demanded in vain to be given immediate possession of Aquitaine. Philip encouraged him to rebel, welcomed him as an intimate friend, and joined him in a campaign against Henry II. Henry, betrayed by his companions, was defeated and died soon afterward. He was buried in the church at the abbey of Fontevrault in Anjou in 1189.

Richard, king of England, now became the rival to fight. The inevitable war was delayed, however, because the two "friends" had sworn to go together on the Third Crusade. But after a few months in the Holy Land, Philip declared that he was ill and set out for home alone. He had promised Richard to protect his possessions "with the same concern that he would show in defending his own city of Paris." Yet Philip had scarcely arrived home, in December 1191, when he made a secret agreement with John Lackland, Richard's brother, to support him in his seizure of the throne of England in exchange for the cession of upper Normandy and Touraine. Informed of these developments, Richard hastened toward home. But en route he was taken prisoner by the Duke of Austria, who delivered him to his enemy the emperor, Henry VI. Philip Augustus intervened in order to prolong his captivity.

Free at last in February 1194, Richard sought to wreak vengeance on the perfidious Capetian. The merciless war that he waged lasted five years. Beaten and driven to extremities, Philip had to beg the pope to intervene in order to secure a truce. Richard seized the opportunity it offered to go settle accounts with one of his vassals in Limousin, and was mortally wounded at Chalus near Poitiers.

John Lackland succeeded Richard on the English throne. The Plantagenet possessions on the Continent were fought over in the name of his nephew, Arthur of Brittany. Philip, who at first took Arthur's side, eventually agreed to leave John all his French fiefs provided that John acknowledge himself a vassal of the king of France.

Shortly thereafter Philip Augustus made use of his right as John's lord to intervene in a conflict between John and one of his vassals in Aquitaine. When John was called to appear before the French king, he refused to come. In accordance with feudal law, he was then declared a felon and condemned to lose all his fiefs. Executing this judgment, Philip Augustus seized Normandy, then Anjou, Touraine, Maine, and Poitou. These were easy conquests, because John had alienated the towns and lords of these provinces. The only serious resistance was encountered at the imposing fortress of Château Gaillard, built by Richard the Lionhearted on a tongue of land in the Seine Valley. It surrendered only after a six-month siege.

Bouvines. At first John appeared to accept his losses, but in 1213 he put together a vast coalition against the king of France. His allies included the counts of Flanders and Burgundy, the German emperor Otto IV, and a host of lesser lords. This northern coalition attacked in the summer of 1214 while John landed at La Rochelle and carried the offensive to the Loire. Prince Louis, son of Philip Augustus, routed the English army at La Roche-aux-Moines on July 2. Three weeks later, on July 27, the king himself defeated the Flemish and the imperial troops at Bouvines, near Lille. This striking victory, in which soldiers from the towns distinguished themselves as brilliantly as the knights, aroused enormous enthusiasm throughout the kingdom. It assured the king of France not only of increased prestige, but also of the undisturbed possession of his conquests, which had practically quadrupled the size of his domains. The victory at Bouvines also had consequences abroad: in Germany the emperor Otto lost his crown to Frederick II, and in England King John, faced with a revolt by his barons, was forced to grant them a great charter (Magna Carta), considered to be the first foundation stone of the British parliamentary system.

Internal Government. Less spectacular but just as important for the future of the monarchy was the king's perseverance in extending and consolidating his authority throughout his realm. The financial and military obligations of the lords in his immediate domain were expanded and specified. Supervising these lords and the royal provosts was a new class of officials created by Philip Augustus. These *baillis* (bailiffs) were charged with centralizing financial receipts and carrying out the royal justice.

In addition, the king made good use of the provisions of feudal law to reduce the domains of the great vassals in various ways from within. Marriages, inheritances, minorities, and various conflicts were all pretexts for his intervention. His "fee" was the surrender of estates or rights, on which new encroachments could be based. The same result was secured by the exercise of patronage and royal protection of bishops and monasteries, and the founding of urban communes that were granted immunities by royal charter. The great principalities, riddled with enclaves that depended directly on the crown, could no longer compete with it. Significantly, Philip Augustus was the first king of his dynasty who could dispense with having his heir chosen and consecrated during his own lifetime.

Louis VIII (1223–26). King at age thirty-six, Louis VIII vigorously carried on his father's work. When Henry III of England, son of John Lackland, was so rash as to declare war, Louis quickly seized Aunis, Saintonge, Limousin, and Perigord. Only Bordeaux held out against him.

His main effort was directed against Languedoc, in the south. The strong local loyalties of this area's population had found religious expression in the strange heresy of the Cathari, or Albigensians. The Count of Toulouse, Raymond VI, secretly supported it, and in 1209 Pope Innocent III launched a crusade against him. Philip Augustus refused to take part in it, but he allowed his vassals to enlist, and in 1215 he even permitted his son to do so on his own account. Under the leadership of Simon de Montfort, a lesser baron from the Ile-de-France, an army of northern knights invaded the south and massacred the heretics without pity. Simon de Montfort, invested with the domains of Raymond VI, acknowledged himself a vassal of the king of France. But after his death in 1218, his son Amaury was unable to repress the rebels in Languedoc, and in 1225 he sold his rights to Louis VIII. The king soon dispatched a powerful expedition, which occupied the country almost without a fight. The Count of Toulouse, Raymond VII, was permitted to retain a part of his territory, on condition that his daughter and sole heiress marry Alphonse, second son of Louis VIII. Thus the whole of Languedoc reverted to the Capetians.

While returning from this expedition, Louis VIII fell ill from dysentery and died prematurely. His reign, brief as it was, had resulted in the extension of the royal domain to the shores of the Mediterranean.

III. ST. LOUIS (1226–70)

The King's Minority. Louis IX was only twelve when his father died. The regency was assumed by his mother, Blanche of Castile. A woman as intelligent as she was energetic, Blanche exercised power for several years after her son attained his majority, and again from 1249 to 1254, while the king was in the East. The regent had to face several rebellions of great lords who believed "that a woman should not govern so great a thing as the kingdom of France." All these attempts were crushed, as was that of the king of England, Henry III, who landed at St. Malo in 1229 with the intention of recovering the former domains of the Plantagenets.

The King. Of all the French rulers during the Middle Ages, Louis IX is the one whose personality is best known, thanks to the reports of those who witnessed his canonization proceedings, including the incomparable Sire de Joinville.

Joinville tells us that Louis IX was of above-average height and blond, with "the face of an angel" and an affable, dignified manner. In combat he was courageous to the point of rashness. As king he knew how to combine kindness with firmness; he listened to counsel but made decisions alone, and he was harsh when he had to be.

Most of all, both in his personal life and in his royal duties Louis sought to follow the Christian precepts that Blanche of Castile had taught him. In accordance with the medieval ideal, his religion was expressed in quasi-monastic piety, physical penance, and charity to the poor. The hospital of the Quinze Vingts, founded to house three hundred poor blind persons, and the Sainte Chapelle, constructed to serve as a repository for the relics of the Passion of Christ, still bear witness to the religion of the saintly king.

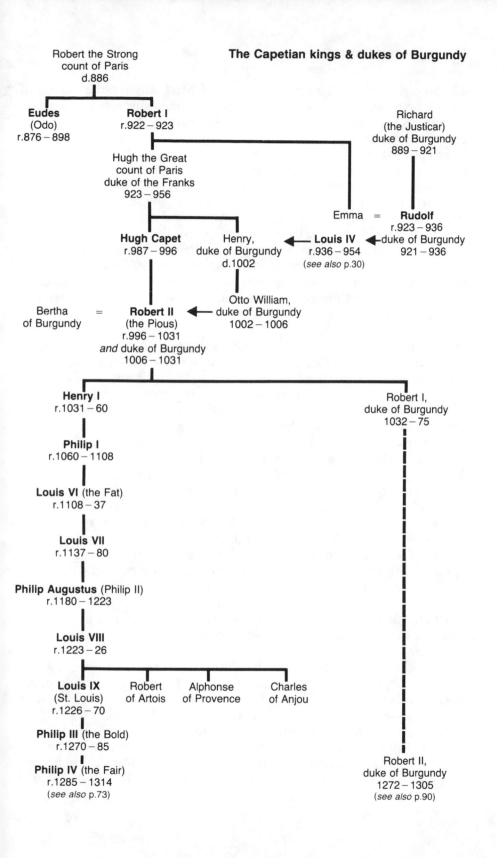

The Capetian kings & dukes of Burgundy

Robert the Strong
count of Paris
d.886

Eudes
(Odo)
r.876 – 898

Robert I
r.922 – 923

Richard
(the Justicar)
duke of Burgundy
889 – 921

Hugh the Great
count of Paris
duke of the Franks
923 – 956

Emma = **Rudolf**
r.923 – 936
duke of Burgundy
921 – 936

Hugh Capet
r.987 – 996

Henry,
duke of Burgundy
d.1002

Louis IV
r.936 – 954
(*see also* p.30)

Bertha
of Burgundy

= **Robert II**
(the Pious)
r.996 – 1031
and duke of Burgundy
1006 – 1031

Otto William,
duke of Burgundy
1002 – 1006

Henry I
r.1031 – 60

Robert I,
duke of Burgundy
1032 – 75

Philip I
r.1060 – 1108

Louis VI (the Fat)
r.1108 – 37

Louis VII
r.1137 – 80

Philip Augustus (Philip II)
r.1180 – 1223

Louis VIII
r.1223 – 26

Louis IX
(St. Louis)
r.1226 – 70

Robert
of Artois

Alphonse
of Provence

Charles
of Anjou

Philip III (the Bold)
r.1270 – 85

Philip IV (the Fair)
r.1285 – 1314
(*see also* p.73)

Robert II,
duke of Burgundy
1272 – 1305
(*see also* p.90)

The Seventh Crusade. The mystical love of St. Louis for the person of Jesus Christ inspired in him the politically indefensible scheme of retaking the Holy Land from the infidels. He believed that the best way to go about it would be to strike the Saracens at the heart of their power—in Egypt. A Franco-Genoese fleet transported the king and his army to Damietta, which was easily taken in May 1249. After this first success, however, several months passed before the force marched against Cairo. The Crusaders' army suffered a disaster before the stronghold of Mansurah, and the king himself fell prisoner to the Saracens. They treated him with respect, and he freed himself by paying a heavy ransom and abandoning Damietta. He then traveled to Palestine, where he occupied himself with visits to the shrines and fortifications of the Christian citadels. The death of his mother, who was again regent of the kingdom in his absence, moved Louis to return home at last in April 1254. He had been gone for five years.

Internal Government. Louis IX sought to bring his subjects the benefits of peace, justice, and Christian order. He forbade his lords to resort to arms and to disturb their vassals. On his own agents—*baillis*, seneschals, and provosts—he imposed a moral code spelled out in a series of great ordinances. Bishops were on occasion vigorously recalled to their duties and to the respect they owed the crown. Popular imagery has Louis personally rendering justice to the people in improvised open-air sessions at the foot of an oak tree in Vincennes. But the history of institutions places more emphasis on the creation of a specialized section within the royal court to administer royal justice. Here lay the origin of the highest French courts, the parlements. Another commission, charged with supervising the financial operations of royal agents, gave rise to the Court of Accounts (Cour des Comptes). To ensure the honesty of operations, Louis ordered the minting of a royal coinage, which circulated throughout the kingdom. Other existing coinages were tied to it at fixed and stable rates.

The Peacemaker. The whole of Louis's foreign policy was inspired by his concern to renounce the spirit of conquest and ensure peace among Christian princes.

He himself set the example by the way he ended the long conflict between Capetians and Plantagenets. In 1242 Henry III of England once again attempted to gain from a rebellion by several barons in Aquitaine—the only such revolt that took place during Louis's reign—by landing an army at Royan. Louis moved against him and defeated him at Taillebourg. The long truce that followed left the claims of Henry III intact. Returning from the East, Louis initiated discussions that resulted in the Treaty of Paris in 1258. The king of France restored to the English monarch the most recent conquests of his father, Louis VIII, in exchange for Henry's renunciation of his claims to the far richer and large domains conquered by Philip Augustus; and as lord of his continental possessions Henry paid homage to the Capetian king.

That same year Louis concluded the same sort of agreement with the king of Aragon, who yielded his claims to the county of Toulouse while the king of France abandoned his suzerainty over Roussillon and Catalonia.

The renown of the saintly king and the confidence that his fairness inspired were so great that from all sides appeals were brought to him for adjudication rather than to the emperor or the pope. A notable case was that of the English barons, who asked Louis to arbitrate their dispute with King Henry III in 1264. In the duel to the death between the papacy and the empire during that period, St. Louis always refused to side with either power, seeking only to restore peace and ensure the independence of the Holy See. It was against his will that his younger brother, Charles of Anjou, already king of Provence, agreed in 1263 to assume the title of king of Naples. Aided by the papacy and displaying savage energy, Charles established the so-called Angevin dynasty, which ruled in southern Italy until the mid-fifteenth century.

The Last Crusade. Charles of Anjou aspired to nothing less than a vast Mediterranean empire. This dream did not run counter to the fateful direction chosen by Louis IX in his last undertaking. The king had never resigned himself to the failure of his first crusade. Overruling all counsels of caution, Louis decided in 1267 to try again. His brother Charles, master of Sicily and eager to establish himself in Tunisia, convinced Louis that the emir of that country was ready to convert and persuaded him to send a substantial body of cavalry to aid him. The expedition, which was carefully planned over three years, arrived at Carthage in 1270, at the worst possible time of year—mid-July. Badly situated, poorly supplied, and prey to plague and dysentery, the army dissolved in the summer heat. The king, already sick when he landed, succumbed to exhaustion on August 25, 1270.

His death crowned his saintliness with the halo of martyrdom. The historical image of St. Louis, the perfect model of a Christian king, gave the crown of France and the Capetian dynasty a religious aura that did as much as its material power to ensure its preeminence among the royal families of Europe.

IV. PHILIP THE FAIR (1285–1314)

Philip III (the Bold). The fifteen years of the reign of Philip III (1270–85) seem to be barren of any memorable event. His uncle Charles of Anjou gained strong influence over him and dragged him into an offensive beyond the Pyrenees against his rival the king of Aragon. It was an unfortunate expedition, which was ended by the king's death at Perpignan in October 1285.

The Legalists. With Philip IV (the Fair) royal authority took on an overbearing, brutal, cynical quality. It is impossible to say, however, whether this change of direction was due to the king himself or to his entourage of advisers, who by now had gained great influence. These advisers have been called the legalists because they sprang from the group of legislative experts that had emerged at the royal court as its judicial functions increased. These men attempted to revive a principle they had discovered in ancient Roman law, which declared that the will of the sovereign was law: "The king's wish is the law's wish." On this basis, and contrary to feudal law, there was no longer any limit to royal power.

The Conflict with the Pope. The king's pretensions collided with the no less exorbitant ones of Pope Boniface VIII, also a legalist, who claimed that the papacy had supreme authority over all Christian rulers. The conflict arose in 1301, when the pope decided to create a new French bishopric at Pamiers without seeking the king's consent. The king arrested the bishop named by Boniface VIII. The pope announced that he would convene the French bishops at Rome to examine Philip's conduct. The king's chief adviser, William of Nogaret, a man totally without scruples, published a version of the pontifical letter that was scandalously falsified so as to wound French pride. The indignant Boniface excommunicated the king and released his subjects from their oath of fealty. Nogaret responded by drawing up a set of charges against the pope, replete with every crime imaginable, to justify his deposition. He then moved quickly into Italy. With a band of mercenaries swelled with personal enemies of Boniface VIII, Nogaret sought to surprise him at Anagni, the pope's summer residence. Called upon to abdicate and covered with abuse by Nogaret and his men, the eighty-six-year-old pope remained unshaken. After two days the people of Anagni rose in support of Boniface VIII, and Nogaret had to flee.

Shortly thereafter the pope died, broken by the ordeal. His successor, Benedict IX, lifted the excommunication against the king but refused to absolve Nogaret. Nogaret had him poisoned. Philip then managed to secure the election of a man of his own choice, the archbishop of Bordeaux, Bertrand de Goth, who took the name of Clement V. Fearing the hostility of the Romans—with good reason—Clement V settled at Avignon in southern France in 1309, under the protection of

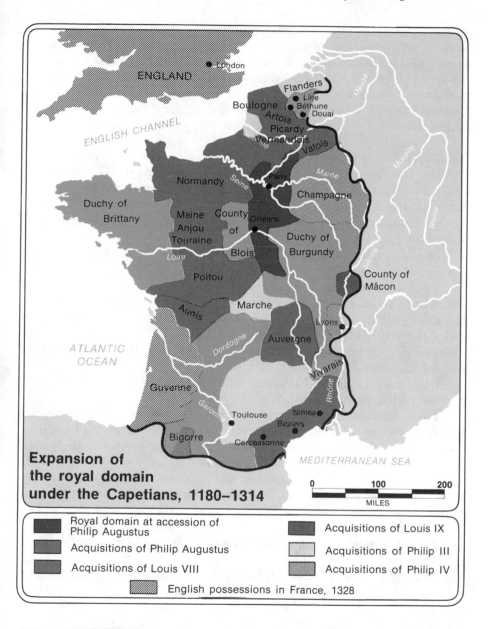

Expansion of the royal domain under the Capetians, 1180–1314

0   100   200
MILES

- Royal domain at accession of Philip Augustus
- Acquisitions of Philip Augustus
- Acquisitions of Louis VIII
- Acquisitions of Louis IX
- Acquisitions of Philip III
- Acquisitions of Philip IV
- English possessions in France, 1328

the king of France. His successors, who were also French, maintained the seat of the papacy there for almost a century.

This conflict and its outcome had enormous consequences for France, Europe, and all of Christendom. The total independence of sovereigns and states was secured at the expense of the popes' dream of a united Christendom. The decline of the papacy, which for a time became an instrument of the French king, deprived Christianity of an arbiter and conciliator capable of checking national aggression and ambition. The popes' stay at Avignon prepared the way for the Great Schism within the church at the end of the fourteenth century, a schism that contributed to the corruption of the clergy and the disintegration of Christendom.

The Government of the Kingdom. Philip the Fair attempted, without much success, to add two of the largest fiefs to his crown. To the south, Guyenne was twice conquered and twice restored to the king of England, in exchange for an arrangement that later proved to be particularly unfortunate—the marriage of the daughter of Philip the Fair to King Edward II.

To the north, the king of France attempted to seize the domains of the Count of Flanders, who made the mistake of allying himself with the English king. But the powerful townships of the area rebelled against the royal agents. The army Philip sent to suppress them was ignominiously defeated by Flemish troops at the battle of Courtrai, also called the Battle of the Golden Spurs, on July 12, 1302. The king had his revenge two years later at Mons-en-Puelle, a victory that gave him full control over Lille, Douai, and Béthune. The rebellious townships reverted to the Count of Flanders, who agreed to renew his homage as a vassal of the French king.

These adventures cost the king dearly. As a result, Philip the Fair had to resort to all kinds of operations to secure money. The feudal obligation of military service was a pretext to establish a tax called "army aid," imposed throughout the kingdom by the royal agents. It was the beginning of royal taxation and of a centralized administration imposed on the great fiefs as well as on the royal domains. The king also resorted to underhanded manipulation of the exchange rate and of the value of coinage; to forced loans, which struck hardest at Lombard and Jewish businessmen; and finally, to simple and brutal confiscation.

The Affair of the Templars. As an example of greed, nothing surpasses in cynicism the way the Templars were treated. Founded in the Holy Land two centuries earlier, this religious and military order had become a true financial and territorial power. The Templars served as bankers for Christian princes and possessed numerous domains, called "commanderies." Their fortress in Paris, the Temple, was the repository of the royal treasury. In October 1307 the king ordered all members of the order arrested and their property seized. His pretext was immorality and heresy. A trial was held under Nogaret. Confessions were extracted by torture and used to force Pope Clement V to suppress the order.

The grand master, Jacques de Molay, and fifty-eight knights retracted their confessions before they perished at the stake.

These were not the only atrocities that gave a sinister cast to the reign of Philip the Fair. Among the many cases that can be cited was that of two knights accused of adulterous relations with the king's daughters-in-law. Philip had them castrated, flayed, and quartered. The Christian justice of good king St. Louis was nothing more than a wistful memory. *The wicked Isabella learned her tricks from her father.*

SUGGESTIONS FOR FURTHER READING

Brown, R. A. *The Normans and the Norman Conquest*. New York, 1968.

Fawtier, Robert. *The Capetian Kings of France: Monarchy and the Nation (987–1328)*. New York, 1960.

Hallam, Elizabeth M. *Capetian France, 987–1328*. London, 1980.

Kelly, Amy Ruth. *Eleanor of Aquitaine and the Four Kings*. Cambridge, Mass., 1950.

Luchaire, Achille. *Social France at the Time of Philippe-Augustus*. New York, 1912.

Runciman, Stephen. *A History of the Crusades*. 3 vols. Cambridge, Eng., 1955.

Strayer, Joseph R. *The Albigensian Crusades*. New York, 1971.

Villehardouin, Geoffrey de, and Jean de Joinville. *Chronicles of the Crusades*. Harmondsworth, Eng., 1963.

Fau, Guy. *L'Affaire des Templiers*. Paris, 1972.

Labal, Paul. *Le Siècle de Saint-Louis*. Paris, 1972.

Levron, Jacques. *Saint-Louis, ou l'apogée du Moyen Age*. Paris, 1969.

5
The Capetians: Society and Economy

The political achievement of the Capetians took place against a background of great changes that affected both the material and the spiritual life of the French nation: growth of population, progress in agriculture, the revival of trade relations, the development of urban life, the increased hold of a purified religion, and the flowering of arts and letters.

I. ECONOMY AND SOCIETY

Agricultural Progress. The end of the invasions and the relative security ensured by the strengthening of royal power and the peaceful influence of the church (see p. 67) would alone have favored the progress of agriculture. So did the increased use of iron in traditional farm implements. But the Middle Ages also produced several remarkable technical innovations:

- The horse collar and iron horseshoes, which permitted the more effective use of horses in tilling and transport, in place of yoked oxen and human muscle.

- The moldboard and wheeled plow, which permitted deeper and more frequent tilling, and the tilling of soil obstructed by roots and stones.

• The water mill, which served not only to mill grain but also to crush materials used by industry (such as tanniferous bark, clay, and pigments), to sharpen tools, and to saw wood.

• Crop rotation, which reduced the area of land left fallow.

Not only was output increased, but cultivated areas expanded rapidly at the expense of wasteland, swamps, and forest edges. These clearings are today recalled in the innumerable place names based on the roots *essarts*, *sarts*, and (in the south) *artigue* (i.e., cleared ground). Grapevines also expanded rapidly over hillsides, furnishing a product of great commercial value, which permitted agriculture to emerge from the narrowly bounded, self-sufficient economy based on simple subsistence.

Growth of Population. This great progress was both made possible and assisted by an extraordinary rise in population. The causes and phases of the phenomenon are little known, but the signs of it are indisputable, as in the fragmentation of rural farmland and the increased number of parishes. (The word *villa*, which had hitherto designated a large estate, now took on the modern meaning of village.) There was also a multiplication of rural communities newly created by the lay and ecclesiastical lords concerned with putting their land into production. These places were called "new towns" (*villes neuves*), "franchises," "refuges," and "burgs." Peasants were drawn to them by concessions that freed them from many services that farmers elsewhere had to render. The establishment and growth of towns, the proliferation of monastic orders, and finally the rise of emigration periodically poured forth surplus French warriors into Spain, southern Italy, and the East.

A conservative estimate of the population in the territory directly controlled by the king in 1328 is 12 million persons, as compared to only 4 million in 1086. Thus the population may have tripled in two and a half centuries, a growth rate unequaled in French history. The whole of the kingdom, including major fiefs, may have had between 16 and 17 million people at that time.

The Reawakening of Trade and Industry. The surplus of agricultural production had a stimulating effect on the other sectors of the economy. To the manorial lords and landowners, who were the main beneficiaries of these advances, increased income brought the means and desire to improve their lot. For the nobles this new affluence meant that stone could replace wood in the construction of their fortresses, that they could improve their defensive and offensive arms, and that they could clothe and feed themselves with greater refinement. For the clergy it meant the capacity to build even larger and more splendidly decorated churches and monasteries.

Since these consumer goods generally had to be imported from afar, there was a revival of trade between regions within and outside the kingdom. To the north and south of France a host of seaports opened, some on the Baltic and North seas after the Vikings became Christianized, others—the most important—on the Mediterranean. This great interior sea, which had been closed to Christian trade for three centuries by the Arab conquests, was now reopened by the Crusades. Venice, Genoa, Pisa, Barcelona, and Marseilles became centers for trade in the goods of the East—spices, perfumes, incense, fine fabrics, carpets, weapons, and jewelry.

The merchants who transported and sold this merchandise were forced to join together to defend themselves against the bands of thieves they met en route, and even against the exactions of the lords whose lands they crossed. The merchant associations, called "guilds," "hanses," "fraternities," or "brotherhoods," sometimes stimulated the growth of urban communities. One such group was the hanse of merchant-boatmen of Paris, whose important role is recalled by the ship that today appears in the city's coat of arms.

Fairs. In order to resupply themselves with trade goods under conditions of optimum choice and security, the wholesale and retail merchants, who often traveled long distances, gathered at fixed times at certain places, generally close to an important town. These fairs lasted several weeks. An ingenious system of accounts based on credits enabled merchants to transact an infinitely greater volume of business than the available money supply would have allowed. In the thirteenth century the most important fairs in the West were held in Champagne, at Troyes, and Provins, in an area where trade networks came together from the north down the Meuse and the Scheldt, from the Atlantic in the west along the Seine and the Marne, and from the Mediterranean via the Rhône and the Saône.

Towns. The reawakening of trade stimulated the revival of urban life. Near ancient centers, narrowly confined within their ramparts, appeared *faubourgs* (suburbs) inhabited by merchants and artisans. These tradespeople also formed guilds, and their numbers were increased by the surplus labor available from the neighboring countryside. The artisans essential to daily life—butchers, millers, bakers, coopers, shoemakers—were everywhere, but a town became truly important wherever there were textile industries that produced for export. This was particularly so in the clothmaking towns that developed in the region between the Somme and the Scheldt.

Occasionally these were entirely new centers, towns that grew up on sites favorable to trade and industry—at crossroads, fords, and river junctions, where water favored the establishment of mills and seaports. Once they became fairly important, suburbs and towns were enclosed with walls.

In a society based entirely on the needs of rural agriculture and feudal relations, these middle-class centers represented a foreign and unassimilable element. Thus, once they became strong enough, the heads of the trade and craft guilds organized "communes"; that is, they joined together by taking an oath (*conjuration*) with the aim of wresting charters of concessions from the local lord, which would create a government better adapted to their activities. These charters limited and defined the taxes due to the lord; created a special tribunal and a uniform judicial code recognized by members of the commune, whatever their origin (former serfs, freemen, or foreigners, who had previously been subject to diverse legislation and authority); granted exemption from tolls and other exactions levied elsewhere in the lord's estates; and authorized the formation of defensive militias. Such charters were often secured by violent insurrection but more often by the payment of money. Once freed from the feudal regime, a commune established a municipal government elected by the well-to-do middle class. In northern France these magistrates were known as *échevins* and in the south as consuls, a reminder of Roman institutions.

Of all the towns of the kingdom, Paris already held the highest position, for it was not only a center for merchants and craftsmen but the seat of royal administration and of the most prestigious university in the West. In St. Louis's time its population may have reached 50,000. Under Philip Augustus the spacious suburbs that had developed on the two banks of the Seine, outside the original nucleus on the Ile de la Cité, had been surrounded by a fortified wall approximately 9,000 yards long. Portions of it are still visible.

Knighthood and Nobility. In the long run the new urban society and the money economy on which it was based served to break down the social order that originated in the feudalism of the high Middle Ages. "Some pray, others fight, and the rest work"—such was the picture drawn in 1031 by Adalberon, bishop of Laon, and this image endured long after it ceased to mirror reality.

The warrior class (*milites*) included diverse elements: great lords, princes, and knights; lesser lords who lived on a modest estate attached to a castle and were always ready to respond to the call of their suzerain, whose reserve they formed; and lastly, landless warriors who lived in the fortress with the lord.

All these men were linked by the common occupation of warrior, which was their reason for being. They all called themselves "knights" (*chevaliers*), for it was ownership of a horse (*cheval*) that allowed them to take part in expeditions. Entry into "knighthood" through the ceremony of "dubbing" raised the warrior into the class of privileged men, destined to live on the labor of those they oversaw and—in principle—protected.

However, as the order imposed by the king and the church reduced their opportunity to fight, as wealth less often took the form of war prizes than of feudal dues regularly paid, and as armies of lawless mercenaries grew, another idea, that of lineage, overtook knighthood in the definition of noble status. This was the idea of a community of interests that brought together the descendants of an ancestor who passed on a heritage that was the basis of a family's power and fame. The authority of the head of the house, always the eldest male, eclipsed that originating in ties of vassalage. A sign of this development was the spread of the use of a surname drawn from the name of an estate, castle, or town.

The Rural World. The development of the peasants' world, which came slowly and in any case varied widely from region to region, was moving in the direction of legal equality as it related both to land and to persons.

Around the ninth century, besides the estates that were held directly as fiefs, two kinds of land were generally distinguished—*censives* and *alleux*. The *censive* was granted by a lord to a farmer in exchange for the payment of dues either in money or in kind (a *cens*). The *alleu* was free land that a person held by inheritance. Over the course of centuries, these *alleux* gradually disappeared. Most of them became regular *censives*, and some—the most important—were transformed into fiefs. The enfeoffed lands themselves were subdivided, for purposes of farming, into *manses* or *coutures*, granted to serfs or free peasants. The result was that all the land became a network of small family farms called *feux* (hearths), generally grouped into parishes and paying various dues to the local lord, who was said to hold the *ban*.

A similar development tended to equalize conditions among men. Former slaves became serfs attached to the farms they had been granted. Gradually their condition tended to resemble that of freemen or *colons*, who became dependents of a lord on the *manse* or *couture* that had been granted to them, and of the *hôtes* (denizens) who were drawn to land that needed clearing. Following the example of the towns, these peasants of various backgrounds occasionally joined together to secure charters that fixed and limited their obligations. Occasionally they took advantage of their lord's need for money to buy back certain burdensome obligations.

At the end of this development the people who worked the land, who were held in disdain by bourgeoisie and nobles alike, were more sharply separated from the nobles than they had been in the Carolingian period. From this situation came the more or less pejorative sense acquired by words that originally had concrete meanings: *vilain* (villain, a farmer attached to a large estate or villa); *manant* (laborer, a man attached to a *manse*, from the Latin *manere*, to reside); *rustre* or *rustaud* (rustic, a man from the country, from the Latin *rus*); *roturier* (commoner, a farmer settled on a piece of land granted for the purpose of clearing, from the Latin *ruptura*).

II. THE CHURCH

An Essential Institution. Whatever his political allegiance or social status, every Frenchman, from the king to the lowliest "villain," considered himself to be first and foremost a Christian, a member of the vast society of the church. The church was expected to provide the assistance and instruction that enabled one to attain the final goal, the blessings of Paradise. Its rites and sacraments encompassed the life of each person from birth till after death. Its instruments of hierarchical rule covered society at every level like a vast net, its efficacy enhanced by the fact that its earthly representatives were generally a moral and intellectual elite. To be a cleric in this period was by definition to be an educated man. As the clergy was subject to the rule of celibacy, it could renew itself only by recruiting from all levels of society. As a result, it was not a separate caste; on the contrary, its life was intimately linked with that of the Christian laity.

But since the church was deeply rooted in human society it was infected by society's weaknesses and vices, and its institutions reflected in many ways those developed by civil society in every age.

Finally, the preeminent role of what was specifically French in the rise of Christianity in the twelfth and thirteenth centuries must be emphasized. The popes more than once took refuge in France during their struggle with the German emperor and held their councils there. It was in France that the idea of a crusade arose. France was the birthplace of great monastic orders that spread throughout Europe. In France developed that incomparable center of intellectual activity, the University of Paris. Finally, it was France that provided Western Europe with the basis for a new architecture and a new art.

The Secular Clergy. The secular clergy, so called because it lived "in the world" (*saeculum*), mingled with the Christian population and thus was vulnerable to contamination by a brutal society. The considerable wealth acquired by the bishops and the income attached to all ecclesiastical functions attracted the greed of the laity. In the tenth century the princes, lords, and knights managed to convert the dignities and offices of the church into hereditary property that could be distributed to a faithful follower or a member of the family, or even sold to the highest bidder. The papal throne at Rome itself was disputed between Italian lords and the German emperor.

Appointed under these conditions, many bishops lived like secular lords, fighting, hunting, and keeping concubines, while the parish priests, who lived modestly, were scarcely distinguishable from their flocks.

Two factors in particular helped to bring the church out of this sorry state of affairs, beginning in the eleventh century:

First, a kind of spiritual awakening at the thousandth anniversary of the death of Christ. Because of a mistaken interpretation of Scripture, a belief sprang up that the end of the world and the Last Judgment were imminent. The calamities that were then afflicting Christendom—plague, famine, war, heresy—were those mentioned in the Apocalypse as the signs of the last days. The anguish awakened in one's conscience prepared one to do penance and to reform oneself so as to appease the wrath of God. The persistence of this idea, even apart from the terrors of the year 1000, which have been exaggerated by the Romantic historians of the nineteenth century, no doubt explains why the theme of the Last Judgment appeared on the tympanums of all new churches.

Second, the investiture controversy. Pope Gregory VII, a Benedictine monk trained at Cluny in France, led a memorable struggle against the German emperor and succeeded in establishing the principle that the dignities and powers of the church could no longer be conferred by kings, princes, and lay lords. The bishops, who henceforth were to be elected by the canons and the people, would receive their spiritual powers from the pope through the intermediary of the archbishops. At most the ruler or lord would have the authority to invest the chosen individual with the temporal property associated with his office.

This Gregorian reform, introduced into France and applied by kings as pious as Louis VII and St. Louis, created an episcopate of great merit. The bishops, in turn, tried to raise the dignity of the parish clergy, particularly by fighting concubinage. But for lack of sufficient education, the country priests preserved a religion that was still permeated with the beliefs and practices of paganism.

The rebirth of towns was a boon to the bishops and the clergy in urban parishes. Helped by the spirit of competition among professional guilds and urban communes, they brought forth on French soil that "white robe of new churches" that the monastic chronicler Raoul Glaber glorified as early as the beginning of the eleventh century. Though we must leave to art historians the task of describing the development of medieval architecture, we cannot fail to mention here that its most original creations, the great Gothic cathedrals, were born on French soil, and more precisely in the royal domain. The most perfect example of the new style was the royal abbey of St. Denis, whose basilica Suger reconstructed between 1132 and 1144. For all of Christian Europe that imitated it, it was the *opus francigenum* (work of France).

Monastic Orders. Because of the importance of the domains that depended on them, monasteries were also often the prey of lay lords. Here, too, the introduction of Gregorian reforms permitted monks to devote themselves more faithfully to their essential function of raising heavenward the perpetual prayer that brought redeeming grace to the living and the dead. To those men and women who were sickened by the brutality and immorality of feudal society, the monastic orders offered a peaceful refuge. To the peasants in their vicinity the monasteries were holy sanctuaries against soldiers, and to the children of noble families and future clerics they were schools.

An abbey that became too populous, or one that simply had received another estate, might establish offshoots. Such new houses were called priories when they remained associated with their mother institution.

The papacy, once its independence from secular rulers was established, recognized the advantage that the head of the church might derive from monastic institutions. The pope placed monasteries in his direct service by exempting them from the bishops' jurisdiction. The abbots, elected by the monks, thus received their spiritual powers directly from the Holy See. The king's consent was still necessary, however, because of the immense territorial wealth over which the abbots presided. In the feudal sense, they were lords.

Cluny. A third element in the reform and prosperity of monastic institutions was the birth of vast brotherhoods of monastic houses that depended on a single authority and observed the same rule. The example was set by Cluny, a Benedictine abbey that enjoyed the privilege of immunity from its founding in 910. Around the year 1000, the abbot Odilon managed to free the daughter houses, too, from the authority of the bishops, and made their heads, whether abbots or priors, subordinate only to the abbot general, the head of the mother house. Thus the same discipline could be imposed everywhere. The Cluniac order expanded enormously under the rule of two exceptional men: Odilon, from 994 to 1049, and Hugh the Great, from 1049 to 1109. At Hugh's death the order numbered 1,184 dependencies, a veritable empire, whose head was almost as powerful as the pope. At Cluny itself, where more than 300 monks lived with hundreds of lay brothers, or servants, Hugh built the largest basilica in Christendom—613 feet at its greatest length, 239 feet wide in five naves, and 985 feet high under the central nave.

Citeaux. By the twelfth century, the life of the Cluniac monks had come to be organized around the celebration of a lavish liturgy, and their ownership and management of vast estates had made them rich and worldly. The life they offered no longer satisfied those who thirsted for evangelical perfection. Other monastic orders took up the task. The Carthusian order was established by St. Bruno on a virtually inaccessible mountain and was devoted to a life of total solitude. The Cistercian order, founded by Robert de Molesmes at Citeaux in 1098, was even more austere.

The Cistercians claimed to be returning to the original rule of St. Benedict in all its purity, rejecting all unnecessary ornamentation in worship and buildings. Practicing abstinence and silence, and dressed in undyed coarse wool, they divided their time between prayer and manual labor. The better to flee the world, the Cistercians established monasteries in wastelands and forests, which they cleared and cultivated with only the help of their lay brothers, for they desired neither servants nor vassals. They shunned the monarchical system of the Cluniacs and placed supreme authority in the hands of an assembly or general meeting held each year at Citeaux.

The order's expansion was due primarily to the influence of Abbot Bernard of Clairvaux (1091–1153). Preacher, reformer, author of books on spirituality and theology, counselor of kings and popes, St. Bernard joins St. Louis as an incarnation of the medieval soul. At his death the Cistercian order numbered 343 abbeys, and by 1300 there were nearly 700.

The Mendicant Orders. The search for evangelical perfection in utter poverty inspired a new way of religious life at the beginning of the thirteenth century. At about the same time (1210 and 1215) the Italian Francis of Assisi and the Spaniard Dominic of Osma, who had gone to Languedoc to fight the Albigensian heretics, secured approval from Rome to establish mendicant orders that would possess neither land nor houses, and would live on alms alone. Unlike the Carthusians and Cistercians, who sought salvation in a complete separation from the world, Franciscans and Dominicans wanted to mingle with the people and preach by example and word. Thus they lived primarily in the cities. Although of foreign origin, these two orders spread rapidly in France. Just as the eleventh century had been the age of the Cluniacs and the twelfth century that of the Cistercians, the thirteenth century was the age of the mendicants.

The need to learn how to teach and to strengthen doctrine, in order to defend it against the deviations of an era fertile in daring ideas, led some mendicants, such as the Franciscan St. Bonaventure and the Dominican St. Thomas Aquinas, to take an eminent place among the doctors of the University of Paris.

The University. Each cathedral church was required in principle to organize a school to educate clerics. The school established by the church of Notre Dame of Paris naturally gained the greatest fame. Men came to it not only from all provinces of the kingdom but from foreign countries as well. Around those teachers authorized by the bishop to grant diplomas and degrees there gradually gathered an ill-defined host of independent teachers. At first ordinary tutors, these teachers without official rank eventually eclipsed those of the episcopal school. With their students' support they demanded the right to organize along the lines of other urban trades. After epic struggles with the bishop and the king's representatives, the pope intervened and the teachers secured satisfaction. Two pontifical acts of 1215 and 1231, accepted by the king, made the Universitas Magistrorum et Scolarum an autonomous corporation, totally independent of the bishop and endowed with judicial immunities.

There were no buildings intended especially for courses, and students lodged as they could in the quarter that had grown up on the site of the ancient Roman city between Mount St. Geneviève and the Seine —the Latin Quarter.

The most fortunate were those who were accepted as scholarship students in the "colleges," which were similar to those of the *Cité Universitaire* in Paris today; there they often found themselves among other students from their native regions. The most famous of these colleges, founded by Robert de Sorbon, chaplain to King Louis IX, accepted only theology students. The teachers at the "Sorbonne" became the most respected doctrinal authorities of Christendom. As one contemporary put it, the University of Paris was the "oven where the intellectual bread for the whole world was baked."

Pilgrimages. Christian life in medieval France and its material and artistic coloration were marked almost as much by pilgrimages as by the rise of monastic orders. Pilgrimages were a sublimation of the natural urge to see other lands and a Christianized survival of primitive magical practices. Pilgrims were moved by their belief in the supernatural power of contact with or nearness to sacred remains, relics of Christ's passion, and by the feeling that at certain sites—particularly those blessed by the earthly passage of Jesus—the grace of purifying redemption and even physical cures might be obtained. To these lures was added the redeeming ascetic value of a long journey, with its fatigue and dangers.

The profits to be gained by a flow of pilgrims led the abbeys to secure remarkable relics (genuine or false) and to magnify the virtues and miraculous powers of the saints whose remains they preserved. The alms they collected were used to construct shrines glittering with gold, precious stones, and enamels, and to build increasingly elaborate sanctuaries. The most distant journeys did not deter crowds of pilgrims of all classes; they thronged to the sepulchre of Christ in Jerusalem and the tombs of the apostles Peter and Paul in Rome. But many other holy places were closer; the most popular were undoubtedly the tombs of St. Martin at Tours, St. Benedict at Fleury-sur-Loire, and above all the apostle St. James at Compostela, in Spain. Along the routes leading to Compostela the Cluniacs organized a kind of relay system of monastery-hostels, which spread across southern France and into Spain the architecture developed in Burgundy.

The Church and Peace. When feudal wars broke out during the tenth and eleventh centuries, and royal authority proved unable to resolve them, the church—that is, the bishops, assembled in council, or even by individual judgments—took a whole series of initiatives to limit the scourge and protect the weak against the brutality of the powerful:

- Refuges: zones marked by crosses, which protected the property of churches, peasants, and other workers, under threat of excommunication.

- Oaths of peace, based on the oath of vassalage, which pledged men of arms not to attack the persons and property of clerics and others who were unable to defend themselves.

- Peace associations, whose members pledged to fight together against troublemakers.

- The truce of God, a ban on fighting on certain days of the week and during certain periods of the liturgical year, such as Advent, Lent, Christmas, and Easter.

At the same time the church asserted its right to perform the ritual of "dubbing," whereby young men rose to the rank of knighthood. The blessing of arms and the oaths taken made the Christian knight the protector of the clergy, women, and orphans. The virtues of loyalty, charity, and honesty were held up to him as ideals fully as important as physical courage and the use of arms.

In the last analysis the only fighting that remained legal was that undertaken against the enemies of God and of the poor.

The Crusades. The movement for the peace of God naturally developed into that of holy war—the Crusade. In this movement were found also the motives of pilgrimages, for the first crusades were undertaken to assure Christians of free access to the tomb of Christ.

There is no need to detail here the history of the eight crusades that led armies recruited from all parts of Christendom to the East from the eleventh to the thirteenth century. Still, we must remember that it was in France, at Clermont, that Pope Urban II launched the First Crusade in 1095, and that St. Bernard launched the second at Vézelay in 1146. France furnished by far the largest number of crusaders, including three kings—Louis VII, Philip Augustus, and St. Louis. Consequently, it was in France that the Crusades had their greatest repercussions on European society.

In the East the crusaders discovered the attractions of a more refined society and brought back a taste for luxury. To satisfy this new taste, trade routes were established across the Mediterranean and through the port towns into the cities of the interior. From this development, as we have seen (see p. 58), grew the prosperity of the merchant class. The Crusades may also be credited with introducing into France certain kinds of trees and useful plants, and with the diffusion of certain artisanal techniques.

The Crusades were a force for internal order and peace, since they directed abroad the military unrest and ambitions of the warrior class. They weakened the power of the nobles, for thousands of them lost their lives, and the survivors were impoverished by the debts contracted to pay the costs of their travel. The king benefited from this situation by strengthening his authority and seizing many estates left without heirs. Urban and rural communities were able to purchase charters of freedom.

In all the lands that bordered the eastern Mediterranean, French crusaders implanted the use of their language and the terrifying or fascinating memory of their exploits and their military outposts—an influence that successive governments of France exploited as late as the nineteenth century.

SUGGESTIONS FOR FURTHER READING

Adams, Henry. *Mont-Saint-Michel and Chartres.* Garden City, N.Y., 1959.

Benton, John, ed. *Self and Society in Medieval France: The Memoirs of Abbot Guibert of Nogent (1064–1124).* New York, 1970.

Bloch, Marc. *French Rural History: An Essay in Its Basic Characteristics.* Berkeley, 1966.

Duby, Georges. *Early Growth of the European Economy: Warriors and Peasants from the Seventh to the Twelfth Centuries.* Ithaca, N.Y., 1974.

———. *The Age of the Cathedrals: Art and Society.* Chicago, 1981.

Evans, Joan. *Life in Medieval France.* 3d ed. London, 1969.

Haskins, Charles H. *The Rise of the Universities.* New York, 1923.

Knowles, David. *The Evolution of Medieval Thought.* New York, 1964.

Ladurie, Emmanuel Le Roy. *Montaillou: The Promised Land of Error.* New York, 1979.

Ozment, Steven. *The Age of Reform, 1250–1550: An Intellectual and Religious History of Late Medieval and Reformation Europe.* New Haven, 1980.

Pirenne, Henri. *Medieval Cities: Their Origins and the Revival of Trade.* Princeton, 1952.

Southern, R. W. *Western Society and the Church in the Middle Ages.* Harmondsworth, Eng., 1970.

Wolff, Philipe. *The Awakening of Europe.* Harmondsworth, Eng., 1968.

Pirenne, Henri. *Histoire économique de l'occident medieval.* Bruges, 1951.

6

The Hundred Years' War

*T*he gains of the Capetian dynasty and France's splendid achievements in the
thirteenth century were compromised by a century and a half of disasters. An
interminable and savage war ravaged the country, aggravating the effects of the
plague and famine that decimated the population. The authority of the crown
was challenged, but in the end it emerged stronger than ever, as did the territorial unity and morale of the nation.

I. PHILIP VI OF VALOIS AND THE ORIGINS OF THE WAR

The Accession of the Valois Family. The eldest of the three sons of Philip
the Fair, Louis X (the Quarrelsome), succeeded him without difficulty
in 1314. Louis died after two years on the throne, leaving only a daughter, but his wife was pregnant. The brother of the late king, Philip the
Tall, declared himself temporary regent. The queen gave birth to a
male heir, who was proclaimed king as John I, but the child died almost
immediately afterward. According to feudal custom, John's sister, Joan,
then eight years old, should have succeeded him. But Philip, with the
consent of his family and the nobles of the kingdom, had himself recognized as King Philip V.

Thus was established a precedent that came into play in curiously similar circumstances when Philip V himself, and later his brother, Charles IV (the Fair), both died without male heirs. Philip of Valois, eldest cousin of the three late kings, was recognized as regent, then as king in 1328. This decision, taken by an assembly of prelates and barons, was contested by the king of England, Edward III, grandson and son of the eldest daughters of two kings of France. But no one wanted an English ruler in any circumstance. To justify his exclusion, which went beyond the precedents so recently established, a custom of the Salian Franks was dredged up, according to which a woman could neither accede to the throne nor transmit to her son a right she did not possess. This so-called Salic Law, resorted to or invented to fit the circumstances and applied by no other reigning family, was henceforth the rule of succession in France. It permitted the monarchy to avoid the inconveniences of marital arrangements that often accompanied the accession of a young queen elsewhere.

For the moment, however, this questionable succession brought long and disastrous wars upon the country.

The Time of Calamities. The scourge of war was only one in a series of calamities of all kinds. At the beginning of the fourteenth century the economic conditions that had favored the rise of Capetian France and sustained it so well had deteriorated. The extension of arable land by clearing seemed to have reached its natural limits. Harvests were reduced by unprecedentedly cold and rainy summers, signs perhaps that the climate had entered a cooling phase. Famines and bad weather decimated the population, which in some places had grown enormously, and reduced the birth rate. Trade was greatly affected by the drop in agricultural income and by the diminishing supply of precious metals and the resulting currency fluctuations. The fairs of Champagne went into rapid decline. Trade between Italy and Flanders was increasingly carried on by sea.

At the end of 1347 the "black plague" (the term designates bubonic plague, but pneumonic plague was rampant as well) was carried from Central Asia by Italian ships that plied the Black Sea and introduced into France by way of Marseilles and Avignon. The scourge spread in 1348 with frightening speed and devastation. Its severity varied from place to place, but on the average it struck down between a third and an eighth of the population; in some towns more than half of the inhabitants succumbed. All forms of activity were suspended, even war. For almost a century after this first general catastrophe, the disease was virtually epidemic, flaring up from time to time in localized outbreaks. In 1361 the epidemic again spread across the entire country.

Famine, plague, and wartime conditions (for war was not van-

The first Valois and the House of Navarre

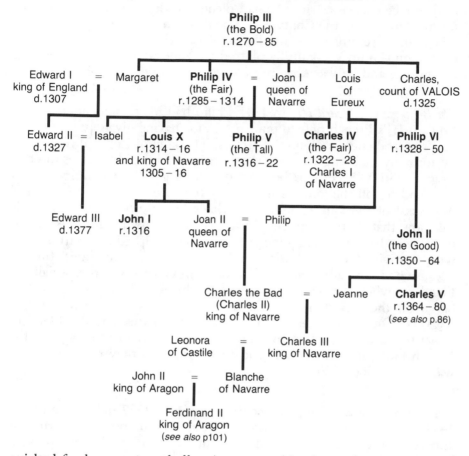

Philip III
(the Bold)
r.1270–85

Edward I = Margaret | Philip IV = Joan I | Louis | Charles,
king of England | (the Fair) | queen of | of | count of VALOIS
d.1307 | r.1285–1314 | Navarre | Eureux | d.1325

Edward II = Isabel | Louis X | Philip V | Charles IV | Philip VI
d.1327 | r.1314–16 | (the Tall) | (the Fair) | r.1328–50
| and king of Navarre | r.1316–22 | r.1322–28
| 1305–16 | | Charles I
| | | of Navarre

Edward III | John I | Joan II = Philip
d.1377 | r.1316 | queen of
| | Navarre
| | | John II
| | | (the Good)
| | | r.1350–64

Charles the Bad = Jeanne | Charles V
(Charles II) | r.1364–80
king of Navarre | (*see also* p.86)

Leonora = Charles III
of Castile | king of Navarre

John II = Blanche
king of Aragon | of Navarre

Ferdinand II
king of Aragon
(*see also* p101)

quished for long, as we shall see) now combined to reduce the population of the countryside so drastically that by the end of the fourteenth century many villages were completely abandoned and the land was overgrown. The remnant of the agricultural labor force that survived became more expensive. As a result, lords and landowning city dwellers had more difficulty in collecting their dues. As their incomes fell, they resisted ever more strenuously the tax demands of their sovereign, himself impoverished and hard pressed by the needs of war. Thus assemblies of gentry and burghers sought to impose control over the royal government.

To all of these afflictions were added political struggles that turned into veritable civil wars, and social unrest that revealed the exacerbation of class conflicts by the economic downturn.

The Beginning of the Reign of Philip VI. The reign of Philip VI of Valois began well. Edward III, engaged in a war against the Scots, had seemed to renounce his claims since he had pledged fealty to the king of France for his domains on the Continent. The Flemish, who had again risen in rebellion, were crushed at the Battle of Cassel and subjected to brutal repression. Philip VI skillfully plotted the annexation of Dauphiné[1] and Burgundy, and he was seriously considering a plan for a crusade.

The Break with Edward III. In 1337 Philip had his parlement confiscate Edward III's French fiefs to punish him for having given asylum to the king's mortal enemy, Robert of Artois. The king of England responded by formally claiming the crown of France. Why did he dare to challenge Philip VI? Perhaps because he saw a good opportunity to end once and for all the long-term anomaly that made the king of England the vassal of the king of France; perhaps because he found his hands free now that he had conquered the Scots; perhaps because he wished to recover the lands in Aquitaine that Charles VI had taken from him, which provided England with wines and other commodities; finally, because he found allies on the Continent, in Germany and especially in Flanders, where he resorted to economic blackmail by placing an embargo on the exportation of English wool, indispensable to Flemish weavers. Once war was declared, as he had expected, the Flemish, under the leadership of Jacques van Arteveld of Ghent, rose against the French king, and when trade had been reopened they recognized Edward III as king of France.

The Character of the War. The conflict begun in 1337 did not end until 1453. Those 116 years were broken by numerous periods of truce or apparent peace—sixty years in all—but the respites did not prevent local hostilities. On the other hand, the fortunes of war left certain regions untouched. The armies that the king of England had at his command were far smaller than those of his opponent, but they were much more homogeneous and disciplined, for they were not feudal armies, but professional ones, recruited by voluntary enlistment and compulsory service, and seasoned in the struggles against the Scots and Welsh. Avoiding formal battles as much as possible, the English practiced a war of attrition, either by cavalry raids that ravaged everything in their path or by surprise attacks carried out by garrisons stationed in captured fortresses.

Against such tactics the feudal host of the French kings, slow to mobilize and disorderly and undisciplined in the field, was usually powerless. Thus the kings increasingly had to resort to mercenaries

---

1. From this time on the heir to the French throne took the title of dauphin.

grouped into "companies," "bands," or "routes," which were recruited from the mass of small ruined nobles, peasants, and artisans driven from their villages and towns, and adventurers from abroad, particularly Genoese crossbowmen.

In its chronological development the war had two periods of major French disasters, each followed by complete recovery.

II. THE FIRST PERIOD: FROM PHILIP VI TO CHARLES V

The First Reverses. At the outset Philip VI had a large fleet, which might have enabled him to take the offensive against England. But it was surprised and destroyed in June 1340 at Sluys, off the Flemish coast. Edward III was therefore able to land at will on the Continent without having to fear an invasion at home.

He attacked first in Brittany, where two pretenders were in contention—Charles of Blois, supported by France, and John of Montfort, backed by England. This first expedition, which was halted by a truce, resulted in the creation of an English party in this province, which conducted a small-scale war linked to the main conflict. This "war of the two Joans" (Joan of Penthièvre, wife of Charles of Blois, who was captured by the English, and Joan of Montfort, widow of the pro-English pretender) was marked by the first exploits of Bertrand Du Guesclin.

In 1346 Edward III landed in Cotentin and led a destructive expedition across Normandy to the gates of Paris. He then beat a retreat toward the north, pursued by the army of Philip VI. Philip's army, which was far superior in numbers, finally caught up with Edward at Crécy and forced him into battle on August 26, 1346. The lack of discipline of the French knights and the skill of the English archers turned it into a disaster for the king of France.

Edward III was then able to mount a siege of Calais at his leisure. The town surrendered only after seven months of resistance. The angry king wanted to massacre the entire population, but when six burghers offered themselves as sacrifices, the townspeople were spared, though they had to go into exile to make way for Englishmen.

The war was interrupted by the pope's intervention, then resumed in 1355. Meanwhile, John II (the Good; that is, the Brave) succeeded his father in 1350. A brave knight, to be sure, but, as the chronicler Froissart said, he was "quick to make up his mind and slow to get an idea out of his head once he had put it in." This time the English attacked in the south under the command of Edward's eldest son, called the Black Prince. After ravaging Languedoc, they advanced into Touraine. John II rushed to cut off their retreat, but the Battle of Maupertuis, near Poitiers, ended in a new disaster for the French. The king himself was taken prisoner on September 19, 1356.

The Political Crisis. The kingdom sank into chaos. Bands of mercenaries, left without leadership, pillaged the countryside. In the area north of Paris an uprising of peasants, called the "Jacques," broke out and led to the massacre of manorial lords and the burning of their châteaux.

The dauphin Charles, a frail young man of eighteen, and his discredited advisers remained in Paris with neither troops nor resources. The opportunity was ripe for ambitious men, among them his brother-in-law Charles the Bad, a descendant of Philip the Fair through the female line, and the provost of the merchants of Paris, Etienne Marcel, a rich cloth merchant.

When the estates of Langue d'Oïl (the north of the kingdom) met in Paris, these ambitious men seized the opportunity presented by the gathering to join forces and wrest from the dauphin a "Great Ordinance" similar to the English Magna Carta, instituting a kind of parliamentary system. When the dauphin tried to trick them, Etienne Marcel had two of the prince's advisers murdered before his eyes. The dauphin managed to escape the capital and appealed to the provincial estates for support. In open rebellion, the provost of Paris made contact with the Jacques and permitted the English, who were in the pay of Charles the Bad, to enter the city. This was too much for the majority of middle-class Parisians, and on July 31, 1358, Etienne Marcel was murdered by followers of the dauphin, who returned to his capital and retrieved the reins of power.

The Treaty of Brétigny. In agreement with John the Good, who was still a prisoner, Charles negotiated peace. By the Treaty of Brétigny, in May 1360, Edward III received full sovereignty over Ponthieu and Calais, on the English Channel, and a considerably expanded duchy of Aquitaine. In exchange he renounced the crown of France and the other fiefs held by his ancestors. Without waiting for payment of his ransom of 3 million écus, John II obtained his freedom by leaving his two sons in England as hostages. A few months later one of them escaped. Honoring his word as a knight, John the Good returned to London as a prisoner. He died there on April 8, 1364.

Charles V. In both physique and morals the new king, Charles V, presented a complete contrast with his two predecessors. Ungainly and sickly, he was nonetheless gifted with fine and thoughtful judgment and lively intellectual curiosity—he created a rare library of a thousand manuscripts—and his piety recalled that of his model, St. Louis.

Charles the Wise adhered to a policy of strengthening the royal dignity by surrounding it with an illustrious framework of renovated or newly constructed palaces: the Louvre, Vincennes, and St. Paul in Paris. He did not lack for money. With the aid of carefully chosen officials, the royal administration was reorganized to raise taxes both

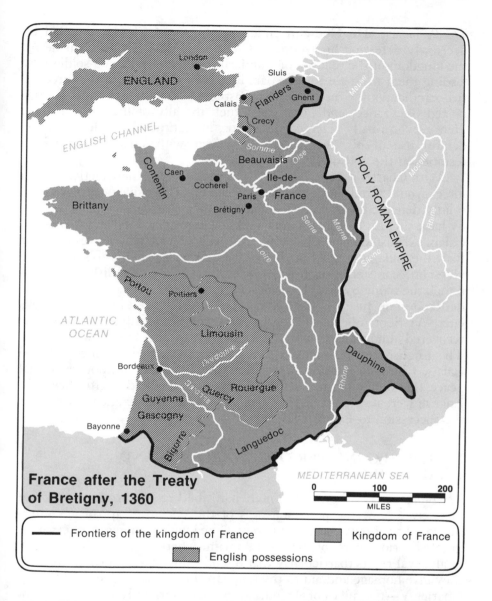

France after the Treaty of Bretigny, 1360

0   100   200

MILES

—— Frontiers of the kingdom of France   Kingdom of France

English possessions

direct (*fouages*) and indirect (excise taxes and the salt tax). With these resources he rebuilt and armed fortresses, manufactured cannon, built ships, and strengthened the discipline of his troops by paying them regularly.

Charles V found an excellent instrument for the waging of war in the person of Bertrand Du Guesclin. The king made this son of a minor Breton nobleman the supreme commander of his armies and gave him the title of constable, once reserved for the greatest lords.

The Reconquest. Du Guesclin ended the hopes of Charles the Bad by decisively defeating his troops at Cocherel in May 1364. Then he rid the kingdom of the scourge of wandering bands of pillaging soldiers by leading them to Spain to take part in a civil war between the forces of two candidates for the throne of Castile—Henry of Trastamara, supported by France, and Peter the Cruel, the ally of the Black Prince. Henry, who finally emerged the victor, in gratitude lent Charles V the helpful use of his fleet in Charles's war with Edward III, which resumed at the end of 1368.

With Charles's approval, Du Guesclin adopted a new tactic. French forces would avoid set battles and instead take defensive positions inside solidly defended fortresses, from which they would exhaust the enemy by harassing his rear guard and flanks. Three great English raids out of Calais exhausted themselves one after the other, with no result other than the pillaging and burning of hapless villages. For his part, Du Guesclin, concentrating his forces against isolated English fortresses, retook them one by one. Du Guesclin died at the siege of Châteauneuf-de-Randon on July 14, 1380, and Charles V followed him a few weeks later, on September 16. By that time their carefully laid plans had recovered almost all of the territories ceded by the Treaty of Brétigny. The English retained only a few coastal enclaves in France, around Calais, Cherbourg, Brest, Bordeaux, and Bayonne. Without a formal peace, this situation continued for thirty-six years in a de facto truce. The English were now absorbed by struggles among aristocratic factions over the succession to Edward III, who died in 1377.

III. THE SECOND PERIOD: CHARLES VI AND CHARLES VII

The Beginnings of Charles VI. The heir to the French throne was a child of twelve. Now the perniciousness of the system of appanages introduced by St. Louis became apparent. The king's younger brothers were granted various parts of the royal domain, where they exercised virtually all royal rights (particularly that of collecting taxes) on condition that they give homage and aid to the king. In this way the three brothers of Charles V—the dukes of Anjou, Berry, and Burgundy—and his brother-in-law, the duke of Bourbon, had been generously endowed. These uncles of the young king hastened to take control of the central government and royal treasury while assuming the role of true kings in their own appanages.

When Charles VI reached the age of twenty, he summoned the courage to free himself from his guardianship. He dismissed his uncles and recalled his father's former counselors—the "Marmousets" (the kids), as the ousted great lords called them derisively.

Their wise administration was beginning to bear fruit when in August 1392 Charles was struck by a first attack of madness during an inspection tour near Le Mans. Other attacks followed, broken by moments of lucidity. The unhappy king soon became no more than a puppet in the hands of an entourage of princes who fought over the material advantages of power.

Armagnacs and Burgundians. The contenders eventually became polarized into two factions: on one side, the followers of Philip the Bold, duke of Burgundy and count of Flanders, whose son John the Fearless succeeded him in 1404; on the other, those of Louis of Orléans, the king's younger brother, who was allied with the unscrupulous Isabella of Bavaria, Charles's queen.

The quarrel assumed the character of a war to the death in November 1407, when John the Fearless had Louis of Orléans assassinated in a Paris street. The king's uncles and the queen united against the murderer. The marriage of the young Charles of Orléans, the victim's son, to the daughter of Count Bernard of Armagnac brought them the support of this respected warrior and his Gascon mercenaries. The Orléanist or princely faction thus came to be called the Armagnacs.

Burgundians and Armagnacs fought particularly over possession of Paris, where John the Fearless had won popularity by flattering the bourgeoisie and the guilds with plans for reforms that would limit the crown's authority. Both parties lost and regained the capital in turn, inflicting terrible massacres. They went so far as to appeal to England for aid.

The Resumption of the War. King Henry V of England, insecure upon his throne, saw here a splendid opportunity to gather his unruly aristocracy around him. In September 1415 he retook Harfleur, then turned his small army toward Calais. The task of fighting the invader fell to the Armagnacs, who then controlled Paris and the royal government. Consequently, it was this faction that was fatally hurt by the defeat at Agincourt on October 25, 1415, when for the third time the marksmanship of the English archers overcame the unbridled impetuosity of the French knights. Henry V returned in triumph to London with his prisoners, among them Charles of Orléans.

The Treaty of Troyes. In the following years Henry V returned to the Continent and undertook the methodical conquest of "his" duchy of Normandy. Two rival French governments confronted him: that of Burgundy, who took advantage of the disarray of his enemies to return to Paris and secure the person of the king, and that of the dauphin Charles, a young man not yet twenty at this time, weak and irresolute, who had taken refuge at Bourges. Queen Isabella, who had settled at Troyes, mediated between the two sides.

John the Fearless and the dauphin Charles finally agreed to meet. The meeting, which took place on the bridge at Montereau, ended tragically when John the Fearless was killed by the dauphin's partisans.

The new duke of Burgundy, Philip the Good, sought vengeance by allying himself with the king of England. The Treaty of Troyes, in May 1420, stipulated that Henry V would marry Catherine of France, daughter of Charles VI, and that he would become his father-in-law's guardian and would rule the kingdom before he acquired it by right of succession. The "so-called dauphin" was completely disinherited.

Divided France. Two years later, in August 1422, Henry V died at Vincennes, and the unhappy Charles VI followed him shortly afterward, in October. The young Henry VI, the ten-month-old infant born of the marriage of Catherine of France and Henry V, was immediately proclaimed king of France and England. His uncle, the Duke of Bedford, exercised control over the regency. For his part, the dauphin proclaimed himself king under the name of Charles VII.

There were thus two or even three Frances, for the Duke of Burgundy, whose policy remained ambiguous, tolerated no English presence in his own states. They were so well administered that they were sheltered from the ravages of war and banditry, and brought their owner wealth far greater than that of either of the two rival kings.

The "King of Bourges," as his enemies called him, was recognized by all the provinces south of the Loire except Guyenne, which was firmly held by England. Even in the northern part of the country, controlled in principle by the English, the people were hostile to the foreigners and supported bands of rebels and fortified places loyal to Charles VII. But he lacked resources, and his will seemed to fluctuate with the rivalries of his unworthy favorites. Encouraged by this inertia, Bedford decided to strike a hard blow. In October 1428 he besieged Orléans; if he could capture it, he could take the Loire Valley. In the spring of 1429, after six months' siege, Orléans's situation seemed hopeless. Then came the miraculous intervention of Joan of Arc.

Joan of Arc. In the entire history of France there is no more stirring figure than the young peasant girl from Lorraine who became the soul of national resistance. Since the details of her extraordinary career are well known, only its major phases need concern us here.

In February and March 1429 Joan traveled from Vaucouleurs, in the east, to meet Charles VII at Chinon. She informed him of her mission to save Orléans and to drive the English from the kingdom.

In March and April, after long delays, the decision was made to

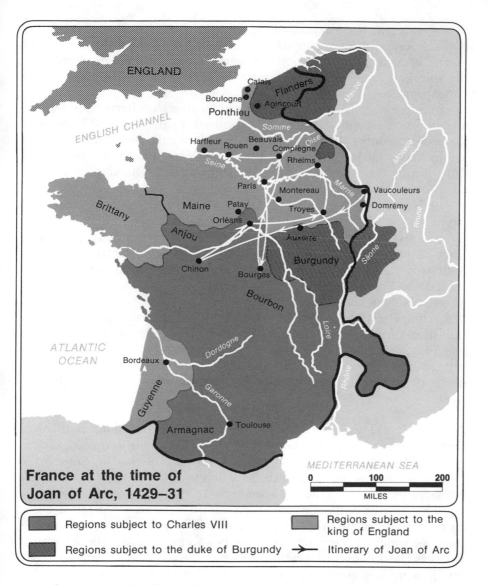

France at the time of Joan of Arc, 1429–31

0	100	200
MILES

Regions subject to Charles VIII

Regions subject to the king of England

Regions subject to the duke of Burgundy

→ Itinerary of Joan of Arc

seize the opportunity Joan offered and to place several thousand soldiers at her disposal.

On April 29 Joan crossed the Loire with several men and entered Orléans. Her arrival quickly raised the morale of the besieged.

Joan roused the French at the risk of her life, and from May 4 to 8 they seized the thirteen "bastilles" or fortifications established by the besiegers on the approach roads. The English retired in confusion.

In June an English army commanded by Falstaff and Talbot was routed at Patay.

In July, at Joan's insistence, Charles VII quickly marched on Rheims across country supposedly held by his enemies. In the eyes of all the French, the coronation ceremony on July 18, 1429, made him the sole king, chosen by God. His support grew in the provinces of Champagne and Picardy.

In September Joan was wounded in an attack on Paris. Charles VII abandoned a second attempt and withdrew to the Loire. Throughout the winter months the Maid (as she was then called) was inactive.

In May 1430, on her own initiative, Joan went to the aid of Compiègne, which was under siege by the Burgundians. On May 23 she was taken prisoner.

In November the Maid was delivered to the English in return for payment of a large sum, and they took her to Rouen.

The trial of Joan of Arc took place from January to May 1431. The English sought to prove that her mission was a diabolical fraud and thus to destroy the great wave of religious and patriotic enthusiasm that had roused the French against foreign domination. The instrument of this effort was Cauchon, bishop of Beauvais and president of the court, a man completely dedicated to the Anglo-Burgundian party. After an unjust and hypocritically meticulous trial, Joan was condemned to life imprisonment as a heretic. Finally a recantation torn from her by trickery (she quickly retracted it) permitted the court to sentence her to death as a "relapsed" heretic. She was burned at the stake on May 30, 1431.

Charles VII and Jacques Coeur. Charles VII, who had done nothing to rescue Joan, seemed to change after her death. He acquired such a remarkable group of civil and military counselors that he came to be known as Charles the Well Served. Among the foremost of his counselors were the constable de Richemont and especially Jacques Coeur.

This son of a modest merchant of Bourges was typical of those enterprising men for whom war becomes an opportunity to make enormous fortunes. Taking advantage of connections at the royal court of Bourges, he became its great supplier of products from the East. By building up a commercial fleet and trading posts, he eliminated the need to use Italian middlemen, and he established sales outlets in most of the large towns of France and neighboring countries. He also owned silk-weaving establishments in Italy, silver-bearing lead mines in Beaujolais and Lyonnais, and other properties. Charles VII, to whom he lent money, conferred various important offices on him: he was master of the mint, finance minister (*grand argentier*), and inspector general of the salt tax. These posts provided him with opportunities to become even richer and to acquire numerous estates. The hôtel or palace that he built at Bourges, still standing, gives some idea of his luxurious style of living.

The Beginning of Recovery. Deciding that the English cause was lost, the Duke of Burgundy resolved to withdraw from the conflict. By the Treaty of Arras, in September 1435, Charles VII ceded to him all of the towns that he had conquered on the Somme, and more important, dispensed him from all homage, making him an independent ruler.

Almost at once Paris opened its gates to Charles VII. The central organs of royal administration could now be reestablished there, but the king preferred to continue to live in his châteaux in Touraine.

Sporadic hostilities continued, interrupted by a rebellion of dissatisfied lords called the "Praguerie," which the king had much trouble repressing. All of these troubles encouraged the proliferation of armed bands, which the people called the "Fleecers" (*Ecorcheurs*)—a name that says much about the nature of their sinister exploits.

The Reorganized Army. A truce concluded in May 1344 gave Charles VII and Richemont the breathing spell they needed to reorganize the army. They eliminated the Fleecers by ordering the dauphin Louis to lead them off to fight the Swiss on behalf of Austria. The best forces were formed into fifteen artillery companies of 600 men each. Regularly paid and billeted at the king's expense, these horsemen, most of them nobles, were subject to strict discipline. This permanent battle corps replaced the old knights of the royal army. In addition, each group of sixty "hearths" (houses) had to support one archer or crossbowman, always ready to respond to the king's call. Finally, the brothers Gaspard and Jean Bureau organized an artillery mobile enough to play a role on the battlefield.

The End of the War. When the war resumed in the spring of 1449, this reorganized French army enabled Charles VII to reconquer his kingdom quickly. Normandy was taken in several weeks. A relief army sent from England was crushed at Formigny on April 15, 1450. The next year it was Guyenne's turn. The elderly Talbot went to its rescue, but he was beaten and killed at the Battle of Castillon on July 12, 1453. This was the end of England's rule on the Continent. It kept only Calais.

General Consequences. The lengthy conflict between the two great Western monarchies thus ended without a formal treaty. Despite its defeat, England retained its role as an island power. As for France, though it was frightfully ravaged and depopulated, it had finally thrown off the burden that had weighed upon its territorial integrity since the fateful marriage of Eleanor of Aquitaine and Henry Plantagenet.

Royal power was at last consolidated when circumstances enabled the crown to win the country over to a system of regular taxes and to create a permanent professional army. Most important, their ordeal had aroused in the French people a sense of national unity centered on a monarchy freed from the constraints of the feudal system.

SUGGESTIONS FOR FURTHER READING

Comines, Philippe de. *The Memoirs of Philippe de Commynes*. 2 vols. Columbia, S.C., 1969, 1973.

Fabre, Lucien. *Joan of Arc*. New York, 1954.

Fowler, Kenneth. *The Age of Plantagenets and Valois: The Struggle for Supremacy, 1328–1498*. New York, 1967.

Lewis, Peter S. *Later Medieval France: The Polity*. New York, 1968.

Lucie-Smith, Edward. *Joan of Arc*. New York, 1977.

Perroy, Edouard. *The Hundred Years' War*. New York, 1951.

Vaughan, Richard. *John the Fearless: The Growth of Burgundian Power*. New York, 1966.

Duby, Georges. *Le Procès de Jeanne d'Arc*. Paris, 1973.

7
The Dawn of
Modern Times,

1461-1515

The half century that separates the accession of Louis XI from that of Francis I can be seen as a period of transition. During the reconstruction that followed the Hundred Years' War the outlines of new institutions and new modes of thought and behavior appeared among the ruins of the medieval order. The personality and accomplishments of Louis XI reflect this mixture of ancient and modern.

The change in direction was particularly noticeable in foreign policy. Until then—except for the adventure of the Crusades—the vision of the French kings stopped at the boundaries of the kingdom. Now that they enjoyed undisputed authority at home and the strength provided by military and financial power, they could seek an active role in Europe—as the adventure of the wars in Italy demonstrates.

I. LOUIS XI (1461–83)

An Unusual Personality. When Louis XI became king at thirty-eight, he was repulsive to look at. His small body, thin and potbellied, was set on crooked legs. His bald head was dominated by a large nose that hung over thin lips. He shook continually with nervous agitation. He dressed more poorly than the poorest nobleman, in clothing of coarse gray fabric and a felt hat decorated with lead medallions. He hated ceremonies and celebrations. On the other hand, he delighted in traveling through his kingdom accompanied only by five or six close friends. Arriving unexpectedly in a town he would unceremoniously invite himself into the home of some rich burgher. His character was composed of a curious mixture of undesirable traits—a hard heart, despotism, knavery, cynicism, and superstitious piety—and royal qualities—intelligence, a lively curiosity, ease of expression, a sense of humor, enthusiasm for work, and total dedication to the interests of the crown. He preferred to negotiate with his enemies rather than confront them on the battlefield. If he could not win them over, he tried to immobilize them by secret maneuvers, trickery, and corruption. The web of his secret intrigues, reaching throughout Europe, made him the "universal spider," as Charles the Bold called him.

From Charles V to Francis I

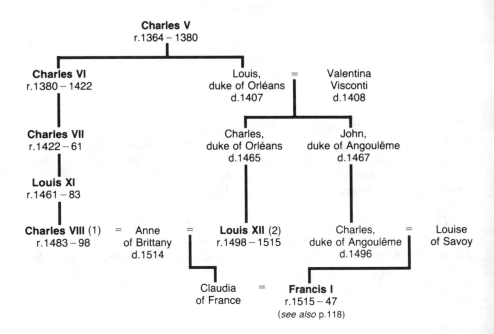

Internal Government. While he was still dauphin, Louis had intrigued against his father, Charles VII, who eventually sent him off to the province of Dauphiné. There he continued to defy the king by marrying the daughter of the Duke of Savoy against the royal will. Things reached such a pass that Charles VII invaded Dauphiné. Louis took refuge with Philip the Good, duke of Burgundy, who received him eagerly. Charles VII died in July 1461, convinced that he had been poisoned by his son. Louis XI made his entry into Paris accompanied by his "good uncle," the duke of Burgundy.

He immediately dismissed his father's counselors, only to recall the best of them once his first wave of anger had passed. But he firmly intended to be the sole master. Distrustful of the great lords, he treated them harshly. He was pitiless toward those who betrayed him. He had Constable St. Pol beheaded and Cardinal Balue imprisoned in an iron cage. He showed confidence in a small number of associates, some of lower-class origin: his doctor, Coitier; his barber, Olivier le Dain; and Tristan the Hermit, head of a special tribunal charged with summarily judging the king's enemies.

Although Louis XI spent very little on himself and his court, he did need considerable money to support ubiquitous informers and agents, make allies, and disarm enemies, and consequently he greatly increased the burden of taxation. He was so concerned with expanding taxable wealth that he took many measures to encourage trade and industry. For example, he encouraged English merchants to return to Bordeaux, tried to secure the Levant trade for Marseilles, sent trade missions abroad, established fairs, and introduced the silk industry to Lyons and Tours. He is also credited with establishing the first primitive royal postal system, and he planned to regularize weights and measures. This aspect of his achievement makes Louis XI seem the first modern ruler, the first one sensitive to economic realities.

The Struggle against the Nobility and the House of Burgundy. During the first ten years of his reign Louis XI had to struggle against the great nobles of his kingdom, who resented being deprived of power. Their opposition became increasingly dangerous when they found allies within the king's own family—his brother Charles—and abroad, in the king of England and the dukes of Brittany and Burgundy.

Burgundy was far and away the most dangerous of enemies. Ever since John the Good had given the duchy of Burgundy as an appanage to his son Philip the Bold, this branch of the Valois family had enormously increased its territorial might. Through marriage Philip the Bold had acquired Franche-Comté, a territory of the Empire; Flanders and Artois, which were still dependencies of the crown; and the county of Nevers. His grandson Philip the Good had inherited Hainaut, Brabant, and the Netherlands, and he had purchased Luxembourg and received Picardy from Charles VII by the Treaty of Arras.

To forge a state similar to other great Western monarchies, the powerful duke of Burgundy needed only to merge the two separate blocs of his possessions, on opposite sides of the line that divided the

Holy Roman Empire from the kingdom of France. The danger of this prospect to France—as great a threat as the Anglo-Aquitainian state had once been—explains the clear-sighted ferocity with which Louis XI worked to prevent it. The inevitable conflict was delayed by the caution of Philip the Good and Louis XI's continuing gratitude to him; but it broke out once Philip's impulsive and ambitious son, Charles the Bold, succeeded him in 1465.

The Leagues of the Commonweal. On three occasions the duke of Burgundy joined the rebellions of the great French nobles, who disguised their selfish aims under the convenient name of "Leagues of the Commonweal."

On the first such occasion, in 1465, the king had to do personal battle against the coalition of armies at Montlhéry, and he showed real courage. Afterward he appeased them by concessions. During the second feudal coalition, in 1468, Louis XI fell victim to his own treachery. He went in person to Péronne to try to negotiate an agreement with Charles the Bold. He hardly had entered the Burgundian fortress when Charles received word of an uprising at Liège in which agents of the French king had openly taken part. The furious Charles had Louis XI arrested. The king escaped only by bribing the duke's counselors and giving in to all of his demands, the most humiliating of which was that the king would join in punishing the rebels. Thus Louis XI silently watched the thorough looting of the town and the massacre of the people who were appealing for his protection. Once free, the king renounced most of the pledges he had made under duress.

During the third war Charles the Bold suffered defeat at Beauvais, where the resistance found its heroine in the person of a young woman named Jeanne Hachette. When the duke retreated, Louis XI put down the rebels one by one. Shortly afterward Prince Charles, the king's brother, died. He had been the hope of the malcontents and the focus of their intrigues. No one ever dared to challenge the authority of Louis XI again.

The Collapse of the Burgundian Dream. No longer able to find allies in France, Charles the Bold transferred his efforts to the lands of the Holy Roman Empire. He seized Gelderland in the northern Netherlands, purchased the rights of the duke of Austria over upper Alsace, and imposed a protectorate on the young duke of Lorraine. All of these moves were steps toward the long-desired consolidation of his holdings.

In 1473 he met with Emperor Frederick III of Hapsburg at Trier and asked him to raise Burgundy's German fiefs to a kingdom. The emperor at first appeared to agree, then abruptly refused. This about-face was the work of the secret diplomacy of Louis XI, who had spared no expense.

Using similar weapons the king fomented a revolt in the towns of upper Alsace and brought about an alliance among their league, the Swiss cantons, and the duke of Lorraine. Charles the Bold, for his part, secured the intervention of his brother-in-law and ally, the king of England. Edward IV landed with 13,000 men, but Louis XI quickly persuaded him to abandon this very dangerous game and negotiate. By the Treaty of Picquigny, in August 1475, Edward abandoned his claims to the French throne in exchange for 75,000 écus and a 50,000-livre pension—a considerable sum for a ruler whose budget depended on the whims of a parliament.

Meanwhile, Charles the Bold decided to deal with the Swiss, those "cowherds" who dared to resist him. But at Grandson on March 2, 1476, and at Morat on June 22, their infantry dealt him humiliating defeats. Retreating toward his possessions in the north, Charles tried to recover Nancy from the duke of Lorraine. The Swiss and Alsatians attacked him, and on January 5, 1477, the Burgundian army was once more ignominiously defeated. Two days later, Charles' body was found half frozen in an icy marsh.

The Burgundian Succession. A great political struggle developed around the inheritance of Charles, which fell to his only child, Mary, then thirteen years old. As her suzerain and natural guardian, Louis XI was in a good position, but the indecent haste with which he acted compromised his efforts. He first sought to have Mary wed his own son, the dauphin Charles. But since Charles was only seven years old, the marriage could obviously not take place immediately, and Louis seized the duchy of Burgundy and the county of Burgundy (Franche-Comté), Picardy, and Artois without waiting. Pressed by her subjects in the Netherlands, who feared the same fate, Mary gave her hand to Maximilian of Hapsburg (later Holy Roman emperor Maximilian I), son of the Holy Roman emperor. An indecisive war broke out in Hainaut and Flanders. Mary's accidental death on March 27, 1482, led the two adversaries to negotiate a compromise. Louis XI retained Picardy and the duchy of Burgundy. Eventually France also received Franche-Comté and Artois, which constituted the dowry of Princess Margaret, daughter of Mary and Maximilian, whose hand was promised to the dauphin Charles. The rest of the inheritance went to their son, Philip I (the Handsome), king of Spain.

Other Acquisitions. Louis XI had better luck with the house of Anjou. The last survivor of this powerful line of appanaged princes, the "Good King René" (the dethroned king of Naples), willed him all his possessions—Anjou, Maine, and, outside the feudal limits of the kingdom, Provence. With them came claims—fraught with consequences for the future—on the kingdom of Naples.

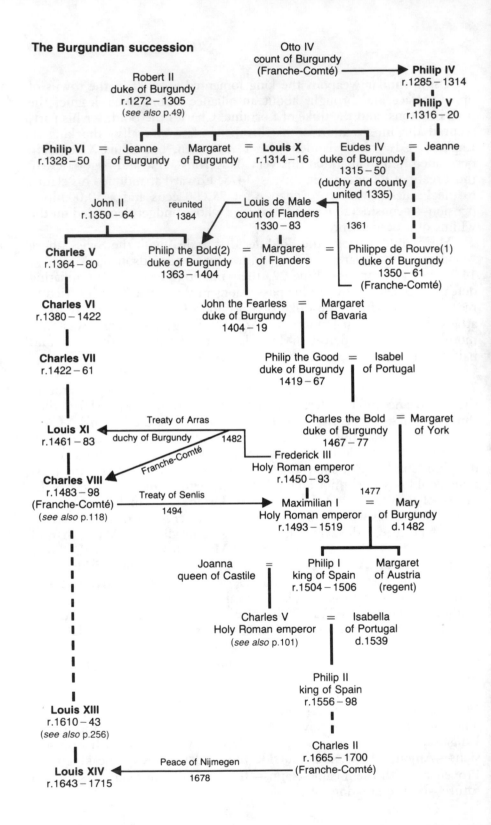

The Burgundian succession

Otto IV
count of Burgundy
(Franche-Comté) ⟶ **Philip IV**
r.1285 – 1314

Robert II
duke of Burgundy
r.1272 – 1305
(*see also* p.49)

Philip V
r.1316 – 20

Philip VI = Jeanne   Margaret = **Louis X**   Eudes IV = Jeanne
r.1328 – 50   of Burgundy   of Burgundy   r.1314 – 16   duke of Burgundy
                                     1315 – 50
                                       (duchy and county
                                       united 1335)

John II
r.1350 – 64   reunited   Louis de Male
          1384   count of Flanders
                       1330 – 83   1361

Charles V
r.1364 – 80   **Philip the Bold(2)** = Margaret = Philippe de Rouvre(1)
            duke of Burgundy   of Flanders   duke of Burgundy
            1363 – 1404   1350 – 61
                                       (Franche-Comté)

Charles VI
r.1380 – 1422   John the Fearless = Margaret
               duke of Burgundy   of Bavaria
               1404 – 19

Charles VII
r.1422 – 61   Philip the Good = Isabel
             duke of Burgundy   of Portugal
             1419 – 67

Louis XI ⟵ Treaty of Arras   Charles the Bold = Margaret
r.1461 – 83   duchy of Burgundy   1482   duke of Burgundy   of York
                             Frederick III   1467 – 77
               Franche-Comté   Holy Roman emperor
                       r.1450 – 93

Charles VIII ⟵   1477
r.1483 – 98   Treaty of Senlis
(Franche-Comté) ⟶   Maximilian I   =   Mary
(*see also* p.118)   1494   Holy Roman emperor   of Burgundy
                       r.1493 – 1519   d.1482

                                  Philip I   Margaret
           Joanna   =   king of Spain   of Austria
           queen of Castile   r.1504 – 1506   (regent)

                     Charles V   =   Isabella
                     Holy Roman emperor   of Portugal
                     (*see also* p.101)   d.1539

                             Philip II
                             king of Spain
                             r.1556 – 98

Louis XIII
r.1610 – 43
(*see also* p.256)

                             Charles II
                             r.1665 – 1700
Louis XIV ⟵ Peace of Nijmegen ⟵ (Franche-Comté)
r.1643 – 1715   1678

In addition, in a very debatable diplomatic and military action, Louis XI annexed Roussillon.

Beginning in 1482, Louis XI fell prey to sickly terrors of death and conspiracy, and withdrew to his small château at Plessis-les-Tours, where he huddled behind iron fences, moats, and traps. He surrounded himself with astrologers and soothsayers, while also seeking relief in the touch of sacred relics and the cures of charlatans. He nevertheless died with equanimity on August 30, 1483.

II. CHARLES VIII AND LOUIS XII

The Beaujeu Regency. Since the dauphin Charles was only sixteen, the regency was controlled by his older sister, Anne, and her husband, Peter of Beaujeu. Louis XI's daughter had inherited her father's political genius and cold determination. The government of the Beaujeus was excellent in all respects.

They succeeded in controlling the reactions that were inevitable after such a tyrannical reign. The Estates General, a kind of national assembly summoned in 1484 and composed of representatives of the clergy, the nobility, and the Third Estate or commoners, served as a safety valve for accumulated grievances. Concessions here, promises there, a few reforms, and everything fell into place.

The death of Duke Francis II of Brittany in 1491 introduced a problem of succession similar to Burgundy's, since Francis' only heir was a thirteen-year-old daughter, Anne. At first she believed she could defend Brittany's independence by offering her hand to Maximilian of Hapsburg, the most powerful of France's potential enemies. But he was too far away. The Beaujeus hastened to invade Brittany. To preserve at least the autonomy of her duchy Anne agreed to marry Charles VIII, and even promised that if she became a widow, she would marry the successor to the French throne. This was in fact what happened.

Charles VIII. On balance, the personal reign of Charles VIII (1491–98) was extremely negative for France. All of the young king's attention and the kingdom's resources were dedicated to futile enterprises in Italy. To them he cheerfully sacrificed some of the gains secured by Louis XI. To ensure the neutrality of Maximilian of Austria he restored Artois, Franche-Comté, and Charolais to him. Similarly, he returned Roussillon and Cerdagne to the king of Aragon. Finally, at a cost of 745,000 gold écus, he purchased the withdrawal of King Henry VII of England, who was besieging Boulogne. The accidental death of Charles VIII at Amboise on April 8, 1498, fortunately put an end to his dangerous fantasies.

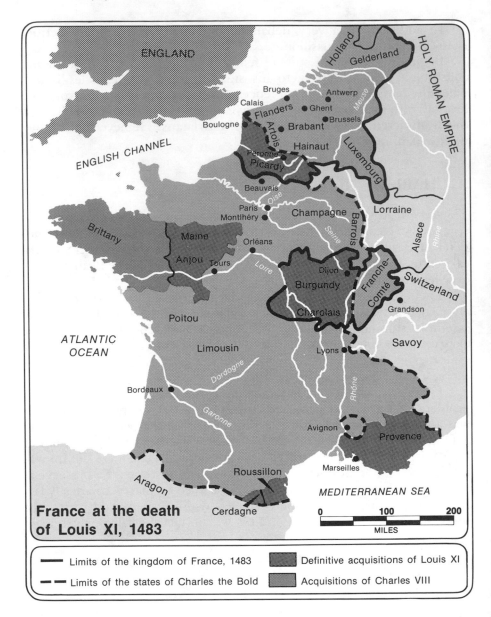

France at the death of Louis XI, 1483

Limits of the kingdom of France, 1483

Definitive acquisitions of Louis XI

Limits of the states of Charles the Bold

Acquisitions of Charles VIII

Louis XII. His successor and cousin was also caught up in the Italian mirage, but at least his internal government showed some merit.

As the representative of the cadet branch of the Valois, Duke Louis of Orléans had been involved in all of the revolts and feudal intrigues against the throne. Louis XI had punished him severely and, the better to bring about the extinction of this inconvenient line, had cynically compelled him to marry his own daughter, Joan, a poor little hunchback incapable of motherhood.

Once he became king, Louis XII hastened to annul this unnatural marriage. He then married Anne of Brittany, in accordance with the agreement she had made before she married Charles. Their only daughter, Claudia, was to wed the heir to the throne, the duke of Angoulême, the future Francis I. Thus the duchy of Brittany entered the kingdom permanently and without a tremor.

The personality of Louis XII—simple, generous, genial—imprinted a paternal character on his government in other respects as well. The reign had the good fortune to coincide with a period of strong economic growth. This prosperity was the result of the work of the three generations that had repaired the ruins of the Hundred Years' War, and undoubtedly also reflected generally favorable long-term conditions. But the king was given credit for it. The very rapid increase in population and overall wealth permitted the country to bear the financial burden imposed by Louis XII's adventures in Italy without much difficulty. Moreover, income from indirect taxes increased so much that the king lowered the far more hated direct tax of the *taille*. For contemporaries and posterity, nothing could have served better to establish the image of the good king. In 1506 the Estates General bestowed upon him the title "father of his people."

III. THE ITALIAN WARS

Origins. Italy had, of course, much to attract the French, and no other country was so well known to them. Added to the permanent connections that resulted from relations with the papacy were political relations born of the enterprises undertaken by French princes for their personal benefit in the thirteenth century. Conversely, the struggles within the Italian states had washed waves of refugees into France, as the vanquished parties hastened to seek the aid of their powerful neighbor. Finally, ever-growing trade had brought dynasties of Italian bankers and merchants to France.

Italy also seemed a prize easy to capture. The principal states, too weak to absorb the others and too strong to be absorbed, were always ready to enter into some coalition. They had no national armies because they had eventually found it more practical to have their wars fought by condottieri, military adventurers whom they could always hire or neutralize at a price.

As we saw earlier, Louis XI had inherited rights to Naples from the house of Anjou, but he had been too wise to stir up that hornet's nest. Charles VIII, raised on tales of chivalry and surrounded by young men who knew nothing of the horrors of the Hundred Years' War, dreamed of leading a crusade against the Turks, donning the imperial crown at Constantinople, and delivering Jerusalem. The first step on this glorious road was the reconquest of the kingdom of Naples.

The death in 1494 of King Ferdinand I of Naples, bastard son of the house of Aragon, provided an unexpected opportunity. Encouragement came from Italy—from the Borgia pope Alexander VI, whose opposition was the Duke of Milan, Ludovico Sforza; the reform party of Savonarola in Florence; and the Neapolitan nobility, restive under the yoke of Aragon.

The Expedition of Charles VIII. With all this support, the French expedition into Italy at first took on the aspect of a military promenade. One after another the cities gave Charles a triumphal welcome. On February 22, 1495, he made his entry into Naples, riding in a chariot drawn by four white horses, the imperial crown on his head.

The pretensions and greed of the foreigners, to whom they themselves had appealed, reawakened national feeling among the Italians. An anti-French league was formed under the leadership of Venice and with the support of King Ferdinand of Aragon and the emperor Maximilian. In danger of being trapped in his own conquest, Charles decided to scurry back to France. The allies tried to block his way through the Appenines near Fornovo, but their army was thrown into disorder by the furious charges of the French cavalry on July 5, 1495. The garrison that Charles left in Naples held out for many months but was finally forced to surrender in February 1496.

Louis XII and Milan. The accession of Louis XII gave the French activities in Italy a new dimension. A grandson of Valentina Visconti, Louis considered himself to be the legitimate heir to the duchy of Milan, where the Visconti had been replaced by an ambitious mercenary, Francesco Sforza. In preparation for war to take this inheritance, Louis embarked on an ambitious diplomatic campaign. He made alliances with Venice and with the Swiss cantons and assured himself of the benevolent neutrality of the emperor Maximilian and Pope Alexander VI. In April 1494 Ludovico Sforza, known as The Moor, was defeated at Novara. Betrayed by his own troops, he was delivered to Louis XII in an iron cage. He perished, a miserable prisoner, in the Château of Loches in central France.

The emperor Maximilian recognized Louis XII as the sovereign of Milan, and the wise and liberal rule of Cardinal Georges d'Amboise, Louis's representative in the duchy, established a solid foundation for his authority there.

The Second Conquest of Naples. The success of this operation encouraged Louis XII to try to retake Naples. Spain's intervention was feared, since Ferdinand of Aragon, already master of Sicily, would naturally defend his cousin, Frederick III, restored at Naples in 1496. Louis XII proposed that they undertake the conquest together and share the spoils. And so it was done. During the summer of 1500, the French and Spanish armies quickly seized the kingdom of Naples, and Frederick III abandoned his title to Louis XII. But the ruler of Aragon had never intended to share the prize. He contrived to provoke a rupture with Louis, and his army, capably commanded by Gonzalvo de Córdoba, the foremost soldier of the day, set about driving the French from Naples. The French, despite the legendary exploits of Bayard, the "knight without fear and without reproach," were finally forced to give up the struggle in 1504. Louis XII managed to save face, however, for Ferdinand of Aragon, widower of Isabella of Castile, married a niece of the French king, Germaine of Foix. Her uncle granted her his rights to Naples in exchange for 900,000 florins paid by the Spanish monarch.

Julius II against the French. Since the king of France had renounced Naples, the Italian wars might have ended there. They were reignited by Giuliano della Rovere, installed as Pope Julius II in 1503, who was more concerned with strengthening his temporal power than with fulfilling his religious functions: he dreamed of establishing his political supremacy over the Italian states. To do so, he had first to crush the Venetians, who had seized Ravenna from the Papal States. That done, he busied himself with freeing Italy from the yoke of the foreigners—the "barbarians," as Julius II called them.

The League of Cambrai, composed of the pope, the Florentines, and three foreign rulers—Louis XII, Maximilian of Austria, and Ferdinand of Aragon—was organized against Venice. The French army, the first to mobilize, bore the burden of the war alone and defeated the Venetians at Agnadello in May 1509.

Julius II took advantage of the French victory to negotiate the return of Ravenna. His diplomacy then turned the coalition against France. The Swiss and the young king of England, Henry VIII, also joined this Holy League.

The Fall of Milan. At first the war went well for the French. Louis XII had given command of his army in Italy to his nephew Gaston de Foix. This twenty-two-year-old man proved to be a gifted general. The speed of his movement and the daring of his maneuvers surprised his enemies and inflicted three successive defeats on them. Unfortunately, on the evening of his third victory, before Ravenna on April 11, 1512, he fell victim to his own impetuousness. His successor, Marshal de la Palisse, was forced to evacuate the duchy of Milan.

Early the next year France, once again beaten in Italy, found itself attacked on all sides at once: in Burgundy by the Swiss, in the Pyrenees by the Spanish, and in the north by the English and imperial forces. The death of Julius II in February 1513, however, deprived the League of its prime mover, and Louis XII negotiated truces with his enemies one by one.

He did not long enjoy the newly won peace. When Queen Anne died, Louis XII, as a token of his reconciliation with England, married the sister of Henry VIII. Ardent and frivolous, the young queen Mary led her elderly husband into a whirl of festivities and pleasures that hastened his death. He died on January 1, 1515.

Francis I. The young and impetuous new king, dreaming of gaining glory in war, quickly determined to conquer "his" duchy of Milan. Early in August 1515 he set out at the head of an army of 33,000 men—the largest and most splendid that had been seen for a long time. He crossed the Alps over the passes of Larche and Argentière, which were considered impassable by a large army and all its train—to the surprise of the Swiss, who were defending the traditional invasion routes at Mount Cenis and Mount Genèvre. Francis entered Turin and approached Milan. The Swiss attacked him at his camp at Marignano on September 13. In the fierce battle, which lasted two days, the French artillery, 300 cannon strong, played an important role for the first time. The king's victory was finally ensured by the opportune arrival of Venetian troops. Francis I, who displayed considerable valor, gained immense glory by beating the Swiss infantry, which until then had been invincible.

Negotiations began shortly thereafter. Francis I met with Pope Leo X at Bologna. From their meeting came the Concordat of 1516, which covered both political relations between the two temporal rulers and the statutes of the Church of France (see p. 108). The Swiss, duly appeased with gold, signed a "perpetual peace" by which they pledged never to serve as mercenaries against the king of France. Finally, by the Treaty of Noyon, the emperor and the king of Spain recognized Francis I's possession of the duchy of Milan in exchange for a second renunciation of all claims to Naples.

Conclusion. The Italian wars were thus ended. Actually, French armies again fought more than once beyond the Alps, but these operations were only secondary features of a far wider conflict between the houses of France and Austria for predominance in Europe.

The spending of such great resources and so much effort on the brief possession of the duchy of Milan is generally condemned as a senseless waste. Still, the results were not totally negative for France. Like the Crusades, the Italian wars provided an outlet for unruliness and a spirit of adventure that might otherwise have undermined the domestic peace of the kingdom. More important, they contributed to the triumph of Italian Renaissance art in France.

SUGGESTIONS FOR FURTHER READING

Calmette, Joseph L. A. *The Golden Age of Burgundy: The Magnificent Dukes and Their Court*. New York, 1963.

Huizinga, Johan. *The Waning of the Middle Ages*. New York, 1927, 1963.

Kendall, Paul M. *Louis XI: The Universal Spider*. New York, 1971.

Bartier, John. *Charles le Téméraire*. Brussels, 1946.

Delaborde, Henri. *L'Expédition de Charles VIII en Italie*. Paris, 1888.

8

The Birth of the
Absolute Monarchy,

1515-1559

During the first half of the sixteenth century, in the reigns of Francis I and Henry II, the kingdom suffered but survived the struggle against the house of Austria. In the end royal power was consolidated. Under Francis I new institutions strengthened royal power. The luxury with which the king surrounded himself and the protection he gave to literature and the other arts contributed to the incomparable prestige of the crown. Finally, economic progress brought about a transformation in the social order.

I. THE STRUGGLE AGAINST HAPSBURG HEGEMONY

Francis I. King at twenty, Francis I quickly charmed the French. He was tall, vigorous, brave in battle, cheerful, likable, generous, a lover of sports, tournaments, and hunting. He was endowed with a very keen taste for arts and letters, composed verses and songs, and was a brilliant conversationalist and writer of charming letters. But above all, he was a spoiled child all his life. He had been raised in an atmosphere of permissive adoration by his mother, Louise of Savoy, and his elder sister, Margaret of Angoulême. Impulsive and fickle, easily bored by serious affairs of state, he displayed an egotism that nonetheless helped to strengthen royal authority, for he could not bear to have his wishes thwarted.

He wasted the royal treasury to feed his appetite for pleasure and luxury and then exhausted his subjects by excessive demands for more money. Very much a ladies' man, he had official mistresses—the last of them was the duchess of Etampes—and innumerable passing affairs, which seem to have contributed to his premature exhaustion and death at the age of fifty-three.

Henry II. Francis' son, Henry II, as vigorous and enthusiastic about physical exercise as his father, had neither his lively mind nor his taste for the arts. Mistreated and kept in the background by Francis I, he had grown up lonely and withdrawn, a bit removed from a court that was too licentious for his taste. Once he was king, he did away with much of the lavishness of royal life and introduced stricter ways. These virtues did not prevent him from inflicting on his wife, Catherine de Médicis, a kind of *menage à trois* with his mistress, Diane of Poitiers, a woman twenty years his senior. Beneath an apparent crudeness and obstinacy, Henry II poorly concealed a real weakness of will and an inferiority complex. Here lies the explanation for the blind trust he placed in an all-powerful favorite, an old man who was narrow-minded, arrogant, and authoritarian—constable Anne de Montmorency.

Charles V. The principal political problem of the reigns of Francis I and Henry II was the struggle against the predominance of the house of Austria, represented by the emperor Charles V, and after 1556 by his son Philip II.

An extraordinary series of successions had bestowed the territorial inheritance of four monarchies on the young prince Charles, born in 1500. To this inheritance was added the immense colonial empire conquered by his subjects in America. He was the first of the rulers on whose lands "the sun never set."

Even in Europe, with his possessions encircling France from Flanders to the Pyrenees, Charles was a coalition all by himself. He hoped to make good use of his power to bring down France and to recover the whole of the Burgundian inheritance, which he considered had been unjustly taken from him.

This inevitable conflict, arising from geography and history, was poisoned by the personal dislike between the two rulers. Charles was as cold, vengeful, methodical, and austere as Frances I was lively, generous, fickle, and prodigal.

The Imperial Election. Their rival ambitions clashed in 1519 over the imperial crown of Germany. Although elective in principle, this crown

Richard Duke = Cecily Nevill
of York
(d.1460)

harles = Margaret
re Bold of York
t Burgundy 1446-1503
467-77 no issue

m → of Burgundy
d.1482
abella
o Bourbon

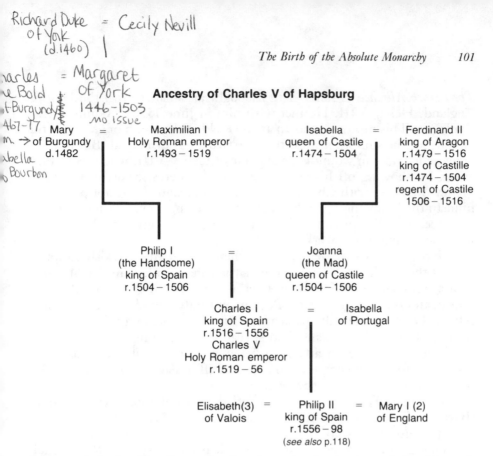

Ancestry of Charles V of Hapsburg

| Mary
of Burgundy
d.1482 | = | Maximilian I
Holy Roman emperor
r.1493 – 1519 | | Isabella
queen of Castile
r.1474 – 1504 | = | Ferdinand II
king of Aragon
r.1479 – 1516
king of Castille
r.1474 – 1504
regent of Castile
1506 – 1516 |

Philip I
(the Handsome)
king of Spain
r.1504 – 1506

=

Joanna
(the Mad)
queen of Castile
r.1504 – 1506

Charles I
king of Spain
r.1516 – 1556
Charles V
Holy Roman emperor
r.1519 – 56

=

Isabella
of Portugal

Elisabeth(3)
of Valois

=

Philip II
king of Spain
r.1556 – 98
(*see also* p.118)

=

Mary I (2)
of England

had not left the Hapsburg family since the beginning of the fifteenth
century. Charles, grandson of the last emperor, Maximilian, expected
to succeed him. But Francis I, pressed by several German princes,
declared himself a candidate. A pamphlet campaign sought to influence
German opinion, and his agents spread money by the fistful to buy the
electors and their counselors.

With the support of a syndicate of bankers, Charles carried the
election, but it cost him a sum equivalent then to 3,300 pounds of gold.
This gives some idea of what Francis' dream must have cost him. All he
gained was the permanent resentment of his rival, who became the
emperor Charles V.

The Nature of the Conflict. The struggle that began in 1520 went on for
thirty-nine years. Those who started it did not see its conclusion, for it
ended only with their sons, Philip II of Spain and Henry II. Six periods
of open warfare were broken by truces and treaties that were violated
almost instantly. Each of the two adversaries sought allies, so that most
European states were involved in the conflict at one time or another. As
a result, diplomacy took on major importance in the sixteenth century.
It went hand in hand with military action, and often proved more decisive.

The French Alliances. Francis I first sought an alliance with the king of England, Henry VIII. He met with him in June 1520 at Guînes, near Boulogne. This meeting, known as the Field of the Cloth of Gold, is still famous for the sumptuousness that the two kings displayed. But Francis I succeeded only in wounding the pride of Henry VIII, who was as vain as he, by showing off his superiority in all spheres. Shortly afterward Henry VIII met with Charles V at Calais and signed a secret pact with him. In the following years Henry changed camps several times, pursuing a seesaw policy intended to prevent either of the great rival monarchs from becoming too powerful.

More useful to France was its alliance with the Turkish Empire, then at the height of its power under the rule of Suleiman the Magnificent (1520–66). The Ottoman fleet dominated the eastern Mediterranean and roamed the coasts of Spain and Italy from its bases in North Africa. On land the sultan's armies, after overwhelming the Christian principalities of the Balkans, had spread into the Hungarian plain, taking Budapest and even attacking Vienna. On several occasions these offensives forced the emperor to relax his efforts against France in order to ward off danger from the east.

In 1543 a Turkish fleet commanded by the famous Khair ed-Din (Barbarossa) joined with the French to capture Nice. Once Francis I even permitted them to establish a land base at Toulon.

This alliance between the Very Christian King and the Infidel, however, scandalized Christian princes, alienated the pope, and provided the emperor with arguments in his diplomatic struggle against France. So Francis I, after attempting to minimize its impact, eventually renounced it.

Still, a very useful trade treaty, which had been concluded in 1535 under the name of Capitulations, remained in effect. Only ships engaged in French trade had the right to dock in ports of the Turkish Empire. The king of France was recognized as the protector of the shrines in Palestine. Consequently, his representatives on the scene, the consuls, had sole jurisdiction over all foreign Christians. Thus the political and commercial influence that France retained in the Near East until the nineteenth century was, curiously, the result of the contest between Francis I and Charles V.

The alliance between the king of France and the Protestant princes of Germany was almost as scandalous, since these princes were enemies of the papacy and Catholicism. But Francis I could not fail to support the emperor's enemies wherever he found them. The alliance between the king and the Protestant princes, already joined against the emperor in the Schmalkaldic League, was formed in 1532. The king more than once provided them with subsidies, and in exchange was permitted to recruit German mercenaries, who in France were known as *reîtres* (mounted troops, from the German *Reiter*, rider) and *lansquenets* (foot soldiers, from the German *Lanskuecht*, trooper).

The alliance grew tighter and more profitable during the years of Henry II. The Protestants, who had recently suffered a great defeat, signed a treaty in 1550 that secured them a regular subsidy; in exchange, according to the treaty, "it has been found equitable for the king of France . . . to take possession of towns that have at all times belonged to the emperor, although the German tongue is not used there, namely, Toul in Lorraine, Metz, and Verdun." The terms were carried out immediately. The acquisition of the "Three Bishoprics" was the most notable result of the long war between France and the Empire. It marked the first step in what has been called "the policy of natural boundaries," whose eastern objective was the Rhine River.

First Setbacks. Francis I made the mistake of failing to take advantage of the difficulties that beset Charles V in 1520, when he was challenged by the revolt of the *comuneros* in Spain. When he finally decided to intervene by attacking Navarre on behalf of his ally and relative Henry d'Albret, in March 1521, the right moment had passed, and the war dragged on there with no decisive outcome.

On the northern front, the imperial forces, supported by the English, on one occasion advanced to within twenty-nine miles of Paris. An unexpected gain for the emperor came in 1523 with the treason of the duke of Bourbon, constable of France. Dissatisfied with a verdict issued against him in a lawsuit involving the queen mother, Louise of Savoy, Bourbon offered his services to Charles V. But, contrary to his expectations, his vassals and clients rallied to the king. The treasonous constable fled to the emperor, who gave him a large army and sent him to attack Provence. Bourbon invaded the territory and laid siege to Marseilles, but the town held out until a French relief army could arrive. Having lost a large part of his artillery, he was forced to fall back to Italy.

But the main battlefield was northern Italy. The duchy of Milan, to which Francis I was most strongly attached, was three times lost and retaken. The third French counteroffensive ended in disaster. While besieging Pavia, Francis I was attacked by an imperial army commanded by Bourbon and the Belgian Lannoy. His lack of caution led to a crushing defeat in which 8,000 of the finest French knights perished. The king himself was forced to surrender to Lannoy on February 25, 1525. On the evening of the catastrophe, Francis I wrote to his mother the famous letter beginning: "Madame, to let you know how the remnants of my fortune fare, not a thing remains to me but my honor and my life, which is spared." The phrase has been condensed by popular history into "Madame, I have lost everything save honor."

The Treaties of Madrid and Cambrai. Relying on the code of chivalry, Francis I believed he could extricate himself by paying a large ransom. But the emperor treated him as a political pawn and had him transferred to Madrid, where he was held prisoner in a gloomy tower for more than six months. Ill and at the end of his patience, Francis signed an exceptionally harsh treaty to regain his freedom. He renounced all of his claims in Italy and French sovereignty (largely theoretical, it is true) over Flanders and Artois. He returned all property and dignities to the traitor Bourbon. Most important, he restored to Charles V the duchy of Burgundy and its dependencies. To guarantee the fulfillment of these terms, he turned his two sons over to the emperor.

Nonetheless, once the king had returned to France, in March 1527, he refused to abandon Burgundy, whose representatives protested that they wished to remain French. He was encouraged by allies who were drawn to him by fear of imperial hegemony. The Medici pope Clement VII, who had joined England in the League of Cognac in May 1526, was severely punished as a result. An army of imperial mercenaries, commanded by Bourbon, seized Rome in May 1527, and pillaged it unmercifully. The city took more than ten years to recover.

The war resumed on a grand scale, particularly in Italy, where two French armies in succession were lost. Finally, threatened by the Turkish siege of Vienna and by uprisings of German princes, Charles V agreed to negotiate a new peace. It was concluded at Cambrai in August 1529. This time he relinquished Burgundy, but Francis I confirmed the other concessions that he had made in the Treaty of Madrid. Bourbon was no longer a problem, for he had been killed during the attack on Rome. To recover his children, who were still prisoners in Madrid, the king had to pay an enormous ransom of 2 million écus. The future Henry II was to retain a long-standing hatred of the emperor as a result of his lengthy and harsh captivity.

The Last Wars of Francis I. The king used the few years of peace that followed to prepare his revenge. The alliances that he sought with the Turks and German Protestants did not deter him from seeking the support of the pope and the powerful Medici family at the same time. The latter objective was secured by the marriage of the king's son Henry to Catherine de Médicis, niece of Clement VII, who went in person to Marseilles to meet with Francis at the ceremony.

The king also strengthened his military might. He ordered the formation of seven provincial legions, each composed of 6,000 volunteers. Ordinary soldiers were well paid, and they might rise through the ranks to captain, thereby acquiring nobility. By this means he created a body of national infantry of 54,000 well-disciplined men—42,000 pikemen and 12,000 crossbowmen. This was the origin of the regiments, each bearing the name of a province, that formed the basis of the French army until the end of the monarchy.

Francis I reopened hostilities in 1536 by conquering Savoy and Piedmont. The emperor responded with an invasion of Provence, which the French met with a scorched-earth policy. The famished imperial troops were forced to retreat. Other attacks by the imperial forces in Roussillon and Picardy were also unsuccessful. A truce was declared in 1538.

The war resumed in 1542 with mixed successes and failures on the various fronts. The French enjoyed one great victory at Cerisole, in Piedmont, in April 1544. Charles V invaded northern France in force with English help and advanced to Epernay and Château-Thierry, some sixty miles from Paris. Exhausted, the two enemies signed another inconclusive peace at Crépy-en-Laonnais in September 1544.

The Wars of Henry II. Henry II's acquisition of the three bishoprics in Lorraine seemed an intolerable provocation to Charles V. He sent a powerful army of 60,000 men to retake Metz, and even though he was ill, he went in person to direct the siege operations from October to December 1522. Admirably defended by Francis, duke of Guise, the fortress resisted all assaults, while the imperial army's strength was drained away by disease and supply problems. On January 1, 1553, it beat a retreat, having lost two-thirds of its effectives.

Two years after this humiliating defeat, Charles V abdicated, leaving the imperial crown and the old Hapsburg states to his brother Ferdinand, and Spain with its Italian and Dutch possessions to his son Philip II. Philip had married the queen of England, Mary Tudor. Thus he had a formidable force at his command. *1555*

This fact became obvious in 1557, when the French rashly resumed hostilities with an untimely invasion of Italy. Under the command of the able Emmanuel Philibert, the dispossessed duke of Savoy, Philip's army invaded northern France. Near St. Quentin it inflicted a stunning defeat on Constable Montmorency and took him prisoner. But the Spanish failed to press their advantage, and lingered to beseige St. Quentin, valiantly defended by Coligny. Francis of Guise was recalled from Italy, where he had fought to no purpose, and given full authority to deal with the situation. In a brilliant surprise operation he seized Calais from the English in January 1558, and then occupied Luxembourg.

The Treaty of Cateau-Cambrésis. The two adversaries, exhausted and short of money, finally negotiated a peace that was signed on April 3, 1559, at Cateau-Cambrésis. Henry II gave up all his claims in Italy and even returned possessions of the duke of Savoy that the French had occupied for twenty-nine years. He retained the three bishoprics of Toul, Metz, and Verdun, and Calais as well.

As a token of reconciliation, Philip II, who had become a widower at the death of Mary Tudor, pledged to marry Henry II's daughter Elizabeth. The marriage took place in Paris to great rejoicing. Henry, eager to take part in a tournament, jousted with Montgomery, the captain of his guards. Montgomery's lance shattered and the jagged end lifted the king's visor and pierced his eye. Henry died ten days later, on July 10, 1559.

Conclusion. Though France was at last driven from Italy, the loss proved to be beneficial to the cohesiveness of the kingdom. France was compensated by the far more useful acquisitions of Calais and the three bishoprics. Most important, France had successfully resisted the attacks of an enemy who had seemed far more powerful.

This kind of negative success, gained despite an often incoherent policy and numerous setbacks, can doubtless be explained by the fact that the French kings, unlike Charles V, could depend on a country strongly united under its ruler's control, and on their people, who were moved by a strong national feeling and were ready to accept any sacrifice to defend its independence.

II. INTERNAL GOVERNMENT

A Prosperous Country. If Francis I was able to find the money necessary to carry on his wars at the same time that he was supporting a luxurious court, it was because until mid-century the country enjoyed the same favorable economic conditions that it had known under Louis XII.

Population had grown so rapidly that by 1500 it had reached and surpassed the level attained in the first decades of the thirteenth century —15 to 18 million inhabitants. Fallow land had been brought back into cultivation, forests had dwindled, and once abandoned villages and hamlets had been repopulated. Grapevines had spread widely, and so had crops useful in industry—linen and hemp in the north, mulberry trees and wood in the south. But since agricultural techniques had made scarcely any progress, food production had an upper limit, and symptoms of overpopulation reappeared in the fragmentation of farms and local famines, particularly after 1560. In addition, the climate became noticeably cooler, and civil war ravaged the interior of the country, which until then had been spared foreign invasions.

On the other hand, industry benefited from numerous technical innovations and the increasing demand for useful and luxury goods. The rise of printing, for example, led to the creation of paperworks and type foundries. The needs of war developed metallurgy, as in the manufacture of crossbows at St. Etienne. Iron forges or blast furnaces multiplied so quickly that in 1543 Francis I had to issue an ordinance that limited their number in order to protect the forests.

The great trade and banking center was not Paris but Lyons, where Italian, German, and Swiss merchants met at four annual fairs. Of the 209 societies of merchant-bankers that are known to have existed in sixteenth-century France, 169 were established there.

Seaports also experienced a remarkable development, notably Le Havre, which was created by order of Francis I to replace the port at Harfleur, which had silted up. Ango, a shipbuilder at Dieppe, sent explorers to the coast of Brazil and financed the expedition of Verrazano. In 1524, while searching for the Northwest Passage to the Far East, Verrazano discovered the present-day site of New York. Jacques Cartier of St. Malo explored the Gulf of St. Lawrence between 1534 and 1543 with the same goal.

Social Changes. This economic progress was accompanied by inflation of the currency, attributable in part to the increased tempo of trade between towns and country and among the provinces, and in part to the influx of precious metals, first from the mines of Germany, then, in growing quantities, from America.

This inflation brought about not only the devaluation of money of account but also a real rise in the cost of living, estimated at between 300 and 400 percent in the course of the sixteenth century. This phenomenon led to pronounced social changes.

All people whose incomes were calculated in money saw their value decline. Such was the case of the workers in the towns and countryside. It has been calculated, for example, that the equivalent of 60 hours of work was needed to pay for a quintal of wheat in Strasbourg around 1500, and 200 hours in 1570. By the end of the century the lower classes had become virtually pauperized, and their problems were worsened by the overpopulation of the countryside. The towns began to fill with beggars.

The lesser nobility were also affected by the decline in purchasing power of their dues and rents, which were fixed payments measured by depreciating money of account. These people were compelled to sell off their lands or enter the king's service.

Wealth increased for peasant landowners, for farmers protected by long-term leases, for wholesale merchants in grain, hay, and wood, and for farmer-collectors charged with collecting taxes in kind and indirect taxes for the king and nobility. In the towns, guildmasters, businessmen, and moneychangers also benefited. These prospering members of the middle class purchased estates put up for sale by the nobility, thereby becoming holders of fiefs and manors. They even acquired judicial and financial offices sold by the crown, thus achieving noble status.

The Reinforcement of Royal Power. The theory then generally accepted was that the king's will was the sole source of law. At the close of his ordinances, Francis I began to use the formula "For such is our pleasure." His person was the object of adulation and almost idolatrous worship. No opposition was able to develop, for a man who might be all-powerful one day might be thrown into prison the next. The Estates General did not meet between 1506 and 1560, and when the parlements dared to present remonstrances, they were sharply rebuked.

Impoverished and gradually displaced from their local functions by the acts of royal bureaucrats, the nobles had to rely on the king's largess, and they congregated at court. To domesticate them the king turned to the immense fortune of the clergy. The Concordat of 1516 had given him the right to fill bishoprics and abbacies as he wished; the pope's role was merely to lend automatic canonical legitimacy. By such appointments the king forged ties with influential families and by the same token ensured a docile clergy.

Lastly, royal authority also benefited from the progressive unification of the kingdom. The last great appanage, Bourbon, was dismantled. Royal bureaucrats, who multiplied for financial reasons, worked in their particular areas to strengthen the king's authority while they strengthened their own. The ordinance of Villers-Cotterêts of 1539 had great significance for the linguistic unity of the kingdom: it determined that judicial acts would henceforth be "pronounced, recorded, and delivered . . . in the native French language, and not otherwise." The same ordinance also prescribed the keeping of records of births, marriages, and deaths.

Instruments of Power. The king governed with a small number of men chosen by him; the group has been called the "secret council," the "council of affairs," or the "little council." Generally one councillor emerged who, under the title of first councillor, was in fact prime minister. Decisions were put in the proper form and transmitted by a corps of royal secretaries—about 120—who worked under the direction of the chancellor. Under Henry II, four of these functionaries were placed at the head of four sections, each charged with administering a geographic area of the kingdom and overseeing relations with the lands that bordered his sector. This was the origin of specialized ministerial departments.

Legal matters were brought before the royal council by the masters of requests of the king's household. The sovereign sometimes designated one of them "appointed commissioner" and sent him to visit the provinces to see that the royal decisions were carried out.

Finances. In 1522 taxes of all kinds—income from the royal domain and feudal dues (called ordinary receipts); royal taxes, the *taille*, indirect taxes, and the salt tax (called extraordinary receipts)—were centralized in a single collection agency, the Treasury, under the direction of a controller general, a virtual minister of finance.

In the provinces sixteen receivers general collected the taxes gathered in their "generality" and deducted regional expenses before sending the remainder—the "good returns"—to the Treasury.

The need for money was so great that the Treasury was constantly empty, despite continual tax increases. The *taille*, for example, had more than tripled. All kinds of expedients were resorted to, among them loans and the sale of offices.

Loans. In 1522, for the first time, the king demanded that all of his subjects lend him money at 8 percent annual interest, secured by the income from indirect taxes collected in Paris. These "annuities on the Town Hall" later served as models for other loans. By 1559 this public debt had risen to 43 million livres.

Sales of Offices. For the men who filled them, the various offices in the royal service meant not only appointments but also such advantages as exemptions from taxes and honors. The highest ranks were even raised to the nobility. Thus when the idea of selling these offices was conceived, there was never any lack of purchasers among the rich bourgeoisie. The kings multiplied the number of these more or less useful offices, especially in the area of justice. Later even military offices were sold.

This system of putting offices up for sale had grave political and social consequences. First it turned the middle-class elite away from productive careers in agriculture, industry, and commerce, which were considered to be less respectable. This deep-seated prejudice has a long history in France.

Second, the judges of the parlements, who had property rights in their offices, could resist the kings without fear of losing their seats. Their opposition eventually played a part in the downfall of the monarchy.

Third, the offices, which were purchased at great cost, became part of an estate transmitted by inheritance; if a title of nobility went with an office, the title, too, passed to the heirs. Thus from the sale of offices sprang a new aristocracy of bourgeois origin, called the "nobility of the robe" to distinguish it from the ancient feudal and military nobility, the "nobility of the sword."

Francis I, Protector of Arts and Letters. Humanists and writers enjoyed constant favor during the reign of Francis I. Printing, introduced into Paris around 1470, developed rapidly. An estimated 25,000 publications were produced during the sixteenth century by Paris printshops, most notably by the Estienne family of humanist scholars and master printers. Shops in Lyons may have published some 13,000 works.

The royal library, directed by the great scholar Guillaume Budé, was enormously enriched by the requirement that printers send it a copy of each of their publications.

In 1530 Francis I instituted a college of royal lecturers where such new subjects as Hebrew, Greek, Latin philology, and science might be taught, free from the narrow control of the Sorbonne. This was the origin of the modern-day Collège de France.

More important still, Francis I exercised a decisive influence on the spread of Italian art in France. The châteaux that he built or remodeled for his pleasure—Blois, Chambord, St.-Germain-en-Laye, Fontaine-bleau—served as models for those built by the aristocracy. The painters, sculptors, goldsmiths, furniture makers, and tapestry weavers who worked for the court conformed to the Italian style that the king preferred. From Italy Francis I summoned such great artists as Leonardo da Vinci and Benvenuto Cellini. Francesco Primaticcio and Il Rosso, who decorated the château at Fontainebleau, created a true school whose conventions became the rule for all French painting.

SUGGESTIONS FOR FURTHER READING

Blunt, Anthony. *Art and Architecture in France, 1500–1700.* Harmondsworth, Eng., 1970.

Denieul-Cormier, Anne. *A Time of Glory: The Renaissance in France, 1488–1559.* Garden City, N.Y., 1968.

Hackett, Francis. *Frances the First.* New York, 1935.

Ladurie, Emmanuel Le Roy. *The Peasants of Languedoc.* Urbana, Ill., 1976.

Mandrou, Robert. *Introduction to Modern France, 1500–1640: An Essay in Historical Psychology.* New York, 1976.

Stone, Donald. *France in the Sixteenth Century: A Medieval Society Transformed*. New York, 1969.

Hauser, Henri, and A. Renaudet. *Les Débuts de l'Age moderne: La Renaissance et la Réforme*. 4th ed. Paris, 1956.

[Handwritten annotation at top of page:] In this account, the Wars of Religion are simply a continuation of war in general, business as usual. How do these wars differ from François I vs Charles V; Louis XI's seizure of Burgundy, Anjou, Provence; Armagnacs & Burgundians fight for the crown; the 100 Years war with England. Religious doctrine is not discussed — was it not important? The only difference is that the masses seem to be involved in the Wars of Religion.

9

The Wars of Religion

The introduction of the Protestant Reformation into France unleashed the cruelest of civil wars. If the Protestants, despite their initial successes and fanatical zeal, failed to triumph here as they did in other states, it was because the monarchy remained faithful to the Catholic church and the great majority of people violently resisted religious innovations. Unable to destroy each other in thirty years of fighting, Protestants and Catholics had to learn to coexist.

I. THE BEGINNINGS OF THE PROTESTANT REFORMATION IN FRANCE

The Meaux Circle. It was not only in Martin Luther's Germany that the corruption of the clergy and the inadequate response of the church establishment to spiritual unrest inspired a desire for reform. Even before Luther's doctrines became known in France, the return to Scripture and a more personal religion has been preached by Jacques Lefèvre d'Etaples. This gentle scholar produced a French translation of the New Testament in 1523. His friend the bishop of Meaux, Guillaume Briçonnet, brought him to Meaux, and the two established a small circle of disciples. The sister of Francis I, Margaret of Angoulême, had to protect them against censure by the Sorbonne.

The Penetration of Lutheranism. Luther's works had begun to reach France by 1520, and a first French translation was produced in 1526 by Louis Berquin. Their spread was basically an urban phenomenon, gaining headway among those social classes that had access to the printed word: jurists, doctors, teachers, city nobles, and middle-class professionals. But it is difficult to measure how far Lutheran Protestantism spread, since there were no publicly organized groups and most of the first Protestants continued to attend Catholic churches. French people who were attracted by the reassuring doctrine of justification by faith, the study of the Bible in their own language, the condemnation of superstitious practices, and the advancement of the laity nevertheless tended to be wary of the Germanic and authoritarian aspects of Lutheranism, as well as certain excesses of the Reformation in Germany.

Calvin. Only a Frenchman could provide his compatriots with a form of Protestantism well suited to their way of thinking. John Calvin, born in 1509 at Noyons, had studied law and classical letters at Orléans, Bourges, and Paris. Converted probably around 1532, he was threatened by the first persecution of Lutherans ordered by Francis I and took refuge first in Strasbourg, then in Basel. His most important work, *The Institutes of the Christian Religion*, was published in Basel in 1536. It appeared first in Latin, then was made accessible to all French readers in a French version published in 1540 under the title *L'Institution chrétienne*. Written in plain language, the book was an enormous success, for it lent the Protestant religion the support of a rigorous logical structure based firmly on Scripture.

The Success of the Calvinist Reformation. Calvin also provided French Protestants with an institutional framework. Finally settling at Geneva he transformed the city into a kind of theocratic republic with himself as all-powerful prophet. There he established a seminary where ministers or pastors were trained to carry the good word to France and organize communities or churches on the Geneva model; that is, to establish meeting places for the celebration of communion according to the new rite, consistories of laymen responsible with an elected pastor for internal discipline, and synods to ensure uniformity of faith among the various communities. By the end of 1561 there were 670 "established" Calvinist churches and a large number of small, less organized groups. A national synod, held secretly at Paris in May 1559, adopted a "confession" of forty articles in which Calvin's doctrines were codified. Because of their ties with Geneva, the French Calvinists were called Huguenots, from the German *Eidgenossen* (confederates).

Meanwhile, an important change had affected the social composition of French Protestantism. Nobles flocked to it in large numbers, among them two princes of royal blood, Anthony of Bourbon, king of Navarre, and his brother Louis, the prince of Condé, and three high-placed nephews of the powerful constable Montmorency: Cardinal Odet de Catillon; Henry d'Andelot, colonel general of the infantry; and Admiral Gaspard de Coligny. This movement may perhaps be seen as the nobility's protest against the economic and political strangulation they were suffering, perhaps also as the resurgence of the southern heretical temper, and more generally as provincial regionalism set against monarchical consolidation. In any case, this massive shift of the nobles to Protestantism, just at the moment when peace deprived their aggressive instincts of an outlet in war, brought the newly organized reformed church the dynamic element that made it a political party, a virtual state within the state.

First Persecutions. If Francis I had a tolerant disposition, the same cannot be said of the Sorbonne and the Parlement of Paris, which supported the capital's lower classes in their hatred of heresy. The first Lutheran martyr was condemned to the stake as early as 1523, and he was followed in 1529 by Berquin, the translator of Luther's works. But these remained isolated cases. The rashness of a few Protestant fanatics unleashed the first systematic persecution. In October 1534 they printed a violent and abusive manifesto against the Catholic mass and posted copies in Paris and the provinces, even on the door of the king's chambers at Amboise. Francis I ordered the prosecution of the people who disseminated the heresy and those who gave them shelter. In Paris alone there were some forty executions within a few months. Later an edict of amnesty suspended the persecution. During the remaining years of Francis' reign, repression remained sporadic. The king's alliance with the Protestant princes of Germany obviously contributed to this semi-tolerance.

Pressed by Montmorency, Henry II declared a pitiless war against the Protestants, whose organization and daring seemed to pose a serious threat to royal authority. A "burning chamber" was created by the Parlement of Paris to track down heretics. The Edict of Compiègne in 1557 established a single penalty for them: death. In 1559 any rebellious or fleeing Protestant was ordered slain without trial. It was largely because he wanted to devote greater effort to the rooting out of heresy that the king signed the Peace of Cateau-Cambrésis.

II. THE FIRST STAGES OF THE CONFLICT

After the death of Henry II, royal power passed successively to his three sons, all of whom were young and either weak or degenerate.

Their mother, Catherine de Médicis, who was officially regent from 1560 to 1563, exerted the dominant influence over crown policies until her death. She was indifferent in matters of religion yet was much given to magicians and astrologers. An exceptionally intelligent and cultivated woman, she was realistic and unscrupulous. In keeping with the teachings of her fellow Italian Niccolò Machiavelli, she had no morality other than reasons of state; the preservation of royal power was all she cared for. The twists and calculated deceptions of her policy earned her the nickname "Madame Snake."

In these conditions royal power became the stake in a struggle between the great aristocratic factions more or less closely connected to the throne (see the accompanying genealogical chart). They made use of religious passions, and in the process gave them the solidarity and organization of political parties. This combination of political and religious hostilities, which were also personal and even social and regional, brought the horrors of a long civil war to France.

The Conspiracy of Amboise. The Guises enjoyed the initial advantage. Their niece, Mary Stuart, had just married the young King Francis II, who at sixteen was weak and sickly, quite unable to govern for himself. Queen Mary had no trouble persuading him to place all power in the hands of her uncles: Francis duke of Guise, the popular conqueror of Calais, and Charles, cardinal of Lorraine, a tough and ambitious man.

Presenting themselves as the champions of Catholicism, they pursued and intensified the persecution of Protestants. Their authoritarian ways offended many people. Some Calvinist noblemen, inspired by a man named La Renaudie, dreamed up a plot to kidnap the royal family. Their purpose, they claimed, was to withdraw them from harmful influence and place them under the guidance of the Protestant Bourbon princes. Several hundred conspirators converged on the spot where they thought the court would pass on its way from Blois to Tours. Francis of Guise, warned of the plot, brought the king to the safety of the château of Amboise. The groups of Calvinist conspirators were surprised separately and destroyed. Those who were not killed on the spot were summarily tried and executed. For lack of enough gallows, prisoners were even hanged from the battlements of the walls of Amboise.

Louis, the prince of Condé, suspected of being the instigator of the plot, was arrested. The Guises had him condemned to death, but he was saved by the premature death of Francis II on December 5, 1560.

An Attempt at Toleration. His brother Charles IX, the heir to the crown, was only ten years old. The queen mother secured the regency in negotiations with the first prince of the blood, Anthony of Bourbon: the regency in exchange for the pardon of his brother, the prince of Condé.

Catherine de Médicis' plan was to establish peaceful coexistence between Catholics and Protestants by appealing to the most moderate elements of both parties. The Guises were shoved aside, and Bourbon and Coligny entered the council. The regent found an eloquent defender of her policy in the new chancellor, Michel de l'Hospital. He addressed an appeal for toleration to the Estates General assembled at Orléans: "The knife is of little use against the spirit . . . ; kindness avails more than severity. Let us throw out those diabolical names designating parties, factions, and seditions—Lutherans, Huguenots, Papists—and keep the name of Christians."

The regent then convened a gathering of theologians of the two faiths in the hope of leading them to find a common ground. But this "Colloquy of Poissy" dragged on from September to October 1561, with fine arguments but no results. Catherine then resolved to impose her policy of toleration by decree. The Edict of January (January 17, 1562) authorized the Protestants to worship publicly outside city walls and to hold synods.

The Massacre of Vassy. Emerging into the open, the Protestants soon exceeded their rights where they had the strength to do so. At Montpellier, for example, they closed the cathedral and drove out the priests. The Catholics reacted with violence. One serious incident unleashed civil war.

While passing through Vassy on Sunday, March 1, 1562, the duke of Guise and his entourage came upon Protestants conducting a service in a barn, in violation of the Edict of January. When a fight broke out, Guise's men massacred twenty-three Protestants and wounded about a hundred.

In Paris, Condé called on Protestants to unite and arm in self-defense. The regent, who was then in residence at Fontainebleau, was uncertain as to what course to take. She was practically sequestered by the leaders of the Catholic party, who had formed a triumvirate for defense: Francis, the duke of Guise, the constable Montmorency, and Marshal Jacques d'Albon de Saint-André. Condé then left Paris and with his small army quickly captured Orléans and several other cities on the Loire. Everywhere Protestants and Catholics clashed fiercely. The civil war, unavoidable now, was on.

III. THE WARS UNDER THE LAST VALOIS

General Features. Historians have generally counted eight successive wars; that is, the number of truces and treaties that halted or slowed hostilities and were violated almost immediately. Actually the struggle was practically continuous for more than thirty years.

The last Valois, the Bourbons, and the Montmorencys in the sixteenth century

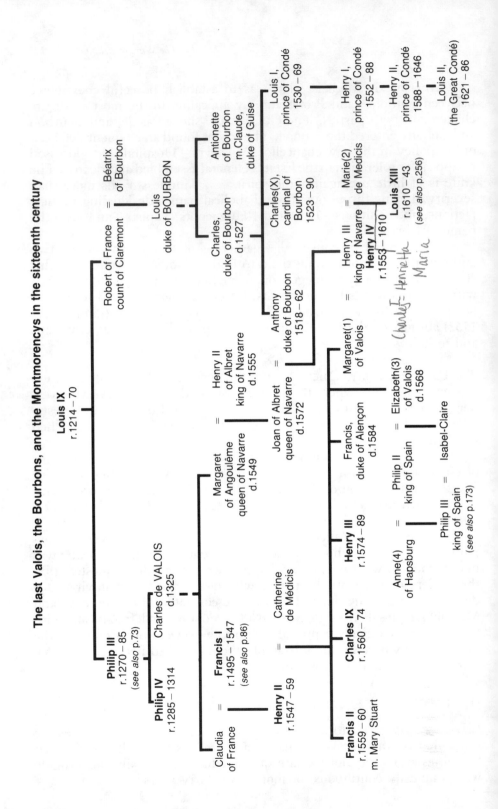

The Last Valois, Bourbons, and Montmorency in the Sixteenth Century

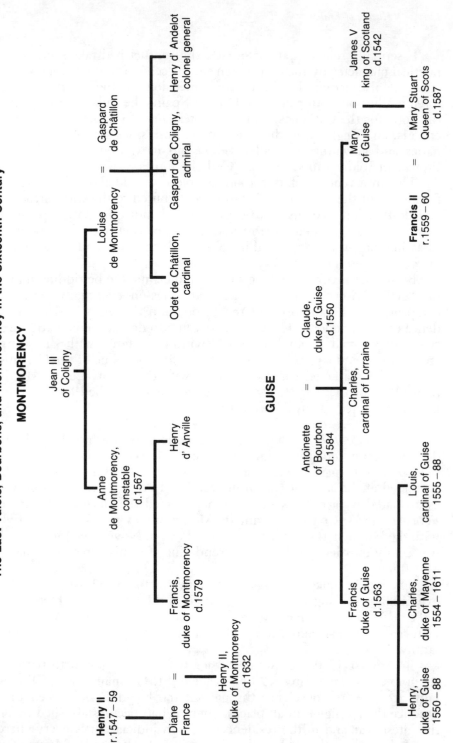

MONTMORENCY

Henry II
r.1547 – 59
=
Diane
France

Francis,
duke of Montmorency
d.1579

Henry II,
duke of Montmorency
d.1632

Anne
de Montmorency, constable
d.1567

Henry
d' Anville

Jean III
of Coligny

Louise
de Montmorency
=
Gaspard
de Châtillon

Odet de Châtillon,
cardinal

Gaspard de Coligny,
admiral

Henry d' Andelot
colonel general

GUISE

Antoinette
of Bourbon
d.1584
=
Claude,
duke of Guise
d.1550

Francis
duke of Guise
d.1563

Charles,
cardinal of Lorraine

Louis,
cardinal of Guise
1555 – 88

Mary
of Guise
=
James V
king of Scotland
d.1542

Mary Stuart
Queen of Scots
d.1587

Francis II
r.1559 – 60

Henry,
duke of Guise
1550 – 88

Charles,
duke of Mayenne
1554 – 1611

Essentially religious at the outset, the conflict had taken on a more political character by the end, when the succession to the throne was at stake. It also acquired a European dimension by the intervention of foreign allies on both sides: the king of Spain, the duke of Savoy, and the pope for the Catholics, and the Protestants of Germany, the Netherlands, and England for the Huguenots. Both sides appealed to mercenaries and adventurers of all nations, and it was not unheard-of for Protestant soldiers to serve with Catholic forces.

The intervention of this rootless soldiery, added to the religious fanaticism of the French combatants, contributed to the war's atrocities and destruction. Towns were captured and indiscriminately pillaged; prisoners and wounded were massacred; hideous cruelties and political assassinations were committed in cold blood; churches and works of art, of course, were not spared.

Both sides invoked the king's name and claimed to be ridding him of his "evil advisers." Actually their carryings-on eventually seriously compromised the authority of the throne and the unity and independence of the kingdom. The Calvinists came to defend democratic theories and formed a kind of state within a state, with an army, strongholds, and a parallel government under the name of the Calvinist Union. The Catholics confronted them with their Holy League. In the final phase of the war Paris and other towns established local governments that rejected royal authority.

Charles IX (1560–72). The first three periods of warfare brought no decisive result for either side. But they did see the disappearance of several of the main antagonists. Anthony of Bourbon was mortally wounded at the siege of Rouen in October 1562. Francis of Guise was assassinated by a pistol shot while he directed the siege of Orléans in February 1563. Constable Anne de Montmorency was killed in a fight with the Huguenots outside the gates of Paris in November 1567. Condé was coldly murdered as he was surrendering after his defeat at Jarnac in May 1569.

The regent took advantage of these deaths to reestablish her control over affairs, shifting between the two sides. Her third son, Henry, the duke of Anjou, was given command of the royal army in 1569, and his victories at Jarnac and Moncontour raised the prestige of the royal family.

In August 1570 the queen mother felt strong enough to try once again to compel coexistence. The Peace of St. Germain granted Protestants freedom of conscience throughout the kingdom and freedom to practice their religion in all places where it had been established before the latest war and in the residences of high judicial lords everywhere. They also received four "places of security": La Rochelle, Montauban, La Charité, and Cognac.

Saint Bartholemew's Day. In token of peace Coligny was recalled to the royal council. There he won the confidence of Charles IX, who at age twenty suddenly displayed a desire to free himself from his mother's guardianship. Coligny proposed a glorious undertaking to the king—an offensive into Belgium against the Spanish in conjunction with the rebellious Protestants in the Netherlands. Firmly committed to peace, Catherine had the council reject Coligny's scheme. Nonetheless, he openly began to recruit an army of volunteers. The queen was persuaded that this man was becoming as dangerous to the peace of the kingdom as to her own influence and must be eliminated at any price.

The occasion presented itself during the festivities held at Paris to mark the marriage of Margaret of Valois, sister of Charles IX, to the young king of Navarre, Henry of Bourbon—a union that was a great success for Catherine's diplomacy. A hired assassin in the service of the Guises was ordered to murder Coligny on August 18, 1572. But his badly aimed arquebus shot only wounded the admiral in the left arm. Furious, Charles IX hastened to assure Coligny that the guilty parties would be punished. But who were they? All signs pointed to the queen mother and the duke of Anjou. The Protestant nobles, who had come to Paris in large numbers, talked of taking justice into their own hands. Panicking, Catherine persuaded her son that the royal family was in mortal danger and that only the elimination of all of the Protestant leaders present in the capital at one stroke could save them. Charles IX gave in. Henri de Guise, who was charged with carrying out the order, personally presided over the murder of Coligny, whom he believed to be responsible for the assassination of his father in 1563. Almost all of the other leading Huguenots were surprised and killed in the same way. The aroused Parisian populace joined in with the soldiers and for three days, August 24–27, massacred everyone whom they suspected of being a Protestant, without distinction of sex or age.

Similar massacres took place in several provincial towns. The number of victims has been estimated at 8,000. A good number of Protestants abjured their faith under threat of death, among them the young king of Navarre Henry of Bourbon. On St. Bartholemew's night he was dragged before the king, and under threat of being slain on the spot, he signed an act of abjuration.

The massacre galvanized the energy of the survivors. La Rochelle became their main rallying point. The town successfully withstood an eight-month siege by the duke of Anjou. War weariness led to a truce in July 1573. By the Edict of Boulogne, all Protestants were granted freedom of conscience, but freedom of worship was permitted in only three towns—La Rochelle, Montauban, and Nîmes.

Charles IX, consumed by remorse and tuberculosis, died shortly afterward, on May 30, 1574. The crown passed to his brother, the Duke of Anjou, who had recently been elected king of Poland and was then in Krakow. He lost not a minute in deserting his new subjects and returning to France.

Henry III. The third son of Catherine de Médicis was her favorite. He had many of the qualities that his two older brothers had lacked—fine bearing, keen intelligence, a gift for speaking and writing, a taste for arts and letters, and courage in battle. But he was brought into disrepute by his extravagant behavior and especially by his homosexual tendencies and the scandalous favors he showered on his entourage of "darlings."

During the first years of his reign, the parties realigned themselves with new leaders and in new groupings. It was at this time that the Calvinist Union, a veritable shadow government, was born. It relied on young King Henry (III) of Navarre, who had reaffirmed his allegiance to Protestantism once he had escaped from court. It also had the secret support of the king's brother, Francis, duke of Alençon, who became duke of Anjou after the accession of Henry III.

Francis was an ambitious and deceitful man, and he incited the Protestant leaders to encourage the German princes to intervene. An invasion by a German army of 20,000 men, who joined the rebel forces inside France, caught Henry III unprepared. In May 1576 he resigned himself to signing the Peace of Monsieur or Edict of Beaulieu, which gave the Protestants much of what they wanted: complete freedom of worship everywhere but in Paris, rehabilitation of the victims of St. Bartholemew, and eight places of security.

Feeling themselves deserted by the king, the Catholics then established their Holy League under the leadership of Henry of Guise, called Le Balafré (the Scarred). The king sought to counter this blow by declaring himself head of the League, a move that soon led to its dissolution.

Nevertheless, the war had spontaneously reignited everywhere. To rid himself of his brother, the king let him embark on a vain attempt to conquer the Netherlands with the help of Queen Elizabeth of England, whom Francis hoped to marry.

The War of the Three Henries. The death of Francis of Anjou on June 10, 1584, put an end to this adventure, but at the same time it created a new situation that was even more threatening to internal peace.

The natural heir to the throne was now Henry of Navarre, and Henry III was inclined to recognize him as such. But in no way would the Catholics accept a relapsed heretic as king. The pope himself declared him ineligible to rule. The Guises and their clients recognized Charles, the old cardinal of Bourbon, as the heir. They revived the League and won the support of Philip II of Spain, who dreamed of seeing his own daughter—born of his marriage with Elizabeth, sister of

Henry III—ascend the throne of France. Without money or an army, the king yielded to the League's demands. By the Treaty of Nemours in July 1585, he stripped Henry of Navarre of his rights to the throne and revoked all concessions that had previously been granted to the Protestants. The war immediately resumed on a grand scale. Henry of Navarre, who proved to be an excellent military commander, crushed the Catholic army commanded by the king's favorite, the duke of Joyeuse, at Coutras. Meanwhile, Henry of Guise drove back the army of German Protestants in Champagne.

Guise's successes raised his popularity to new heights. Against the wishes of Henry III, he went to Paris to be acclaimed by the Leaguers. Humiliated and isolated, the king was forced to name him lieutenant general of the kingdom. Shortly thereafter, the meeting of the Estates General at Blois again brought into relief the discredit into which the king had fallen. While Guise was fawned upon, all his own demands for money were insultingly refused. Some delegates even talked of deposing Henry III and replacing him with Guise, whose Carolingian ancestry was conveniently recalled.

Playing his last card, the king drew his rival into carefully planned ambush and had him assassinated by the royal guard. The duke's brother Louis, the cardinal of Guise, was seized and murdered the next day, December 23, 1588. "Well cut, my son," the queen mother (who was then near death) reportedly said, "but now you must sew the pieces back together."

The Death of Henry III. At the news of this sensational development, Parisians, led by Guise's brother Charles, duke of Mayenne, formed a rebel government that declared the king deposed. Although a prisoner, the cardinal of Bourbon was recognized as king under the name of Charles X, and Charles, the duke of Mayenne, last survivor of the three Guise brothers, was chosen lieutenant general of the kingdom.

Henry III reached a new agreement with Henry of Navarre, whom he recognized as his heir. Joining forces, they besieged Paris. There Henry III was assassinated by a young fanatic, a Dominican monk named Jacques Clément, on August 1, 1589. Before dying, the last Valois pleaded with his cousin to become a Catholic. Recognized as king by the army, Henry of Navarre ascended the throne as Henry IV.

IV. HENRY IV AND THE END OF THE WARS

Four Years of Warfare. The new king soon found himself in a critical situation. Catholics left his army in droves, and even some Protestants joined the exodus, disgusted by Henry's repeated advances toward his opponents. The king then lifted the siege of Paris and withdrew to

Dieppe, where help might reach him from England. The army of the League, commanded by Mayenne, attacked him and was severely beaten at Arques in September 1589.

After wintering at Tours, the king resumed the offensive in the spring and took possession of Normandy. Then he marched on Paris. On March 14, 1590, at Ivry, near Evreux, he again defeated the Leaguers, although they outnumbered him two to one. A surprise attack on Paris failed, and he tried to reduce the city by starvation. After a four-month siege the Parisians were saved by the arrival of Spanish armies commanded by the viceroy of the Netherlands, Alexander Farnese, who was as good a general as Henry IV. Throughout 1592 the two opponents maneuvered indecisively in Normandy.

The Abjuration of Henry IV. The death of the phantom king Charles X in January 1593 created a crisis for the Leaguers. Several candidates presented themselves as his replacement, the most serious among them being the Princess Isabel Claire, daughter of Philip II, whose troops already occupied numerous strongpoints in France. Gathering in Paris, the Estates General angrily rejected the Spanish proposal, and the Parlement of Paris issued a solemn decree that forbade the placing of a foreign prince on the French throne.

During these debates Henry IV, who had put an end to hostilities, gradually disarmed his enemies by his courage and good grace. The weary French wanted to have done with it all. The Parisians in particular had had enough of the fanatical tyranny of the Sixteen who had taken power in 1589. Henry IV finally decided to take the step that the majority of his subjects desired, and on July 23, 1593, in the basilica of St. Denis, he made a solemn profession of Catholicism. The disappointed Calvinists took their revenge by attributing to him the famous saying "Paris is well worth a mass." In effect, the struggle was now won, and the king's coronation in the cathedral at Chartres on February 27, 1594, brought him a flood of supporters.

On March 22 the governor of Paris opened the city to him. The submission of the chief Leaguers in the provinces was won at high cost. But Henry IV wanted to end the bloodshed; he wanted to forgive and forget. Other than a few temporary exiles, there were no reprisals.

The War against Spain. Abandoned by his League allies, Philip II pursued the struggle on his own. The indecisive war centered mainly on the strongholds in Picardy and Burgundy. There was only one notable episode, the battle at Fontaine-Française in June 1595, when Henry IV was surprised by the enemy and extricated himself by charging wildly an enemy cavalry that outnumbered him five to one. The weariness of the two opponents led them to make peace at last. The treaty of Vervins, signed on May 2, 1598, simply restated that of Cateau-Cambrésis in 1559.

The Edict of Nantes. At almost the same time, Henry IV consolidated peace at home by an act intended to reassure the Protestants who were still resisting. The concessions included in the Edict of Nantes on April 13, 1598, comprised a kind of summary of measures that had been promised at various times during the thirty years of civil war:

- Freedom of conscience throughout the kingdom.

- Freedom of worship where it had been previously recognized, and also in noble households and in at least two towns in each bailliage.

- The authorization of provincial and national synods.

- An end to religious discrimination in the distribution of offices and honors.

- A double chamber, called the Chamber of the Edict, instituted in each parlement to ensure equitable justice to Protestants.

- Some 100 places of security granted to Protestants for eight years.

It was only with great difficulty that the king managed to get the Parlement of Paris and other parlements in the provinces, which spoke for the silent Catholics, to register this edict.

Conclusion. The system established by the Edict of Nantes had the defect of establishing and consolidating a kind of foreign body within the nation, with privileges that were certain to seem excessive to the rest of the population. Sooner or later this anomaly would become intolerable.

On the other hand, by separating religious and political obedience, France set an unprecedented example of religious toleration, then a strange notion in all other states, both Protestant and Catholic.

SUGGESTIONS FOR FURTHER READING

Erlanger, Philippe. *St. Bartholomew's Night: The Massacre of Saint-Bartholomew.* New York, 1962.

Grant, Arthur J. *The Huguenots.* London, 1934.

Héritier, Jean. *Catherine de Médicis.* New York, 1963.

McNeill, John T. *The History and Character of Calvinism.* New York, 1954, 1967.

Roelker, Nancy L. *Queen of Navarre, Jeanne d'Albret*. Cambridge, Mass., 1968.

Sichel, Edith M. *Catherine de' Medici and the French Reformation*. London, 1969.

Sutherland, Nicola Mary. *The Massacre of Saint-Bartholomew and the European Conflict*. London, 1973.

Thompson, James Westfall. *The Wars of Religion in France, 1559–1576*. New York, 1957.

Leonard, Emile G. *Histoire générale du Protestantisme*. Vols. 1 and 2. Paris, 1961.

IO

The Recovery
under Henry IV
and Louis XIII

U nder the benevolent government of Henry IV, the country began to repair the destruction of the civil wars. But the tragic death of the king left power in incompetent or unworthy hands, and anarchy reappeared among the nobility. In the person of Cardinal Richelieu Louis XIII found a minister capable of righting the situation. His cold, hardheaded efficiency broke all resistance and established monarchical absolutism. In addition he successfully resumed the struggle against the house of Austria.

I. THE REIGN OF HENRY IV

The King. With peace ensured by the Treaty of Vervins and the Edict of Nantes both in the interior and on the borders, Henry IV set about the very necessary task of guiding the country's recovery and restoring royal authority.

The king, born in December 1563 at Pau, was at forty-five a man filled with vitality and hardened by the wandering life of a partisan leader. The countless dangers and difficult situations that he had faced had forged his character and sharpened his political judgment. Having traveled all over his kingdom and mingled with his most humble subjects, he had acquired an understanding of their ways of thinking and a sympathy for their needs—exceptional qualities in a king. He charmed people with his high spirits, his good humor, his familiar manners, his witty jests, his quickness to forgive, and his way of making orders seem like friendly requests. Nonetheless, he had a lofty idea of royal authority, and he knew full well how to make it clear that he alone was in charge. Marshal Armand de Biron, the governor of Burgundy and his boyhood friend and comrade at arms, allowed himself to be led by ambition into conspiring with the duke of Savoy and then with the king of Spain. Henry pardoned him for his first treason. The second time, still ready to forgive, the king demanded only that Biron recognize his error. When he obstinately refused, the guilty man was tried and beheaded.

Henry's great weakness was his uncontrolled passion for women. To satisfy his desires, the *Vert-Galant* (Ladies' Man) committed more than one folly. In 1599, for example, he wanted to marry his favorite mistress, Gabrielle d'Estrée, who had already borne him two illegitimate children. Only her accidental death prevented him from carrying out a scheme that would have compromised the future of the dynasty.

His Marriage. His first wife, Margaret of Valois—"Queen Margot"— had given him no children and had lived apart from him since 1585. The king was rightly concerned about the troubles that would certainly arise if he died without legitimate heirs. He secured a papal annulment of his first marriage and asked for the hand of the niece of the grand duke of Tuscany. One reason for his choice was the importance of her dowry—600,000 gold écus—which permitted him to repay part of the crown debts. Moreover, Marie de Médicis, as she was known in France, or the "banker," as the courtiers styled her, in time fulfilled the king's hopes by bearing him two sons.

Sully and Finances. Of all Henry IV's collaborators the most effective and most devoted was Maximilien de Béthune, duke of Sully. This lesser nobleman of Flemish birth and Calvinist religion—he remained a Calvinist until his death—had shared the king's adventurous life from the beginning. Henry recognized in his friend a practical business sense that was unusual in one of his class. In 1598 he made him superintendent of finance. Sully also acquired the positions of grand commissioner of roads, superintendent of buildings and fortifications, and grand master of artillery.

He established rigorous economy and order in the handling of finances. He made embezzling tax collectors and purveyors disgorge their ill-gotten gains. He recovered the royal rights that had been turned over to private citizens in exchange for loans. He annulled outright part of the crown debt and repaid the rest, and reduced by half the interest on the loans that were still outstanding.

Forty thousand people who had taken advantage of the troubles to secure exemption from the direct tax of the *taille* were restored to the tax rolls. On the other hand, Sully forgave the poorest their back taxes and then reduced the rate of the *taille*. The only new tax he established exploited the immoderate French taste for royal judgeships and financial posts: owners of these offices who wanted to pass them on to their heirs had to pay an annual tax. Since its collection was, according to the custom of the day, farmed out to a private citizen, a man named Paulet, the tax came to be called the *paulette*. Its historical importance lies in the fact that it helped to perpetuate heredity of office. By all these measures Sully not only balanced the budget but also created a surplus of 30 million livres.

Economic Life. Henry IV was concerned about the lot of the peasants. He wished, he said, that each of them could have "a chicken in the pot" on Sunday. For fiscal reasons Sully shared this concern. "Grazing and farming," he wrote, "are the two breasts on which France feeds, the true mines and treasures of Peru."

Manorial lords were forbidden to hunt in cultivated fields and vineyards after March of each year. Pillaging by soldiers was severely punished. Most important, tax collectors were barred from seizing the cattle and tools of peasants who could not pay their taxes. But more effective than all these measures were the dozen years of peace that permitted the countrymen's work to restore the country's wealth.

The luxury industries, which had flourished under Francis I, had suffered greatly during the wars. Aided by Barthélemy Laffemas, controller of commerce, Henry IV encouraged their revival. Sully gave them indirect aid by forbidding (though without much success) the importation of luxury goods from Italy. He created new industries, setting up royal manufactories—more than 200 in all—and importing foreign craftsmen to work in them. To ensure the supply of raw silk to the silk industry, mulberry trees, on which the silkworm feeds, were introduced into France.

As grand commissioner of roads, Sully had highways rebuilt and bridges reconstructed. At Paris the Pont Neuf was completed, and work was begun on the Place Royale (today the Place des Vosges) and the Place Dauphine. The palaces of the Louvre and the Tuileries were joined by the construction of the Long Gallery, parallel to the Seine. The Royal Library was moved from Fontainebleau to Paris and made accessible to the public. Work was begun on the Briare Canal, linking the Seine and Loire rivers. Trade treaties were concluded with England and Turkey. Unlike his predecessors, Henry IV wanted to found an empire based not on gold but on colonization and agriculture. He supported the voyages of Samuel de Champlain, who, following the path opened by Jacques Cartier during the reign of Francis I, founded a settlement at Quebec in 1608. French peasants began to emigrate to Canada.

Foreign Policy. Peace abroad, restored by the Treaty of Vervins, was broken in 1600 by a minor war against the duke of Savoy. After a rapid campaign in which Chambéry was captured, Henry IV forced the duke to cede all his possessions beyond the Rhône—Bresse, Bugey, and the region of Gex. After that the king was generally satisfied to exert his influence through active diplomacy.

In 1609, however, an occasion to resume the traditional struggle against the house of Austria arose. When the Rhenish duchies of Cleves and Juliers became vacant, the emperor Rudolf sought to place a Catholic prince on the throne. Henry IV determined to support the claims of Protestant princes and began great military preparations.

The Death of the King. The thought of seeing France return to war, and on behalf of Protestants, was very unpopular. The old hatreds of the Holy League, which still lay dormant, reawakened and inspired a madman, François Ravaillac, to stab Henry IV to death on May 14, 1610, as he was riding in his open carriage on his way to confer with Sully at the Arsenal.

This tragic end served the king's posthumous glory by preventing him from pursuing an adventure that would have compromised the work he had accomplished. In their shock and confusion the French forgot their old and recent quarrels. In contrast with the rulers who succeeded him, he became magnified in memory as "good king Henry," the brave soldier, the merry man of Béarn, the friend of the humble, the restorer of the peace and unity of the kingdom.

II. LOUIS XIII AND RICHELIEU

The Regency. The new king, Louis XIII, was not yet nine years old, so Marie de Médicis had herself recognized as regent by a declaration of the Parlement of Paris. She was a large woman with common features, a narrow outlook, a childish personality, and a stubborn and temperamental character. She allowed herself to be dictated to by her foster sister, Leonora Galigai, who had come with her from Florence. Leonora's husband, a swashbuckler named Concini, was immediately made marquis of Ancre and a marshal, and he practically governed France.

The heads of the major families, led by Henry II, the prince of Condé, the first prince of the blood, demanded a share in the privileges of power. Concini sought to appease them by showering them with large pensions. The treasury that Sully had accumulated disappeared.

When agitation nonetheless continued and spread to all classes, the traditional expedient of summoning the Estates General was tried. It met at Paris in October 1614. Its desire to gain control over the monarchy was soon relegated to second place by the quarrels between the nobility and the third estate, composed of representatives of the upper bourgeoisie who held royal offices. Bursting with contempt for these "vile upstarts," the nobility demanded the abolition of the *paulette*—in other words, the heritability of offices. The third estate struck back by complaining to the queen about the pensions paid to the nobles, "who are so unrestrained that there are great and powerful kingdoms that have less income than what you give your subjects to buy their loyalty." After speaking and arguing at length, the deputies were dismissed in February 1615 without having secured anything more than vague promises. The Estates General did not meet again until 1789.

The Fall of Concini. Although Louis XIII was declared of age at fourteen, the queen mother and Concini continued to govern as before, buying off the opposition with cash. All the same, Condé became so dangerous that the queen had him imprisoned in the Bastille. Concini began to behave like the unchallenged master.

Furious that he was being treated like a little boy, the young king threw his support to a plot led by his falconer, Charles de Luynes, and the captain of his guards, Vitry. Chosen to arrest Concini by surprise in the courtyard of the Louvre, Vitry killed him with a pistol shot on August 24, 1617.

The Government of Luynes. The queen mother was sent off to Blois, and Luynes replaced Concini in the role of all-powerful favorite. "It's the same tavern," people said, "they've only changed the sign." His greed in gathering offices and favors for himself and his family roused the nobles to new disturbances in 1620, which had the support of the queen mother. They collapsed before the vigorous action of the royal soldiery, personally led by Louis XIII.

More dangerous was the revolt that broke out at almost the same time among the southern Protestants, who had been angered by Louis's restoration of Catholic worship in the old independent kingdom of Béarn. Luynes was promoted to the rank of constable and sent to put down the rebellion, but he displayed pitiful ineptness. After suffering defeat near Montauban, he caught an infectious fever and died in December 1621.

Richelieu in Power. Marie de Médicis returned to court and recovered a degree of influence over her son. In April 1624 she managed to have her confidant, Richelieu, admitted to the king's council. Three months later he was head of the council, or prime minister.

This ambitious man had long hungered for power. Born in 1585 to a minor noble family in Poitou, Armand Du Plessis de Richelieu had originally been destined for a career in the army. He became a priest only to keep the bishopric of Lucon, which his older brother had given up for monastic life, in the family. Richelieu had gained prominence as spokesman for the clergy at the Estates General of 1614. Marie de Médicis made him her chaplain, and Concini put him in charge of foreign affairs for a time. Caught in the queen mother's disgrace, he humbled himself and diplomatically reconciled mother and son. As a result, he was named cardinal in 1622 and resumed his role in public affairs.

Louis XIII. Anxious to preserve his authority, the king was hesitant to confide in Richelieu, and the cardinal never wholly succeeded in winning his affection. But since Louis XIII considered him to be the only person capable of conducting affairs of state, he supported the cardinal against the world. This self-denial and loyalty are good indications of the character of this king, who was above all profoundly religious and honest. Despite his poor health and the inadequacies that he was the first to admit, "Louis the Just" carried out his duties with admirable conscientiousness and courage. Of a sickly and melancholy temperament, he was at home only among his troops, whom at times he commanded ably. His only amusement was hunting, and he had built a modest lodge at Versailles, destined to become the nucleus of his son's immense palace. Finally, quite unlike his father, Louis XIII was always very reserved toward women—so much so that he has been described (though without any proof) as having homosexual tendencies.

In 1615 Louis XIII married Anne of Austria, the eldest daughter of the king of Spain. But this union long remained barren, and misunderstandings developed between the couple. A fortunate incident in December 1637 reconciled them, however, and a dauphin was born on September 5, 1638, followed by a second son not long afterward. The unexpected royal births brought great joy throughout the kingdom. The queen, for her part, showed her gratitude to God by building the majestic church of Val-de-Grâce in Paris.

III. THE INTERNAL GOVERNMENT OF RICHELIEU

Policies. "Ruin the Huguenot party, humble the pride of the nobles, compel all subjects to their duty, and raise the name of the king among foreign nations to the point where it should be." Such were the objectives that the new minister proposed to his master from the very start.

He was to follow this program point by point, sustained by an inflexible will and the talents of a mind that was both imaginative and realistic. Richelieu had few friends other than a Capuchin monk, Father Joseph du Tremblay, "the Gray Eminence," who was his right arm in diplomatic negotiations.

The Struggle against the Protestants. The Protestants were unwise enough to open hostilities in October 1627 by taking up arms in the south and appealing to England. Richelieu determined to strike the rebellion at the heart of its power—La Rochelle. Along with Louis XIII he personally directed the siege of the stronghold. To close the harbor to English aid he constructed a stone dike 4,920 feet long across the harbor entrance and lined it with batteries of cannon. The siege lasted nearly a year. On October 29, 1628, exhausted by hunger, the people of La Rochelle finally had to surrender.

Louis XIII next turned against the Protestant towns of the Cevennes and seized the two most important strongholds, Privas and Alais. When negotiations where suggested, Richelieu replied that the king would not bargain with rebellious subjects but would grant them what seemed fair to him. By the Peace of Alais, or Peace of Grace, of June 28, 1629, the Protestants lost their places of safety, the right to hold general assemblies, and all the other political privileges granted them by Henry IV. But they were still guaranteed freedom of worship and equal treatment with Catholics.

The Struggle against the Nobility. The conspiracies of the nobles were longer and harder to crush because more often than not they were joined by the king's own brother, Gaston of Orléans, heir to the throne until the tardy birth of the dauphin, and by the two queens, Marie de Médicis and Anne of Austria.

On one famous occasion, when the two women believed they had nudged the prime minister out of the king's favor, all the cardinal's enemies openly rejoiced. But that very evening they had to sing a different tune when Louis XIII came back to his senses and reaffirmed his full confidence in Richelieu. After this "Day of Dupes" (November 10, 1630), the queen mother was exiled.

Plots and rebellions were pitilessly repressed. Highly placed conspirators were beheaded, notably Marshal Marillac, one of those compromised on the Day of Dupes; Henry, the duke of Montmorency, governor of Languedoc, who had tried to rouse his province to rebellion; and Cinq-Mars, grand equerry, convicted of plotting with Spain. Others were thrown into the Bastille or dragged before "special commissions," extraordinary tribunals composed of the cardinal's men. A network of secret informers completed the apparatus of tyrannical

repression. In the provinces Richelieu systematically dismantled fortified châteaux that royal troops could not occupy. The governors, transferred and dismissed, were watched or checkmated by intendants
(counselors of state or masters of requests) frequently sent on missions
with dictatorial powers.

Never had the nobles suffered such constraints, and among them
the memory of Richelieu, considered to be the person most responsible
for their decline, would long be cursed. Yet many measures taken by
the cardinal in favor of the nobility demonstrated that he did not want
to see it disappear, but only to free it from its feudal outlook and to
place it at the service of the modern monarchical state.

The Economy and Society. The influx of American gold and silver into
Europe in the sixteenth century had set in motion forces that in time
profoundly changed the French economy and undermined the old social
order (see p. 107). The economic base of the nobility's power—that is,
income from land—was threatened by inflation and by the rise of new
forms of wealth. The immediate effects were tempered by the privileges
that nobles held from the crown, notably exemption from taxes and
income from public and clerical offices. Consequently, the nobility in
the seventeenth century retained their preeminence in society.

The bourgeoisie of business had greatly increased their wealth but
socially remained inferior to the privileged class of nobles. They still
aspired, moreover, not to supplant the aristocracy, but to join it by
purchasing public offices that carried titles of nobility. By the mid-
seventeenth century a large number of new "nobles of the robe" had
taken their places beside the old "nobles of the sword." Many of them
held offices in the parlements, and they increasingly led the aristocracy
in its battles with the crown.

About 90 percent of the 16 million French subjects at the beginning
of the seventeenth century were peasants. A few owned their own land,
animals, and tools, but most were tenants, sharecroppers, and laborers.
Agricultural techniques were primitive—fallowing, common pasturing
of all animals, absence of fertilizer were the rule. Yields were low, and
the peasant's life was a constant struggle for an uncertain existence.
Many people found no secure place in the economy, and they provided
the recruits for bands of beggars and vagabonds that were part of the
everyday scene.

Life was precarious for everyone. Average life expectancy at birth
was about twenty years. To achieve the rare old age of forty was to
become a community elder.

Peasant Revolts. Peasant poverty grew more oppressive under Louis XIII
as inflation continued, taxes mounted, and the looting and devastation

of war returned; and when peasants protested violently from time to time they also suffered from Richelieu's harsh repression. Serious peasant revolts occurred in Burgundy in 1629–30, in Périgord and parts of the Midi in 1636–37, and in Normandy in 1639. They were not without precedent. Violent protests against taxes, sometimes bloody and usually made more devastating by food shortages or epidemics, were part of an old peasant tradition in France, and word of them, if not the actual practice, was passed down from generation to generation. The serious revolts of Louis XIII's reign occurred in provinces that had once been independent of the king and that still retained at least a tradition of fiscal autonomy. Violence usually started as protests against *new* taxes and *new* collection agents; in part it was the protest of an old society against increasing impositions by the new central state. Local authorities and militias handled the lesser disturbances gently, but if royal troops were sent to the scene, the repression became brutal; unfortunate peasants were hanged in wholesale lots.

The Navy and Commerce. Richelieu was well aware of the strength that powerful navies gave England and the Netherlands. He created the title of "Grand Master and Superintendent General of Navigation" and assumed the post himself. Brest and Toulon became the sites of important fortified arsenals. The vessels that were constructed or purchased were formed into two fleets: the Levant or Mediterranean fleet, composed primarily of galleys, and the ocean or Atlantic fleet, which in 1642 was made up of some forty large sailing ships.

Richelieu would also have liked to secure the benefits of colonial and overseas trade for France. He encouraged the establishment of large privileged companies on the model of those that enriched the Dutch and the English. An ordinance authorized nobles to engage in overseas commerce without losing their status as gentlemen. A special company called the Hundred Associates (*Cent-Associés*) resumed the systematic colonization of New France, in Canada, and a Company of the Isles undertook to colonize the French West Indies.

The Direction of Thought. As a cardinal of the Catholic church, Richelieu of course had a duty to protect the clergy, but in giving it protection he also made sure that its influence was exercised in the service of the state, and he tolerated no deviation (see p. 148–49).

He established a kind of press office to issue brochures and books defending his policies. The Parisian physician Theophraste Renaudot had begun to publish the *Gazette de France*, the first French newspaper, in 1631; Richelieu made it into the unofficial mouthpiece of the government. A few men of letters had fallen into the custom of getting together more or less regularly; Richelieu organized the group and put it to use. Thus in 1634 was born the French Academy, with Richelieu as head and protector.

The College of the Sorbonne, seat of the highest authorities in matters of theology, felt compelled to elect Richelieu as its rector. At his own expense the cardinal reconstructed its buildings and added a fine church. Someday, he decided, he would be buried there.

Of perhaps even greater influence on the course of history than Louis XIII or Richelieu was the contemporary mathematician and philosopher René Descartes (1596–1650). He founded analytical geometry and established the principles of geometrical optics. His insistence that all accepted knowledge be totally reexamined and his method of deductive reasoning, which offered a fruitful substitute for the ad hoc procedures of medieval science, were basic to the scientific revolution of the seventeenth century.

IV. FOREIGN POLICY

The Thirty Years' War. When Richelieu rose to power, central Europe was suffering the ravages of a vast religious and political conflict known as the Thirty Years' War. The Hapsburg emperor Ferdinand II had undertaken to restore Catholicism in the German states and to strengthen the authority of the imperial crown by making it hereditary rather than elective, as it had been. At first it seemed that he would be successful. One by one his armies crushed the Czechs, whose rebellion had unleashed the war; the elector of the Palatinate, leader of the Calvinist Evangelical Union; and finally the king of Denmark, whom the Protestants had called to their aid.

Would the Holy Roman Empire, which until then had been divided and impotent, be transformed into a centralized monarchy like that of France or England? A formidable power would then be in the hands of a Hapsburg, who was closely allied with the other Hapsburgs, who ruled Spain, Milan, and the Netherlands. As in the days of Charles V and Francis I, France felt the noose tightening and had to react.

Indirect Intervention. Because of difficulties at home, Richelieu could not yet intervene openly. Besides, his policy was and always would be marked by a fundamental contradiction: the knowledge that he, a cardinal and minister of a king who protected the Catholic church, supported German and Dutch Protestants against Catholic rulers. This fact scandalized many Frenchmen and was a constant theme of the cabals organized against Richelieu in France.

During the first years, then, Richelieu had to be content with checkmating the house of Austria through diplomacy and by intervening quickly and promptly, as he did in the Valteline, an Alpine valley of great strategic importance through which the Spanish might pass from the duchy of Milan to Germany. Richelieu dispatched his best agent, Father Joseph du Tremblay, to undermine the plans of Ferdinand II. "The Capuchin disarmed me with his rosary," Ferdinand is supposed to have commented. "As narrow as his cowl was, he could cloak six electors in it."

Lastly and most important, in the same year, 1630, Richelieu raised a new and formidable enemy against the emperor—King Gustavus Adolphus of Sweden. A genius of a soldier, he had revamped both arms and tactics. To help him realize his ambitious plans of conquest in Germany, France made favorable agreements with him and promised him an annual subsidy of a million livres.

The well-disciplined Swedish army marched from victory to victory, until even Richelieu was embarrassed, for Gustavus Adolphus, a fervent Protestant, threatened to destroy the Catholic principalities in southern Germany that were allies or clients of France. But in November 1632 the Swedish king was killed at the Battle of Lützen. Two years later the Swedes and their German allies suffered total defeat at Nördlingen. Again master of the situation, Ferdinand II saw the German princes, both Catholic and Protestant, flock to him. If France now abandoned to their own resources the two last allies still in the struggle, Sweden and the United Netherlands, would they not also want to come to terms with Ferdinand? The king of France would then find himself isolated before the house of Austria.

Open War. Richelieu therefore decided it was time to act openly. In 1635 war was officially declared against the king of Spain and the emperor. Despite the large number of troops that Louis XIII mustered, some 100,000 men in five armies, the war did not go well for the French. Burgundy and Picardy were invaded. The Spanish took Corbie, seventy-five miles from Paris, and their scouts got as far as Pontoise, only about twenty miles distant. Panic began to spread in the capital. To raise morale, Richelieu drove through the streets, apparently unshaken. In a surge of patriotic self-preservation, the Parisians improvised a new army of 40,000 men and forced the Spanish to retreat.

The following years saw the armies of Louis XIII regain the advantage on all fronts. In Artois the main Spanish fortresses that protected the route to Flanders were captured. In the east, Alsace, which had been seized for himself by Bernard of Saxe-Weimar, a daring soldier of fortune, fell to the French. Finally, on the Pyrenees front the Catalans rebelled against Philip IV, the king of Spain, and while he was thus occupied the French stepped in and took Roussillon. Louis XIII went in person to put the final touch to the business by capturing Perpignan in September 1642.

By this time the new emperor, Ferdinand III, was discouraged by his failures in Germany and agreed in principle to a negotiated settlement. As Richelieu lay dying in December 1642, he could believe that his objectives were close to being realized.

SUGGESTIONS FOR FURTHER READING

Buissert, David. *Sully and the Growth of Centralized Government in France.* London, 1968.

Burckhardt, Carl Jacob. *Richelieu and His Age.* 3 vols. London, 1967–70.

Lough, John, ed. *An Introduction to Seventeenth-Century France.* 2d ed. New York, 1969.

Seward, Desmond. *The First Bourbon: Henry IV of France and of Navarre.* London, 1971.

Treasure, Geoffrey. R. R. *Seventeenth-Century France.* New York, 1966.

Wedgwood, C. V. *Richelieu and the French Monarchy.* New York, 1949, 1962.

_____. *The Thirty Years' War.* Garden City, N.Y., 1961.

Pagès, Georges. *Naissance du grand siècle: La France de Henri IV à Louis XIV.* Paris, 1948.

Tapié, Victor L. *La France de Louis XIII et de Richelieu.* 2d ed. Paris, 1967.

II
Anne of Austria and Mazarin

The regency of Queen Anne of Austria was marked by a reaction against the oppressive rule of Richelieu. After a long period of disorder, known as the Fronde, the authority of the throne emerged stronger than ever. Armed with the queen's trust, Cardinal Mazarin governed in the name of the young Louis XIV and put an end to the wars against the house of Austria. During this period Catholicism experienced a renewal in France.

I. THE REGENCY AND THE FRONDE

The Regency. Louis XIII survived his minister by only seven months. His death on May 14, 1643, left the throne to a child of four years and eight months. The late king had altered nothing in Richelieu's policies and had even tried to ensure their continuity by creating a regency council in which the queen and Gaston, the duke of Orléans, his brother—two people he distrusted equally—would be neutralized by Richelieu's old associates. But Anne of Austria appealed to the Parlement of Paris, and the Parlement, only too happy to annul a royal decree, hastened to declare her regent with full authority.

While the queen, then forty-one, was not truly beautiful, she had the appearance and grace of a great Spanish lady tempered by a desire to please. Though she was not a woman of great intelligence and had no practical knowledge of affairs, she showed good sense. Her natural pride and her great piety helped her to sustain her role with dignity. Her son always showed her unfailing respect.

Mazarin. Anne's first act was to choose Cardinal Mazarin as head of the council. Everyone was surprised and many were disillusioned. Still, it was a judicious choice, for Mazarin, Richelieu's confidant in his last years, was the only person who knew the ins and outs of the important diplomatic negotiations that were then under way. Moreover, as a foreigner who had no ties to noble or parlementary factions, and who owed his rise solely to the queen's favor, he would be completely loyal to her. As we shall see, feelings also entered the picture.

The career of the man who thus rose to power was one of the most astonishing in French history. The father of Giulio Mazarini was a Sicilian who had become the steward for the great Colonna family of Rome. After a stint as an officer in the papal army, the son had entered the diplomatic service. He then took his first minor orders and donned a churchman's robes, but he did not join the priesthood. His rapid rise took him to Paris in 1634 as nuncio, or papal ambassador. Richelieu appreciated his cleverness, and Mazarin himself believed that he had more to gain in France than in Italy. He therefore entered the service of Louis XIII. After the death of Father Joseph, Richelieu made him his chief assistant for foreign affairs and secured a cardinal's hat for him in 1642.

Mazarin had been careful to win over the queen. About her own age, he was handsome and charming. Deprived of her husband's affection, Anne of Austria was taken by the flattering and sensitive attention he paid her. Eventually he came close to occupying a husband's place in her affections. When she left the Louvre to reside in the Palais Royal—Richelieu's old residence, which he had willed to the king—Mazarin was given an apartment close to the queen's. "And so," it has been written, "by a game of love and chance—two very great forces in history—the French monarchy fell into the hands of a Spaniard and a Neapolitan." Unlike Richelieu, Mazarin never had to fear disgrace or to struggle to get the sovereign to accept his views. He was as humble, obliging, and gentle toward others as Richelieu was haughty, imperious, and hard. Guile, tenacity, and persuasion were his weapons. "I never approached the cardinal," one contemporary said, "without believing that I would be speaking to the greatest of knaves, and I never left him without being charmed."

The Opposition. All those who had been bullied by Richelieu, beginning with the princes and nobles, lifted their heads again and formed a "cabal of the worthies." As in 1610, an effort was made to win them over with money, but this time there was no cash in reserve. On the contrary, tax revenues had been mortgaged for four years in advance. Yet with the war continuing, the armies had to be maintained and allies provided with subsidies.

The Superintendent of Finances, Particelli d'Emeri, an Italian brought to France by Mazarin, found ingenious ways to pressure taxpayers, invent new taxes, and delay payments due to bondholders, suppliers, and officials. Exasperation increased among the Parisians, who were particularly hard hit by these measures.

The Claims of Parlement. In 1648 Mazarin and Particelli, who had run out of expedients, announced that in exchange for a nine-year resumption of the system of hereditary offices sanctioned by the *paulette*, the king would withhold the salaries of officials of the supreme courts (Court of Accounts, Court of Indirect Taxes, Grand Council) for four years. Though they had wisely stopped short of extending the measure to the Parlement, the members nevertheless seized the occasion to assert their claim to be the nation's natural representatives, a kind of permanent commission of the Estates General. They boasted of the example presented by the English Parliament in its rebellion against Charles I. They forgot that the English Parliament and the Parlement of Paris were similar in name only. The former was a true representation of all the ruling classes; the latter was a group of judges whose power was delegated by the throne.

They declared their solidarity with the members of other sovereign courts and invited them to a joint session to discuss the reform of the kingdom. The regent banned the meeting, but it was held anyway. In June 1648 it adopted a declaration "of the Chamber of St. Louis," inspired by the English Magna Carta—twenty-seven articles that formed a true declaration of rights.

The regent pretended to accept it. Two months later, she seized the opportunity provided by the public celebrations over the victory of Lens and arrested the ringleaders of the parlementary opposition. Almost at once a hundred barricades sprang up in Paris, blocking all troop movements and isolating the Palais Royal. On August 28, 1648, Anne of Austria once again gave way.

The Parlementary Fronde. Shortly afterward, when peace had been restored by the Treaties of Westphalia, the regent summoned the troops commanded by the young and popular Louis II, prince of Condé. As soon as they were near, on June 6, 1649, the queen slipped away by night with the young king and Mazarin and settled in the château of St. Germain, a dozen miles west of Paris.

Parlement declared itself in rebellion, not against the king, but against Mazarin. The people of Paris took up arms enthusiastically, encouraged by the bishop coadjutor of Paris, the ambitious Paul de Gondi. The princes and their entourages of restless lords also took part, in a spirit of fun or quixotic adventure. Their wives and lovers seized the opportunity to conspire and show themselves off. All these antics gave a frivolous quality to this "little war"; hence the name given to it, the Fronde—a children's game, to be sure, but a dangerous one.

Condé blockaded the city. Resistance eroded quickly, undermined by divisions among the rebels. The nobles reproached the "square caps" of Parlement for their paralyzing concern not to overstep legality. The members of Parlement were scandalized by the blustering and thoughtlessness of the nobles, who spoke of calling for foreign assistance. Both sides were afraid of mob violence. The good bourgeoisie wearied of their hardships and were upset when they realized that no one was protecting their suburban homes against pillage.

The execution of Charles I in London on January 30, 1649, showed just how far a rebellion might go. Mathieu Molé, first president of the Parlement, took it upon himself to begin discussions. These talks resulted in the Peace of Rueil on March 30, 1649. As for the princes, they made individual arrangements to sell their surrender at the highest price.

The Fronde of the Princes. Condé considered himself to be the savior of the kingdom. His demands and arrogance exasperated Anne of Austria. Would he go so far as to try to drive out her dear Mazarin? On January 18, 1650, the regent had Condé, his brother the Prince of Conti, and his brother-in-law the Duke of Longueville arrested without warning at the Palais Royal.

The prisoners' wives and friends went off to stir up rebellions in several provinces. Happily, the army remained loyal, for it was firmly led by an officer corps that was seasoned and loyal to the crown. The local disturbances were quickly repressed.

The Union of the Two Frondes. This "Fronde of the Princes" seemed to be all but put down when it received unexpected aid from a revival of the Parisian and parlementary Fronde—the work largely of the ambitious Paul de Gondi, with the support of the king's uncle Gaston of Orléans and his followers. The Parlement once again demanded Mazarin's dismissal. Mazarin decided that the wisest course was to disappear for a while; if he were removed from the scene, the motley coalition of his enemies would fall apart. He freed Condé, slipped away to Germany, and quietly continued to pull the regent's strings from there.

The months that followed were filled with confused and absurd happenings. Condé, as predicted, made himself intolerable to Paris, and he returned to his province of Guyenne, where he rallied a large part of the nobility about him. Set up like a king in Bordeaux, he even signed a treaty of alliance with Spain. The queen and her son fled to Poitiers under the protection of the faithful royal army, now commanded by Henri de Turenne, the only general thought capable of standing up to Condé. In the spring of 1652 Condé felt strong enough to try to assume the leadership of his partisans north of the Loire. After a series of successful maneuvers Turenne cornered him just outside Paris, in the Faubourg St. Antoine. Condé avoided being captured only by fleeing into Paris, which until then had been closed to his troops. Once again he alienated the bourgeoisie and the members of Parlement, and he was refused provisions for his soldiers. He then fled to his Spanish allies in the Netherlands. Several days later the young king and his mother were humbly entreated to return to their "good city." Disgusted by the disorder and stupidity of the *frondeurs*, the people of Paris gave the two a triumphal welcome on October 21, 1652. The ever-cautious Mazarin preferred to let the passions of the moment subside; he did not return to Paris until the beginning of February 1653.

The Results of the Fronde. The Fronde not only inflicted destruction on the country and useless suffering on the people, it also turned public opinion more strongly than ever in favor of absolute monarchy. The nobility and the Parlement of Paris, the two political forces that had sought to limit arbitrary royal power—and not without good reason—had conducted their undertaking so ineptly that they were discredited and discouraged for many years to come. The people, who hoped for order and security, were ready to accept strong authority gratefully.

The End of Mazarin. Mazarin was the first to benefit from this state of mind. Until his death on March 8, 1661, he enjoyed unchallenged power. Although Louis XIV was of age, he left Mazarin in complete charge of the government. The cardinal, for his part, showed him fatherly affection and quietly prepared him for his duties as king. He also gave him a remarkable sign of his devotion. The young king was smitten by a niece of the cardinal, Marie Mancini, and wanted to marry her. Mazarin was unbending in his refusal, and despite the young couple's tears, he sent Marie away. And yet enriching and promoting his family's fortune had been one of his chief concerns. As far as he himself was concerned, he took ample care of his own interests and was not overscrupulous as to the means. The fortune he left to his heirs has been estimated at 200 million gold francs, plus an immense number of art objects. Perhaps to show that he was no less generous than Richelieu, Mazarin willed 2 million francs to found a college of the "four nations," that is, the four provinces annexed by the Treaty of the Pyrenees. The majestic building constructed after his death today houses the Institute of France.

II. MAZARIN'S EUROPEAN POLICY

The Victory of Rocroi. The Spanish in the Netherlands attempted to profit from the disorder in France caused by the deaths of Richelieu and Louis XIII. A powerful army took the offensive on the northeastern border. Despite its numerical inferiority, the French army of Picardy moved rapidly to relieve the besieged fortress of Rocroi. At its head was a twenty-two-year-old general, the Duke of Enghien, the future Prince of Condé. The stunning victory that he won on May 19, 1643, revealed his military genius. The terrible losses inflicted on the famous Spanish infantry regiments, the *tercios viejos*, shattered forever their fighting power and their reputation for invincibility.

The Offensive in Germany. During the following years the French military effort was directed mainly against the imperial forces in the east. There the reputation of another great French soldier, Marshal Turenne, was established. The arrival of reinforcements from the Duke of Enghien permitted him to take the offensive in Germany, and he defeated the enemy at Fribourg in 1644 and at Nördlingen in 1645. But Mazarin's niggardliness kept him too short of supplies to win decisively. Finally, in the spring of 1648, he linked up with Karl Gustav Wrangel's Swedish army in Bavaria. Together they crushed the imperial troops at Zusmarshausen on May 17, 1648. With his capital threatened, the emperor came to terms.

The Treaties of Westphalia. The negotiations, which opened in 1644, were carried on in the two cities of Münster and Osnabrück simultaneously. Taking part were the representatives not only of the belligerents—the emperor and the kings of France, Spain, Denmark, Sweden, and the Protestant Netherlands—but also those of all the German princes and the mediating powers, the pope, and Venice. It was, in short, a virtual European congress, the first of its kind.

The Treaties of Westphalia, signed on October 24, 1648, were concerned mainly with Germany:

First, the princes had the right to impose their religion on their subjects, according to the principle of *cujus regio ejus religio* (loosely, "the king's religion is the kingdom's religion"). Dissenters had only the right to emigrate.

Second, the imperial crown remained elective, and the princes retained all their sovereign rights, including that of concluding alliances with foreigners; the only reservation was that no alliance could be directed against the emperor.

Third, the treaty's provisions in regard to the status of Germany were guaranteed by all the signatory powers.

Fourth, among numerous territorial changes confirmed by the treaty, France acquired Alsace, except for Strasbourg and Mulhouse.

But in addition the new constitution of the German state indirectly gave France immense political advantages, for it confirmed the fragmentation of Germany and perpetuated the impotence of the imperial crown, reducing it to an empty symbol. France was given not only a guarantee of its security but also the means to intervene constantly in the affairs of the empire on the pretext of safeguarding "German liberties." It is not surprising that until the end of the eighteenth century the chief concern of French European policy was to maintain these Treaties of Westphalia, which were considered the masterpiece of its diplomacy.

The War against Spain. Spain's representatives withdrew from the congress after concluding a separate treaty that recognized the independence of the United Provinces. The war then continued between the French and Spanish alone.

The victor of Rocroi, who became prince of Condé, quickly took the offensive in Flanders, capturing Dunkirk and winning a brilliant victory at Lens on August 20, 1648. But these triumphs proved hollow when the Fronde paralyzed France and encouraged Spain to continue the war.

In 1657 Mazarin, braving public opinion, entered into negotiations with the regicide dictator Oliver Cromwell, ceding him Dunkirk in exchange for an alliance with England. A Franco-British army commanded by Turenne defeated the Spanish at the Battle of the Dunes on June 14, 1658, and went on to attack strongholds in Flanders. The king of Spain at last decided to negotiate.

The Peace of the Pyrenees. Mazarin went in person to discuss terms in meetings held on a small island in the Bidassoa River, on the border between the two countries. This so-called Peace of the Pyrenees recognized France's possession of its recent conquests—Roussillon and Cerdagne in the south, and Artois and several strongpoints in Flanders and Luxembourg, including Thionville, in the north.

In exchange, Louis XIV pardoned the prince of Condé, and, most important, married the eldest daughter of King Philip IV of Spain, the infanta Marie Theresa. The wedding, celebrated with great pomp at St. Jean de Luz, opened prospects for French ambitions, for the degenerate royal family of Spain seemed to be on the way to extinction. The Spanish ministers had indeed sought to dispel such a danger, for with her marriage the infanta renounced all her rights to the Spanish succession—but on condition that her promised dowry of 500,000 gold écus would be paid in full. This escape clause was inserted by the wily Mazarin, who suspected it would not be fulfilled; and in fact it was not.

The two treaties of Westphalia and the Pyrenees marked the triumph of France over the two branches of the house of Austria and made it the dominant power in Europe.

III. THE CATHOLIC RENAISSANCE

A Spiritual Awakening. It was also toward the middle of the century that the Catholic renaissance in France reached its height. Many aspects of this movement gave a very distinctive quality to French society in the seventeenth century. It was of course linked to the Counterreformation, which the church set in motion a half century earlier at the Council of Trent; but the impetus felt at the top was blocked in France by the wars of religion until the end of the sixteenth century. On the other hand, the wars perhaps contributed to the religious revival by impelling many Christians to understand and to live their commitment more fully. Also strides in printing favored the spread of treatises on spirituality and books on piety. Numerous translations now made available to French Catholics the works of ancient and modern spiritual writers, notably those of the great Spanish mystics of the sixteenth century, Luis de Granada, St. John of the Cross, and St. Teresa of Avila.

Two French writers in particular helped to nourish the piety of Catholics in those years—the bishop (later saint) Francis de Sales (1567–1622) and the cardinal Pierre de Bérulle (1575–1629). In his *Introduction to the Devout Life* (1608), Bishop de Sales led the laity along paths to spiritual perfection that until then had seemed suitable only to monks and nuns removed from the world. Pierre de Bérulle was perhaps known less for his written work—the exalted quality of its mysticism made it difficult to grasp—than for his personal influence on a whole generation of priests and monks, and among the parlementary circles from which he sprang. He was also at the source of Catholic opposition to certain aspects of the government of Richelieu, who tended to place religion and the clergy at the service of the state, and whose foreign policy served the interests of Protestantism in Germany.

Religious Communities. The proliferation of religious communities remains one of the most visible aspects of the Catholic renaissance. In Paris alone about a hundred new religious houses were established within a half century. Bérulle played no small part in this development, for he had introduced the Spanish contemplative order of the Carmelites into France, and in 1611 had founded the Oratory, a society of secular priests devoted chiefly, but not exclusively, to the education of youth. By 1629 the "Oratorians" had some sixty houses throughout the country. Other such societies were born a short while later. Vincent de Paul founded the Priests of the Mission, called Lazarists or Vincentians; Jean Eudes founded the order of Jesus and Mary, whose members were called Eudists; and Jean Jacques Olier the Society of St. Sulpice. The Sulpicians devoted themselves exclusively to the training of priests in seminaries; the other two orders organized preaching missions and retreats in country and city.

The Jesuits, driven from France by an act of Parlement in 1594, had been authorized to return ten years later. Their colleges, which numbered seventy in 1640, educated the sons of the upper classes, bourgeois as well as aristocratic. The daughters of these families were taught by the Ursulines, a society of Italian origin, and by the sisters of the Visitation, founded by St. Francis de Sales and St. Jeanne de Chantal. The mendicant religious orders—Capuchins, Cordeliers, Minimes, Recollets—were more concerned with the urban poor. Finally, the great old orders—Augustinians, Benedictines, Cistercians—were roused from their lethargy or decay by a generation of reforming abbots. Several new congregations of nuns were established.

The Secular Clergy. Because the Concordat of 1516 allowed the king to name bishops, the quality of the upper clergy depended on the way the sovereign understood his duty. Henry IV perpetuated the worst abuses of the preceding century; one of his bastards was given the see of Metz at the age of six! Such scandals no longer occurred under Louis XIII.

But Richelieu still promoted men who were known more for their political talents than for their religious virtues, and abbeys and other church benefices were still considered the equivalent of cash in the state coffers, available to pay for services rendered or expected. The abbé *in commendum*, who was occasionally a layman, had to do nothing but collect his income, while a "claustral prior" performed the duties of the office. At length Anne of Austria entrusted the "list of benefices" to Vincent de Paul, and from then on the choices were excellent.

As for the lowly parish clergy, who were quite neglected, the efforts made to provide them better training produced results only very slowly.

The Laity. Never had such a large proportion of upper-class men and women shown such an interest in theology or applied themselves so assiduously to piety and good works.

At one time the most active were gathered in a secret society, the Company of the Holy Sacrament. It had been founded around 1630 by the Duke of Ventadour to link all the works intended to aid the sick and the poor, uplift society, and convert heretics. The hidden power of this "cabal of the devout," and the indirect control it exerted over morals, eventually caused concern, and Mazarin dissolved it.

Among the works it supported, the missions preached in the countryside had the most lasting effect. They dispelled religious ignorance, and the brutality and paganism that flourished during the wars of religion declined.

Vincent de Paul. The social and charitable side of the religious revival was incarnated in St. Vincent de Paul (1576–1660). This son of poor peasants had known the misery of small country parishes before he became a tutor in the home of Philippe de Gondi, commander of the galleys. He took advantage of this post to try to improve the frightful conditions among the convicts who were condemned to row them. His increasing contacts within high society eventually brought him the confidence of the queen mother. He became her counselor in religious matters, "a minister of charity."

With Louise de Marillac he established the Congregation of the Daughters of Charity in 1633 to help the sick and poor; today it has spread throughout the world. Another of his lasting works was the Home for Foundlings, which took in babies abandoned in the streets by the poor or by unwed mothers.

Jansenism. The effort at renewal led some people to extremes that fomented discord within Catholicism. This "Jansenist" tendency owed its name to a bishop of Ypres named Cornelius Jansen or Jansenius. In a book titled *Augustinus*, he interpreted St. Augustine's doctrine on the influence of divine grace and human free will in a way that approached Calvin's theory of predestination. The propagator of Jansenism in France was Jean Duvergier de Hauranne, the abbé de St. Cyran, a disciple of Bérulle. He held his followers to an inflexible standard; he rejected any compromise with the lures of worldly life, and the conditions his followers were required to meet before they could receive the sacraments were hardly human.

The main center of Jansenism in Paris was the monastery of Port Royal, whose young abbess, Angélique Arnauld, placed herself under St. Cyran's guidance after energetically reforming her community. The Arnaulds were very influential among the upper-middle-class judicial officials in Paris, and through them Jansenism made headway in parlementary circles. Some of these men withdrew from the world to the lonely Port Royal des Champs, south of Paris. Their writings and example had great influence on the society of the period.

First Jansenist Controversy. Richelieu took umbrage at the way St. Cyran, like Bérulle before him, condemned his foreign policy and in general all intervention by the state in the life of the clergy. "That man," he said, "is more dangerous than six armies." He had him imprisoned at Vincennes.

The implacable struggle between the Jesuits and the Jansenists—a struggle that was to continue until the end of the eighteenth century—began under Mazarin. The Jansenists charged that the Jesuits compromised with worldy power and readily accommodated their morality to the temper of the times. The Jesuits counterattacked on doctrinal grounds. In 1653 they obtained the pope's condemnation of five propositions or theses in which the Sorbonne summarized Jansenius' doctrines. The Jansenists, who wanted above all to avoid the appearance of heresy, argued that the five heretical propositions did not appear in Jansenius' *Augustinus*. The battle raged around this point. The Jansenist cause had a highly original defender in the person of Blaise Pascal. His *Provinciales*, letters to a provincial, a masterpiece of seventeenth-century literature, seriously damaged the reputation of the Jesuits. Mazarin, growing weary of the dispute, banned the *Provinciales* and dispersed the hermits at Port Royal.

Despite the persecutions—and perhaps in part because of them—Jansenism had enormous influence on the French Catholicism of the seventeenth century. Catholicism in France took on a gravity, intensity, and moral rigor that contrasted sharply with the more relaxed Catholicism of Italy, Germany, and the Austrian states.

SUGGESTIONS FOR FURTHER READING

Abercrombie, Nigel. *The Origins of Jansenism*. Oxford, 1936.

Carré, Henri. *The Early Life of Louis XIV (1638–1661)*. London, 1951.

Hassel, Arthur. *Mazarin*. New York, 1911.

Kossman, E. H. *La Fronde*. London, 1954.

Moote, A. Lloyd. *The Revolt of the Judges: The Parlement of Paris and the Fronde*. Princeton, 1972.

Sedgwick, Alexander. *Jansenism in the Seventeenth Century: Voices from the Wilderness*. Charlottesville, Va., 1977.

Méthivier, Hubert. *Le Siècle de Louis XIII*. 4th ed. Paris, 1977.

12
Louis XIV: Internal Government

Just as St. Louis had provided the medieval West with the model of the ideal Christian king, Louis XIV provided his own time and history with the archetype of the absolute monarch. By a determined effort, sustained for almost a half century, the king subjected all parts of his nation to his authority and created an effective and centralized administration. If the persecution of the Protestants seems a disastrous mistake, his reign can also be credited with France's rise to virtual supremacy in intellectual and artistic pursuits.

I. THE KING AND HIS GOVERNMENT

The King Takes Power. Louis XIV was not quite twenty-three years old when Mazarin died. The young king surprised everyone by indicating that the cardinal would have no successor and that henceforth he intended to be his own first minister. And in fact, until his death fifty-four years later, Louis XIV was to exercise fully, day after day, what he called "the great, noble, and delectable" profession of king. He regularly spent long hours studying affairs with his ministers, presiding over councils and ceremonies, and reading and listening to reports. It might be added that the example of the assiduous and regular labors performed by the head of state inspired unusual efficiency in all parts of the government.

The King. Saint-Simon, the great memorist of the reign, wrote of the king:

> His entire manner [was] so naturally imbued with the most imposing majesty that it stood forth even in his least gestures and his most ordinary actions, with no trace of pride, but with simple gravity. . . , perfect manners, with the grandest bearing and grandest air that a man ever had. No fatigue, no effect of the weather troubled him. Drenched with rain, snow, cold, sweat, covered with dust, he was always the same. . . . A voice that went with all the rest, a facility for speaking well and listening politely . . . much reserve . . . a politeness that was always serious, always majestic, always appropriate to age, condition, and sex . . .

If he had only average intelligence, he showed solid good sense. "He loved truth, fairness, order, and reason," Saint-Simon says; "he even loved to be got the better of by them." Cautious and distrustful, he made decisions only after taking time to reflect and make inquiries. "I shall see" was his initial reply to any request. Finally, in defeat he displayed a moral courage that compelled the admiration of his enemies.

In contrast to these truly royal qualities, Louis XIV developed the defects inherent in any holder of absolute power. Convinced that he was God's agent on earth, he believed he had the absolute right to control the property, the freedom, and even the lives of his subjects, so long as he observed the divine and natural laws that Providence had assigned him to protect. This belief, coupled with the adulation that surrounded him from his earliest youth, nurtured in him such pride and egoism that he adopted the sun as his emblem. Love of glory was the moving force of his life; the well-being of his people was too often sacrificed to it.

Divine-Right Kingship. A compelling theoretical base and religious justification for Louis's absolute rule was provided by Bishop Jacques Bossuet (1627–1704). In his sermons and writings he presented Louis as God's representative on earth, divinely ordained to rule a society that was the culmination of the Judeo-Christian tradition. The individual subject owed obedience to the king as to God himself, and there could be no appeal against the king's decisions except through prayer.

The King's Private Life. The king's Christian faith, real though not very enlightened, did not often deter him from giving in to his sensual impulses. Although he respected the unattractive wife whom politics had bestowed upon him—the insignificant little queen Marie Theresa—he kept mistresses: Louise de la Vallière, Marie Angélique de Fontanges, and particularly the imperious and witty Marquise de Montespan, who

ruled over the pleasures of the court for more than ten years. He legiti-
mized the children they bore him and married them to princes or princesses of the royal family. After the death of the queen in 1683 Louis XIV
did give a more dignified air to his private life by secretly marrying
Francoise d'Aubigné, marquise de Maintenon, a woman of rather humble
origin but of great wit, who had been the governess of the king's illegitimate children by Madame de Montespan. From that moment on the court
changed its tone: the liveliness and licentiousness that had characterized
it at the beginning of the reign gave way to relative piety and austerity.

The Court. The unbridled development of court life in the age of Louis
XIV and the veneration of the king's person had a political aim: it was
intended to neutralize the dangers arising from the existence of an idle
and unruly nobility. By drawing the nobles to court with the lure of a
brilliant and festive life, by requiring them to appear there to obtain the
slightest favor or office, and by inciting them to spend too much in
order to cut a fine figure, he made them more and more narrowly
dependent on royal power.

To justify such an assemblage he multiplied the useless or purely
honorific posts that together made up the king's civil household—several hundred persons divided into six services. The queen and the royal
princes and princesses also had their households. To these people were
added all those who were not yet provided for but who came to put
themselves on display in the hope of obtaining some share of the boun-
ty. In addition, the palace guard in the king's military household offered young noblemen an equally enormous number of honorable and
paid positions. All told, the court numbered between 4,000 and 6,000
individuals.

Life at court was ordered by minutely observed rituals of etiquette.
Every action in the king's day, from getting up to going to bed, constituted a public ceremony that was minutely regulated as to role and
precedence. The king himself conformed precisely to the established
timetable. "With an almanac and a watch," wrote Saint-Simon, "one
might say exactly what he was doing at a distance of three hundred
leagues."

Versailles. The worship of the Sun King required a fairly vast temple to
assemble all the officials and the faithful. That temple was the palace of
Versailles, the supreme expression of the absolute monarch but also the
most impressive accomplishment of the art of the age, integrating architecture, sculpture, painting, and furniture, not to mention the gar-
dener's art and the fountain builder's skill.

Louis XIV's decision to establish his residence outside of Paris can
undoubtedly be explained by his memories of the Fronde. The choice

of site was probably determined by the existence of the small château built by Louis XIII near forests filled with game. Like his father, Louis XIV loved the outdoor life and hunting. The construction of the palace at Versailles practically never ceased to occupy the king until his death. Rebuilding, expansion, and beautification went on year after year. To improve the gardens, the site itelf was transformed by immense labors as terraces were formed and trees planted. At Marly a marvelous machine was constructed to raise water from the Seine to the level of the aqueduct that would feed the numerous fountains in the park of Versailles. The name of André Lenôtre, who created this immense park, is still associated with the "French style" of garden, designed in geometric patterns. The architects Louis Le Vau and Jules Hardouin-Mansart are associated with the construction of the palace itself, and the painter Charles Lebrun with the interior decoration.

The immense royal palace became an overcrowded hotel. Louis XIV wanted to have more agreeable and intimate residences. These were the Trianons, quite close to the palace, and, a little farther away, Marly, the summer residence, surrounded by greenery and cooled by a profusion of fountains.

Louis XIV has often been blamed for his excessive taste for building, whose cost may have consumed 3 to 5 percent of the annual budget. In any event, he reproached himself for it on his deathbed. Today we can be less harsh, for aside from the political aspect of this accomplishment—an effective instrument of prestige for the king and the monarchy—these undertakings gave a powerful spur to the arts. Thousands of workers and craftsmen were set to work, and they made lasting contributions to the nation's artistic heritage.

Protector of Arts and Letters. At Versailles as in the other buildings of the period (the grand colonnade of the Louvre, the hospitals of the Invalides and La Salpetrière), in all the plastic arts, and even in music itself we can see the king's preference for the Italian art of the day, but with a distinct note of sobriety, regularity, measured majesty, and somewhat cold grandeur. The French Academy of Rome, founded in 1666, enabled young French artists to study the models of antiquity and the Renaissance on site, while the Academy of Painting and Sculpture in Paris, under the direction of Charles Lebrun, saw that the rules of "good taste"—that is, the king's taste—were observed. More than any other ruler, Louis XIV looms as the virtual creator of a style that was imposed on a generation of artists of all types. French art became the model for all Europe and was copied in every royal and ducal court.

In the literature of the period, too, the king's standards of perfection triumphed: imitation of ancient authors, a concern for clarity and simplicity in composition, and propriety and nobility in language. This discipline was imposed by the French Academy, and still more by the king's pronouncements. Louis XIV knew how to single out such talents as Molière and Racine and to encourage them by generous pensions and even by marks of esteem that helped to raise the social position of writers.

The king appointed a superintendent of music, the Italian Jean-Baptiste Lully (1632–87), to develop musical composition and performance. Lully obtained a virtual monopoly on musical productions in France, and he used his position particularly to establish and develop French opera.

The sciences were also encouraged, notably by the founding in 1666 of the Academy of Sciences, the establishment of the Paris Observatory, and publication of the first scientific journal, the *Journal des Savants*.

Government. "It was important," wrote Louis XIV, "that the public should know by the rank of those who served me that I had no intention of dividing my authority, and that they themselves, understanding what they were, should cherish no higher hope than that which I might give them." That is why, in governing the state, the king wished to be served only by bourgeoisie. The nobles were admitted to careers only in the army or the navy, or as court functionaries. Yet those bourgeoisie who were singled out in this way quite quickly received titles of nobility, and through marriage their descendants soon merged with the old nobility.

Elsewhere Louis XIV was content to use the institutions of central government that had gradually developed since Francis I, while specifying their powers: a chancellor, who was in charge of justice; a controller general of finances; four secretaries of state, each combining control over the administration of one part of the country with responsibility for a specialized ministry (Royal Household, Foreign Affairs, War, Navy); and a royal council, unitary in principle but in fact functioning through a number of specialized sections: the High Council (Conseil d'en Haut), the Council of Dispatches, the Council of Finances, and the Council of Pleas. In the provinces the principal innovation was to make the intendants' posts permanent and fixed. Until then their functions had resembled the *missi dominici* of Charlemagne, who were inspectors and traveling controllers. Now the intendants would be the king's eyes and arms in the provinces, invested with full power.

Confronted with this all-powerful administration, the other groups of royal officials were forced into silent submission. The town governments were closely controlled by the intendants, and in Paris the task of maintaining order was entrusted to a lieutenant general of police. The provincial estates were only rarely allowed to assemble. The right of the parlements to issue remonstrances was virtually eliminated. Abuses and injustices committed by the local nobility were more likely now to be brought to light and checked.

II. THE WORK OF COLBERT

Colbert and Fouquet. The chief architect of this powerful monarchical administration was Jean-Baptiste Colbert. This son of a merchant draper from Rheims had been the confidant of Mazarin, whose immense fortune he had carefully managed. As the cardinal lay dying, he had strongly recommended Colbert to the king. The first service Colbert rendered the king was to make him aware of the corruption of the Superintendent of Finances, Nicolas Fouquet. Fouquet had succeeded too well in enriching himself at the expense of the royal treasury, and the insolent luxury he flaunted—particularly in building the marvelous château of Vaux-le-Vicomte—had offended the king. In September 1661 Louis had him arrested without warning. Fouquet enjoyed so much sympathy that even though this trial threw a spotlight on his dishonesty, it ended with a simple sentence of banishment. On his own authority the king changed it to imprisonment for life. Shortly afterward Colbert was named controller general of finances, and in 1669 he also assumed the offices of secretary of state for the royal household and secretary of the navy. For almost twenty years he held the entire administration of the kingdom in his hands, with the exception of the ministries of war and foreign affairs. After his death in 1683 there was never again such a concentration of power.

Colbert turned to these crushing tasks with a true passion for work, a clear and methodical mind, and an absolute dedication to the greatness of the king and the country. Nor did he forget to advance the interests of his family, which in the course of a half century supplied Louis XIV with no fewer than five ministers. His harshness and stern demeanor made him the terror of bureaucrats and favor-seekers.

Finances. Colbert introduced rigorous accounting methods that permitted income and expenses to be known month by month, and established an annual budget. A special chamber of justice prosecuted financiers who, like Fouquet, had enriched themselves dishonestly; they were forced to return 110 million livres to the treasury, the equivalent of a year's ordinary receipts. The excessively high rate of interest on various kinds of loans could then be reduced.

Out of a concern for fiscal justice, Colbert hunted down designing noblemen who had secured exemption from the *taille*. He reduced by 16 percent the income from this direct tax, which weighed only on the mass of people with no special privileges, but at the same time quadrupled the income from indirect taxes, which weighed on everyone: the excise taxes on beverages, duties (internal customs), and *gabelles* (salt taxes). To these resources Colbert added others from stamped paper, the marking of gold and silver objects, stamps on playing cards, and a monopoly on the sale of tobacco—all of which are still part of the French fiscal system.

Until 1672 Colbert succeeded in balancing expenses and receipts, but after that deficits began to recur; court expenses, construction, and particularly war costs exceeded the normal revenues of the kingdom. It was necessary to return to borrowing and the sale of offices.

Legislation. In order to "speed up the conduct of business by eliminating numerous delays and unnecessary measures," Colbert issued three great ordinances: the Civil Ordinance of 1667, the Criminal Ordinance of 1670, and the Commercial Ordinance of 1673. Many of their provisions were later incorporated in the Napoleonic codes. The Ordinance on Water and Forests (1669) preserved France's woodland heritage by regulating its exploitation. The Navy Ordinance (1681) and the Colonial Ordinance (1685) were so well conceived that England adopted their chief provisions.

Colbertism. Colbert's economic policy was inspired by a few simplistic ideas. To be strong, the king had to be rich. Wealth meant gold and silver. Since the kingdom did not produce them, it had to secure them by foreign trade. Therefore it had to purchase as little as possible and sell as much as possible.

Industry. Industry was the keystone of this system. It had to be developed till it could provide the French with what they had hitherto procured from other countries, and at the same time offer products that would be attractive to foreigners. A pilot role was given to the "king's manufactories," or state enterprises. The most important of these firms, that of the Gobelins in Paris, produced not only the tapestries that made it famous but all kinds of furniture and art objects. The "royal manufactories," or private enterprises, were encouraged by subsidies, exemptions from taxes, and monopolies. Colbert brought in skilled workers from abroad, such as glassworkers from Venice, who helped to set up glassworks first in Paris and then at St. Gobain. Product quality was ensured by a corps of inspectors and minute regulations. Craftsmen who worked independently were obliged to join trade guilds, in which work was controlled by bonded inspectors. To ensure the supply of labor, Colbert forbade emigration to foreign countries, worked to attract immigrants, and encouraged early marriages and large families by tax exemptions. To increase productivity he set long workdays, reduced the number of holidays, and forbade strikes.

The woolen textile industry suggests the effects of Colbert's efforts. It occupied a major place in French industry, both as an export industry and as an employer in all parts of the kingdom. For a quarter of a century Colbert lavished it with his attention. In 1708, near the end of Louis XIV's reign, the volume of its production was more than 50 percent above the level in the 1660s, and the value of its product had increased 170 percent in the same period.

Commerce. Once industry produced the goods, it was up to commerce to bring in the gold and silver from their sale. On the one hand, Colbert sought to strangle foreign imports by prohibitive customs duties; on the other, he wanted to develop a merchant marine to rival the British and Dutch fleets. French shipowners received incentives to construct or purchase ships.

Colbert organized five large joint-stock companies qualified by royal privilege to extend French trade into the East Indies, the West Indies, the Near East, the North Sea, and Senegal. Three of the companies were threatened with failure and were dissolved in Colbert's own lifetime. The East and West Indies companies suffered considerably from the continual wars. Nonetheless, in the last years of the reign the impetus provided by these companies was felt by shipbuilders and private companies, and several French ports, among them St. Malo, Nantes, and Marseilles, enjoyed great prosperity based on foreign trade.

Internal trade was encouraged by the safety of communications, the reduction of internal customs barriers, and work on roads, bridges, and navigable canals. The Canal des Deux-Mers, planned and supervised by Pierre-Paul Riquet, took fifteen years to complete (1667–81). When it was finished, it linked Toulouse, on the Garonne, with the port of Sète, on the Mediterranean. With its 179-mile length and the 190 locks needed to lift a boat 590 feet, the canal was admired as the greatest feat of modern times; but its use never altogether met expectations.

Agriculture. Despite all the efforts to promote industry and commerce, the French economy was overwhelmingly agrarian at the end of Louis XIV's reign, as it has been at the beginning. Most of the royal revenues came from taxes on land, paid by peasants. Agriculture benefited from no infusion of new technology, productivity remained low, and harvests were still uncertain and unpredictable.

Colonies. Colbert's determination to free France from foreign trade led him to encourage colonial enterprises. Black slaves purchased on the coast of Senegal were transported to the West Indies to expand the sugar plantations there. New France, in Canada, received several thousand peasants from the western provinces, and a royal administration was established there, with a governor, an intendant, and a bishop. A Quebec businessman, Louis Jolliet, and a Jesuit, Father Jacques Marquette, explored westward from Lake Michigan and reached the headwaters of the Mississippi, which they named Colbert River; they followed it several hundred miles south to the mouth of the Arkansas River. Later Robert La Salle traveled the length of the Mississippi and reached the Gulf of Mexico. He called the country he had discovered Louisiana, in honor of the king. In India the French trading centers of Pondichéry and Chandernagor were established.

The Navy. The protection of trade and colonies presumed a war fleet. Mazarin allowed the one created by Richelieu to decay, and by 1661 the king had no more than eight ships and six galleys that were seaworthy. At first Colbert purchased ships from Italy, Holland, and Denmark. At the same time he developed the powerful arsenals and shipyards at Toulon, Rochefort, Brest, and Dunkirk, and methodically organized the resources of the forests and national industries. By 1670 he could write proudly to the king: "Everything that can be used for the construction of vessels is at present available in the kingdom, so that Your Majesty need no longer resort to foreigners for his navy." In 1681 the royal fleet numbered 176 vessels, of which 120 were ships of the line and 30 were galleys.

To acquire crews Colbert devised a system of naval registration and compulsory service that forms the basis of the system in force today. All men in coastal areas who were not farmers were required to serve one year out of three, four, or five (depending on their family responsibilities). As compensation they enjoyed certain privileges, including old-age pensions.

Finance after Colbert. Even before Colbert's death, budget deficits reappeared. The enormous expenses incurred by the wars could not help but increase them. Two new taxes were created:

First, the capitation. Beginning in 1695, all the king's subjects were divided into twenty-two classes on the basis of their social rank and taxed accordingly: from 2,000 livres for the first class down to one livre for the twenty-second, artisans and day laborers.

Second, the *dixième* (tenth), instituted in 1710, which was a tax on income of all kinds.

But because of an inadequate administrative system and stubborn resistance by the nobility and clergy, the burden of these new taxes fell most heavily on those who already paid the *taille*.

In the same period all forms of expedients were used to raise money:

- Loans, on which interest was not always paid regularly.

- Lotteries.

- The sale of increasingly useless and ridiculous new offices ("supervisor-inspector of wigs," "taster of butter and cheese").

- Currency manipulation, in which the relationship between money of account (the livre) and the coins in circulation was arbitrarily changed. The livre, whose value had been fixed at 8.33 grams of fine silver (0.29 ounces) between 1641 and 1689, was worth no more than 5.33 grams (0.18 ounces) in 1715. To coin money Louis XIV melted down most of the silver and precious ornaments from Versailles.

And still the deficit and the public debt continued to grow. By the end of his reign bankruptcy was thought to be inevitable.

III. RELIGIOUS AFFAIRS

Louis XIV's idea of the rights and duties of a Catholic ruler led him, on the one hand, to place his power at the service of Catholic orthodoxy, and, on the other, to reject all interference by the pope in the life of the Church of France.

The Conflict with the Pope. When a bishopric fell vacant, custom permitted the king not only to appropriate its revenues but also to fill vacant offices in the diocese until a new bishop was installed. These were called "regalian rights." Until then, however, these rights had not applied to sixty dioceses in the south. In 1673 the king decided to put an end to this exemption. Two bishops alone protested and appealed to the Holy See. Pope Innocent XI condemned the king's conduct.

With the support of the majority of royal bureaucrats and officials, Louis XIV asked the French clergy to back the liberties of the Gallican church against the "ultramontane" claims. An extraordinary assembly of the clergy, a kind of national church council, met in 1681–82 and gave him what he asked for by adopting a solemn declaration in four articles:

First, in temporal matters kings and rulers are not subject to any ecclesiastical authority.

Second, the pope's supreme authority in spiritual matters cannot annul that of universal councils.

Third, the customs and rules of the Gallican church must remain inviolable.

Fourth, the pope's judgment in matters of faith is not in itself irreversible.

The historical importance of this "Declaration of the Four Articles" stems from the fact that from then until the nineteenth century it was invoked as the most authentic expression of what has been called "Gallicanism."

At the time it aggravated the conflict between king and pope. Louis XIV meant to require all churchmen to accept it formally. Innocent XI, for his part, refused investiture (that is, the granting of spiritual powers) to bishops who had been named by the king and who subscribed to the declaration. As a result, when Innocent XI died in 1689, thirty-five French bishoprics had no incumbents.

Difficulties in Louis's foreign policy finally persuaded him to yield on this matter. In 1693 he announced that the declaration would no longer be taught, and agreed that the bishops he named would sign a retraction before being installed by the pope. In exchange Pope Innocent XII recognized the extension of regalian rights to the entire kingdom.

Jansenism. Louis XIV detested the Jansenists. With their opposition and quibbling, they reminded him of the parliamentary circles to which many of them belonged. Outwardly obedient, the sect had continued to win followers, thanks to the support provided it by the Gallican doctrines. By the end of the reign, Jansenism had become a form of protest against the regime.

Louis XIV grew angry, and in 1709–10 he brutally dispersed the nuns at Port-Royal-des-Champs, the sect's headquarters, and tore down the buildings. In 1713 the king secured a new and solemn papal condemnation of Jansenist doctrine. Those who refused to subscribe to this document, the bull *Unigenitus*, risked exile or imprisonment.

The Revocation of the Edict of Nantes. To Louis XIV, as to all comtemporary rulers, the existence of subjects whose religion differed from the ruler's was abnormal and dangerous to the state. Further, the more his policy set him in opposition to the pope, the more he sought to pose as a defender of Catholicism. In the last years of his life, under the influence of Madame de Maintenon, he even made it a duty of conscience. And he had little reason now to show consideration for the Huguenots, for the great majority of noble Protestant families had returned to Catholicism so as not to be excluded from the king's favor.

Louis XIV had, in fact, adopted the principle of granting no personal favor to dissenters. He had also been quick to forbid them anything that was not expressly stated in the Edict of Nantes. Since no specific provisions had been made for funerals, for example, all Protestant burials were forbidden between six in the morning and six at night. In 1676 he established a Conversion Fund, intended to provide cash payments to encourage recantations. This unworthy scheme had little success.

Persecution was intensified in 1680 by a series of measures that contradicted even the letter of the Edict of Nantes. Those who held to the R. P. R. (*Religion Prétendue Réformée*, or Supposedly Reformed Religion) were excluded from all public offices and liberal professions, such as medicine, law, and printing. The intendant of Poitou even thought of applying a form of pressure occasionally used with unwilling taxpayers: billeting bailiff's men in their homes—soldiers they would have to feed. These draconian measures did in fact secure so many outward conversions that Louvois, the minister of war, made them the rule on his own authority. Kept in ignorance as to the true nature of the operation, Louis XIV was impressed by these apparent signs of a massive wave of conversions. He believed, apparently in good faith, that there were no Protestants left but a stubborn minority, and that it was pointless to continue a special arrangement for them. On October 18, 1685, he signed the Revocation of the Edict of Nantes. Public worship was forbidden, all houses of worship were to be demolished, and pastors were driven from the kingdom. The ordinary faithful, on the other hand, were forbidden to leave France on pain of being condemned to the galleys if they were caught.

Fateful Consequences. The decision was hailed with enthusiasm by the great majority of the French. In fact, it was to have the most disastrous of consequences.

First, despite the penalities they risked, 200,000 to 300,000 Protestants fled the country, leaving everything behind. The exodus of this elite, which included many skilled artisans, intellectuals, and experienced soldiers and sailors, weakened France. In several provinces the textile industry was threatened with ruin. In the countries that gave them asylum, on the other hand, these people became a force for prosperity, notably in Prussia, where more than 20,000 French Protestants settled.   ε Northern Ireland

Second, the hatred that this persecution aroused in all the Protestant states of Europe helped to create and sustain the coalitions that Louis XIV had to fight beginning in 1688.

Third, in 1702 the Calvinist peasants of the Cevennes rebelled. They were called *Camisards* because they wore white shirts (*chemises*) in order to recognize each other during their nighttime attacks. A civil war—a guerrilla war—lasted three years, from 1702 to 1705, immobilizing thousands of the best troops. Marshal Claude de Villars finally induced leaders to submit by offering an amnesty and promises of toleration, but troubles continued until 1710.

All these persecutions failed to stamp out Protestantism in France.

On the contrary, it eventually regained its strength. A few days before the death of Louis XIV, a secret synod of southern Huguenots convened near Nimes.

SUGGESTIONS FOR FURTHER READING

Ashley, Maurice P. *Louis XIV and the Greatness of France.* New York, 1965.

Bradby, Godfrey F. *The Great Days at Versailles: Studies from Court Life in the Later Years of Louis XIV.* New York, 1927.

Church, William F. *Louis XIV in Historical Thought from Voltaire to the Annales School.* New York, 1976.

Cole, Charles W. *Colbert and a Century of French Mercantilism.* 2 vols. New York, 1939.

Erlanger, Philippe. *Louis XIV.* New York, 1970.

Goubert, Pierre. *Louis XIV and Twenty Million Frenchmen.* New York, 1970.

Lewis, Warren H. *The Splendid Century: Life in the France of Louis XIV.* Garden City, N.Y., 1957.

Mitford, Nancy. *The Sun King: Louis Fourteen at Versailles.* New York, 1966.

Ranum, Orest A. *Paris in the Age of Absolutism.* New York, 1968.

Rule, John C., ed. *Louis XIV and the Craft of Kingship.* Columbus, O., 1969.

Saint-Simon, Louis de Rouvroy, duc de. *Historical Memoirs of the Duc de Saint-Simon.* 3 vols. London, 1967–72.

Mandrou, Robert. *Louis XIV en son temps.* Paris, 1973.

13
The Foreign Policy of Louis XIV

The objectives of Louis XIV's policy were in accordance with the national interest and were even rather reasonable, but he pursued them with a concern for his personal glory and an arrogance that aroused all other countries against him. Four wars that grew increasingly long and difficult—thirty years in all—required tremendous effort and left France exhausted, but also with valuable gains.

I. OBJECTIVES AND MEANS

Objectives. In its inspiration and style, Louis XIV's foreign policy reflected the dominant traits of his personality—his proud drive for supremacy and his passion for glory. History and the popular imagination, fascinated by the memory of Alexander the Great and Julius Caesar, wreathed kings and princes in an aura that grew in brilliance in proportion to their military exploits and conquests. That was the glory Louis wanted. On the other hand, one may see in him also perseverance and even, in many instances, discretion. The concrete objectives he pursued conformed to the policy that Richelieu and Mazarin had set to serve the national interest—to destroy the dangerous predominance of the house of Austria and enlarge the kingdom so as to strengthen its borders. Under the circumstances that prevailed at the time, it was largely at the expense of the Spanish monarchy that Louis XIV sought to obtain those advantages.

Louvois and the New Army. As the principal instrument of foreign policy, the army received Louis's full attention, and it underwent great changes during his reign. Louis XIV's desire for continuity was strikingly shown in the administration of the army. Michel Le Tellier, secretary of state for war under Mazarin, kept his office for more than thirty years. When he became chancellor in 1677, he was succeeded by his son, the Marquis of Louvois, and in 1691 by his grandson, Louis de Barbezieux. Associated with his father since 1662, Louvois was the most powerful of Louis XIV's ministers after the death of Colbert. As a member of the High Council, he had a voice in all the major business of the state. From 1683 on, the king also put him in charge of construction. To retain the king's favor, Louvois too often told him what he wanted to hear and so helped to push him into some of his most unfortunate decisions, among them the Revocation of the Edict of Nantes. Toward everyone else Louvois was haughty and surly. Nonetheless, by his administrative talent and tireless labor he endowed France with the most powerful army of its day.

Military Reforms. First came an increase in size. From fewer than 40,000 men in 1661 the peacetime standing army was increased by stages to 125,000 infantrymen and 47,000 cavalrymen. In wartime Louis XIV had as many as 300,000 men under arms. Because recruiting efforts did not always yield enough volunteers, Louvois organized a form of compulsory service in 1688. Each parish had to provide a certain number of militiamen drawn by lot from among bachelors between twenty and forty years of age.

Second, discipline suffered from the fact that the ranks of colonel and captain were purchased, like judicial and financial posts. Louvois created the new ranks of major and lieutenant colonel, which did not have to be purchased, and from these ranks poor and worthy officers could rise to the higher ranks of brigadier, major general, and lieutenant general. All of them were subject to the authority of inspectors general and civil commissioners of war. The name of one such man, Jean Martinet, feared by all for his meticulous severity, has entered the language. Louvois also established cadet companies in which future officers were trained.

As for the enlisted men, their maneuvers and orders were standardized. Each soldier had to wear the distinctive uniform of his regiment. To remove any excuse for looting, soldiers were paid a regular wage,

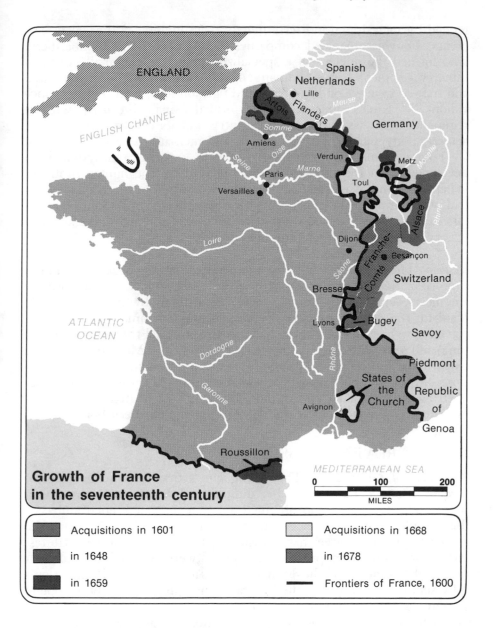

Growth of France in the seventeenth century

Acquisitions in 1601		Acquisitions in 1668	
in 1648		in 1678	
in 1659		Frontiers of France, 1600	

and in the field they were assured of supplies by a network of store-houses and a transport service.

For old, poor soldiers and the permanently disabled, the Hospital for the Disabled (Hôtel des Invalides) offered a dignified and relatively comfortable retirement home.

A third reform was specialization. Until now cannon had been tended by men drawn indiscriminately from infantry and cavalry regiments. Louvois organized companies of cannoneers and bombardiers, who formed the nucleus of a specialized branch of the artillery. Each infantry regiment had a company of grenadiers. Dragoons, equipped and trained to move on horseback and fight on foot, were another innovation. The King's Household alone formed a small elite army, with its regiments of Swiss and French infantry and its cavalry corps—musketeers, bodyguards, light horsemen, and men-at-arms.

Fourth, armament was improved. The musket, a heavy weapon developed from the arquebus, was replaced by the lighter flintlock. When a bayonet was attached to it, the distinction between musketeers and pikemen disappeared. As a result, tactics were revolutionized. Certain cavalry units received short-barreled carbines. Finally, the artillery was provided with lighter cannon of uniform caliber.

Vauban. The campaigns of the era generally were organized around the capture or defense of fortresses; hence the importance of the Corps of Engineers, created by Louvois and commanded by the Marquis de Vauban, the greatest military engineer of modern times. Vauban conceived new methods of attack (ricochet fire, parallel trenching and sapping) and personally directed more than fifty sieges. Most important, he constructed more than 300 fortresses, using a system of low fortifications of his own devising, which was soon imitated throughout Europe. A string of particularly strong and admirably coordinated citadels compensated for the lack of natural defenses on the northern border.

II. THE GREAT SUCCESSES (1661–79)

The Policy of Magnificence. The young king's first acts in the realm of foreign affairs demonstrated his intention of being dominant everywhere. He demanded and obtained agreements that French ambassadors would take precedence over Spanish ambassadors. Similarly he forced England to agree that British ships would fire the first salutes. After soldiers of the pope's Corsican guard were involved in an altercation with members of the French ambassador's staff in Rome, Louis XIV sent troops to occupy the Comtat Venaissin and forced the pope to extend solemn and humiliating apologies to him.

When the Turks attacked the Holy Roman Empire, the king sent 6,000 reinforcements to the armies raised by the emperor. To commemorate their brilliant role in the decisive battle of St. Gothard, in Hungary, on August 1, 1664, the king had a medal struck bearing the proud legend *Germania servata* (Germany saved).

The War of Devolution. The death of the king of Spain, Philip IV, in

September 1665, provided Louis XIV with the occasion for his first war of conquest. The heir to the Spanish domains, Charles II, was a sickly child of four, born of the second marriage of Philip IV. Marie Theresa, the queen of France, who was born of Philip's first marriage, claimed the succession on the ground that her renunciation of her claims, written into the Treaty of the Pyrenees of 1659, was voided by Spain's failure to pay the promised dowry (see p. 145). Affecting a magnanimous moderation, Louis XIV demanded "only" Flanders, basing his claim on the "right of devolution," an ancient Netherlands custom that gave children of a first marriage prior claim to an inheritance.

Spain obviously was not going to yield without a struggle. So Hugues de Lionne, the outstanding secretary of state for foreign affairs, worked to isolate it by a network of alliances linking the king of France with numerous German princes, the Dutch Netherlands, and the king of England, Charles II. In exchange for 5 million livres, Charles surrendered Dunkirk to France.

In the spring of 1667 a French army, acting on Turenne's orders, seized the principal Spanish strongholds in southern Flanders. When Spain refused to accept this loss, Louis sent another army, commanded by Condé, into the Franche-Comté, then Spanish territory.

Holland and England became alarmed by the sight of French power expanding into an area where it might challenge their commercial supremacy. With Sweden they formed the Triple Alliance of The Hague, which offered to mediate the dispute. Threatened by his former allies with a general war, Louis XIV swallowed his irritation and agreed to negotiate. All the same, the peace signed at Aix-la-Chapelle in May 1668 granted him possession of eleven fortresses captured in Flanders, among them Lille and Douai. Spain recovered the Franche-Comté.

The Dutch War. Experience had shown that any French thrust into Belgium would encounter opposition from the Dutch. Louis XIV resolved to bring down the insolent nation of merchants that had dared to resist him. For once Colbert encouraged his master's warlike mood, for the opportunity to destroy the commercial supremacy of the United Provinces seemed to be at hand.

A methodical preparation of enormous military might was launched, in tandem with a new diplomatic campaign to buy the neutrality of any potential allies of Holland. The military campaign opened in June 1672 with a brilliant operation, the fording of the Rhine at Tolhuys. Taken from behind, the Dutch defenses crumbled. To save Amsterdam and The Hague, the Dutch took the heroic measure of opening the dikes that protected the low-lying plains against sea water and rivers. The flooding halted French progress.

The government of the United Provinces—the Estates General and the Grand Pensionary, Jan De Witt—wanted to negotiate. Driven by his resentment and pride, Louis XIV then made the mistake of imposing excessively harsh and humiliating conditions. Outraged national feeling in the Netherlands erupted in a revolt against the middle-class republican government, which was held responsible for all the disasters. The revolt brought to power the leader of the party that urged resistance to the death, the young prince William of Orange, with the titles of *stathouder* and captain general.

As Dutch resistance hardened in response to the hardships and devastation brought by the French, William of Orange managed to organize Spain, the Holy Roman emperor, and most of the German princes in a coalition against France.

With his armies still immobilized by the flooding in the Netherlands, Louis XIV withdrew them before the end of 1673 and sent them to take Franche-Comté from Spain again. In 1674 he also was forced to go on the defensive on his northern border. Condé trounced a powerful coalition army at Seneffe. In the east the imperial forces invaded Alsace, but Turenne expelled them in a brilliant winter campaign that is still famous in military history. Six months later, when he was leading an offensive west of the Rhine, he was killed by a cannon ball. After the death of this matchless leader, operations dragged on there with no decisive outcome.

In Flanders, however, the French recovered the advantage. Vauban laid methodical siege to Spanish fortresses, and they fell one by one. In the Mediterranean the new French fleet, commanded by Abraham Duquesne, crowned Colbert's efforts by beating the Spanish and Dutch forces led by the Dutch admiral Michel de Ruyter, the most famous naval commander of the day.

The capture of Ghent by the French in March 1678 strengthened the peace party in Holland. The merchants feared that Antwerp would suffer the same fate, and then Amsterdam's prosperity would be destroyed. Louis XIV took advantage of this opportunity to have done with a costly and seemingly endless war. In a preliminary treaty signed at Nijmwegen in August 1678 he offered the Dutch very advantageous conditions, including the abolition of tariff barriers raised against them by Colbert. After that, the other members of the coalition had to submit to the king's will in one way or another. Spain gave up the Franche-Comté and twelve additional strongholds in Flanders. Fortified by Vauban, they were to become part of the great defensive system known as the "iron border" (see p. 168).

III. TO THE LIMITS OF POWER

The Policy of Reunification. In his pride at having stood his ground against Europe, Louis XIV now believed he could do as he pleased. The treaties of Westphalia and Nijmegen declared that the territories and cities ceded to France were transferred with their dependencies. The king interpreted these clauses to cover all places that had had any tie of dependency with the ceded territories in the past, no matter how remote. The French courts charged with deciding these cases never failed to rule in the king's favor. Louis XIV then occupied the coveted territories, among them the county of Montbéliard, the Saar, and part of Luxembourg.

In the case of Strasbourg there was not even a pretense of legality. This free city, liberated from the Holy Roman Empire, guarded one of the few bridges across the Rhine. Three times during the recent war the imperial troops had used it to invade Alsace, despite the supposed neutrality of the little republic. In September 1681 a surprise attack organized by Louvois captured its outlying defenses. The Strasbourg senate recognized the futility of resistance and agreed to the city's annexation to France in exchange for a promise that its privileges would be respected and that its Protestants might practice their religion freely. With great pomp, Louis XIV went in person to take possession of it. A medal struck for the occasion proclaimed *Gallia Germanis clausa* (Gaul closed to the Germans).

The War of the League of Augsburg. The princes who were affected by the encroachments of this "devouring and aggressive peace" at first did no more than protest. In 1682 the emperor and Spain joined forces against France, but the emperor was suddenly immobilized by a fierce invasion by the Turks, who got as far as the gates of Vienna. Spain thus had to bear alone the wrath of the French king, who resumed his attack on the Spanish towns in Belgium. A truce signed at Regensburg in August 1684 seemed to confirm the unopposable hegemony of the Sun King.

A few years later, however, the balance of power was shifted by a conjunction of several factors. First, the indignation aroused by the Revocation of the Edict of Nantes lost the king his support in Protestant countries, notably Holland and England. Second, once the emperor had driven back the Turks, he was able to take a more active role in the west. With the major German princes and the kings of Sweden and Spain he formed a vast coalition, purely defensive in principle—the League of Augsburg. Third, Louis XIV unwisely provided the emperor with an excuse to reopen hostilities by taking two new arrogant actions—the occupation of the electorate of Cologne, where he swept aside the candidate favored by the pope and the emperor for the office of Elector and installed his own man, and the invasion of the Palatinate on the pretext of defending the rather dubious rights of the Duchess of Orléans, sister of the late ruler. Fourth, Louis XIV had counted on England and Holland to remain neutral, since they were then occupied by a struggle between the Protestant majority in England, supported by

William of Orange, husband of Mary Stuart, against King James II, supported by the Catholics. The speed of events dashed Louis XIV's plans. Installed as king of England by the Glorious Revolution of 1688, William of Orange hastened to send the aid of both England and Holland to the coalition powers.

An Indecisive War. The French armies repulsed the coalition's repeated offensives on all fronts. The victories won by Marshal Luxembourg at Fleurus, Steinkirk, and Neerwinden, in Belgium, won him the nickname "draper of Notre Dame" because of the number of flags taken from the enemy and hung according to custom in the cathedral's arches. On the Alpine border Marshal Nicolas de Catinat distinguished himself. Of middle-class origins, he had won his high rank by abilities that called Turenne to mind—a mixture of daring and cautious deliberation. Finally, the French fleet, commanded by Tourville, won many brilliant victories over the far superior forces of the English and Dutch, while the privateers René Duguay-Trouin, from St. Malo, and Jean Bart, from Dunkirk, inflicted enormous losses on enemy commerce—some 4,000 ships in nine years.

Louis XIV also suffered his share of losses, notably in his attempt to restore James II to the English throne, which met defeat at the famous Battle of the Boyne in 1690.

The Peace of Ryswick. Nine years of useless struggle finally wore the coalition powers down, and they became resigned to listening to Louis XIV's peace proposals. They proved to be surprisingly moderate. In a series of treaties signed at Ryswick, the king yielded most of the territories annexed since the Peace of Nijmegen, retaining only Strasbourg and Sarre Louis. He recognized William of Orange as king of England and pledged to give the dethroned Stuart dynasty no further support.

IV. THE WAR OF THE SPANISH SUCCESSION

If the king was accommodating, it was because he saw approaching the moment he had been awaiting for more then thirty years. The death of King Charles II without heirs would open up the enormous question of the Spanish succession, in which France's rights to the crown were weighed against those of the Hapsburgs of Vienna.

The Negotiations. Louis XIV had prepared for this moment with consummate care. His aim was to secure the desired results for France without having to undertake a new war. Since the emperor Leopold I had agreed to partition of the Spanish possessions, the best means to

The Spanish accession

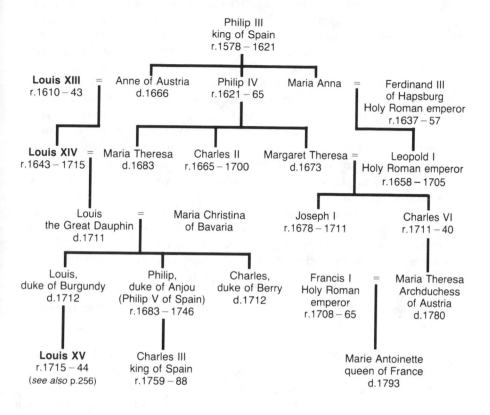

ensure its peaceful execution was to secure in advance the consent and guarantee of the two most potentially dangerous opponents, England and Holland. They gave him what he wanted in a treaty signed in London in March 1700. The most important part of the Spanish legacy —Spain, the Netherlands, and the colonial empire—would go to the archduke Charles, second son of the emperor Leopold I. The king of France reserved for himself only the Spanish possessions in Italy—not to keep them, but merely to use them as pawns to round out the kingdom. The duchy of Milan would be exchanged for Lorraine, and Naples and Sicily for Savoy. But the emperor stubbornly refused to give up Milan.

The Will of Charles II. This splendid arrangement was undone by a burst of Spanish pride. The advisers of Charles II convinced him that honor and conscience required him to preserve the monarchy intact at any price. The will that the king signed just one month before he died, on

November 1, 1700, provided that the sole heir would be Philip, the duke of Anjou, second grandson of Louis XIV, but only on condition that the crowns of Spain and France would never be united. Should he refuse, the entire legacy would pass to the archduke Charles of Austria.

Louis XIV found himself in a painful dilemma. To accept the Spanish offer would be to break the Treaty of London and to face the certainty of a difficult war. To hold to that treaty was no less dangerous, for he would have to fight the Spanish and the emperor, who had not accepted the partition agreed to at London; and if he won, he would have the English and Dutch at his back again. Since war could not be avoided in any event, the king and his counselors reasoned that it would be better to wage it alongside Spain than against it, and for the whole succession rather than a small portion. On November 16, 1700, Louis XIV announced his acceptance in a scene worthy of the magnitude of the event. The Spanish greeted their new king, Philip V, enthusiastically, giving rise to the famous expression that Voltaire incorrectly attributed to Louis XIV, "The Pyrenees no longer exist."

In a note to the other powers Colbert observed, correctly, that Louis XIV's repudiation of any attempt to enlarge his own kingdom was a sign of moderation. England and Holland seemed to accept this point of view; with all the other rulers except the Holy Roman emperor, they recognized Philip V as king of Spain.

The Grand Alliance of 1701. William of Orange, however, had accepted Philip only under pressure for peace from the ruling classes, and he had to struggle to rouse them against Louis XIV. Louis eased his task by several unwise steps. He had the Parlement of Paris affirm Philip V's eventual rights to the French crown, and he had his troops occupy the Spanish strongholds in the Netherlands. The English and Dutch merchants were deeply disturbed to see French commerce insinuate itself into the Spanish colonies. Finally, English indignation erupted when Louis XIV recognized James III, son of the Stuart king James II, as the rightful heir to the throne when his father died in exile in France in 1701.

The Grand Alliance of England, Holland, and the Empire was concluded at The Hague in September 1701. They were joined by Denmark, Portugal, the Duke of Savoy, and most of the German princes.

The War. The War of the Spanish Succession lasted thirteen years. This time France had to defend not only its national boundaries but also the vast territory controlled by Spain, which was incapable of sustaining the struggle with its own resources.

The Allies had the benefit not only of resources but of the talents of two great warriors: the Duke of Marlborough, Queen Anne's favorite, who controlled policy after William of Orange died, and Prince Eugene of Savoy, who had been born in France and entered the service of Austria out of spite when the king refused him a regiment.

The French first took the offensive in Germany and Italy and won several victories. But in August 1704 their main army in Germany was virtually destroyed at Blenheim by the combined armies of Marlborough and Prince Eugene. In May 1706 Marlborough inflicted another disastrous defeat on the French army in the north, commanded by the incompetent marshal Nicolas de Villeroy. The Spanish Netherlands had to be abandoned. Invading France, the Allies besieged Lille and captured it in October 1708. Meanwhile the Austrian pretender, Archduke Charles, landed in Portugal and with English help set out to conquer Spain. At one point he even succeeded in entering Madrid to have himself proclaimed king of Spain as Charles III.

A severe winter and widespread famine in 1709 added to France's woes. Louis XIV resigned himself to suing for peace; he was ready to recognize Archduke Charles as king of Spain; and even to give up Lille and Strasbourg. But the Allies demanded that the king join them in dethroning Philip V. Louis XIV rejected this outrageous demand. "Since war must be waged," he said, "it is better to wage it against my enemies than against my children."

Spanish and French of all classes showed their approval by a burst of patriotism that spurred the two kings to continue the struggle. In various theaters of operations the balance began to turn in favor of the Franco-Spanish forces.

The End of the War. Weary after so much vain effort, the English turned strongly in favor of peace when they learned that Archduke Charles had become Emperor Charles VI upon the sudden death of his older brother, Joseph I, in 1711. The fear of seeing the empire of Charles V reborn outweighed hatred for Louis XIV. Talks between French and English diplomats resulted in a preliminary peace agreement.

The Dutch and the emperor, who were not pleased by England's defection, decided to finish off an opponent who seemed to be on his last legs. On the orders of Prince Eugene, a massive army of 130,000 men invaded France and swept everything before it. Louis XIV had only 70,000 men to throw against it. By a skillful maneuver, however, Marshal Villars managed to surprise and defeat Prince Eugene at Denain on July 24, 1712.

The Dutch and all of their allies except the emperor signed the Treaty of Utrecht in April 1713. Charles VI held out until Villars led another victorious campaign in Germany. The treaty signed at Rastatt in March 1714 at last restored peace to France and Europe.

Philip V kept Spain and its colonies, but he renounced his rights to the French throne. Emperor Charles VI received the Netherlands and Spain's possessions in Italy except for Sicily, which went to the Duke of Savoy. England got Gibraltar and Minorca and won a foothold in New France by acquiring Newfoundland and Acadia.

Apart from these distant territories and four strongholds on the northern border (Tournai, Ypres, Furnes, and Menin), Louis XIV kept all his conquests, which had so noticeably strengthened the strategic boundaries of France.

These results, plus the fact that the Spanish monarchy at last slipped from the house of Austria and entered France's orbit, leads us to conclude that Louis XIV's foreign policy did not end on an altogether negative note, despite his obvious errors and failures.

V. THE END OF THE REIGN

The Poverty of the Kingdom. Against these advantages must be set the financial distress of the kingdom, the crushing weight of taxes of all kinds (see p. 159), the ruin of luxury and export industries once they were deprived of state support, and the wretchedness of the lower classes. The king's policies were not entirely responsible for this misery. All of Western Europe experienced an economic downturn during this period, and France suffered serious food shortages stemming from severe weather conditions, particularly in the harsh winter of 1709, when the Seine froze from Paris to Le Havre. Famine and epidemics recurred, and violence born of misery broke out in the towns.

Opposition to the Regime. This accumulation of disasters aroused the critical spirit. The basis of the absolute monarchy and of royal policies was attacked even within the king's entourage. Bishop François Fénelon, tutor to the heir to the throne, Louis, duke of Burgundy, demanded representative institutions, and Vauban sought equal taxation. Catholic doctrine, a prop of the monarchy, was itself attacked by certain writers, called "freethinkers" (*libertins*), who applied to religion the spirit of doubt and free investigation made popular by the philosopher René Descartes (see p. 136).

The Unhappy Last Years. To the humiliation of defeat, the bitterness of great schemes gone awry, regret for past errors, and a chorus of complaints from all parts of the kingdom was added a series of domestic calamities that further darkened the last years of Louis XIV. Within a few months in 1711–12 a smallpox epidemic carried off in quick succession the king's only legitimate son, Louis the Great Dauphin, his two grandsons, Louis, the duke of Burgundy, and Charles, the duke of Berry, and the first of his great-grandchildren. Only the last, frail child of the duke of Burgundy, the little duke of Anjou, Louis (later Louis XV), born in 1710, survived this disaster.

The Death of Louis XIV. The king bore these tragedies with exemplary stoicism and dignity. In all circumstances he conducted his daily affairs as usual, maintaining the same apparent calm and affability toward everyone. Six days before his death he again treated his court to the spectacle of a public dinner to the music of violins. Untreatable senile gangrene had already developed in his leg. With perfect self-control he arranged all the details of his funeral and succession, said his farewells to all, and received the last rites of the church. He died on the morning of September 1, 1715, faithful to the last to his own ideal of royal dignity.   aged 76

SUGGESTIONS FOR FURTHER READING

Bamford, Paul W. *Forests and French Sea Power, 1660–1789*. Toronto, 1956.

Hatton, Ragnhild L. *Louis XIV and His World*. New York, 1972.

Priestley, Herbert I. *France Overseas through the Old Regime: A Study in European Expansion*. New York, 1939.

Wolf, John B. *Toward a European Balance of Power, 1640–1715*. New York, 1969.

Wrong, George M. *The Rise and Fall of New France*. 2 vols. New York, 1928.

André, Louis. *Louis XIV et l'Europe*. Paris, 1950

Méthivier, Hubert. *Le Siècle de Louis XIV*. 8th ed. Paris, 1980.

14
The Reign of
Louis XV

The reign of Louis XV has produced conflicting judgments. On the one hand, the decline of authority, the moral corruption encouraged by the example from above, the waste of public funds at court, the preservation of unjustified privileges, the inconsistency of the king's foreign policy, the humiliating defeats, and the loss of colonies have all been criticized, and with good reason. On the other hand, the economic and social progress, the decline of the scourge of war, the real liberalism and benevolence of a government that was a tyranny in appearance only, the intelligence and effectiveness of administration, and the vitality of thought and of the arts have been praised, also with good reason.

I. THE REGENCY (1715–23)

Philip of Orléans. The Sun King was succeeded by a little five-year-old orphan. By law the regency of the kingdom went to the first prince of the blood, Philippe, duke of Orléans, nephew of Louis XIV. A mature man—he was forty-one in 1715—he was naturally affable, generous, honest, eloquent, and cultivated. Unfortunately, his laziness and his complete lack of moral sense kept him from putting his talents to use. All his evenings were devoted to dissolute pleasures in the company of fellow debauchees who were called *roués*—that is, deserving to be broken on the wheel (*roue*).

The court was brought back to Paris from Versailles and followed the regent's example. The Regency period bears the stamp of high society gone wild. Suddenly freed of the constraints imposed by the preceding regime, the court gave itself over to unrestrained pleasure. Even in clothing and furniture there was a "Regency style," lighter and more imaginative than earlier styles. The paintings of Antoine Watteau are reflections of it.

Domestic Policy. The great nobles, who had been held in check by Louis XIV, thought their moment to regain power had come. Inspired by the Duke of Saint-Simon, the regent began by replacing the ministers with six councils made up of members of the upper nobility. But this system, called the Polysynody, was soon discredited by their incompetence and ineffectiveness. In September 1718 the regent returned to "the governing style of the late king, so convenient and so absolute."

Likewise, the Parlement of Paris, which had rediscovered the right of remonstrance in 1715 and used it to paralyze the government, was sharply recalled to obedience by summary judgment and exile.

The System of John Law. Louis XIV had left the kingdom's finances in a shambles; normal receipts no longer even covered the interest due on a public debt of more than 2 billion livres. Running out of expedients, the regent let himself be dazzled by the daring ideas of the Scottish financier John Law. In 1716 Law was authorized to establish a private bank. The shares that constituted its capital were payable one-fourth in hard currency and the remainder in government bonds.

The "General Bank" accepted deposits by private persons and discounted commercial paper. In a great innovation, it made its payments in notes that were redeemable on demand. The public quickly became accustomed to them. By 1717 the regent permitted these banknotes to be used for payments to and by the state treasury. Soon Law's bank became a "royal bank" and began to issue paper money as legal tender. Law himself became controller general of finances early in 1720.

In Law's scheme, the accumulated capital, supplemented by credit, was supposed to be used to promote large-scale enterprises. His first creation, the Western or Mississippi Company, was granted a monopoly to develop Louisiana. Then Law bought out the existing trading companies one by one and merged them into a single great firm, the East India Company. This company was granted monopolies on the coining of money, the sale of salt and tobacco, and even the collection of various indirect taxes.

Excited by the promises of huge profits and the frequent issuing of new shares, the public stampeded to invest its savings, sometimes even going into debt in the hope of quick riches. Speculators went to work, and the price of shares rose to dizzying heights. Every day crowds thronged the Rue Quincampoix, site of the bank and its annexes.

These excesses of speculation brought the system crashing down. The shrewder capitalists began to sell their overvalued shares, causing a drop in prices that became as precipitous as the earlier rise. Loss of confidence spread like a contagion to the banknotes; everyone wanted to be reimbursed in gold or silver for the paper he held. But the amount of paper money in circulation was five or six times the total of specie then available in France. The crowding and panic at the cashiers' windows turned into a riot. The regent ordered the bank closed, thus sanctioning the bankruptcy of the system. John Law fled to the Netherlands.

The episode left deep scars. The French public long remained hostile to credit institutions and paper money, the mainsprings of a modern economy. The ruin of numerous families, in sharp contrast to the sudden wealth of a few fortunate speculators, upset established social relationships and encouraged cynicism and immorality. Respect for royal authority also suffered. Still, there were at least two positive results: a noticeable reduction in the public debt and a stimulus to overseas trade provided by the East India Company and the creation of the ports of Lorient in Brittany and New Orleans in Louisiana.

Foreign Policy. In foreign policy the regent was advised and assisted chiefly by his former tutor, Abbé Guillaume Dubois, whom his contemporaries depicted as an unscrupulous rogue, an unbeliever, and a rake. This did not prevent the regent from naming him archbishop of Cambrai and then cardinal.

Dubois negotiated a triple alliance with England and Holland to guarantee the fulfillment of the Treaty of Utrecht, which King Philip V of Spain still refused to accept. Philip, pressed by his second wife, Elizabeth Farnese, and by his chief minister, the Italian Julio Alberoni, wanted to retake Spain's former possessions in Italy. At the same time he reaffirmed his claims to the French throne, while his ambassador to Paris stirred up opposition against the Duke of Orléans. Open hostilities began in July 1718, when a Spanish army landed in Sicily. England and France declared war on Philip V, and the Austrian emperor, Charles VI, joined them. When Spain suffered defeats on all fronts, Philip V had to dismiss Alberoni and seek peace. The settlement that Dubois's diplomacy contrived for him was honorable. By finally giving up all claims to the French throne and accepting the Treaty of Utrecht, Philip V assured his young son, Don Carlos, of possession of the duchies of Parma and Tuscany. As a token of the reconciliation between France and Spain, it was understood that Louis XV would marry the infanta Anna Maria, Don Carlos' sister.

II. THE INTERNAL GOVERNMENT OF LOUIS XV

The King's Marriage. When Louis XV reached the age of thirteen in 1723, he was declared to be of age, but the Duke of Orléans continued to govern as first minister. The duke's sudden death later that year placed power in the hands of another royal prince, the Duke of Bourbon.

The only notable event of his government, which was otherwise rather dismal, was the marriage of the young king. The little infanta, who had been brought to the French court, was still only seven in 1725. Bourbon considered it unwise to postpone Louis's marriage, and thus the opportunity to produce an heir, until the infanta grew up. To the great indignation of Philip V, he sent her back to Spain and had the king marry Maria Leszczyńska, daughter of the dethroned king of Poland, in August 1725. Since this princess of modest origins was obliged to him for her rise in the world, Bourbon counted on her to consolidate his influence.

Cardinal Fleury. Nonetheless, Bourbon was suddenly dismissed less than a year later. The problem was that he had tried to get rid of a man who enjoyed the complete confidence of the young king—his tutor, the bishop of Fréjus, André Hercule de Fleury.

A curious bond of affection had been established between this hearty, good-natured, sly old man and the adolescent monarch; they were like grandfather and grandson. Louis XV left the task of governing to him. His title was simply minister of state, but soon another was added: cardinal. Fleury was seventy-three when he came to power; he was to keep it until his death in 1743. This long ministry brought the country what it needed most—peace and reordered finances at home and a cautious and generally peaceful policy abroad.

The chief troublemakers at home were the unsubdued Jansenists. They gave notable demonstrations of collective euphoria in hysterical scenes at the tomb of one François de Paris, a Jansenist deacon, in the cemetery of St. Médard. More serious than the excesses of these "convulsionaries" was the support the Jansenists found among the members of the Parlement of Paris, who opposed all measures to restrain dissenters.

The Work of Orry. Excellent management by the controller general, Philbert Orry, improved financial conditions. In 1739 a miracle unknown since the time of Colbert occurred—a balanced budget. This improvement owed much to the growth of the country's economy (see p. 189). The most important of the measures taken to encourage prosperity was a return to a stable currency. A decree of 1726 had established a fixed relationship between metallic currency and money of account. The silver écu was now worth five livres, the louis d'or twenty. These two coins—the livre and the louis d'or—had the same weight and quantity of precious metal as in the past. These relationships remained unchanged until 1790. In addition Orry undertook a vast program of road construction.

Louis XV. "Well, here I am prime minister," Louis XV is supposed to have said when he learned of the death of the old cardinal. At age thirty-three it was time for him to take on the full role of king. He lacked neither the intelligence nor the good sense needed for the job. He showed courage occasionally, real humility, and faithfulness to his friends. But the unusual education he had received had developed serious character defects in him—egoism, dissimulation, laziness, and lack of self-confidence. He tended to follow the contradictory advice of his immediate circle and his ministers. Paying only half-hearted attention to affairs of state, he sought to relieve his boredom by hunting, which he did passionately several times a week, and by all kinds of other costly amusements—building, festivities, travel.

Madame de Pompadour. His other ruling passion was women. The good queen Maria, seven years older than her husband and exhausted by ten successive pregnancies, no longer satisfied him. The king did not resist advances by ladies at court, who were attracted as much by his looks as by the advantages of the position of royal favorite. After several high-born mistresses, the king turned his affections to a young woman from a family of middle-class financiers, Jeanne Poisson. He made her the marquise de Pompadour and settled her at Versailles, below his own apartment. Beautiful and witty, Madame de Pompadour loved literature and the arts, and she encouraged authors and gave work to artists and craftsmen. Under her influence court life blossomed. For twenty years (1745–64) she was not only the king's minister of pleasure but also his chief political adviser, a power who could make and unmake ministers, generals, and ambassadors.

Madame de Pompadour was still young when she died in 1764, wasted by tuberculosis. During her last years she encouraged the king to indulge in affairs with lower-class women that could only bring discredit upon him. Once she was gone, Louis XV abandoned himself to them all the more readily. He eventually became attached to a lower-class woman, Jeanne Bécu, who for reasons of convenience became the countess Du Barry, and he installed her at Versailles, to the great horror of the court.

The Failure of Fiscal Reform. Forced from favor by Madame de Pompadour, Orry was replaced by Jean-Baptiste Machault d'Arnouville. A tax, the *vingtième*, which he proposed in 1749, would have affected all incomes without exception and would have been an important first step toward fiscal justice. But all the bodies that represented the privileged classes—parlements, provincial assemblies, the Assembly of the Clergy —raised vehement protests. The king gave Machault only feeble support, and finally he had to come to terms and agree that the privileged would in large measure escape the burden. Eventually it fell on the third estate (the commons). The failure of this useful reform is to be counted among the underlying causes of the Revolution of 1789.

The Opposition of the Parlements. In other areas, too, the government's efforts were continually blocked by opposition from the parlements. Not only the Parlement of Paris but also the twelve provincial parlements, which considered themselves to be its equals as members of a single body, claimed a power of control over royal authority. This opposition intensified, particularly between 1752 and 1757, over religious questions: the members of the parlements supported the Jansenist clergy against the archbishop of Paris and the king. The unrest that this foolish quarrel stirred among the people incited a madman named Robert Damiens to attempt to stab the king. The affair had important political consequences, for the shocked parlement was less aggressive for some time afterward, and Machault lost his post for daring to try to take advantage of the emotion of the moment to remove Madame de Pompadour from the court.

Choiseul. After Machault was eliminated, the predominant influence in the government for a dozen years (1758–70) fell to a protegé of Madame de Pompadour, the Duke of Choiseul. Along with the Ministry of Foreign Affairs, he also controlled the ministries of the army and the navy. Unfortunate in his foreign policy (see p. 189), he at least must be given credit for beginning to rebuild the country's military might and for securing the annexation of Corsica to France in 1768.

Choiseul also sought to win the support of the Paris intellectuals, a liberal and unruly lot. An opportunity arose to please both them and the Jansenists in the parlements. The Jesuits, after a trial in which one of their members was involved, were rash enough to appeal to the Parlement of Paris. The Parlement got hold of the Jesuit statutes, declared them to be contrary to the laws of the kingdom, and in 1762 abolished the Society of Jesus in France. Choiseul wrung from the king an edict that supported this decision. Moreover, his diplomatic maneuvers helped to get the same measure adopted in Spain, Naples, and Parma, and finally to have the Society dissolved by Pope Clement XIV.

The Triumvirate and Judicial Reform. This victory further emboldened the parlements, which pursued their war of harassment against the king's agents with increasing vigor. Louis XV finally determined to act. He dismissed the too complaisant Choiseul in December 1770 and turned the direction of affairs over to three men who were resolutely hostile to the parlements' pretensions: René de Maupeou as chancellor, Abbé Joseph Terray as controller general of finances, and the Duke of Aiguillon as secretary of state for foreign affairs. This "Triumvirate" was to govern until the king's death.

Maupeou seized upon a new act of defiance by the Parlement of Paris early in 1771 to launch a complete overhaul of judicial institutions. The Parlement of Paris was abolished and replaced by six Superior Councils. Instead of owning their offices, their members were appointed and paid by the king. Justice was to be rendered without charge, whereas before judges had reimbursed themselves for the purchase of their offices by charges (*épices,* or "spices") imposed on litigants. These reforms were soon extended to the provincial parlements. Those former members of parlement who refused to accept the new arrangements were exiled and stripped of their offices.

The magistrates thus affected posed as victims of royal despotism, and a large segment of the public failed to understand the genuinely salutary and progressive nature of Maupeou's reforms.

At the same time Abbé Terray earned a richly deserved unpopularity by the harsh measures he took to avert the bankruptcy of the royal treasury: forced conversion of state financial obligations, reduction of the interest rate on government bonds, creation of new indirect taxes, and other measures. These sacrifices were accepted less than enthusiastically in view of the shameless waste displayed by the king, his new favorite, Madame Du Barry, and the many grasping and idle courtiers.

Louis XV died on May 10, 1774, of smallpox, after duly but belatedly begging forgiveness for the scandals of his private life. But public opinion against him was now so strong that his body was taken to St. Denis by night, along a route that bypassed Paris, for fear of hostile demonstrations.   aged 64

III. FOREIGN POLICY

The War of the Polish Succession. In the eyes of Cardinal Fleury, the chief objective of foreign policy was the peace of France and Europe. Without abandoning the alliance that Dubois had made with England, he counterbalanced it by renewing cordial ties with the king of Spain, who had been seriously offended by the duke of Bourbon's return of the infanta (see p. 182). His efforts to normalize relations with Austria as well were opposed by a powerful faction at court and within the government. Its leading figure, Germain de Chauvelin, secretary of state for foreign affairs, took advantage of the affair of the Polish succession to revive the traditional French rivalry with the house of Hapsburg. In 1733 Stanislas Leszczyński, Louis XV's father-in-law, was again elected king of Poland. His unhappy rival, the elector Augustus III of Saxony, appealed to Emperor Charles VI, and an Austro-Russian army ousted Stanislas. Louis XV's honor did not permit him to remain idle. War was therefore declared against Austria, in alliance with the king of Spain. But Fleury took care to limit operations to Italy and to negotiate a compromise peace as soon as possible. It might be said that if Chauvelin tricked the cardinal into war, the cardinal made off with the peace. Sealed by the Treaty of Vienna in 1738, the settlement consisted of a kind of exchange of royal pawns on the European chessboard: Naples and Sicily, which were ceded by the emperor, went to Don Carlos (later Charles III), along with the title of king of the Two Sicilies. Don Carlos' father, Philip V, the king of Spain, had been ruler of the duchies of Parma and Tuscany since 1721. These duchies returned to the son-in-law of Charles VI of Austria and heir presumptive to the imperial crown, Duke Francis of Lorraine. Finally, Francis ceded his hereditary states, the duchy of Lorraine and the county of Bar, to Stanislas Leszczyński with the understanding that at his death they would revert to the king of France. France's annexation of this important province was thus assured. Moreover, the establishment of a new Bourbon monarchy in southern Europe offered certain advantages, for until the end of the century the alliance of the three crowns worn by the Bourbons—"the family pact"—was to weigh heavily in European politics.

The War of the Austrian Succession. If the emperor Charles VI proved conciliatory, it was because he foresaw the difficulties that his daughter, Maria Theresa, would soon encounter in gaining the succession to all her various states. In most of them, tradition barred women from the throne. By an act called the "Pragmatic Sanction," issued in 1713, Charles VI had set aside these traditions. Since then his principal concern had been to have the act solemnly recognized both by his subjects and by the other powers.

It was a wasted effort, for Charles VI had scarcely closed his eyes when all the pledges were forgotten. First, the king of Prussia, Frederick II, pounced upon Silesia. France was not directly interested, and neutrality was all the more imperative since Spain would have to be supported against the English, who had declared war on Spain just a year earlier, in October 1739. That was the first thought of Louis XV and Fleury, but once again they allowed themselves to be influenced by the powerful anti-Austrian faction, now led by the brilliant marshal Charles Fouquet de Belle-Isle. Without a declaration of war, French armies were sent to Germany to support the elector of Bavaria, who claimed the imperial crown. Belle-Isle seized Prague, and his candidate had himself crowned emperor in January 1742 under the name of Charles VII.

Maria Theresa, who was at first overwhelmed, held on courageously, and the situation turned in her favor. She had the support of England, and she bought off Frederick II, her most dangerous opponent, by ceding him Silesia. The Franco-Bavarian forces were driven from Bohemia. The opportune death of the ephemeral emperor Charles VII in 1745 enabled Maria Theresa to have her husband, the former duke of Lorraine, crowned emperor as Francis I. The war nonetheless continued for Austria's possessions in Italy and the Netherlands. Beaten south of the Alps, the French armies were successful in Belgium. There Marshal Maurice de Saxe won the three victories of Fontenoy (1745), Rocourt (1746), and Lawfeld (1747). The first of these battles in particular, fought in the presence of Louis XV against a powerful Anglo-Dutch army, has remained in French military annals the most glorious episode in a reign that boasted few victories.

In the wake of these victories Louis XV found himself in possession of Belgium, but he was weary of a war that was dragging on interminably. In the Treaty of Aix-la-Chapelle, in October 1748, he purchased the peace he wanted by giving up all his conquests—not only Belgium, but Savoy and Nice as well. The establishment in Parma of another Spanish Bourbon, Don Philip, who was to marry a daughter of Louis XV, did not compensate for these losses. The principal beneficiary was Frederick II of Prussia, who had his possession of Silesia guaranteed. France, it was said, had "worked for the king of Prussia."

The Seven Years' War. It was with equal reluctance that Louis XV was led into the third and most disastrous war of his reign. It was forced on him first by England and then by the skillful diplomacy of the Austrian government.

The British saw all their commercial and colonial advantages threatened by the rapid expansion of French commercial shipping and colonization. In the Far East the daring action of Joseph Dupleix, governor of the French East India Company, laid the basis for a virtual empire, far larger than the one then held by the rival English company. His ambition frightened the company's directors, who forced his recall in 1754. Particularly in North America the relative positions of France and Britain made a conflict inevitable. Masters of Newfoundland, Acadia, and Hudson's Bay, the British encircled Canada, but they were barred from any expansion into the interior by French settlements in the Mississippi and Ohio valleys. It was there that hostilities erupted in 1754, instigated by British colonists from Virginia commanded by George Washington. Under pressure from the Virginians, who were supported by London merchants, the British government itself entered the struggle with an attack that resembled piracy. In June 1755, without a declaration of war, the British seized three warships and 300 French merchant vessels, thereby depriving France of a great part of its maritime might.

Still, if France joined all its forces with those of its Spanish allies, it might still fight successfully. Unfortunately, Louis XV squandered his resources in a continental war in which Austria had involved him. The empress Maria Theresa was firmly determined to take her revenge on the king of Prussia, and she needed the aid of France to do it. Her advances, at first rejected, were finally welcomed when it was learned at Versailles that Frederick II, despite his great debt to France, had concluded an alliance with England in January 1756. Louis XV thus entered a European coalition formed by Austria against Frederick II. This reversal of alliances and the abandonment of France's traditional policy were considered the most sensational diplomatic event of the age. But the sole advantage that Louis XV might have gained from it was the possibility of striking indirectly at England by seizing Hanover, the personal possession of King George II.

Indeed, by 1757 Hanover was occupied by a French army commanded by the duke of Richelieu. But after this first success, the armies of Louis XV suffered a series of reverses. The most humiliating was Frederick's defeat of a Franco-German army far superior in numbers at Rossbach on November 5, 1757. Hanover itself was lost the next year. The poorly led French forces then exhausted themselves in secondary operations between the Rhine and the Weser, while the decisive events were taking place farther to the east, among the great armies of Prussia, Austria, and Russia.

The British, meanwhile, made full use of their superiority at sea to capture French overseas positions, to which the homeland could send only minimal aid. French Canada, valiantly defended by the Marquis de Montcalm and the Duke of Lévis, finally fell in September 1760. In India all the gains made by Dupleix were lost by his incompetent successors. The last of them, Thomas de Lally-Tollendal, was finally bottled up in Pondichéry, where he had no more than 700 soldiers to resist a British army of 22,000 men supported by a fleet of fourteen ships. The surrender of this stronghold, in January 1761, at last gave Britain dominion over the immense Indian empire.

The Treaty of Paris. All these defeats were greeted with indifference in France. Why, asked Voltaire, should they fight "over a few acres of snow in Canada"? As for the war in Germany, the intellectual set praised the successes of the "philosopher king" Frederick II to the skies, while damning Austria, that bloodsucker that grew fat on the money and men that France squandered in vain.

By the end of 1762 Louis XV and Choiseul were resigned to cutting their losses and negotiating directly with England. Under the Treaty of Paris of February 10, 1763, France gave up part of the French colonies won by the British in the West Indies and Senegal. In the Orient the French East India Company recovered five trading posts on condition that they be totally demilitarized. Finally and most important, with a stroke of the pen Louis XV surrendered everything that the struggle and sacrifice of several generations of Frenchmen had won in North America. All of Canada east of the Mississippi passed under British rule. The territories to the west of the Mississippi, all that was left of Louisiana, were ceded to Spain to compensate it for Florida, which it lost because it had fought on the side of France.

IV. SOCIAL AND ECONOMIC CONDITIONS

A Prosperous Country. On the whole, the France of Louis XV seemed to be a prosperous country, particularly in comparison with the France of the preceding century. An indisputable sign of progress was the relatively rapid and regular growth of population (see Table 2).

Table 2. Population of France, 1700 – 80 (in millions)

YEAR	POPULATION
1700	21.5
1720	22.6
1740	24.6
1760	26.7
1780	27.5

France had long been the most populous country of the West. In the eighteenth century only Russia among European nations even approached it in population. Russia then had about 12 million, England 5 to 6 million, Spain 6 to 8 million, and the Austrian Empire about 8 million.

Recurring demographic "catastrophes," striking approximately every thirty years, had limited population growth in preceding centuries. Wars, epidemics, and famines increased mortality, decreased the number of marriages, and led to sharp drops in the number of births. The last great catastrophe in France occurred in 1740–42. Thereafter the demographic crises became progressively less severe, as agriculture became more productive, improved transportation permitted grain to be moved quickly to meet local shortages, incomes increased, and the government devised efficient administrative machinery to deal with shortages. The old brakes on population were removed, and France's population increased relatively sharply in the second half of the century, until it exceeded 27 million in 1780.

At least 85 percent of the population remained rural. Only about twenty cities could count their inhabitants in the tens of thousands. Paris, with a population estimated at 510,000 in 1719 and 577,000 in 1763, was by far the largest city of the kingdom, but only about 2 percent of the national population lived within its walls.

An Enlightened Administration. The growing prosperity and the increase in population were certainly due in part to a generally honest and enlightened administration that managed to harmonize the centralizing policy pursued since Colbert with the many provincial privileges and customs defended by local assemblies, as in Languedoc and Brittany. The intendants in the thirty-three "generalities" usually remained on the scene long enough to understand their regions fully and to promote improvements in agriculture, town planning, public works, security, tax collection, and transportation.

Industry. In the eighteenth century France was the world's first industrial power. Its industry, however, consisted not of factories that employed hundreds of workers, but of scattered artisans who worked in their homes or in tiny shops and produced simple products. Woolen textiles were the backbone of the industrial system. Production of woolen goods increased about 75 percent in the course of the eighteenth century, and their value nearly doubled. The increase in value reflected improvements in quality as well as inflation. Overall industrial production increased perhaps 60 percent. Some leading sectors, such as the new cotton textile industry and paper, grew at well above the average rate. The iron industry remained a dispersed, backward, and high-cost industry; only in the 1780s did it even begin to improve—by copying new British methods.

The distinction between industrial workers and peasants was not yet clearly established. Most spinners and weavers and most ironworkers also tilled the land and moved from agriculture to industry and back with the seasons and with the ebb and flow of the economy. Finishing processes of the textile industry—washing, dyeing, printing—tended to concentrate, and there were a few industrial textile towns—Amiens, Rheims, Rouen, Lyons. An industrial proletariat could be found in these towns, but in 1750 it probably did not exceed 100,000 persons in all of France. Some economic historians have placed the beginning of the Industrial Revolution in France in the latter eighteenth century. Industry's share in the gross national product grew significantly in the course of the century—from about 5 percent to about 13 percent—but on the eve of the French Revolution, industry, measured by the value of its product or by its share of the working population, still occupied a subordinate place in the economy.

Agriculture. Agricultural output increased modestly in the eighteenth century, 25 to 40 percent, most of the growth coming in the latter half of the century. This growth was achieved without any major changes in technology or land tenure. It is attributable to minor alterations in methods, introduction of new crops, conversion of wasteland to production, and reduction in the number of small holdings.

For the 85 percent of the population that lived directly from agriculture, life and work remained simple and crude. Except in areas with easily usable stone, peasant houses were made of wood, earth, and straw. With rare exceptions, wood was the only fuel. Tools were fashioned from wood; metal was a luxury of the rich and the military. Peasants ate little meat, and each household tried to produce most of its own needs in vegetables and grains.

Mobility and Transportation. For most people life was narrowly localized, as movement was costly and difficult. The predominantly agrarian economy was served by a multitude of local paths and tracks, six to seven feet wide, now almost entirely disappeared. Somewhat better roads were maintained to serve particular economic needs, such as the "fish-cart roads" between Channel ports and Paris, used to supply the huge market for fish sustained by the church's 150 annual fast days.

In mid-century Daniel Trudaine founded the Corps of Bridges and Roads to improve the design, construction, and maintenance of royal roads, and he planned and began to construct a national system of highways radiating from Paris to the borders. From his initiative came the straight, wide (sixty feet), paved, ditched, and tree-lined highways that were the envy of foreign visitors in the final decades of the century. But throughout Louis XV's reign, most royal roads were unpaved and badly maintained, dusty in dry weather, muddy in wet. They served royal messengers and mail, well-to-do travelers, and long-distance freight. Costs were so high, however, that no agricultural or industrial product of any considerable weight, such as grain or wine, could pay them and still find a market. Consequently, the large volume of freight was moved by coastal waters, rivers, and canals.

Until the late decades of the century the rhythm of the movement of persons and goods had changed little since the Middle Ages, a rhythm set by the pedestrian and the plodding horse. Lyons was a good

[handwritten in margin: 18e Eng experienced great changes in agriculture.]

ten days from Paris at the beginning of the century, Bordeaux fifteen. In 1780, thanks to Trudaine's improved or new roads, a traveler could reach Lyons in five days, Bordeaux in six.

Society. Commercial prosperity and improved administration naturally benefited the bourgeoisie, which grew in numbers, in wealth, and in influence. Its most affluent members tended to split off to form a veritable aristocracy of wealth, which merged with the older nobilities of sword and robe. One group in particular distinguished itself by its opulence: the Farmers General, forty associated financiers who advanced the state the estimated value of indirect taxes and then undertook to collect them in its stead—for a profit. Shortly before 1789 they obtained permission to surround Paris with a continuous wall, the better to control the entry of taxable goods. Careful to combine the beautiful with the functional, however, they hired the avant-garde architect Charles Ledoux to ornament the collection gates with monumental entryways, some of which still survive.

The Salons. Except perhaps during the several brilliant years of the "reign" of Madame de Pompadour, the focus of worldly life and the control center of taste and wit has no longer the court of Versailles but the capital. There everyone who counted in high society—nobles, upper bourgeois, men of letters, artists—assembled in a few salons directed by women of wit, such as Madame Geoffrin, the Marquise Du Deffand, and Madame Helvétius. At these gatherings the art of conversation was developed and refined in a way that has never been equaled. Jean-Jacques Rousseau called it conversation that was "wise without being pedantic, lively without being uproarious, gallant without being vapid." It also had polish and an exquisite politeness made up of natural ease and calculated attentiveness.

The meetings held in cafés were freer. The café dated from the Regency; the most famous was the Café Procope. Numerous provincial towns had their "academies" or "philosophical societies." And finally, Freemasonry, which was imported from England at the beginning of the century, increased opportunities for exchange of ideas through its lodges.

The New Ideas. The conversation at all these meetings was no longer only literary or worldly but what was then called "philosophical." That is, it freely touched on subjects once considered too dangerous or boring—political, social, economic, and scientific questions. And naturally all beliefs and all established institutions were criticized in the name of reason. "To philosophize," as Madame de Lambert, hostess of one of the leading salons of the day, explained it, "is to give reason its full dignity and restore it to its rights; it is to shake off the yoke of accepted opinion and authority."

These critical tendencies received their first stimulus after 1715 in relations with England, where two revolutions had destroyed monarchical absolutism and the grip of Catholicism, and where such daring writers as John Locke had formulated democratic and irreligious doctrines. After 1750 the *philosophes*'s attacks, encouraged by the weakness of a discredited government, became more daring and extensive. It was then that the first volume of the *Encyclopedia* appeared, edited by Denis Diderot and destined to be the catalyst and most effective vehicle of this "philosophy of the enlightened."

In religious matters the *philosophes* violently attacked the Catholic church for its ignorance and intolerance. They sought to replace traditional Christianity with either a sort or rational deism, as in the case of Voltaire, or a sentimental and philanthropic evangelicalism, as in the case of Jean-Jacques Rousseau, or even a purely atheistic materialism, as in the cases of Denis Diderot and Claude Helvétius. In political and social matters they fought royal absolutism and the privileges that perpetuated inequality. With Rousseau and Mably there even appeared purely democratic doctrines, such as the sovereignty of the people, and some ideas that were almost socialistic, such as the limitation of private property. And in economic matters, the school of "physiocrats," which included François Quesnay, Vincent de Gournay, and Anne-Robert Turgot, criticized the Colbertist system, in which industry was strictly controlled and protected from competition, and substituted a system of commercial and industrial freedom whose motto was "*Laissez-faire, laissez-passer*" (Let people do as they please, let them go where they please).

All these doctrines aroused in the educated classes a reformist mentality—discontent with the present and the idea that progress is possible and desirable—that led to the fall of the Old Regime.

The Arts. Under the inspiration of Louis XIV, the artists of the preceding century had produced works that were rather cold but that had a majestic unity of style. In the eighteenth century patronage of the arts expanded to include *nouveaux riches*, and the arts reflected their tastes and requirements as well as those of royal and noble patrons. The work of eighteenth-century artists was distinguished by light gracefulness, imagination, and variety. These qualities appeared particularly in the ornamentation seen in daily life. Painting was especially decorative, something to be added to architectural design. Particularly popular were the mythological and pastoral paintings of François Boucher (1703–70), the sentimental and sometimes erotic pieces of Jean Fragonard (1732–1806), and the portraits and genre paintings of Jean-Baptiste Chardin (1699–1779) and Jean-Baptiste Greuze (1725–1805).

Civil architecture attained an unequaled degree of solid and harmonious elegance, and so did the art of the furniture maker. The first

half of the century loved sinuous lines and an excess of whimsical ornamentation that was familiar and imaginative, the so-called rococo
style. From 1760 onward literary influence and archaeological discoveries prompted a return to the more severe styles of ancient art. Examples
to be found in Paris include the Panthéon, by the architect Germain
Soufflot, the Hôtel des Monnaies, and the Ecole Militaire, and at Versailles the Petit Trianon, the latter two by Jacques Gabriel. Applied to
furniture, this "neoclassicism" introduced the "Louis XVI style"—a mis-
nomer, since it had begun to appear at the end of the preceding reign.

The prosperity of the bourgeoisie and the growth of cities led to
growing attention to urban design. In many small, essentially medieval
cities, efforts were made to provide light and open space, and at the
same time to provide embellishment in the form of royal *places* or
squares centered on a statue of the king. The most celebrated example
is the Place Louis XV in Paris, now the Place de la Concorde. Others
were built in Bordeaux, Rheims, Dijon, Nancy, and a number of other
cities.

France and Europe. The eighteenth century saw the apogee of French
cultural influence over Western Europe. Literature, philosophical theories, fine arts, decorative arts, and most of all the art of living developed
at the court of Versailles and in the Paris salons fascinated the upper
classes of other countries. French artists received commissions from all
points of the compass, and foreigners came to Paris to enjoy the charms
of social life and to absorb French taste. French became the international language of the aristocratic and cultivated classes. Foreign rulers such
as Frederick II of Prussia and Catherine II of Russia even used it in
preference to the language of their own countries and maintained close
relations with such great French writers as Voltaire and Diderot.

SUGGESTIONS FOR FURTHER READING

Becker, Carl. *The Heavenly City of the Eighteenth-Century Philosophers.*
New Haven, 1932, 1936.

Gaxotte, Pierre. *Louis the Fifteenth and His Times.* Philadelphia, 1934.

Gay, Peter. *The Enlightenment: An Interpretation.* 2 vols. New York,
1966–68.

Gooch, George Peabody. *Louis XV: The Monarchy in Decline.* New York,
1956.

Lough, John, ed. *An Introduction to Eighteenth-Century France*. London, 1960.

McDonald, Joan. *Rousseau and the French Revolution, 1762–1791*. London, 1965.

Mason, Hayden. *Voltaire: A Biography*. Baltimore, 1981.

Wilson, Arthur M. *Diderot*. New York, 1972.

Wrong, George M. *The Conquest of New France: A Chronicle of the Colonial Wars*. New Haven, 1918.

Egret, Jean. *Louis XV et l'opposition parlementaire, 1715–1774*. Paris, 1970.

15
Louis XVI and the Crisis of the Old Regime

The accession of Louis XVI at first appeared to presage a fresh start for the nation and the monarchy. But the weakness of the king, the intrigues of his entourage, and the opposition of the privileged class led to the failure of the major reforms that alone might have averted the Revolution. More fortunate in his foreign policy, Louis XVI succeeded in checkmating England, maintaining peace on the Continent, and restoring French influence.

I. THE FIRST YEARS OF LOUIS XVI

Louis XVI. Louis the Dauphin, the only legitimate son of Louis XV, died in 1765. At the untimely loss of this very upstanding man, the crown went to his son, a youth of twenty when he mounted the throne in 1774. He was as honest and moral as his father but lacked experience and self-assurance. From his mother, Maria Josepha of Saxony, Louis XVI inherited a heaviness of build and features that accentuated his clumsiness. In royal bearing he was a pitiful contrast with Louis XIV and Louis XV. He was very pious, and he had received an excellent education; he knew how to work with his hands, draw maps, and make locks. He began his duties with a touching concern for the public good, but his candor and scrupulous conscience, added to his weak will, made him hesitant, and led him to yield to pressures from his entourage.

Marie Antoinette. The young queen Marie Antoinette, daughter of the empress of Austria, Maria Theresa, was lively, elegant, and gracious. During her later ordeals she was to display great character, but at the beginning of the reign she gave the impression of being a frivolous, capricious, extravagant young woman, interested in nothing but pleasure, and ready to throw the rules of royal etiquette joyfully to the wind, even at the risk of her reputation.

The Recall of the Parlements. To guide him in his inexperience, Louis XVI summoned the Count of Maurepas, a former navy minister who had been forced out in 1749 by Madame de Pompadour. This likable old man, who was named minister of state without portfolio, now sought only to please everyone. He advised the king to dismiss Maupeou and the other unpopular ministers of Louis XV and restore the parlements. This last measure caused tumultuous outbursts of rejoicing everywhere, but as a few clear-sighted individuals predicted, it doomed to failure all efforts to reform the regime.

Turgot. Maurepas can at least be credited with bringing to the finance ministry a man of great ability and fine character—Anne-Robert Turgot, son of a former provost of the Paris merchants. A very active member of the physiocratic school, he had had the opportunity to apply —quite successfully—the ideas of Quesnay and Gournay in the generality of Limoges, where he had been the intendant.

What were his plans for royal finances? First, he wanted economies, preferably in the least useful expenditures, such as those of the court; then he sought to increase revenues by a fairer levying of taxes and by developing the country's wealth according to the physiocratic formula, *Laissez-faire, laissez-passer.*

On the first point—economies—Turgot soon encountered opposition from the queen and all those who profited from financial abuses. The measures he took to increase revenues from indirect taxes also drew the dangerous resentment of the Farmers General, whose profits were reduced. The total freedom of the grain trade, proclaimed in September 1774, did not prevent a considerable increase in the price of bread the next spring in the wake of a poor harvest. Riots broke out, directed against grain convoys and bakery shops. The *laissez-faire* doctrine was applied by an edict abolishing craft guilds. Finally Turgot attacked the fundamental problem of equal taxation. His ultimate objective was to replace all the old direct taxes by a single "land tax" based on ownership of land. He began by abolishing the royal corvée, unpaid labor on road construction and maintenance required of peasants, and replacing it with a tax levied on all landowners. This edict aroused the indignation of the privileged classes, and the Parlement of Paris issued solemn remonstrances against it.

In May 1776 a coalition of all the opponents of the plan, headed by the queen, pressured Louis XVI to dismiss Turgot and to restore the guilds and the corvée.

Necker. Shortly afterward, in October 1776, Louis XVI entrusted the administration of finances to the banker Jacques Necker. This Protestant from Geneva had risen to the top ranks of the financial profession in Paris, and had won the favor of a group of *philosophes* whom Madame Necker had attracted to her salon. He strongly opposed the physiocratic theories of Turgot, and helped to bring him down.

At first Necker justified his reputation as a skillful technician by reorganizing the collection of indirect taxes to make the operation more economical, and particularly by financing the costs of French participation in the American Revolution by repeated loans (see p. 201). People were grateful that he did not levy new taxes, but it soon became apparent that his failure to do so had raised the public debt to a catastrophic level.

Necker polished his image as a "philosophical" statesman by such practical humanitarian reforms as improvements in hospitals and prisons, the suppression of judicial torture, and the abolition of the remnants of serfdom on the royal domains. He undertook a liberal decentralization of administration by creating provincial assemblies in the provinces of Berry and Guyenne, on an experimental basis. These assemblies, in which nobles, churchmen, and bourgeois were equally represented, were intended to take over some of the intendants' powers in such matters as the allocation of taxes, welfare, and public works.

Necker's zeal for reform met the usual opposition, and he eventually had as many enemies as Turgot. Necker responded to the lampoons issued against him by publishing his *Compte Rendu au Roi* (Report to the King) in February 1781. There he publicly revealed for the first time the balance sheet of the state's income and expenses. The beneficiaries of the abuses that were exposed in it redoubled their attacks. Abandoned by Maurepas and Louis XVI, Necker submitted his resignation in May 1781. His departure marked the final collapse of the reform effort and of the hopes raised by the accession of the young king.

II. FOREIGN POLICY

Vergennes. Louis XVI had the good fortune to find one of the best foreign ministers who ever served France and the wisdom to keep him in office until 1787. Count Gravier de Vergennes endowed his functions with a regularity and style that were perpetuated into the nineteenth century. Without renouncing the Austrian alliance, which was passionately defended by the queen, he made sure it did not drag France into new adventures. Even though the emperor Joseph II, Marie Antoinette's brother, went in person to Versailles and even offered to cede Belgium to France, Vergennes refused to support his plans for conquest in Germany and in the East. His policy of balance of power and peace and his firm repudiation of any territorial expansion won him the confidence of the smaller states, which were frightened by the ambitions of Austria and Prussia.

The American Revolution. The peace that reigned on the Continent allowed France to take its revenge on England. The rebellion of the British colonies in America and their Declaration of Independence on July 4, 1776, were greeted enthusiastically in France. A number of young officers from the high nobility, among them the Marquis de Lafayette, spontaneously offered their services to the "Patriots." The Continental Congress sent one of its most eminent members, Benjamin Franklin, to France. His calculated simplicity and shrewdness did wonders for the American cause at the court of Versailles and in the Paris salons.

Nevertheless, Vergennes was cautious in his commitments. In the beginning France limited its aid to subsidies and armaments drawn from the royal arsenals. News of Washington's first military success, at Saratoga in September 1777, finally convinced the French government to intervene openly, and on February 6, 1778, it signed a treaty of trade and alliance with Franklin. A declaration of war against England soon followed.

France had recovered its military strength since the disasters of the Seven Years' War. Choiseul and then Count Claude de Saint-Germain, minister of war from 1775 to 1777, had done their work well. Saint-Germain had restored discipline and improved the recruitment and training of officers. He had enabled the engineer Jean-Baptiste Gribeauval to provide the artillery with new equipment so advanced that it served without modification through the Revolution and the Empire. The restoration of the navy, also well begun by Choiseul, was continued by Gabriel de Sartine, a former lieutenant general of police in Paris and an able administrator. At the beginning of 1778 France had 78 well-built and well-armed ships of the line and 186 smaller ships.

When Spain, after long hesitation, entered the war on the side of France in June 1779, extensive preparations were made for a joint landing in the British Isles. But the plan failed miserably when their ships proved unable to win control of the English Channel. Similarly, all efforts to capture the fortress of Gibraltar failed. The only gain in the

Mediterranean was the capture of the important naval fortress of Mahon on the island of Minorca.

Elsewhere, both in the West Indies and in Asian waters, the British and French fleets confronted each other with mixed success. The French admirals Toussaint de La Motte-Picquet, Pierre-André Suffren, and Henri d'Estaing particularly distinguished themselves.

The fate of the war was sealed on American soil. Supported by a small French expeditionary force under Count Jean-Baptiste de Rochambeau and by the French West Indies squadron under Admiral François de Grasse, Washington's army blockaded the main British army in its base at Yorktown, Virginia, and forced General Charles Cornwallis to surrender on October 19, 1781.

When the discouraged British asked to negotiate, the Americans, despite the commitments they had made to France, concluded a separate preliminary peace with England in November 1782. The final and general treaty, prepared by Vergennes, was signed only nine months later, on September 3, 1783, at Versailles. England recognized the independence of the United States and ceded it the territory between the Appalachians and the Mississippi. To Spain it surrendered Minorca and Florida, which it had acquired twenty years earlier. France recovered only what it had lost overseas during this war and a few minor territories lost by the Treaty of Paris of 1763, including the islands of St. Pierre and Miquelon off the Newfoundland coast. Far more important than these symbolic gains was the satisfaction of dealing a fatal blow to England's claims to world hegemony and restoring France's political and military influence.

But the American War of Independence also had important consequences in France. On the one hand, the birth of a republic founded on democratic principles was an encouragement and an example to the critics of traditional monarchy. On the other hand, the cost of the war —more than 1.5 billion livres—completed the ruin of the state's finances and made recourse to the Estates General inevitable. The French Revolution thus appears to have been the daughter of the American Revolution.

III. THE STRUCTURE OF SOCIETY ON THE EVE OF THE REVOLUTION

Nobility. At the top of the social structure stood the hereditary nobility: 110 to 350 thousand individuals, who constituted 0.5 to 1.5 percent of the population. As a class they were distinguished by their wealth, their privileges, and their general acceptance as the nation's natural leaders and social elite. They owned a quarter to a third of the land, collected feudal dues on most that they did not own, held so many offices in the church that they received as much as one-fourth of its revenues, had a virtual monopoly on public offices and *their* revenues, and were the largest investors in heavy industry. Individual and family wealth varied greatly. The lower 20 percent had incomes comparable to those of modestly well-off peasants. At the other end of the scale were some 250 families with annual incomes of 50,000 livres or more. These were the court nobles, whose ostentatious lifestyle discredited the entire noble class in the eyes of those who did not share their privileges. A middle group, about 60 percent of the total, had annual incomes of less than 4,000 livres, which permitted only a modest standard of living.

All nobles were exempt from the *taille*, from obligatory military service, and from having troops billeted in their houses. They enjoyed special treatment in the law courts; for example, a noble condemned to death had the exclusive right to decapitation, which carried no taint of social dishonor. They enjoyed conspicuous symbolic privileges—the right to wear a sword in public, to display a coat of arms, to take precedence on ceremonial occasions. They had the right to a pew in the parish church on the "New Testament" side of the altar—that is, on the right hand of God—and the right to be buried in the choir of the church. Army ranks above captain, with some exceptions, were limited to nobles. In remote areas where there were no royal law courts, nobles administered justice to their peasants, and appeals to royal courts were permitted only with their consent. As patrons of the arts and of intellectuals and as the arbiters of fashion, the nobility still dominated the country's cultural life.

Clergy. The clergy of the Catholic church—the monastic and secular clergy combined—numbered about 120,000, 0.5 to 1 percent of the population. As a class the clergy was rich and privileged, but the benefits were inequitably distributed among its members. The church's revenues were fully as large as those of the government. Its total landholdings can only be estimated. They varied from as much as 20 percent of the land in some regions to as little as 1 percent in others; the national average was between 6 and 10 percent. From its lands the church drew rents and feudal dues, and it also owned and received income from urban real estate and commercial enterprises. It was exempt from taxation but made a gift of about 5 million livres annually to the royal treasury—only about one-tenth of the taxes it would have had to pay if its property had been equitably taxed. From its income the church not only supported the clergy and all its strictly religious functions but also financed almost all hospitals and hospices, orphanages, other charitable services, and schools.

The secular clergy varied enormously in social status and material condition. At the top of the pyramid were the 139 archbishops and bishops, all of noble origin in 1789, and their entourages of grand vicars, comparable in prestige and wealth to the court aristocracy. At the bottom of the pyramid the thousands of parish priests and curates shared the hardships and often the poverty of their peasant flocks. Between top and bottom was a kind of ecclesiastical bourgeoisie—pastors of important urban parishes, well-endowed canons, university professors, and some others.

The monastic clergy, about 25,000 individuals in more than 700 abbeys and 1,800 religious houses, suffered in the public mind from the conspicuous moral laxity of a few. The female orders, with some 40,000 members, generally maintained high standards of piety and charitable zeal, but some houses had degenerated into luxurious retreats for noble spinsters and widows.

Bourgeoisie. The bourgeoisie is less readily defined and enumerated than the nobility or the clergy, for the term has had different meanings at different times. If the class is defined as the nonnoble, well-to-do city dwellers, their numbers may be fixed at about 2.3 million in 1785—approximately 8 percent of the population. It was a growing class, having increased threefold since 1700. Its individual members varied from shopkeepers, skilled artisan-proprietors, and minor bureaucrats through lawyers, doctors, writers, and publishers to rich industrialists, merchants, bankers, and, at the top of the financial scale, tax farmers. They enjoyed no privileges, real or ceremonial, comparable to those of the nobility, and the nobles treated them as social inferiors. The common aspiration of a financially successful bourgeois in the 1780s was still to join the nobility, not to combat it, and to "live nobly." A growing number of bourgeois, however, saw themselves as at least the equals of nobles in ability and merit, and they resented the system of privilege that reserved lucrative public offices and influence to the highborn. To such men the idea of equality was especially appealing, and it was in their ranks that the Revolution was to find its radical leaders.

Peasants. At least 80 percent of all French subjects on the eve of the Revolution—that is, probably about 22 million people—were peasants. As many as three-fourths of them owned some land, and together they held about half of all French land, but only a few owned enough to be self-sufficient. The great majority had to rent or sharecrop additional land or find other sources of income. They and the totally landless worked as agricultural laborers, engaged in such rural industries as spinning, weaving, and lacemaking, or migrated to find seasonal jobs in other parts of France; as a last resort, they begged and stole. These were the rural poor, barely able to survive in good times, reduced to desperate measures in times of economic crisis, as in 1788–89. The situation of all but the self-sufficient peasants worsened toward the end of the eighteenth century as a result of the rise in rural population and the consequent heightened competition for land, increased pressure on local food supplies, and declining wages in a saturated labor market.

Tax burdens on the peasants were heavy. They paid the *taille*, income taxes, headtaxes, and the salt tax. Those who owned land tithed to the church, nominally 10 percent of the annual crop but varying regionally from 3 to 8 percent. To the local seigneur they owed feudal dues, the most onerous being the *champart*, which averaged between 5 and 12 percent of the annual crop but varied greatly from place to place. If they sold their land, they paid the lord a sales tax, and they owed him money payments for the use of his mill, ovens, and winepress, even though these facilities might no longer exist. The total burden of fuedal dues has been estimated at between 10 and 15 percent of the peasant's production.

Other impositions added to peasant grievances. Until 1787, when a money payment was substituted, they were required to give several days of labor on road maintenance each year without pay. They were forbidden to kill the wild game that ate their crops or to chase the lord's pigeons from their planted fields.

Urban Workers. On the eve of the Revolution about 22 percent of the population lived in communes with 2,000 or more inhabitants and were therefore formally urban. Many of them, however, lived in conditions and engaged in work that would now be considerd rural. The nascent urban proletariat was concentrated in the cities, but even these urban workers did not yet form a class-conscious, coherent group.

In Paris about half the population in 1789 (550,000 to 600,000) was composed of workers. Some 90,000 were domestic servants, waiting on the 120,000 nobles, clergy, and bourgeois residents of the city. Best off among the workers were the journeymen, who had skills to sell and unions, illegal but tolerated, to defend their interests. The great mass of casual workers earned at best a subsistence wage. Illness, accident, old age, or economic depression were catastrophic for these people and their families. They could turn to begging and theft, but for some in times of high unemployment and high prices the end was death from hunger and exposure.

IV. THE ARISTOCRATIC REVOLUTION

Calonne. Necker's first two successors did not succeed in reducing the ever-growing deficits of the treasury. In November 1783 Louis XVI summoned the former intendant of Hainaut, Charles Alexander Calonne, who was known for his skill and amiability. This new controller general of finances first sought to restore confidence in the state's credit and revive economic activity by an openhanded policy that had the added advantage of disarming the hostility of the court, which had contributed to his predecessors' failure. In August 1786, when he thought his personal authority was well enough established, Calonne presented to the king a vast program of fiscal and administrative reform inspired by the ideas of Turgot.

The Assembly of Notables. Since all previous efforts to introduce a certain equality into the tax system had been obstructed by the parlements, Calonne tried to have his proposals adopted by an Assembly of Notables. In February 1787, 144 men chosen by the king assembled at Versailles. But these representatives of the privileged class were uncompromisingly opposed to Calonne's plans. Louis XIV replaced him with the archbishop of Toulouse, Loménie de Brienne, who had distinguished himself as a leader of the opposition. But he was no more successful, and on May 25, 1787, the king had to dismiss the notables.

The Revolt of the Parlements. Brienne then had to resort to the traditional method of having edicts approved by the parlements. They proved more unyielding than ever after the attempt to go over their heads. Brienne tried to break their resistance by exiling the Paris magistrates to Troyes. But the provincial parlements showed their sympathy with their Paris counterparts, and public opinion seemed to side with the "victims of despotism." The minister resigned himself to a compromise: the Parlement would be recalled to Paris, and in return would agree to raise the amount of the *vingtième*.

On May 3, 1788, intoxicated by its popularity, the Parlement ventured onto political territory by issuing a kind of declaration of the nation's rights in opposition to the monarchy. Louis XVI now recognized the error he had committed early in his reign when he repealed Maupeou's great judicial reform (see p. 198). The chancellor, Guillaume de Lamoignon, reintroduced it, but this time circumstances were even less favorable, and the royal edicts were greeted by a storm of protests and demonstrations. Nowhere was resistance stronger than in Dauphiné. In July 1788 representatives of the three estates or orders—the nobility, the clergy, and the commoners—met at the château at Vizille and issued an appeal to all provinces, urging them to refuse payment of taxes unless the king convened the Estates General. Louis XVI capitulated, and on August 8, 1788, the Estates General was summoned for May 1, 1789. Several days later Loménie de Brienne was replaced by Necker, who returned in triumph.

The Elections. The debate that quickly began over the methods of elec-

tion and the composition of the Estates General brought into the open
the true character of parlementary opposition. The reformers, who
adopted the proud title of "patriots," demanded that the third estate
have twice as many deputies as either the nobility or the clergy, that
joint deliberations be held, and that each deputy have a vote. The
Parlement of Paris, however, solemnly spoke out for the traditional
procedure, by which the three orders would deliberate in separate halls
and each order would have only one vote. The two privileged classes
would thus be able to block all reforms. Immediately the members of
Parlement were branded as "aristocrats" and lost all popular support.
On December 27, 1788, Louis XVI and Necker sanctioned the "dou-
bling of the third estate," a decision that roused the enthusiasm of the
"patriots"; since the king had separated his cause from that of the privileged classes, the way to reform seemed open.

The elections took place on this basis and in some confusion. Of
1,139 deputies chosen, the clergy elected 291, including at least 200
parish priests, most of whom were receptive to the new ideas. The 270
deputies of the nobility also included some advocates of reform, Lafayette among them. Needless to say, the bulk of the 578 deputies of
the third estate, most of them lawyers, also sought reform.

The Grievance Lists. Following custom, each electoral assembly drafted a
grievance list (*cahier de doléance*) that would transmit its wishes to the
monarch. As a whole such documents represent a sampling of national
public opinion that has unique value. Three general themes emerge
through the differences of opinion that separated the three orders: first,
the desire for reform of the state by means of a constitution that would
limit arbitrary government; second, more equitable taxation and access
to public office; and third, a deep attachment to the monarchy and to
the Catholic religion. Really? The Revolution undid the sovereignty of both

The Economic and Social Crisis. Unfortunately, the Estates General
opened in an atmosphere that was troubled not only by controversies
but also by popular discontent, the result of a severe economic crisis.

For some years an important sector of the economy, the wine industry, had suffered from overproduction, which depressed prices. In 1788
bad weather had wiped out a large part of the grain harvest, so that the
price of wheat and bread increased by 50 percent in the first months of
1789 and reached critical heights just before the new harvest, precisely
at the time the Estates General convened.

These difficulties aggravated the endemic social unrest stemming
from the fact that the increase in population (see p. 189) had stimulated
a rise in land prices and rents, so that young families had great difficulty getting established, and many peasants were forced to move to the

towns, where they fell into the wretched situation of casual laborers or beggars.

Since 1786 industry had suffered from competition by British manufacturers, who took advantage of a trade treaty concluded that year, to flood France with their goods. The sudden contraction of purchasing power, a result of the agricultural crisis, unleashed a veritable catastrophe: many industries were forced to shut down or cut production, dismiss workers, and reduce wages. In Paris, troops had to be called out on April 27–28, 1789, to put down a riot by workers in the Faubourg St. Antoine; many people were killed and several hundred wounded.

The widespread economic malaise that made taxes, debts, feudal dues, and all inequities harsher for all, and a lower class enraged by poverty and haunted by the specter of famine—these in large part explain the explosions of violence that were soon to bathe the bourgeois revolution in blood.

SUGGESTIONS FOR FURTHER READING

Behrens, G. B. A. *The Ancien Régime*. New York, 1971.

Darnton, Robert. *The Business of Enlightenment: Publishing History of the Encyclopédie, 1775–1800*. Cambridge, 1979.

Doyle, William. *Origins of the French Revolution*. New York, 1980.

Godechot, Jacques. *France and the Atlantic Revolution of the Eighteenth Century, 1770–1799*. New York, 1965.

Padover, Saul K. *The Life and Death of Louis XVI*. New York, 1963.

Palmer, Robert R. *The Age of the Democratic Revolution*. 2 vols. Princeton, 1959, 1964.

Egret, Jean. *La Prérévolution française, 1787–1789*. Paris, 1962.

Mornet, Daniel. *Les Origines intellectuelles de la Révolution française*. rev. ed. Paris, 1954.

16

The Revolution
and the End
of the Monarchy

The Estates General, which met to resolve a financial crisis, transformed itself into a Constituent Assembly that shook the old political and social structure from top to bottom. The necessary and salutary work of rebuilding was compromised by the fatal interaction of popular violence and clumsy attempts to respond to it by the king and the privileged classes, which finally resulted in the fall of the monarchy.

I. THE CONSTITUENT ASSEMBLY (MAY 1789–SEPTEMBER 1791)

The Birth of the Assembly. The Estates General opened with solemnity at Versailles on May 5, 1789, and immediately found itself paralyzed by a basic quarrel over procedure: should the deliberations take place jointly or in three separate halls? The deputies of the third estate insisted on the first solution and even refused to proceed with the preliminary formality of verifying credentials until it was adopted. The nobility and the clergy insisted on the traditional procedure; the king encouraged them but hesitated to speak out openly.

Finally, on June 17, the deputies of the third estate, calculating that they represented 96 percent of the nation, declared themselves to be a

France in 1789

——— Provincial boundaries   .... Department boundaries

National Assembly. On June 20, finding their customary meeting place closed, they assembled in a hall that happened to be available, an indoor tennis court, and there took an oath not to separate before they had given the kingdom a constitution.

In the next few days the pace of events accelerated. Some of the clergy and nobility joined the third estate. On June 27 Louis XVI accepted the fait accompli. Finally, on July 9, the National Assembly, with the deputies of all three orders sitting together, declared itself to be a "Constituent Assembly."

Absolute monarchy thus ceased to exist, and this political revolution by aristocrats and jurists had not cost a drop of blood. But just at that moment the mobilization of the lower classes of Paris and the countryside plunged the country into violence.

The Capture of the Bastille. As soon as he yielded, Louis XVI seemed to backtrack. Troops were assembled around Paris and Versailles, and on July 11 Necker was dismissed to make way for a reactionary government. The people of Paris, probably stirred up by agents of the ambitious duke of Orléans, began to seethe. The electors of Paris formed a new city government and decided to establish a middle-class militia, the National Guard, to suppress looting. The popular Lafayette was named its commander.

On the morning of July 14 a mixed crowd marched on the Bastille, the old fortress built by Charles V on the east side of Paris, where they hoped to find arms. Defended by about a hundred disabled veterans under the command of the Marquis de Launey, the Bastille surrendered after a few hours' siege. Launey was killed with six of his men. Shortly afterward, Jacques de Flesselles, the former provost of the merchants (mayor) of Paris; Joseph Foullon, the intendant of finances; and his son-in-law, Louis de Bertier de Sauvigny, intendant of the généralité of Paris, suffered the same fate.

The fall of the Bastille, an event of little importance in itself, later assumed symbolic importance because the fortress had served as a prison for subjects confined by *lettres de cachet*, that is, by arbitrary order of the king issued without a hearing.

At the time, the event spurred Louis to recall Necker (again!) and to go to the Paris city hall to recognize the new city government. It was on this occasion that the tricolor cockade appeared, symbolizing this reconciliation: white, the royal color, between red and blue, the colors of Paris.

The Count of Artois, the king's brother, was among the hard-liners who left the country to save their lives, thereby giving a signal for the emigration of opponents of the Revolution.

The Peasant Revolution. News of the events in Paris stirred similar movements in most towns. In defiance of royal administrators, who were immobilized by fear and by the disobedience of their subordinates, new city governments formed, supported by the bourgeois militias.

In the countryside the accumulated resentments burst into the open. Walls and fences enclosing fields were destroyed, forests pillaged, manorial dues refused. Here and there bands of peasants attacked châteaux and abbeys to burn the archives that contained the records of their burdensome and humiliating obligations.

Several provinces experienced the "Great Fear," a curious phenomenon of collective psychosis. When news of approaching but unidentified brigands spread from village to village, male peasants hastily armed themselves while their wives and children took flight.

The Night of August 4. The shockwaves from the capital had aroused the peasant masses. In turn the shock of this popular revolution pushed the political revolution forward. On the evening of August 4 two liberal nobles proposed to the Assembly that manorial rights be voluntarily relinquished in order to restore calm among the peasantry. Carried along by their zeal to outdo each other in generosity, the representatives of all the privileged bodies—clergy, nobility, magistracies, provinces, towns, and guilds—one by one renounced their special rights. By the end of the session, which lasted until 3 A.M. in an atmosphere of emotional enthusiasm, nothing remained of the old structure of French society based on legal privilege and inequality.

With the ground thus cleared, the Assembly approved the Declaration of the Rights of Man, the preamble of the future constitution, a catechism that codified the basic ideas of the eighteenth-century *philosophes:* the sovereignty of the nation, equality among citizens, personal liberty, freedom of thought and expression, and the inviolability of private property.

The October Days. A new crisis developed during September. The king hesitated to sanction the decrees proclaimed on the night of August 4, and in the Assembly itself a conservative party was taking shape. But in Paris popular agitation was spurred on by food shortages.

On October 5 a band of women led by armed men disguised in skirts marched on Versailles, supposedly to demand bread. The invaded Assembly, all order gone, voted everything they wanted. Louis XVI received a delegation of women and promised to sanction everything the Assembly had done and to distribute food. Exhausted but pacified, the crowd slept wherever they were. But at daybreak on the sixth, some of them forced their way into the palace, killed a number of guards, and reached the apartments of the queen, who narrowly escaped. At last Lafayette arrived with the National Guard and succeeded in evacuating the palace. But the crowd in the courtyard shouted its demand that the king come with them to Paris. Louis XVI appeared on the balcony with the queen and Lafayette and announced his agreement. That evening the royal family, in the midst of a wretched procession and practically prisoners, left Versailles to take up residence in the palace of the Tuileries. A few days later the Assembly moved into the riding school of the palace, which had been turned into a meeting hall.

The Clubs. The legal authorities were now subject to pressures from popular Parisian agitators. Their troops of small shopkeepers and craftsmen were organized by popular societies in the city's various sections (or quarters) which took their orders from the Cordeliers Club, dominated by such violent orators as Jean-Paul Marat, Georges Danton, and Jacques Hébert.

The more bourgeois Jacobin Club included a good number of the deputies of the Assembly's reform party. Its growing power during the Revolution was due to its many branches in other towns, which received directives and ideas for propaganda from Paris.

The Constitution of 1791. The constitution finally adopted in September 1791, after numerous revisions, revealed the bourgeoisie's distrust of the common people.

The complex electoral system, which operated in several stages, seemed to be in flagrant contradiction to the Declaration of the Rights of Man, since it established new inequalities based on income. It denied the right to vote to "passive citizens," those who were too poor to pay a minimum tax. Among the "active citizens" it established a graduated scale of tax requirements that served to restrict election as a deputy to a minority of well-to-do landowners, some 40,000 to 50,000 individuals. Legislative power was entrusted to an indissoluble one-house Legislative Assembly of 745 members elected for two years.

Executive power resided in the king, first servant of the state. He could refuse to approve the Assembly's decrees, but his veto could only suspend them temporarily. All his acts had to be countersigned by a minister who assumed responsibility for them.

To complete this separation of powers—a principle dear to Montesquieu and adopted in the United States—all judges were to be elected.

A new administrative organization that was rational and uniform replaced the old divisions with their confused boundaries and disparate authorities. The country was divided into eighty-three departments of approximately equal size, each subdivided into districts and communes. All of these entities governed themselves by means of elected councils and officials.

Economic Reforms. Application of the principle of *laissez-faire, laissez-passer* led to the elimination of all internal tariffs, city customs, tolls, and other levies. Craft guilds and monopolies held by certain manufacturers were also abolished. Workers, who were henceforth on their own in their dealings with employers, were strictly forbidden to go on strike under the Chapelier Law of June 14, 1791.

A very useful reform was the creation of a uniform system of weights and measures, the metric system, which was developed by the Academy of Sciences of Paris and eventually was adopted throughout the world.

National Property and Assignats. The financial disarray had worsened after May 1789. To avoid bankruptcy, the Assembly decided to "nationalize" (that is, confiscate) the immense fortune that the Catholic church had accumulated over the centuries. Its arable land, forests, and real estate represented perhaps 6 to 10 percent of the national territory. In compensation the state itself would pay the expenses of worship, the material support of the clergy, and the works of charity and education that the church had performed until then.

But how could all this "national property" (*biens nationaux*) be turned into liquid assets? The Treasury issued notes called *assignats*, which were secured by this property and which served as paper money. Naturally, governments in succeeding years yielded to the temptation of raising income by multiplying the supply of *assignats* beyond all measure.

This monetary inflation produced a rise in prices, which increased the misery of the lower classes. The depreciation of *assignats* in relation to gold and silver specie prompted people who received them in payment to get rid of them as quickly as possible by purchasing national property with them. Each purchaser thus became bound to the cause of the Revolution. At the same time, speculators built enormous fortunes at the expense of the state, which sold off valuable property in exchange for paper money that increasingly shrank in value.

The Civil Constitution of the Clergy. Inasmuch as the state undertook to support the clergy, the Assembly held that it could reorganize the Church of France as it might any other public service. It began by abolishing religious vows as contrary to fundamental human liberties (February 1790). The diocesan clergy was given a new organization called the "Civil Constitution," based on that of the general administration. There was one diocese to a department, one parish to a commune. Bishops and priests were elected like other local officials. In a Gallican spirit the Assembly also decreed that the elected bishops would receive spiritual investiture from one of their colleagues, called the metropolitan bishop, and no longer from Rome, as the Concordat of 1516 had ordained. The Holy See would only be "informed" of the elections.

Religious Divisions. The pope could only condemn these changes, which would eventually create a national church separated from Rome and subordinated to the civil power, as in England. The French clergy, who had not resisted the nationalization of their property, now proved far more recalcitrant. To compel them to obey, the Assembly decided that all paid churchmen must take an oath to support the Civil Constitution of the Clergy under penalty of losing their posts. Only seven bishops and about half of the priests agreed to take the required oath. The Church of France was cut in two.

These seeds of trouble and division, added to all the others, were fatal to the work of the Constituent Assembly. Worse yet, for more than a century the cause of the Catholic Church was to be linked with that of the enemies of the Revolution.

The Flight of the King. Louis XVI's religious conscience had been deeply shaken by these latest measures of the Assembly. A wave of reaction or weariness was developing in some sectors of the population, and in the spring of 1791 appeals from émigrés and foreign rulers led him to try to recover lost ground. To do so, he had first to escape the Parisian mob. After careful preparations, he set out on the night of June 20–21, 1791. The heavy coach bearing the king and his family left Paris and headed toward Lorraine, where a loyal army was waiting. It had reached Ste. Menehould, 124 miles from Paris, when the king was recognized by the postmaster, Jean-Baptiste Drouet. Drouet managed to have him arrested a little farther away, at Varennes. Louis XVI and his family were taken back to Paris.

This episode had serious consequences. The humiliation suffered by Louis XVI outraged royalist officers, and they emigrated in large numbers. The patriots, who until then had been loyal to the king, lost confidence in him. The Assembly temporarily suspended the king's powers, and the country experienced a virtually republican government. Foreign rulers at first observed the troubles into which France had fallen without much regret, but this latest event opened their eyes to the dangers that threatened the royal family and the monarchical principle in general. The Austrian emperor, Leopold II, brother of Queen Marie Antoinette, met with the king of Prussia, Frederick William, at Pillnitz in Saxony, and together they issued a threatening manifesto on August 27, 1791.

The End of the Constituent Assembly. The king's flight also caused a split within the Assembly and the Jacobin Club. Some, such as Robespierre, sought to take advantage of the opportunity to get rid of the monarchy. Others, such as Lafayette and his friends, attempted to save Louis XVI. The Cordelier Club organized a demonstration on the Champs de Mars on July 17 to demand the deposition of the king. On Lafayette's orders the National Guard dispersed the crowd by musket fire. The fiction that Louis XVI had been "kidnapped" by aristocrats was concocted, and the king was able to recover his powers on September 14.

Two weeks later, on September 30, 1791, the Constituent Assembly dissolved itself and agreed that none of its members might serve in the next assembly. This was a noble decision but an unfortunate one, since by retiring from the scene, experienced men turned over power to incompetent and presumptuous newcomers.

II. THE LEGISLATIVE ASSEMBLY (OCTOBER 1791– SEPTEMBER 1792)

The War Policy. When the new Assembly met on October 1, 1791, it was guided by a few dynamic members of the left—about 136 deputies out of 745—who had the advantages of an active leader, Jacques Brissot; an illustrious theorist, Antoine Condorcet; and brilliant speakers. Since some of them came from Bordeaux, in the department of Gironde, they were called the Girondists. The party also had its salon, presided over by the young Madame Roland, a deputy's wife, who was steeped in the democratic theories of Rousseau.

The Girondists continually denounced the moderate ministers chosen by Louis XVI and demanded rigorous measures against émigrés and refractory priests, whom they accused of fomenting reaction. According to them, the best means of unmasking traitors and galvanizing revolutionary energy would be a general war that would rouse people everywhere against their kings. Louis XVI was willing to accept this plan, for his best counselors considered it would provide an opportunity to restore discipline in the army and recover some influence for the king. Such in particular was the idea of Charles Dumouriez, a conspiratorial but capable general who was made a minister in March 1792, along with several Girondist representatives.

On April 20, 1792, the Assembly voted by acclamation to declare war, not against the emperor but against the "king of Bohemia and Hungary," thereby indicating that the war was being fought only against "tyrants," not against the people of Germany.

June 20. The French army had become disorganized by emigration and lack of discipline. Its first offensive, against Belgium, ended in a shameful rout. The Girondists, blaming the disaster on treason, voted decrees intended to force the king into a corner—the deportation of recalcitrant priests, dissolution of the king's guard, and the concentration of 20,000 provincial National Guardsmen in Paris. When the king vetoed these decrees, the Girondists set out to intimidate him. On June 20 a crowd of 20,000 people mobilized by the popular clubs invaded the palace of the Tuileries and paraded before Louis XVI, who had been backed into the embrasure of a window. His calmness and firmness disconcerted the demonstrators, who finally withdrew, having accomplished nothing.

The Fall of the Throne (August 10, 1792). Jacobins and Cordeliers decided to be done with the king. The gravity of the danger from abroad was underlined by a decree issued by the Assembly declaring "the country in danger." The excitement of the lower classes was conveniently raised to fever pitch by the Brunswick Manifesto, a proclamation by the leader of the Austro-Prussian armies, who threatened Paris with "military execution and total destruction" if harm came to the king and his family. Volunteers from the provinces flocked to the capital. Those from Marseilles aroused the enthusiasm of the Faubourg St. Antoine by singing the stirring "Song of the Army of the Rhine," composed by Claude Rouget de Lisle and known thereafter as "The Marseillaise."

Openly prepared for, the insurrection broke out on the morning of August 10. While men from the various quarters assembled at the city hall to the sound of church bells and drums, the legal city government was neutralized and replaced by an insurrectionary commune.

The Marquis de Mandat-Grancey, leader of the various companies that defended the royal palace, was drawn into an ambush and killed. Louis XVI and his family took refuge in the hall of the Assembly. The crowd attacked the palace, which was defended by several hundred Swiss guards and aristocratic volunteers. The bloody and indecisive struggle was halted when the king ordered the defenders to lay down their arms. They were massacred in large numbers, and the palace was pillaged.

The Assembly resigned itself to suspending the king's powers and decided that the people, without distinction of wealth, would elect a national convention to draft a new constitution. An executive council of six members would temporarily run the government.

The First Terror. The provinces reacted only slightly to the violence in Paris. The Paris Commune, however, multiplied the number of arbitrary measures, imprisoned the royal family in the tower of the Temple, and filled the prisons with suspects. The Assembly voted to confiscate and sell the property of émigrés, to deport recalcitrant priests, and to take over the registration of births, marriages, and deaths, which until then had been a church function.

Georges Danton, minister of justice in the executive council, took no interest in any of these measures; he was completely occupied with preparing the country's defense against the invaders.

Other leaders, among them Jean-Paul Marat, insisted that before they marched off to war they must secure the state against treason at home by a general liquidation of suspects. Between September 2 and 5 teams of killers invaded the prisons and methodically butchered the prisoners. The exact number of victims is unknown, but it is believed to be between 1,000 and 1,400. The massacres spread to the provinces, where Marat exhorted patriots to follow Paris' example.

Valmy. A strong Prussian army, reinforced by a corps of French émigrés recruited by Louis-Joseph, the prince of Condé (great-grandson of Louis II, prince of Condé), crossed into France on August 19. Under the command of the Duke of Brunswick, it seized Longwy and Verdun and crossed the line of wooded hills of the Argonne, the last natural obstacle on the road to Paris. By a series of skillful maneuvers, General Dumouriez and General François Kellermann forced the Prussians to retreat and face their combined forces near Valmy. On September 20, impressed by the determination of the French and the effectiveness of their artillery, Brunswick decided not to give battle. Weakened and demoralized by illness and lack of food, his army retreated.

Although there was actually no battle, only a prolonged exchange of cannon fire, this "victory" of Valmy took on a symbolic meaning in the eyes of the nation and of Europe. Revolutionary France had repulsed the assault of the monarchies allied against it. "From this place and this day," wrote Goethe, who was present at Valmy, "dates a new era in the history of the world."

SUGGESTIONS FOR FURTHER READING

Brinton, Crane. *A Decade of Revolution, 1789–1799.* New York, 1963.

Cobban, Alfred. *The Social Interpretation of the French Revolution.* Cambridge, Eng., 1964.

Furet, François, and Denis Richet. *The French Revolution.* London, 1970.

Godechot, Jacques. *The Taking of the Bastille, July 14, 1789.* New York, 1970.

Hampson, Norman. *A Social History of the French Revolution.* Toronto, 1963.

Lefebvre, Georges. *The Coming of the French Revolution.* New York, 1957.

———. *The French Revolution.* 2 vols. New York, 1962.

McManners, John. *The French Revolution and the Church*. New York, 1965.

Rudé, George. *The Crowd in the French Revolution*. Oxford, 1969.

Soboul, Albert. *The French Revolution, 1787–1789, from the Storming of the Bastille to Napoleon*. New York, 1974.

Stewart, John Hall, ed. *A Documentary History of the French Revolution*. New York, 1951.

Thompson, James H. *The French Revolution*. New York, 1966.

Godechot, Jacques. *La Grande Nation: L'Expansion révolutionnaire de la France dans le monde, 1789–1799*. Paris, 1956.

Lefebvre, Georges. *La Grande Peur de 1789*. Paris, 1922.

17
The Revolution: The First Republic

Elected to establish a republican government, the Convention governed auto-cratically for three years. Its power was seized by an extremist faction, the Montagnards, and foreign and domestic dangers gave them an excuse to institute a bloody reign of terror. But they did manage to hold out against a Europe united against them. The government of the Directory, which followed the dic-tatorship of the Convention, nurtured economic and fiscal recovery with some success, but it could never establish a stable government at home or fix on a consistent foreign policy. Then, too, the war, which dragged on endlessly, en-abled a victorious general, glorified by his victories, to turn the desire for order and peace to his own benefit.

I. THE CONVENTION: DOMESTIC POLICY (SEPTEMBER 1792–OCTOBER 1795)

The Parties. Elected by a minority of revolutionary voters, the new As-sembly voted at its first session, on September 21, 1792, to abolish the monarchy and establish a republic. The extremists of the earlier Assem-bly, the Girondists, now seemed like moderates. The lawyers and bour-geois among them disapproved of the crimes committed at the beginning of September; those who had been elected from the provinces condemned the dictatorship that the Commune of Paris claimed it had the right to exercise over the state and all the departments. They were also committed to the idea of economic liberty. The Montagnards ("Men of the Mountain"), so called because they sat on the highest benches of the hall, were for the most part deputies from Paris. In permanent contact with the extremists of the popular sections, the *sans-culottes*, they were ready to resort to despotism and violence to deal with political dangers and economic difficulties.

Between these two extremes drifted the mass of deputies of the "Marsh" (*Marais*). Having no aim but to save the Revolution—and their own heads—they swung from one side to the other, depending on circumstances. This explains the amazing shifts within the Convention during the next years.

The Execution of Louis XVI. At the outset the Girondists were in control. Under their direction the Convention took several measures toward pacification. Led by Maximilien de Robespierre, the Montagnards discovered the way to regain the advantage. Louis XVI was to be placed on trial for his counterrevolutionary maneuvers and collusion with the émigrés and foreign rulers. The king's trial took place before the Convention itself. After several dramatic votes, Louis XVI was condemned to death by a narrow majority of 387 to 324. On January 21, 1793, he was guillotined on the Place de la Révolution, today the Place de la Concorde.

As the Montagnards had calculated, regicide prevented the Convention from taking any step backward and launched a fight to the death between the Revolution and its enemies, which seemed to justify the most dictatorial measures.

The Fall of the Girondists. The king's execution immediately brought England and Spain into the war. To French military reverses was added a revolt by the western provinces in the spring of 1793 (see p. 226).

Driven by poverty, the lower classes of Paris turned to the extremists known as the *Enragés* (Madmen) and demanded such measures as price controls on commodities, the requisitioning of grain, and the despoiling of the rich. They threatened to dissolve the Convention.

The Montagnards made use of this popular movement to bring down their enemies. With their approval the Commune had the Convention surrounded by several thousand citizens, who demanded the arrest of the Girondist deputies. The Assembly yielded and decreed the expulsion of twenty-nine of its members on June 2. Others, threatened with arrest, stepped down voluntarily.

In numerous provincial towns, notably Caen and Bordeaux, protests against this seizure of power gave rise to local government bodies in revolt against the dictatorship of Paris. This so-called Federalist movement was soon crushed by forces sent by the Convention. But in the southeast, rebellious royalists gave Toulon over to the British. They turned Lyons into an entrenched camp and held out from August 9 to October 9 against a besieging army dispatched by the Convention. When the city finally fell, two deputies sent by the Convention, Joseph Fouché and Jean Collot d'Herbois, carried out mass executions of rebels.

The Revolutionary Government. The Federalist movement prompted the Montagnards hastily to approve a very democratic constitution, the Constitution of the Year I. But at the same time they decided not to put it in force until peace was restored. In the meantime the government would be "revolutionary"; that is, the Convention could take any measures that circumstances required.

In practice the Assembly had no role other than to approve decrees drafted by its twenty-one specialized committees. Two of them effectively monopolized power: the Committee of Public Safety, the center of political power, and the Committee of General Security, in charge of police and revolutionary justice. The Committee of General Security exercised its authority through the Revolutionary Tribunal, directed by its prosecuting attorney, the sinister Antoine Fouquier-Tinville. Its swift verdicts could not be appealed and were carried out immediately. In the provinces the old local administrations were not officially abolished but were replaced by "national agents" sent out by the central government. They were assisted and kept under surveillance by the revolutionary committees and the branches of the Jacobin Club of Paris. Finally, the Convention sent to some departments, as it did to the armies, "representatives on mission," who were invested with dictatorial powers.

The Terror. By the device of the Terror, which was raised to the level of an institution, a handful of determined men imposed their will on the recalcitrant masses. The Law of Suspects of September 17, 1793, permitted the arrest of all presumed enemies of the Revolution. The revolutionary tribunals in Paris and in the provinces multiplied the number of death sentences until the guillotine became the symbol of the regime. The victims of the Terror numbered between 35,000 and 40,000 executed and more than 300,000 imprisoned.

Dechristianization. The Convention attempted to eliminate Christianity. For the church calendar it substituted a Revolutionary calendar, in which September 22, 1792, became the first day of Year I of the new era. The twelve months of the year bore sonorous and poetic names:

Vendémiaire, Brumaire, Frimaire; Nivôse, Pulviôse, Ventôse; Germinal, Floréal, Prairial; Messidor, Thermidor, Fructidor. Each month was divided into "decades"—ten-day periods that replaced weeks. The Commune of Paris and many others in the provinces that followed its example instituted a "religion of reason." In the cathedral of Notre Dame of Paris, a dancer from the Opera was dressed as Liberty and enthroned upon the altar. Pressure was exerted on constitutional priests to abandon their offices and to marry. Those recalcitrant priests who remained in France were hunted down and executed.

Social Measures. Pressure from the people of Paris and the needs of national defense forced the Montagnards to fix wages and commodity prices, control the distribution of food, and take drastic measures to prevent hoarding. The Ventôse Decrees of February–March 1794 provided that property confiscated from suspects was to be distributed among the patriotic poor. The Convention approved a national plan to provide subsistence to all citizens who were unable to work and to provide health care for the poor.

Leaders of the Convention believed that education, formerly a privilege usually provided by the church, should be a public service provided free by the state. Plans were prepared for a national education system, including compulsory primary schools and secondary schools open to all on the basis of merit. Top graduates would go on to state universities or professional schools. All schools were to be tuition-free, and no church influence was to be permitted in them. The plan was not realized, but it remained a model for later republicans. The Directory established about a hundred secondary schools modeled on the Convention's plan, but tuition was charged, and the advanced curriculum effectively limited enrollment to students whose parents could afford thorough preparatory studies. Two of the great French professional schools of modern times were founded by the Convention—the Ecole Polytechnique, a military engineering school (which became the model for the United States Military Academy at West Point), and the Ecole Normale Supérieure.

The royal academies were replaced in 1795 by the Institute of France, which was divided into sections for science and mathematics, moral and political sciences, and literature and fine arts.

The Dictatorship of Robespierre. By his skill in maneuvering, the firmness of his convictions, the bombastic eloquence inspired in him by Rousseau, and the austerity of his private life, Maximilien de Robespierre, "the Incorruptible," had slowly risen to the pinnacle of authority in the Convention, in the Committee of Public Safety, in the Jacobin Club, and even among the lower-class *sans-culottes*. One after another in the spring of 1794 he eliminated the factions that attacked him, first the *Enragés* or Hébertists, then the Indulgents, led by Danton. Their leaders were guillotined.

For four months Robespierre was a virtual dictator. He instituted an official religion of the Supreme Being, which held its first festival in Paris on June 8, in a great display of civic ceremony. But his reign was also marked by an acceleration of the Terror. In Paris alone 1,376 executions took place between June 10 and July 26.

9 Thermidor. While this bloody frenzy was erupting, the French armies' victories were removing the dangers that might have justified the Terror, and most of the French were sickened by it. This feeling was seized upon by those revolutionaries who for various reasons were themselves afraid of the scaffold. Early in July a coalition of Robespierre's enemies was formed. Finally, on 9 Thermidor (July 27), during a tumultuous and dramatic session, the Convention voted to arrest the "new Cromwell" and his closest collaborators. He was released from prison, however, by the Commune of Paris, which had risen in rebellion. During the night the Convention forces invaded the city hall and again arrested Robespierre, who attempted to commit suicide. The next day he was sent to the guillotine along with his followers.

The Thermidorian Reaction. Power slipped from the hands of the decimated Montagnards into those of the centrists. In their desire for a more liberal regime they were in harmony with the mass of the country, which rejected the harshness of dictatorship. The apparatus of the Revolutionary government was quickly dismantled. Political prisoners were released or pardoned, while several of the harshest Terrorists were sent to the scaffold. The state stopped supporting the constitutional clergy and established freedom and equality of religion.

The complete economic freedom restored by the Convention brought on a rapid rise in the cost of living. The lower classes of Paris saw their poverty deepen. The surviving Montagnards and *Enragés* took advantage of their desperation to stir up riots against the Convention on two occasions: April 1 and May 20, 1795. The Convention called in the army to disarm the *sans-culottes* of the working-class districts.

Royalist Intrigues. Royalists dared to strike back. In the Rhône Valley, armed bands called "Companions of Jéhu" committed bloody reprisals against the Jacobins. A body of émigrés armed by the British landed on the Quiberon Peninsula in June 1795, but they failed to link up with the rebels in the west and were captured and killed.

Taking fright, the members of the Convention hastened to approve a constitution designed to ensure power to the upper bourgeoisie. Free elections, they knew, would sweep away the republicans, so they decided that two-thirds of the new deputies had to be chosen from among the members of the outgoing assembly.

That measure outraged the royalists in Paris. The National Guard in the middle-class sections rebelled and marched on the Convention on October 5, 1795 (13 Vendémiaire). The deputy Paul Barras took command of the loyal troops of the garrison and, assisted by the young general Napoleon Bonaparte, broke up the attack.

II. THE WAR AGAINST THE EUROPEAN COALITION

The First Successes. In the last months of 1792 the armies of the Republic, having repelled the invasion, occupied Nice and Savoy, the German territories west of the Rhine, and finally Belgium, after the brilliant victory at Jemmappes won by Dumouriez on November 6. Divided into departments, these areas were annexed to France, justified by the doctrine of "natural boundaries."

The European Coalition. England could not tolerate the occupation of Belgium. The execution of Louis XVI served as a pretext to enter the war, and England brought most other European states into a general coalition against Revolutionary France.

The Insurrection in the West. At that time (March 1793) France's defenses were disorganized by insurrections at home. The most serious had erupted in the area south of the Loire—in Anjou and lower Poitou—when the Convention tried to call up soldiers there. The Vendéans (as they were wrongly called) seized several important towns, but they failed before Nantes and were exhausted by their unsuccessful attack on Granville, where they might have received help from England. Defeats at Le Mans and Savenay in December 1793 put an end to the major operations of the "Catholic and Royal Army." The insurrection continued in several western departments, however, in the form of a guerrilla war (the *Chouannerie*), despite the most savage efforts at repression, including systematic devastation and the massacre of civilians.

The Major Defeats. The main coalition army, operating in the Netherlands under the Prince of Coburg, defeated Dumouriez at Neerwinden on March 18, 1793. Threatened with arrest, Dumouriez attempted to lead his troops against the Convention and eventually crossed over to the enemy lines with his general staff. This treason demoralized and disorganized the French Army of the North, which evacuated Belgium in panic. On all the other fronts—the Rhine, the Alps, the Pyrenees—

enemy armies regained the territory lost at the end of 1792 and invaded French soil. By mid-1793 the Republic seemed to be near its end.

Carnot. The savage control exercised by the Committee of Public Safety, supported by the patriotic frenzy of part of the nation, nonetheless managed to restore the situation. One man above all deserved to be hailed as "the Organizer of victory"—Lazare Carnot, an officer in the corps of engineers and a member of the Convention and the Committee of Public Safety. A general conscription decreed on August 23, 1793, mobilized all unmarried men between the ages of eighteen and twenty-five. Now France could send into combat a truly national army that was superior in numbers to the mercenary armies of its enemies. Carnot ensured their cohesion by combining elements of the old royal army with the young volunteers and conscripts. Discipline was restored at all levels. The young generals who rose from the ranks used daring offensive tactics that disconcerted the old professionals who opposed them.

The Liberation of the Country. The Republic's salvation was due in large part to the divisions among the allied powers, who never managed to coordinate their plans and movements. In 1794 Prussia and Austria even withdrew part of their forces from the western front in order to crush a last revolt in Poland and complete the partition of that unhappy country.

Republican counteroffensives relieved the strongholds at Dunkirk and Maubeuge, in September 1793, and drove back the enemy in the east, the Alps, and the Pyrenees. Toulon was recaptured from the British in December 1793 after a long siege in which the young artillery commander Bonaparte distinguished himself.

New Conquests. The next June the Army of Sambre and Meuse, commanded by Jean-Baptiste Jourdan, defeated the Austrians under Coburg at Fleurus. Belgium and the Rhineland once again fell into the hands of the French. The Rhine itself was crossed. General Charles Pichegru took advantage of a severe winter that froze rivers and canals to make a quick sweep of Holland. Meanwhile, the French also threatened northern Italy and Catalonia.

The Treaties of 1795. The king of Prussia, in conflict with Russia over Poland, decided to make peace with the Republic. By the Treaty of Basel on April 5, 1795, he recognized France's right to annex the territories on the west bank of the Rhine.

Under pressure from the French, Holland formed a democratic and unitary republic. By the Treaty of The Hague on May 16, 1795, it ceded its provinces south of the Rhine to France.

Finally, Spain, worried by British designs on the West Indies, also withdrew from the coalition by a second treaty of Basel on July 22, 1795.

The war was not over, but Republican France, having held its own against monarchical Europe, could look to the future with confidence.

III. THE DIRECTORY (OCTOBER 1795–NOVEMBER 1799)

The Constitution of the Year III. The ingenious new constitution was devised to avoid the dictatorship of one man or one party. The electoral system ensured the power of an aristocracy of wealthy bourgeois. Elections were conducted in two stages. In the first, only citizens who were at least twenty-five years old and who paid some tax were permitted to vote. They chose the actual electors—fewer than 30,000 men qualified by a prescribed high level of wealth. It was the electors who chose the legislative assemblies and local administrations.

The legislative body consisted of two houses; one-third of each house was elected each year. The Council of Five Hundred initiated and discussed bills, and the Council of Elders rejected them or enacted them into law. The 250 members of the Council of Elders had to be at least forty years old, while those in the Council of Five Hundred had to be only thirty. These requirements reflected distrust of the young, born of experience with young revolutionary zealots in 1793–94.

The executive branch was entrusted to a Directory of five members chosen by the Elders from a list of candidates submitted by the Council of Five Hundred. One of the five was to be replaced each year.

Since the Directory did not have the right to dissolve the councils, and the councils had no means of imposing their will on the Directory, a coup d'état was the only way of resolving an impasse.

Internal Politics. The internal politics of the Directory were dominated by the determination of the former members of the Convention to keep themselves in power, along with their clientele of profiteers from the Revolution. At any cost they had to avoid either a restoration of the monarchy or a return to popular Jacobinism. In both cases they stood to lose either their heads or their recently acquired fortunes.

The first elections, which were rigged by the two-thirds decree (see p. 226), won them a majority in the assemblies. Five regicide members of the Convention were elected to the Directory. Jean-Paul Barras was the only one of the five who managed to hold his office until the end of the regime, and so came to personify it. This nobleman from Provence was intelligent and courageous, but he had become a revolutionary out of self-interest and projected the image of a cynical and corrupt rake.

The elections of the spring of 1797 brought a royalist majority to the councils. The Directory broke it by summoning the troops of the Paris garrison, under the command of General Pierre Augereau, to arrest and deport hostile deputies in the coup of 17–18 Fructidor (September 3–4, 1797). The next year the Jacobins were the victims of a similar coup on 22 Floréal (May 11, 1798). After the deportations and imprisonments following the first of these coups, the regime no longer seemed so liberal. The Catholic clergy suffered new persecutions.

The Economic and Social Situation. The state was constantly paralyzed by financial weaknesses. The badly paid bureaucrats compensated themselves by peddling their influence and selling state property. Bands of brigands called *chauffeurs* (firemen)—they tortured their victims with fire—roamed the countryside, robbing stagecoaches.

Morality declined among the new rich, particularly in Paris. A frantic pursuit of pleasure inspired the extravagant dress adopted by the fops and dandies.

The scandalous display of luxury contrasted with the poverty of the lower classes. Popular agitation in Paris found a leader in the person of Gracchus Babeuf, founder of the Society of Equals, who preached a form of early communism and was preparing to overthrow the regime by force. Warned of the plot, the Directory arrested and executed Babeuf and his accomplices in May 1797.

The War against Austria. As the coalition weakened, France was able to take the offensive. The Directory's initial objective in pushing its armies beyond the natural boundaries was to seize pawns to force its enemies to recognize its new boundaries and also to secure money. But it was soon led into a genuinely imperialistic campaign.

The British, France's most determined enemy, were invulnerable on their island, so Carnot directed the main military effort against Austria. In the spring of 1796, the two armies of Jean Moreau and Jean-Baptiste Jourdan marched across southern Germany and converged on Vienna, but the archduke Charles of Austria managed to beat them separately and forced them back across the Rhine.

The decisive victories were won by the army in Italy, originally charged only with creating a diversion. The twenty-seven-year-old general Napoleon Bonaparte maneuvered his 30,000 men with lightning speed, separated the Austrians from their Piedmontese allies, and forced the latter to sign an armistice on May 7. The victory at Lodi won him passage across the Po and on to Milan. He surrounded the defeated troops in Mantua and successively defeated four relief armies from the north at the battles of Castiglione (August 5), Bassano (September 8), Arcola (November 17), and Rivoli (January 17, 1797). The surrender of Mantua on February 2, 1797, at last brought all of northern Italy into his hands.

Despite the Directory's instructions, he pushed his army across the Alpine passes and came within sixty-two miles of Vienna. The desperate Austrians appealed for an armistice. A preliminary peace was signed at Leoben on April 18, 1797.

The Peace of Campo Formio. The final treaty was signed at Campo Formio on October 18, 1797. Austria recognized France's possession of Belgium and France's boundary on the Rhine. Representatives were to meet at Rastatt to determine the compensation to be awarded the German princes who lost land as a consequence of this shift in the boundary. Austria received most of the ancient republic of Venice, which Bonaparte summarily liquidated on a flimsy pretext. This was the price paid for Austria's recognition of the major changes in northern Italy worked out by Bonaparte—the creation of a Cisalpine Republic centered on Milan and a Ligurian Republic based on Genoa, both bound to France by similar regimes and by treaties of alliance.

The Egyptian Expedition. On his return to France, Bonaparte was hailed as a hero. His popularity irritated the Directory, and to get him out of the way it financed a fantastic undertaking he had devised to increase his personal fame—the conquest of Egypt.

On May 19, 1798, he set off from the harbor of Toulon with a fleet of fifty-five warships and 280 transports laden with 38,000 elite troops, several hundred administrators, scientists, artists, and writers—everything necessary to establish a modern state.

Seizing the island of Malta along the way, the expedition landed without difficulty near Alexandria on July 1. A single battle, the so-called Battle of the Pyramids on July 21, near Cairo, was all that Bonaparte needed to break the military feudalism of the Mamelukes, who were the real masters of the country. Several days later on August 1, the French fleet was surprised by Horatio Nelson at its anchorage at Abukir and almost annihilated. Although the French were sealed off in their conquest, Bonaparte began to organize the country as if he expected to occupy it indefinitely.

The sultan of the Ottoman Empire, the nominal ruler of the country, declared war on France and assembled an army in Syria. Bonaparte decided to march to meet it, perhaps hoping to equal the legendary exploits of Alexander the Great and return to Europe by way of Constantinople. But after crossing the Sinai desert and defeating a Turkish army in Palestine, he failed to take the fortress of St. John of Acre. He was forced to return to Egypt with his forces greatly depleted.

The news that reached him from France shortly afterward decided him to leave without warning on August 22, 1799, abandoning to their fate all those he had involved in the adventure. His successor, the brave general Jean-Baptist Kléber, was assassinated on June 14, 1800. After a humiliating surrender in 1801, what remained of the expeditionary force was finally repatriated by the British.

This fantastic epic, though disastrous in the short run, was not altogether fruitless, for it implanted in Egypt a French cultural influence that persisted there until the beginning of the twentieth century.

The Second Coalition. The news of the disaster at Abukir enabled England to regain allies on the Continent. They were ready to resume the offensive in any case, since the Directory had pursued its imperialist policy by creating "sister republics"—the Parthenopean Republic at Naples, the Helvetian in Switzerland, and the Roman in the Papal States. Pope Pius VI was abducted and taken to France. He died there on August 29, 1799.

This time Austria had the active support of Tsar Paul I, who sent an army commanded by Count Aleksandr Suvorov, a daring tactician and great leader of men. The closely pressed French armies lost all of Italy. But General André Masséna managed to inflict a serious setback on the Russians at the Battle of Zurich on August 25–26, 1799. Shortly thereafter General Guillaume Brune forced the surrender of an Anglo-Russian corps that had landed in Holland.

The End of the Directory. When Bonaparte landed at Fréjus, in southern France, on October 9, 1799, after miraculously evading the British Mediterranean fleet, the military situation no longer required his intervention. But he arrived at an opportune moment to take advantage of the general disgust with the Directory. Undermined by dissension, threatened on its right by new royalist insurrections and on its left by a reawakening Jacobinism, the government seemed to be sinking into anarchy. The former Thermidorians and two of the directors themselves, Emmanuel Sieyés and Roger Ducos, saw no salvation for their republic but a new constitution that would reinforce the executive power.

The enthusiastic welcome that Bonaparte received from the people of Paris on October 14 forced the revisionists to make use of him to carry out their plans. Everything was done to give the coup d'état a semblance of legality. On 18 Brumaire (November 9), according to the agreed-upon scenario, three of the directors submitted their resignations, and the councils voted to move to St. Cloud on the pretext of a phantom conspiracy. Bonaparte was named military commander of Paris. But the next day the Jacobins in the Council of Five Hundred exploded in outrage and even talked of declaring Bonaparte an outlaw. When the general arrived to give an explanation, he was attacked. Finally the deputies were driven from the hall by the grenadiers of the legislative body, commanded by Lucien Bonaparte, Napoleon's brother and president of the Council of Five Hundred. What remained of the councils hastily voted to turn power over to three provisional consuls—Bonaparte, Sieyès, and Ducos —while awaiting a revision of the constitution.

Seeking to consolidate the bourgeois republic, the revisionists opened the way to a one-man dictatorship.

Economic Consequences of the Revolution. The Revolution had contradictory influences on the economy. Inflation and the diversion of capital and labor to the works of war disrupted the long-term growth of productivity and the rise in incomes that had begun in the first half of the eighteenth century. On the other hand, the Revolution, in destroying the remnants of feudalism, freed the economy and the society from a myriad of restraints. It eliminated the privileged classes and made a start toward an equitable system of taxation. It freed the peasants from seignorial dues and tithes. It ended the monopolies of the guilds. It struck down internal tariff barriers and ended local diversity in laws, commercial regulations, and weights and measures, preparing the way for creation of a national market.

The disruption was temporary. The liberation was permanent, and it made possible not only resumption of the earlier economic growth but also the emergence of a capitalist economy and, in the long run, the Industrial Revolution of the nineteenth century.

Rationalism and Religion. The Revolution produced a reaction against the Enlightenment's optimistic faith in reason, progress, and the perfectibility of man. Notable French expressions of this reaction came in 1796 from two exiles, Louis de Bonald and Joseph de Maistre, who argued that a stable society must be based on the authority of the Catholic church and a divinely ordained monarchy. In France, however, their influence was scarcely felt until after the fall of the Empire in 1814. Those in France who disapproved of the Revolution and the ideas it embodied were more likely to find ideological justification for their convictions in religion, and a religious revival was beginning in the late 1790s. The first great literary expression of it did not appear, however, until 1802—François-René Chateaubriand's *Genius of Christianity*.

At the end of the century France continued to be the great bastion of rationalism. Its spokesmen occupied key places in the universities and higher professional schools and in the Institute. Science—the term then was understood to include applied science—was encouraged by the Revolutionary assemblies and taught in the schools, and it flourished. The naturalist Etienne Geoffrey Saint-Hilaire (1772–1844), for example, began his career in 1793 as a professor in the newly established Museum of Natural History, and the young Georges Cuvier (1769–1832), famed for his work on comparative anatomy, became a professor in one of the new state secondary schools in 1796 and published his first scientific papers in that year and in 1798. Napoleon Bonaparte took a team of scientists, scholars, and artists on the Egyptian expedition in 1798, and provided them with an opportunity to study the country, its history, and its flora and fauna. They were the virtual founders of the science of Egyptology.

The Arts. The Revolution freed art from ancient monopolies, aesthetic regulations, and censorship, but it also deprived it of a cultivated royal and noble clientele and turned it to political uses. Efforts were made to convert it to an instrument of moral and republican propaganda, but even then it retained the neoclassical style of the 1780s. The best results may be seen in the paintings of Jacques-Louis David (1748–1825), particularly *The Death of Marat*, a revolutionary Pietà. David became the virtual dictator of the arts under the First Republic, and he organized a number of the great Revolutionary pageants, such as the Festival of Liberty in 1792, the Festival of Unity and Indivisibility in 1793, and the Festival of the Supreme Being in 1794, all of them examples of the use of art as propaganda. In music emphasis was placed on reaching the people through outdoor performances by large instrumental and choral groups.

After 1795 the return to relative calm permitted renewed concern for the amenities of life, and a distinctive style of interior decoration and furniture design appeared. This Directory style combined prerevolutionary elegance with geometric rigor, often inspired by Greek, Etruscan, and Egyptian discoveries.

SUGGESTIONS FOR FURTHER READING

Brinton, Crane. *The Jacobins: An Essay in the New History.* New York, 1930, 1961.

Cobb, Richard. *The Police and the People: French Popular Protest, 1789–1820.* Oxford, 1970.

Herold, J. Christopher. *Bonaparte in Egypt.* New York, 1962.

Mathiez, Albert. *After Robespierre: The Thermidorean Reaction.* New York, 1964.

Palmer, Robert R. *Twelve Who Ruled: The Year of the Terror in the French Revolution.* Princeton, 1959.

Soboul, Albert. *The Parisian Sans-culottes and the French Revolution.* Oxford, 1964.

Thompson, James M. *Robespierre.* 2 vols. New York, 1964.

Thomson, David. *The Babeuf Plot: The Making of a Republican Legend.* London, 1947.

Tilly, Charles. *The Vendée.* New York, 1967.

Wilkinson, Spenser. *The Rise of General Bonaparte.* Oxford, 1930.

Woronoff, Denis. *La République bourgeoise de Thermidor à Brumaire (1794–1799).* Paris, 1972.

18
Napoleon

The Revolution destroyed the old institutions but did not succeed in consolidating liberty and equality, because the republican governments proved unable to ensure order and peace. The necessary and inevitable reaction brought to power an extraordinary personality, Napoleon Bonaparte. The new dictatorial monarchy that he founded consolidated the social results of the Revolution but temporarily destroyed its political gains. Eventually the limitless ambitions of the emperor Napoleon led to a collapse that left France weak and wasted, shorn of even the territorial gains of the Revolution.

I. THE BONAPARTE CONSULATE

The Rise of Bonaparte. Only the immense upheaval of the French Revolution could have provided the opportunities for a career as extraordinary as that of Napoleon Bonaparte. He was born on August 15, 1769, of a noble but poor family of Ajaccio, in Corsica, which had been acquired by France as recently as 1768. (See the genealogical chart.) Awarded a royal scholarship to the military school at Brienne, he became a sublieutenant in the artillery at age sixteen. After 1789 he hoped to play a political role in Corsica, but the separatist party of Pascal Paoli won out over the Jacobin party, to which Bonaparte belonged. He and his family had to take refuge in France. His decisive role at the siege of Toulon (see p. 227) won him the rank of brigadier general and the friendship of the representative on mission, Barras (December 1793). After the fall of Robespierre he languished in Paris in semidisgrace until Barras summoned him to put down the royalist insurrection of 13 Vendémiaire (October 5, 1795). It was also to Barras, now one of the five directors (see p. 228), that Bonaparte owed the Italian command that brought him fame, and even his marriage to a seductive Creole, Josephine Tascher de la Pagerie, widow of General Alexandre de Beauharnais and Barras's former mistress.

The Constitution of the Year VIII. The new constitution, practically dictated by Bonaparte, was put into effect on December 25, 1799. The plebiscite to ratify the fait accompli after the coup did not take place until the following February. Of 7 million potential voters, only 3 million cast affirmative ballots; the rest abstained.

Once this gesture to the principle of sovereignty was made, the citizens' electoral role was limited to making up local, departmental, and national lists of prominent men by a graduated selection process.

The pivot of the regime was the first consul, named for ten years with full executive powers and even a share of legislative power, since it was his responsibility to propose and promulgate laws. The other two consuls served only as window dressing.

Scarcely less important was the role of the Senate. This assembly of eighty members, appointed for life, was originally named by Bonaparte and Sieyès. The Senate was the guardian of the constitution and a virtual electoral college as well, since it chose from the lists of prominent men the consuls and the members of the two legislative assemblies—the 100-member Tribunate, which discussed drafts of bills without approving them, and the 300-member Legislature, which accepted or rejected bills transmitted by the Tribunate without discussing them.

The Council of State, a revival of the old Royal Council, was a "brain trust" in the service of the first consul; it drew up laws and decrees and was also a tribunal that heard all cases involving the administration.

The Reestablishment of Order. The Law of 28 Pluviôse, Year VIII (February 17, 1800), ensured the central government's control over the country, effectively extinguishing the practice of democracy on the local level, where it might have served its apprenticeship. In the departments, arrondissements (which replaced districts), and communes, power was exercised not by elected officials, but by officeholders named in Paris: prefects, subprefects, mayors.

The first consul intervened personally to complete the great work of unifying the various law codes used in France before 1789 and the hundreds of laws passed by the Revolutionary assemblies. The Civil Code, promulgated on March 21, 1804, confirmed and made permanent the Revolutionary legislation that was to become the fundamental law of modern French society—the abolition of feudal privileges, equality before the law, freedom of conscience, secularization of the state, free choice of occupation, and protection of property rights. The Criminal Code and the Criminal Procedures Code established safeguards against arbitrary arrest on criminal charges and ensured equal judicial treatment and equal punishment for all. On the other hand, the Civil Code made women legally subject to their fathers or husbands. The law codes proved to be effective vehicles to carry the principles of the Revolution across Europe.

By instituting efficient and strict procedures for the assessment and collection of taxes and the disbursement of public funds, Napoleon brought order to the state's finances. He balanced the budget, and when emergencies required additional revenues, he raised taxes or cut ordinary expenditures, avoiding the Revolutionary governments' blunder of recklessly printing paper money. In 1801 the principal bankers of Paris were encouraged to join together to found the Bank of France, a central bank created to perform certain financial operations for the state, to serve as the lender of last resort for the national credit market, and to issue paper money.

National Reconciliation. Indicating his desire to bring together the best elements of the old and new societies in the country's service, Bonaparte drew officials from among republicans and moderate royalists. Political prisoners were freed, and émigrés were permitted to return without penalty. The insurgents in the west were disarmed by a mixture of concessions and firmness.

The work of pacification found its most significant expression in the concordat signed in Paris on July 16, 1801, by Cardinal Consalvi on behalf of Pope Pius VII, marking the reconciliation of the Catholic church with Revolutionary France. The pope accepted the nationalization of church property; the dioceses would be reorganized to fit into the departmental administration; and a new episcopate would be established by the procedures used under the old monarchy, with the head of the state naming the bishops and the pope conferring their religious authority. In exchange, the constitutional schism was ended, and the Catholic clergy and worship were protected and paid for by the state.

This arrangement encountered lively opposition from the assemblies and even within the government. To dampen it, Bonaparte added

The Bonapartes

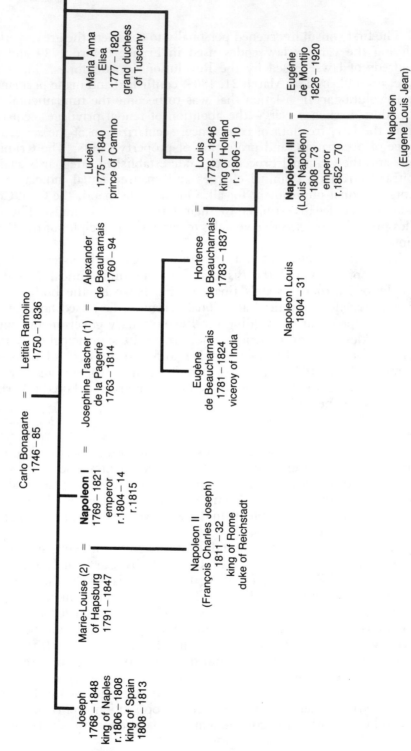

Carlo Bonaparte = Letitia Ramolino
1746 – 85   1750 – 1836

Joseph
1768 – 1848
king of Naples
r.1806 – 1808
king of Spain
1808 – 1813

Marie-Louise (2) = Napoleon I = Josephine Tascher (1) = Alexander
of Hapsburg   1769 – 1821   de la Pagerie   de Beauharnais
1791 – 1847   emperor   1763 – 1814   1760 – 94
                     r.1804 – 14
                     r.1815

Lucien
1775 – 1840
prince of Camino

Maria Anna
Elisa
1777 – 1820
grand duchess
of Tuscany

Napoleon II
(François Charles Joseph)
1811 – 32
king of Rome
duke of Reichstadt

Eugène
de Beauharnais
1781 – 1824
viceroy of India

Hortense
de Beaucharnais
1783 – 1837

Louis
1778 – 1846
king of Holland
r.1806 – 10

Napoleon Louis
1804 – 31

Napoleon III
(Louis Napoleon)
1808 – 73
emperor
r.1852 – 70

Eugénie
de Montijo
1826 – 1920

Napoleon
(Eugene Louis Jean)
1856 – 79
prince imperial

The Bonapartes

Carlo Bonaparte 1746 – 85 = Letitia Ramolino 1750 – 1836

Pauline (Charlotta) 1780 – 1825 m(1)general Leclerc m(2)prince Camilo Borghese

Caroline (Maria Annunciata) 1782 – 1839 m.Joaquim Murat king of Naples r.1808 – 15

Napoleon Archille 1801 – 47

Napoleon Lucien Charles 1803 – 78

Jerome 1784 – 1860 king of Westphalia r.1807 – 14 m(1)Elizabeth Paterson

Catherine (2) of Württemberg 1783 – 1835

Victor Emmanuel II king of Italy r.1861 – 78

Matilde 1820 – 1904 m.Anatoli Demidov

Napoleon (Joseph Paul Charles) (Jerome) 1822 – 91 = Clotilde of Savoy

Charles Joseph 1851 – 1921 U.S. secretary of the navy 1905 – 1906, U.S. attorney general 1906 – 1909

Victor 1862 – 1926 = Clementine of Belgium

Louis Napoleon 1914 – head of the house of Bonaparte

to the concordat several "organic articles" that more closely subordinated the church to the state in the spirit of the old Gallicanism. Bonaparte was to go even further in using the church for state purposes, for he regarded the clergy as a kind of moral police force, assigned the task of ensuring the people's submission.

Foreign Pacification. The French defeats of the summer of 1799 left the Austrians virtual masters of northern Italy. In the spring of 1800 only the stronghold of Genoa, which was defended by André Masséna and besieged by the army of the Austrian general Michael von Melas, still held out. In mid-May, Bonaparte crossed the Great Saint Bernard Pass, which was thought to be not yet open for the year, and suddenly appeared at the rear of the Austrian positions. He entered Milan without firing a shot. Threatened with encirclement, Melas retreated hastily eastward. On June 14 he clashed with Bonaparte's army on the plain of Marengo. Defeated, he signed an armistice.

When peace negotiations did not bear fruit, hostilities resumed at the end of November 1800. The striking victory won by General Jean-Victor Moreau on December 3 at Hohenlinden, in Bavaria, finally forced Austria to submit to the conditions dictated by Bonaparte.

The Treaty of Luneville, signed on February 9, 1801, once again gave France the west bank of the Rhine. In addition Austria surrendered Italy, to Bonaparte's delight; now he could rearrange its boundaries and governments as he pleased.

With Russia also withdrawing from the coalition, Britain found itself isolated and in the grip of serious economic difficulties. Henry Addington, a liberal minister who favored peace, replaced William Pitt, France's implacable enemy, on March 14, 1801. Hostilities ceased on October 1. The final treaty, signed at Amiens on March 25, 1802, established a peace that was inconclusive and riddled with ambiguities. Nonetheless, it ended a decade of war and was hailed with demonstrations of popular rejoicing in both countries.

The Consulate for Life. The restoration of peace raised the prestige of the first consul to new heights. He used it to consolidate his personal power. Bonaparte had himself declared consul for life on August 2, 1801. At the same time, the constitution was amended to reduce the role of the legislative assemblies and reinforce those of the first consul and the Senate. The Senate could henceforth modify the constitution by a simple *senatus consultum*, without a popular vote.

Royalist Conspiracies. At the beginning the royalists had hoped that Bonaparte would crown his work by restoring the Bourbon monarchy, but he disdainfully rejected the pretender's advances. Some extremists then resorted to violence. A first attempt to assassinate Bonaparte, by exploding a keg of gunpowder and scrap iron as he passed by, failed on December 24, 1800. In August 1803 Georges Cadoudal, a leader of the Breton guerrillas, went secretly to Paris to make plans to eliminate Bonaparte, and there he made contact with several enemies of the dictatorship. The plot was exposed and a state of siege was declared in Paris. Cadoudal was hunted down and arrested on March 9, 1804. He and seven accomplices were guillotined.

Bonaparte extended his vendetta to the Bourbon family. He ordered the kidnapping of the duke of Enghien, who lived close to the French border in the grand duchy of Baden. The young prince was taken to Vincennes. On March 21, 1804, after a farcical trial, he was executed by a firing squad. This murder, combined with the violation of foreign territory, aroused the horror of foreign courts and French royalists.

Bonaparte as Emperor. But at the same time Bonaparte reassured the senators who as members of the Convention had voted for the execution of Louis XVI in 1793, and persuaded them to transform the consular dictatorship into a new monarchy. A *senatus consultum* of May 18, 1804, also called the Constitution of the Year XII, proclaimed Bonaparte hereditary emperor under the title of Napoleon I.

Napoleon wanted to consecrate his imperial title twice over, once by a plebiscite—which duly gave him 500,000 more votes than in 1800 —and once by a religious coronation that would eclipse those of the kings of France at Rheims. He was the new Charlemagne: he wanted the pope, and in his own capital. Pius VII submitted to this unprecedented demand, and the sumptuous and theatrical ceremony was held in the Cathedral of Notre Dame of Paris on December 2, 1804.

II. FRANCE UNDER THE EMPIRE

The Despotism. Never had France known a greater concentration of power in the hands of one man. Endowed with a rapid, penetrating, and attentive mind and an amazing capacity for work, the emperor occupied himself with the smallest details. He tolerated neither discussion nor opposition from his subordinates. Ministers and generals were merely agents for transmission or execution of orders. Only two men among them had the stature to pursue a personal policy—Charles de Talleyrand, at the Ministry of Foreign Affairs, and Joseph Fouché, at the Ministry of Police.

Fouché covered the entire country with the nets of the first police state of modern times: a network of official and secret informers, a "black cabinet" that watched private correspondence, and censorship over newspapers (reduced to four in Paris), all other printed matter, and theatrical productions. An order from the emperor, the minister of police, or even a prefect was enough to have a person arrested or to require him to move to an assigned residence. At the beginning of 1814 the number of people held in state prisons without trial rose to 2,500—far fewer, it is true, than in the France of the Terror and in many states since then. Napoleon was intelligent—or humane—enough to realize that by limiting repression he could secure the effects of the Terror without antagonizing public opinion.

The New Aristocracy. During the period of the Consulate, Napoleon attempted to create a new aristocracy of merit—the Legion of Honor. It in fact became a simple decoration.

The establishment of the Empire led to the creation of a court in imitation of the old royal court, with an assortment of grand officers, chamberlains, ladies of honor, pages, and equerries. Napoleon also sought to create a new hierarchical nobility. At the summit were the members of the Bonaparte family, who had become French princes and were well provided for; then thirty large hereditary fiefs, established for the most part in Italy, which brought their holders the title of prince or duke. (Talleyrand, for example, was prince of Benevento, and Fouché, the former regicide, was duke of Otranto.) Titles of nobility—count and baron—also went with the chief military and civil offices. Thus the social inequalities abolished by the Revolution were revived.

Society. Nonetheless, the Napoleonic system contributed to the rise of the bourgeois class. The political institutions gave to the bourgeoisie the right to participate in public life and, practically speaking, access to administrative posts and secondary education, which was monopolized by the Imperial University in its *lycées*. The official encouragement given to bankers, businessmen, and industrialists, as well as the general prosperity, further contributed to its rise.

The rural population continued to swallow up national lands, and the Civil Code's provisions for equal inheritances increased the number of small landowners.

Napoleon's rule had mixed effects on the working class. Real wages increased, and diet and dress improved—at least until the economic crisis of 1811–12. On the other hand, the *livret*, or worker passport, without which a worker could not legally travel or be employed, added to the serious restrictions on freedom of action and movement imposed by the Chapelier Law of 1791, which remained in force (see p. 213). Relations between workers and employers in the last difficult years of the Empire became increasingly tense and hostile.

The Economy. The economic picture in the fifteen years of Napoleon's rule is mixed. Agriculture benefited from the introduction of some new commerical crops, such as sugar beets, but generally the old ways of cultivation and land management persisted. Neither yields nor agricultural incomes changed significantly.

Overseas commerce, which had flourished in the eighteenth century, suffered disastrously from the naval and economic warfare with England. Bordeaux, still a prosperous international port at the turn of the century, now confined its shipping to coastal waters and its role to that of a regional port. Marseilles suffered a similar decline, and the ports of Brittany and the Channel coast suffered nearly total paralysis.

The industrial outlook was brighter. Industry benefited from the introduction of new technology, as in the cotton textile and chemical industries; from large and continuing orders from the army; and from the closing off of British competition in European markets. Still there was no substantial increase in productivity. No definitive records of industrial production were kept, but a recent careful estimate places industrial production in the years 1803–12 a modest 13 percent above that of the 1780s.

Population. In 1800 the minister of the interior ordered the newly appointed prefects to make a complete count of all persons domiciled in their departments. This first national census reported a population of 27,349,000, about the same as in 1789. The census of 1806 showed a population of 29,107,000. In the next eight years it scarcely changed; population numbered 29,340,000 in 1814. Battle deaths, estimated at about 900,000 in the Napoleonic years, account only partially for that minimal growth. The legal requirement that estates be divided among all surviving children, the growing practice of birth control, and increasing alienation of the public from the teachings of the church helped to reduce the birth rate to unprecedentedly low levels.

Education. Napoleon was interested in education primarily as a means to provide trained officers and government officials, and he took care that it was controlled by the central government. He established the Imperial University, an administrative organization that directed the entire national education system, from primary school through the universities and professional schools. Primary education was left to municipal and private initiatives, and neither the Consulate nor the Empire did much to increase its availability. At the heart of Napoleon's interest and his system were the secondary schools, forty-five *lycées* created to train the civil officials required by the expanding imperial administration and to prepare young men for schools of medicine, law, and engineering. *Lycée* students wore uniforms, lived under near-military discipline, and followed a curriculum prescribed by the Imperial University in Paris.

The requirement that students pay tuition fees ensured that these schools would draw their students largely from the bourgeoisie.

Arts and Sciences. Few French rulers did more than Napoleon to encourage the arts and sciences, and under him Paris regained its position as the artistic and intellectual capital of Europe. He saw the arts as an instrument of propaganda to support his regime, a concern reflected in much of the painting, sculpture, architecture, and literature of the time. The arts were by no means limited to this role, however, or to official styles.

In painting activity was intense and varied. Jacques-Louis David was the official painter, and he and his students recorded the great events of the imperial epic in heroic canvases in the neoclassical style. But some of them, and many others, went in quite different directions —toward genre painting, landscapes, primitives. The young Théodore Géricault's (see p. 265) first paintings heralded the new Romantic age.

Literature had its share of official hagiography, and Chateaubriand won official favor with his *Genius of Christianity* because it concurred with Napoleon's policy of religious restoration. Censorship was less rigorous than under the Revolutionary governments, and literary production was large and varied. Yet, except for the books of Chateaubriand and Madame de Staël (1766–1819), it included no memorable works.

Neoclassicism continued to dominate architectural style, and, combined with Napoleon's taste for the grand and monumental, it produced such monuments as the Arch of Triumph of the Etoile, the Church of the Madeleine, and the Vendôme Column, a copy of Trajan's Column in Rome.

The nearest approach to a distinctive Empire style came in interior decoration, especially in furniture design. Like the Directory style, which it continued, it drew on Greek, Roman, and Etruscan models, and especially on Egyptian motifs.

The scientific community enjoyed the emperor's interest and support, and it included a galaxy of names that still shine in the history of science. Among them were the mathematician Charles-Louis Lagrange (1736–1813), the astronomer and physicist Pierre La Place (1749–1827), and the chemist Claude Berthollet (1748–1822). The Ecole Polytechnique was then turning out a generation of young scientists who were to revolutionize modern science in the coming decades and make Paris the world's center of scientific research and education.

The Opposition. Despite its many accomplishments, the Napoleonic regime never succeeded in eliminating widespread opposition in all social classes.

The bourgeoisie chafed under the yoke of army and police, which limited their freedom of expression. The lower classes especially despised the *droits réunis* (taxes on consumption) and conscription. Even in the upper echelons of government many people disapproved of the policy of continual wars and conquest.

Finally, Napoleon's rude treatment of the pope alienated the clergy and the mass of Catholics, whose gratitude he had initially won by the concordat of 1801. In May 1809, on the pretext of securing enforcement of the continental blockade, the emperor decreed the annexation of Rome and the Papal States. Pius VII responded by excommunicating the emperor. On the night of July 5–6, 1809, he was taken from his palace by a French detachment and held in captivity at Savona. Later, in May 1812, Napoleon transferred him to Fontainebleau, where he was kept in close confinement. Pius VII did not regain his freedom until 1814. In the interim, the pope embarrassed the emperor by denying the legitimacy of his second marriage (see p. 250), and even more so by refusing to install the bishops the emperor named. Napoleon tried to get around the difficulty by calling a council of the bishops of his empire in 1811, but the bishops (including the emperor's own uncle, Cardinal Fesch, archbishop of Lyons) sided with the Holy See.

III. THE NAPOLEONIC WARS

The War against England. British merchants soon regretted the Peace of Amiens, which permitted French trade to compete with theirs once again. British leaders grew disturbed by Bonaparte's feverish activity as he moved pawns on the world chessboard—in the Mediterranean, in India, and particularly in the West Indies, where he dispatched a powerful expedition to recover the large island of Santo Domingo. In 1801 he also secured from Spain the return of former French Louisiana in exchange for the installation of a Spanish prince on the throne of Tuscany.

In May 1803 a conflict over Malta, which England refused to surrender, in violation of the Treaty of Amiens, served as a pretext for a break that both sides wanted.

Bonaparte revived plans to invade England, and 150,000 men and 1,200 barges were assembled at Boulogne. But communications difficulties prevented the French and Spanish fleets from coordinating their movements and controlling the English Channel long enough for Napoleon to move his army to the enemy coast. In mid-August 1805 Napoleon learned simultaneously of his fleet's latest failure and of the formation of the third coalition. He abandoned his plans for an invasion in order to lead the army assembled at Boulogne against his enemies on the Continent.

The large-scale maneuvers of the opposing fleets reached their climax off the Spanish coast on October 21, 1805. In the Battle of Trafalgar the British fleet under Admiral Nelson annihilated a Franco-Spanish fleet of thirty-three vessels. Even though Napoleon was victorious on land, he could never again realistically hope to humble England.

The Third Coalition. The Continental powers were becoming alarmed at the cool audacity with which Napoleon intervened in neighboring countries in order to strengthen his own dominance. In 1803 he had himself recognized as "mediator" of the Helvetic Republic, then transformed it into the Swiss Confederation, which became a French satellite. The antique structure of the Holy Roman Empire was totally upset by the Imperial Recess of 1803, imposed on the Imperial Diet by the French, which reduced the number of independent German states from 360 to 82. The Cisalpine Republic, which in 1802 had become the considerably expanded Italian Republic with Napoleon as president, became a kingdom in 1805. Napoleon had himself crowned its king and attached the territory of Genoa.

In April 1805 Tsar Alexander I allied Russia with England to force France to return to its former boundaries. Austria joined the coalition on August 9 and was followed by Sweden and Naples.

At this news Napoleon quickly led his Grand Army from the Channel coast to Bavaria. He encircled the Austrian army of General Charles Mack at Ulm and forced it to surrender on October 20. The French army then moved down the Danube Valley like a flood, captured Vienna on November 15, and marched to meet the Russian and Austrian armies, which had linked up in Moravia. The stunning victory of Austerlitz on December 2, 1805, has remained in the annals of military history as the model Napoleonic battle. While the remnants of the Russian army withdrew to the east, the emperor of Austria was compelled to sign the Treaty of Pressburg, by whose terms he surrendered all his territories in Italy and southern Germany.

The Fourth Coalition. Prussia had remained uninvolved, as Napoleon had promised to cede Hanover, which had been taken from England in 1803, as the price of Prussian neutrality. There was a powerful anti-French party, however, at the court of Berlin. Napoleon strengthened its arguments by his reckless redrawing of the political map of Germany. The old Holy Roman Empire disappeared, giving way to a Confederation of the Rhine, which brought the southern and western states together under the supreme authority of a "protector" (Napoleon, of course) who would direct its foreign policy and command its armies. Included in the Confederation was a new state established on the east bank of the Rhine, the grand duchy of Berg, which Napoleon awarded to Joachim Murat, his brother-in-law. Other members of the imperial clan were similarly provided with crowns: Joseph, the older brother, became king of Naples; Louis, the younger brother, king of Holland; Eugène de Beauharnais, the stepson, viceroy of Italy and son-in-law of the king of Bavaria.

During the summer of 1806 the king of Prussia, Frederick William III, conducted secret negotiations with Russia, and on October 1 he ordered Napoleon to evacuate Germany as far as the Rhine. The emperor was at Bamberg when he received this ultimatum on October 7. On the fourteenth the Prussian army was annihilated at the twin battles of Jena and Auerstadt, and on October 27 Napoleon made his entry into Berlin.

The Russians were still to be dealt with. In December Napoleon occupied part of Poland. In midwinter a Russian army attempted to relieve the siege of Danzig. Rapidly assembling his forces, Napoleon caught up with the Russians at Eylau, where on February 9, 1807, an indecisive and bloody battle took place in a snowstorm.

The emperor returned to Warsaw, reformed his army, and in the spring resumed the offensive. This time he defeated the Russians decisively at Friedland on June 14, 1807. Tsar Alexander I was forced to give in. At a theatrical meeting on a raft in the middle of the Niemen River, the two emperors dramatized their reconciliation. They sealed it by the Treaty of Tilsit on July 8, 1807.

Prussia paid the penalty: it lost all it had acquired in the east by the partition of Poland. Those provinces were brought together in the duchy of Warsaw and given to Napoleon's ally, the king of Saxony. Prussia's possessions west of the Elbe River, with other territory added on, became the kingdom of Westphalia, with Jerome Bonaparte, the youngest of Napoleon's brothers, as king. As for the tsar, he only pledged to declare war on England.

The Continental Blockade. Once again England alone remained intractable and inaccessible. Napoleon sought to break it by economic warfare. The decrees of Berlin (November 21, 1806) and Milan (December 17, 1807) closed the Continent to British trade by ordering the seizure of any vessel, even a neutral one, that carried British merchandise or merely called at a British port.

Despite some privations among the English people, the "Continental blockade" never posed a mortal threat to them. To a certain degree it helped French industry, but it accelerated the decay of the major French seaports. More important, the desire to render the blockade more effective led Napoleon to annex new territories on the North Sea and in Italy and to commit himself to the fatal adventure of a war in Spain.

The Peninsular War. Portugal had refused to break with England, so Napoleon made an agreement with the Spanish government to occupy and partition that small country. A French army commanded by General Andoche Junot entered Lisbon in November 1807, and the royal family fled to Brazil. Napoleon seized the opportunity to remove the weak and corrupt government of the old Spanish king, the Bourbon Charles IV, who was totally dominated by Manuel de Godoy, the queen's favorite. Using the pretext of arbitrating a conflict that had arisen between Charles IV and his son Ferdinand, Napoleon brought them to Bayonne and on May 5, 1808, forced both of them to abdicate. Joseph Bonaparte was immediately made king of Spain, while his brother-in-law Joachim Murat, who had already occupied Madrid, was ordered to replace Joseph as king of Naples

This outrage was met by a patriotic uprising of the Spanish people. A national junta met in Seville and organized resistance in the name of Ferdinand VII. An initial great triumph on July 22 gave the resistance irresistible momentum—the humiliating surrender of a French division trapped in the desolate pass at Baylen. The Portuguese revolted in their turn and were soon supported by a British force commanded by Sir Arthur Wellesley, later the duke of Wellington. Junot was forced to abandon his conquest by signing a convention of surrender at Cintra on August 30, 1808.

Napoleon decided to intervene himself. To do so he was obliged to withdraw a large part of his troops in Germany and to assure himself of the neutrality of Tsar Alexander. In September 1808 he staged an elaborate congress at Erfurt, in Saxony, attended by the tsar and some two score German kings and princes. There the alliance with Russia was renewed and nominally strengthened. From Erfurt Napoleon went to Spain, personally leading an army of 150,000 veterans. Without much difficulty he occupied Madrid on December 4, and from there he loosed a flood of decrees intended to remake the kingdom. Suddenly in mid-January 1809 the emperor quit Spain, leaving to his marshals the task of completing the pacification.

The task proved as impossible as it was costly. For the first time the Napoleonic armies confronted not the usual mercenary or conscript forces of kings, but fanatic guerrilla fighters moved by a moral force as potent as the Revolutionary idealism of the French. His troops, organized, skilled, and experienced as they were, could not overcome the guerrillas. Moreover, the British came to support the Spanish resistance. In 1811 Napoleon gave Marshal Masséna the task of dislodging the British from Portugal. Wellington not only repulsed him but took the offensive, drove King Joseph from Madrid, inflicted the decisive defeat of Vitoria on the French in June 1813, and pushed them back into France at the end of 1813. The final victory of the Allies came early in 1814.

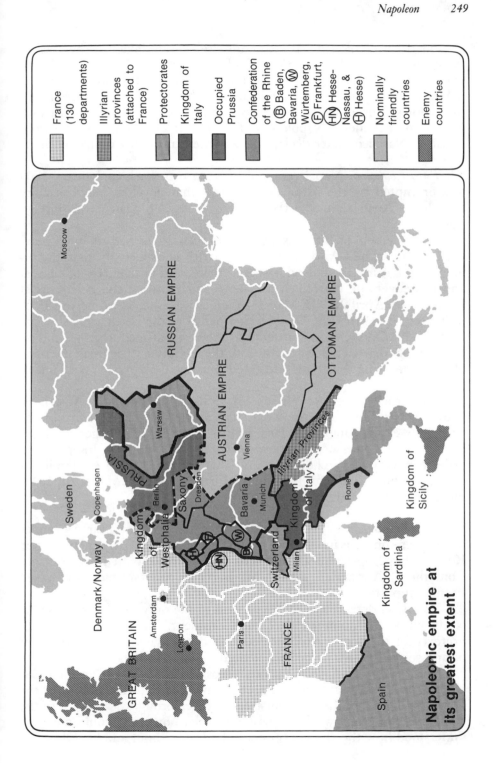

Napoleonic empire at its greatest extent

Legend:
- France (130 departments)
- Illyrian provinces (attached to France)
- Protectorates
- Kingdom of Italy
- Occupied Prussia
- Confederation of the Rhine (Ⓑ Baden, Bavaria, Ⓦ Würtemberg, Ⓕ Frankfurt, ⒽⓃ Hesse-Nassau, & Ⓗ Hesse)
- Nominally friendly countries
- Enemy countries

Moscow

RUSSIAN EMPIRE

AUSTRIAN EMPIRE

OTTOMAN EMPIRE

Warsaw

Vienna

Illyrian Provinces

PRUSSIA

Sweden

Denmark/Norway

Copenhagen

Berlin

Saxony

Dresden

Bavaria

Munich

Kingdom of Italy

Rome

Kingdom of Westphalia

Ⓗ Ⓦ Ⓑ Ⓕ ⒽⓃ

Switzerland

Milan

Kingdom of Sardinia

Kingdom of Sicily

GREAT BRITAIN

Amsterdam

London

Paris

FRANCE

Spain

On the military side, the war unwisely undertaken in the Iberian Peninsula took the lives of 300,000 of the best French troops and provided England with a base of operations on the Continent. On the political side, Spain's example encouraged the spirit of resistance among the peoples of occupied countries, particularly—and ironically—Spain's American colonies. Napoleon's failure undermined his position. "Spain," Napoleon later declared, "was the cancer that destroyed me."

The Fifth Coalition. Napoleon's sudden return to Paris in January 1809 was prompted by the nationalist ferment that developed in Germany and drove Austria to take the lead in a crusade against the foreign power.

With the help of British subsidies, the Austrians had rebuilt a powerful army. In mid-April Archduke Charles unexpectedly took the offensive in Bavaria. Napoleon hastened there, and in five days of combat and maneuvers he regrouped his army and repulsed the Austrians at Eckmühl on April 22. On May 11 Vienna was once again occupied. A first attempt to cross the Danube met defeat at the Battle of Essling on May 21–22. On the second attempt Napoleon managed to cross, and on July 5–6 he waged a bloody battle with the archduke Charles on the plain of Wagram. The Austrians, defeated but not destroyed, asked for an armistice.

The peace signed at Vienna on October 14 deprived Austria of additional territory, but the worst was averted by the sacrifice of the emperor's eldest daughter, Marie Louise of Hapsburg. Eager to assure himself of a successor, Napoleon divorced the empress Josephine in order to marry the archduchess and thereby enter the great family of kings. His hopes were fulfilled by the birth of a son on March 20, 1811. He gave him the title of king of Rome.

The Russian Campaign. The French alliance had brought Tsar Alexander more than one disappointment. The blockade in particular ruined Russia's large agricultural landlords and merchants. Under pressure from them, Alexander opened his ports to neutral trade and taxed French imports.

Napoleon determined to put an end to the only power still capable of disputing his domination of the Continent. There was no lack of pretexts for the break. An enormous military force was gathered, numbering some 500,000 men, half of them from vassal states.

This "army of twenty nations" crossed the Niemen on June 24, 1812. The Russian armies withdrew, leaving a void in the path of the invaders. Two months of exhausting marches brought Napoleon to the approaches of Moscow. The Russian people, however, would not have understood how the "holy city" could be lost without a fight. Old Mar-

[handwritten margin note: sacrifice? How does this arranged m. differ from many others, such as Henry VI of Eng w/ Catherine, d. of Charles VI? Napoleon limited the old ways]

shal Mikhail Kutuzov therefore gave battle at Borodino, on the Moscow River, at a site carefully chosen and fortified with earthen redoubts. The indecisive and extraordinarily bloody battle, on September 7, killed 50,000 Russians and 30,000 Frenchmen. A week later, on September 14, Napoleon entered Moscow. But any resources that the city might have offered were almost immediately destroyed by a huge fire. Napoleon lingered there for more than a month, waiting in vain for peace feelers.

When he finally decided to retreat, on October 19, winter was already well on its way. Harassed by Cossacks and partisans, the army managed to force its way across the Beresina River on November 28–29, but then the increasing cold and hunger killed soldiers by the thousands. Eventually only 100,000 soldiers managed to reach Germany. When he arrived at Vilna on December 5, Napoleon turned the command over to his brother-in-law Murat, king of Naples, and returned in haste to Paris to resume control over a country shaken by the catastrophe.

The Campaigns of 1813 in Germany. The arrival of the Russians at the German border encouraged the king of Prussia to resume the struggle against Napoleon. The French armies were forced to withdraw to the Elbe.

In the spring of 1813 Napoleon resumed the offensive in Saxony. The two victories he won at Lützen and Bautzen, on May 2 and 20, enabled him at first to force his opponents back across the Oder River, but the exhaustion and inexperience of his army, which had been hastily assembled at the beginning of the year, induced him to accept Austria's offer of mediation and to sign an armistice on June 4. The peace negotiations, guided by Metternich, were wrecked by bad faith on both sides. On August 10 Austria, Russia, and Prussia formed a "Grand Alliance." They were joined by Sweden and England, which provided financial aid to the other allies. Napoleon once more defeated an Austro-Prussian army, this time before Dresden on August 26–27, but the losses suffered by his lieutenants in a series of secondary engagements counterbalanced his success. The allies finally managed to concentrate all their available forces—320,000 men—near Leipzig. Napoleon had only 160,000 soldiers there, for he insisted on leaving almost as many in the various strongholds of Germany. The gigantic and furious Battle of the Nations lasted three days, from October 16 to 18, and ended in Napoleon's total defeat. The remains of his army, scarcely 40,000 men, retreated to the Rhine. Behind them the German sovereigns, pressed by their subjects, rallied to the European coalition.

The Campaign of France, 1814. As they were about to begin the decisive struggle in France, the allies proclaimed that they were waging war not on the French nation but only on the emperor. Napoleon, looking to satisfy public opinion, which demanded peace at any price, agreed to negotiate while fighting, but the meaningless "congress" of the Châtillon, from February 4 to March 19, 1814, was a diplomatic comedy played by both sides.

The allied armies, more than 250,000 men strong, penetrated France early in 1814. Napoleon had only 70,000 men to oppose them, but his military genius seemed for a moment to be capable of redressing a desperate situation. The two main allied armies, commanded by the Prussian Gebhard von Blücher and the Austrian prince Karl von Schwarzenberg, separated to march on Paris. The emperor, moving rapidly against one after the other, defeated them and drove them eastward.

At first thrown into disarray, the allies tightened their alliance with England, and by the Pact of Chaumont on March 1, 1814, each pledged not to make a separate peace and to furnish the coalition with 150,000 men.

Napoleon faced this determined coalition with a deteriorating army and eroding popular support. He himself lacked the vigor and ambition of his youth. His top commanders, now middle-aged rich men with much to lose, were reluctant to take risks for additional rewards and glories. The country was exhausted by a quarter century of war, increasingly resentful of conscription and mounting taxes, and disillusioned by Napoleon's multiplying defeats. In Paris supporters of the Bourbons were already plotting his replacement.

The offensive resumed at the beginning of March. This time Napoleon, overwhelmed by numbers, suffered several reverses. He then conceived the rash scheme of moving into Lorraine in order to relieve the besieged French garrisons there and to cut the invaders off from their bases. But Tsar Alexander, informed of the defeatism that prevailed in Paris, persuaded his allies to march on the capital. It was defended by only 40,000 irregular troops. After a day of fighting at the city gates, Marshals Jeannot de Moncey and Auguste de Marmont signed an honorable surrender on March 30. Joseph Bonaparte, president of the Regency Council, fled to Blois with the empress Marie Louise, the little king of Rome, and the principal dignitaries. At noon on March 31 Tsar Alexander and the king of Prussia made their entry into Paris.

The departure of the regency left the field free to the intrigues of Talleyrand. He succeeded in convincing Alexander that only the Bourbons could rally the general support of the nation. A fait accompli worked in their favor, for the entry of the British into Bordeaux on March 12 enabled the royalists to display the white flag of the monarchy to the acclaim of the people in the streets. On the evening of

March 31 the Allies announced that they would no longer negotiate with Napoleon. The next day, April 1, the senators who had remained in Paris named a provisional government headed by Talleyrand, while the city council of Paris posted a proclamation demanding that the emperor be deposed. On April 3 the Senate announced his deposition.

The Fall of the Empire. Napoleon, however, moved toward the capital in forced marches. He halted at Fontainebleau to regroup what remained of his troops with the intention of launching a counteroffensive. But his marshals refused to consider a struggle that would turn Paris into a battlefield. On April 4 the emperor abdicated in favor of his son. For a moment the tsar appeared to favor this solution, but it was learned that Marshal Marmont had abandoned Napoleon and placed his troops at the disposal of the provisional government. Alexander and the French marshals then demanded unconditional abdication. On April 6 Napoleon at last gave in.

The allied rulers proved generous. By the terms of the Treaty of Fontainebleau, Napoleon retained his title of emperor and received sovereignty over the island of Elba and an annual pension of 2 million francs. On April 20 he left for exile after delivering a moving farewell to his old guard, assembled in the courtyard of the château of Fontainebleau. During his journey down the valley of the Rhône, in contrast, he was forced to endure the insults of a population that wanted to lynch him.

Significance of Napoleon's Rule. For all his power and feverish activity, Napoleon had little influence on the deeply rooted tendencies of French history. His political innovations, economic policies, military adventures, and conquests did not significantly speed, slow, or change the direction of the long-term development of French agriculture or industry. The movement of population eluded his control. Most French men and women, moreover, continued to live lives shaped by ancient tradition and folk custom and by the unchanging forces of soil and climate.

Napoleon's influence is to be found largely in the institutions he created. To the Revolution's legacy of a class structure based on private property he gave a firm and lasting institutional and legal foundation, which enabled that society to survive all the revolutions of the nineteenth and twentieth centuries.

SUGGESTIONS FOR FURTHER READING

Bergeron, Louis. *France under Napoleon*. Princeton, 1981.

Bruun, Geoffrey. *Europe and the French Imperium, 1799–1814.* New York, 1938, 1963.

Connelly, Owen. *Napoleon's Satellite Kingdoms.* New York, 1965.

Geyl, Pieter. *Napoleon: For and Against.* New Haven, 1949.

Guérard, Albert L. *Reflections on the Napoleonic Legend.* New York, 1924.

Herold, J. Christopher, ed. *The Mind of Napoleon: A Selection from His Written and Spoken Words.* New York, 1955, 1961.

Holtman, Robert B. *The Napoleonic Revolution.* Philadelphia, 1967.

Knapton, Ernest John. *The Empress Josephine.* Cambridge, 1963.

Lefebvre, Georges. *Napoleon.* 2 vols. New York, 1969.

Markham, Felix. *Napoleon and the Awakening of Europe.* New York, 1954.

Tarlé, Eugenii V. *Napoleon's Invasion of Russia, 1812.* New York, 1942.

Thompson, James M. *Napoleon Bonaparte.* New York, 1952.

Godechot, Jacques. *L'Europe et l'Amérique á l'époque napoléonienne.* Paris, 1967.

Tulard, Jean. *Napoléon ou le mythe du sauveur.* 2d ed. Paris, 1977.

19
The Constitutional Monarchy

The restoration of the Bourbon dynasty in 1814 was accomplished by a compromise between the principles of the old monarchy and those of 1789. The prudence of Louis XVIII enabled him to consolidate this ambiguous regime and to repair the damage caused by the Hundred Days. The intransigence of Charles X revealed the difficulties of reconciling royal prerogative with the rights of national representation. The bourgeoisie was left with the impression that the nobility and clergy were seeking to recover their former privileges.

The Revolution of 1830 replaced the principle of divine right with that of national sovereignty, and reduced the influence of the aristocracy while increasing that of the wealthy upper middle class. But the base of the July Monarchy remained narrow and precarious, for in violation of its own principles, political life was reserved to a minority of those privileged by fortune.

I. THE FIRST RESTORATION AND THE HUNDRED DAYS

The Return of the King. On April 6, 1814, the day Napoleon abdicated, the Senate summoned the brother of Louis XVI, the Count of Provence, to the throne. This prince, who had left France in June 1791, lived in exile in several countries before finally finding asylum in Eng-

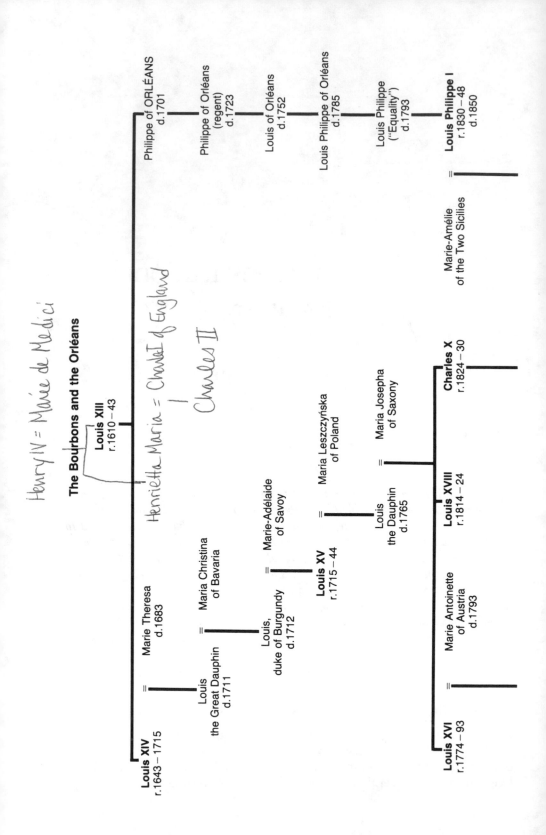

Henry IV = Marie de Medici

The Bourbons and the Orléans

Louis XIII
r.1610 – 43

Henrietta Maria = Charles I of England

Charles II

Philippe of ORLÉANS
d.1701

Philippe of Orléans
(regent)
d.1723

Louis of Orléans
d.1752

Louis Philippe of Orléans
d.1785

Louis Philippe
("Equality")
d.1793

Louis Philippe I
r.1830 – 48
d.1850

=

Marie-Amélie
of the Two Sicilies

Louis XIV
r.1643 – 1715

=

Marie Theresa
d.1683

Louis
the Great Dauphin
d.1711

=

Maria Christina
of Bavaria

Louis,
duke of Burgundy
d.1712

=

Marie-Adélaide
of Savoy

Louis XV
r.1715 – 44

=

Maria Leszczyńska
of Poland

Louis
the Dauphin
d.1765

=

Maria Josepha
of Saxony

Charles X
r.1824 – 30

Louis XVIII
r.1814 – 24

Louis XVI
r.1774 – 93

=

Marie Antoinette
of Austria
d.1793

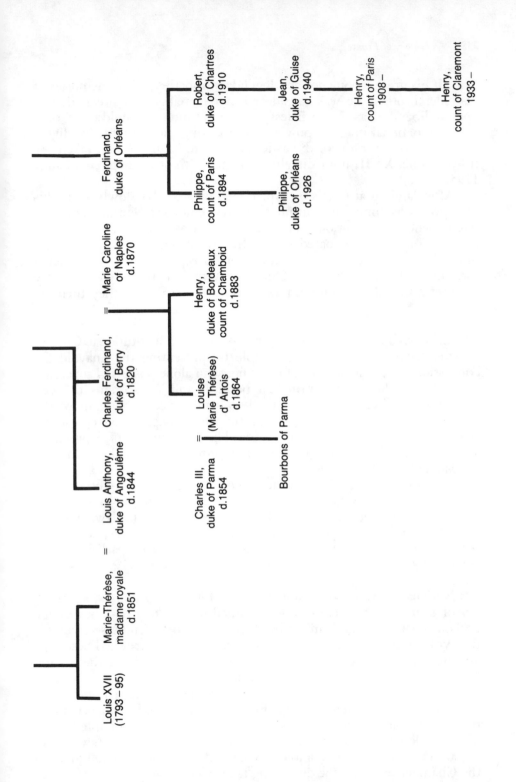

land. If his great corpulence and legendary appetite stirred memories of his older brother, he was considered more intelligent, cultivated, and open to liberal ideas. Nonetheless, he did not intend to hold the throne by some national grant of power. He was king, he thought, by divine right, that is, by right of dynastic succession. Thus he had taken the title of Louis XVIII immediately after the death of his nephew in June 1795.

After landing at Calais on April 24, Louis XVIII slowly made his way to Paris amid an outburst of rejoicing and enthusiasm that strengthened his position. As a result, he was able to set aside the constitution hastily prepared by the Senate, which would have subordinated royal power to that of the people's representatives—the senators. In the Declaration of St. Ouen, on May 2, 1814, he pledged only to grant a liberal constitution guaranteeing conditions as they then existed.

The Charter. The act issued on June 4 as the Constitutional Charter safeguarded the monarchical principle by presenting the unavoidable concessions as a gracious gift of the king, who alone possessed sovereign power. Nonetheless, the principal political and social gains of 1789 were preserved: equal access for all to state offices, the right of the people to consent to taxes and to participate through their representatives in the making of laws, individual liberty, freedom of expression, and freedom of religion, with the added novelty that Catholicism was proclaimed the state religion.

The king retained full executive power and had sole authority to initiate legislation. Article 14 of the charter authorized him to make "the necessary rules and ordinances for the execution of the laws and the security of the State." He freely chose his own ministers, who were responsible only to him. Thus the regime was not truly parliamentary, since a vote of the chambers could not in itself compel a minister to resign.

National representation was provided for by two houses, a Chamber of Peers, whose members were named by the king on a hereditary basis, and the elected Chamber of Deputies, whose members served for five years unless the king dissolved the Chamber earlier. These two assemblies participated equally in the making of laws, but the budget had to be approved first by the deputies.

The electoral system restricted political activity to a minority of those who had the money to qualify for it. To vote a man had to be thirty years old and pay 300 francs in direct taxes; to be eligible for the office of deputy, 40 years and 1,000 francs. Consequently, fewer than 90,000 Frenchmen were eligible to vote and fewer than 10,000 to sit in the Chamber. Because the qualifying taxes were largely land taxes, both the electorate and the Chamber were dominated by substantial land-lords, a large number of them nobles.

The Treaty of Paris. On April 23 Talleyrand signed an armistice agreement that provided for the evacuation of French territory. The final peace treaty was signed at Paris on May 30. France lost practically all the conquests of the Revolution and Empire and returned to its boundaries of January 1791, but retained a third of Savoy and several small territories on the northeastern border. The Allies did not impose a war indemnity or insist on occupation of French territory.

The Congress of Vienna. France also pledged to accept the future territorial arrangement of Europe that would be determined by a congress to be held in Vienna beginning in October 1814.

Talleyrand, who represented Louis XVIII at the gathering, by his skill and personal prestige won an influential role for himself in the congress. Conflicts of interest among the victors even gave him the opportunity to sign a secret treaty of alliance with England and Austria. The final provisions of the Vienna settlement, however, reflected the Allies' determination to protect themselves against any future French adventures. France found itself surrounded by a chain of buffer states: the kingdom of Holland, composed of Belgium and the former Dutch republic; the Swiss Confederation, whose neutrality was guaranteed by the great powers; and the kingdom of Piedmont-Sardinia, which guarded the Alpine border. Most important, Prussia was installed on the west bank of the Rhine, to prevent France from ever recovering that portion of its "natural boundaries."

Public Uneasiness. Unhappiness over the treaty was aggravated by many other disappointments.

The peace dislocated the economy, long geared to the demands of war. The industries that supplied the armies lost their markets. The end of the blockade brought an influx of British goods, which precipitated the ruin of numerous businesses. These developments and the halt of public works created widespread unemployment. Demobilized soldiers added to the ranks of the jobless. The civil servants of previous regimes were shocked by the exclusive preference given the émigrés who returned with the princes. The buyers of national lands were alarmed by the compensation demanded by former landowners and by the anathemas hurled against them by the clergy. In short, the general feeling was that the Old Regime had returned.

The army was deeply embittered. While twelve thousand idled officers were retired on half pay, the privileged King's Guard was rebuilt with former officers who were either émigrés or from the Vendée, the seat of the most militant opposition to the Revolution.

The Return of Napoleon. The former despot soon felt confined in his little island realm of Elba. Aware of the increasing irritation among the French public, he decided to play his last card. Escaping the surveillance of the British, he landed on March 1, 1815, in Juan Gulf, between Cannes and Antibes, with 700 men of his guard. Following mountain roads, he headed for Grenoble. At the Laffrey Pass he met the first detachment sent against him and rallied it to his cause. Each day thereafter the number of his followers was swelled by the addition of new attachments sent to arrest him. Grenoble and Lyons welcomed him enthusiastically. Even Marshal Ney, who had promised Louis XVIII that he would bring Napoleon back in an iron cage, yielded to the general enthusiasm and took his troops over to the emperor.

At Paris, panic and discouragement replaced confidence. Louis XVIII left the Tuileries secretly on the night of March 19–20 and took refuge in Ghent with several faithful followers. On the evening of March 20 Napoleon was again master of France. He had not fired a shot.

Domestic Difficulties. After his triumph Napoleon realized that he could not simply reestablish his regime as it had been before. He sought to conciliate the liberal bourgeoisie by drafting a constitution based more or less on the charter of Louis XVIII. But when this document, titled "Additional Act of the Constitutions of the Empire," was submitted to a plebiscite, three-quarters of the electors abstained. The same thing happened when elections were held for the new Chamber of Deputies. Clearly the most enlightened sectors of the nation realized that the adventure had no chance of success. The royalists gathered themselves together and stirred up an uprising in the western provinces.

Waterloo. As soon as the news of the emperor's return reached the Allies at the Congress of Vienna, they declared Napoleon an outlaw and renewed the Treaty of Chaumont by reaffirming their resolve to continue the war until the scourge of Europe had been eliminated.

Napoleon had to act quickly, before the Russians and Austrians could join their British and Prussian allies, who were concentrating in Belgium. The emperor opened the campaign on June 15 with only 125,-000 men. His plan was to separate and defeat first the Prussian troops of General von Blücher and then the Anglo-Dutch forces commanded by Wellington. On July 16 he thrust at Blücher at Ligny, but the Prussians managed to withdraw, thus forcing Napoleon to detach 30,000 men under the command of Marshal Emmanuel de Grouchy to pursue them.

Meanwhile, Wellington took up a strong defensive position south of Brussels on the plateau of Mont Saint-Jean, near the village of Waterloo. Napoleon attacked him there on June 18. Wellington's army, at first inferior in numbers, held against the furious French assaults, thus giving the Prussians time to arrive. Grouchy had been unable either to catch them or to appear in time to reinforce Napoleon's army. The day ended with the defeat and rout of the French. The Battle of Waterloo, one of the most decisive of modern times, determined the immediate fate of Napoleon and, for long years afterward, that of France and Europe.

The Second Abdication. Returning to Paris, Napoleon was paralyzed by the hostility of the liberals in the Chamber and by the intrigues of Joseph Fouché, his minister of police. On June 22 he abdicated in favor of his son. Fouché, named president of a five-man provisional government, maneuvered to become indispensable to Louis XVIII, whose restoration seemed to be inevitable. He disposed of Napoleon by directing him to the port of Rochefort, where a frigate was waiting to take him to America.

Marshal Louis Davout, who had almost 100,000 men under his command at Paris, became convinced that a new battle was pointless. He concluded a military convention that allowed the Anglo-Prussian forces to occupy Paris, while the French army retired south of the Loire River. This retreat left Fouché's hands free. He hastened to St. Denis to negotiate with Louis XVIII and Talleyrand, who had closely followed Wellington. The king agreed to take the former regicide as his minister. The next day Fouché informed his amazed colleagues that their roles were finished. The king returned to the Tuileries on July 8, exactly 100 days after his departure.

As for Napoleon, he eventually surrendered to the British and was confined on St. Helena, a dot of land in the South Atlantic. He died there on May 5, 1821.

II. THE SECOND RESTORATION (JULY 1815–JULY 1830)

The Second Treaty of Paris. This time the Allies were fully determined to make the incorrigible nation feel the burden of defeat. More than a million soldiers from all parts of Europe flooded across French territory.

The treaty signed on November 20, 1815, was rigorous. France lost the territorial concessions granted in 1814 and had to pay war reparations of 700 million francs plus debts of all kinds contracted abroad by the preceding governments, which eventually amounted to 240 million francs. To see that these obligations were carried out, the northern and eastern departments were to be occupied from three to five years by 150,000 men, at France's expense.

At the same time the Allies signed the Quadruple Alliance, which renewed the Treaty of Chaumont and instituted a form of trusteeship or surveillance over France.

Richelieu. The episode of the Hundred Days dangerously divided the nation. All those who had committed themselves to Napoleon were thrown into irreconcilable opposition, while the royalists demanded punishment for the traitors. Some who accused the king of weakness in this respect became known as ultraroyalists, and this faction dominated the elections of August 1815. Under pressure from the Chambre Introuvable ("Matchless Chamber"), Louis XVIII dismissed Talleyrand and Fouché and entrusted power to Duke Armand de Richelieu, an émigré nobleman who enjoyed the friendship of Tsar Alexander.

Richelieu sought to restrain the reaction by punishing a few of the guilty, among them Marshal Ney, who was condemned to death by the Chamber of Peers and shot on December 7, 1815. Pressed by the Allies, Louis XVIII dissolved the Chambre Introuvable in September 1816. New elections produced a moderate "constitutional" majority, and Richelieu began to repair the disasters of defeat. Thanks to the confidence he inspired and his integrity in carrying out the treaty that he had had the unhappy responsibility of signing, Richelieu secured the complete evacuation of France by the end of 1818. At the Congress of Aix-la-Chapelle, where the Allies decided on the evacuation, France was also admitted as a full member of the concert of great powers.

Decazes. Richelieu retired after this success, and power passed into the hands of Elie Decazes, a relatively young man of thirty-eight. Of modest origins, charming and ambitious, Decazes had managed to win the affection of the old king. But the royalists hated him for his conciliation of the liberal and Bonapartist enemies of the monarchy, and they took advantage of a tragic accident—the murder of Charles Ferdinand, the duke of Berry, the king's nephew, on February 14, 1820—to force his dismissal.

Villèle. A transitional government headed by Richelieu allowed the ultraroyalists to regain power over the machinery of state. As much from caution as from laziness, Louis XVIII resigned himself to governing as a virtual constitutional monarch, allowing his ministers to take full responsibility for their actions once he had chosen them. Count Joseph de Villèle, head of the Royal Council from 1822 to 1824, distinguished himself by bringing order to state finances.

His colleague in the Ministry of Foreign Affairs, the great writer François de Chateaubriand, led France to intervene militarily against the

Spanish liberals, who had imposed a democratic constitution on King Ferdinand VII. Well commanded and crowned with complete success, this expedition served to establish the country's military and political recovery in the eyes of Europe. It also helped to consolidate the regime at home, by demonstrating the loyalty of the army in which many of Napoleon's former officers served.

When Louis XVIII died, in September 1824, France had regained not only peace and order but real economic prosperity.

The Reign of Charles X. The Count of Artois, the brother of Louis XVIII, succeeded him without difficulty. The new king at first charmed his people by his fine figure, spontaneous kindness, and desire to please and behave well. But he had neither the intelligence nor the political tact of his predecessor. The very conscientiousness he brought to his kingly task was to compromise the throne.

At the outset Charles X retained Villèle as the head of his government. His policies disturbed some people, since they gave the impression that the Old Regime had returned. The former émigrés were compensated for the property they had lost during the Revolution. The desire to reinforce the aristocracy inspired a bill to reestablish a form of primogeniture in inheritances. The Catholic church also enjoyed the regime's favor, and a strong current of anticlericalism reemerged. In the election of 1827 Villèle was opposed by a royalist faction, vilified by a daring and brilliant liberal press, and blamed for the economic depression. He lost his majority in the Chamber of Deputies, and Charles X resigned himself to appointing men more acceptable to the opposition.

The next, somewhat colorless ministry gave some satisfaction to nationalist feeling by its successful intervention in the Greek war of independence. Joining forces with the British and Russians, a French squadron destroyed the combined Turkish and Egyptian fleet in the harbor of Navarino. Later a small expeditionary force sent by Charles X intervened between the rebels and the Turkish armies in southern Greece. Thus France played a very active role on the side of England and Russia in the negotiations that founded the new Greek state.

Society and the Economy. Of the 29.5 million French citizens in 1816, about 70 percent lived from agriculture, and they produced three-fourths of the gross national product. Most individual landholdings were small—more than half the agricultural land was owned by small independent proprietors, and archaic methods of cultivation still prevailed. Fallowing was usual, the use of fertilizers rare, and the wooden plow, the spade, and the hoe were the ordinary agricultural implements.

The industrial population was made up largely of artisans who worked in their own homes or in small shops of ten or fewer workers. The factory system, still in its infancy, had as yet touched only the textile industry in Alsace, the north, Normandy, and the Paris region. Ironworks, dependent on charcoal for fuel, were small and widely dispersed in order to be near wood supplies. Except in the few factory towns, the distinction between agricultural workers and industrial workers had not yet been clearly established; men and women moved from the fields to the shop and back with the seasons.

The first half of the 1820s was a period of substantial capital investment in industry. The number of silk looms in Lyons doubled, the number of workers in cotton mills rose by more than a quarter, the production of coal by one-third. A financial crisis that began in 1825 and was intensified by a series of poor grain harvests beginning the next year ended this expansion.

A modest though diminishing excess of births over deaths raised the nation's population from about 29 million at the end of the Empire to more than 32 million in 1830, but the distribution of population was little changed. Eight French people in ten lived in isolated homesteads or in villages of 2,000 or fewer inhabitants. This huge mass of people was scarcely touched by the great world of politics, diplomacy, and commerce. Most peasants were preoccupied with the daily struggle for existence, and as the rural population increased in the first half of the century with no significant change in agricultural technology, their material condition deteriorated. An infant mortality rate of 175 per 1,000 live births—more than seventeen times the present level—and the army's regular rejection of a third of its conscripts on physical grounds indicate the low level of the common standard of living. Social disorganization, which reformers associated with cities, affected rural France as well. Violent crime, illegitimacy, infanticide, and child abandonment were common. Education remained a luxury. More than half the army conscripts in the late 1820s could not read or write.

Although 20 percent of the population were nominally urban, in 1821 only eight cities had more than 50,000 inhabitants, and Lyons and Marseilles, with 149,000 and 115,000 respectively, were the only provincial cities whose populations exceeded 100,000. They and some smaller centers, such as Bordeaux, Rouen, and Lille, retained importance as regional capitals, but they were shortly to lose it to Paris.

Paris, the nation's only really large city, was growing much more rapidly than the country as a whole. Its population in 1817—714,000— was 20 percent larger than in 1801, and it increased another 10 percent in the remaining years of the Restoration. It passed the million mark in the middle 1840s. The largest city on the European continent, Paris under the Restoration recaptured its position as the European capital of fashion and elegance and of the arts and sciences.

Intellectual and Artistic Life. The return of peace and order under a relatively liberal regime not only permitted the nation to repair its physical destruction and begin to catch up with England in industrial development; these conditions also encouraged the revival of arts and letters.

The return of peace, the unusual freedom of expression permitted under the law, and foreign influences carried by returning émigrés and by military and civil officers who served in conquered countries contributed to an intellectual revival. Paris again became the meeting place for all those in Europe who were interested in things of the mind. The physical sciences benefited from the innovative work of Augustin Fresnel in optics, André Ampère in electricity, and Nicolas Carnot in thermodynamics; the natural sciences from that of Jean-Baptiste Lamarck, Etienne Geoffroy Saint-Hilaire, and Georges Cuvier. The courses in medicine given by such experts as Guillaume Dupuytren and René Laënnec drew students from America. Free to express itself, political and social thought founded the principal schools on which the nineteenth century later drew: the liberalism of Benjamin Constant, the traditionalism of Joseph de Maistre and Louis de Bonald, the positivism of Auguste Comte, the eclecticism of Victor Cousin, and even the socialism of Saint-Simon and Charles Fourier.

With the poetry of Alphonse de Lamartine and Victor Hugo, literature experienced a romantic revolution against the rules and limitations of classicism. This revolution helped to bring about a rebirth of historical studies, turning them to the serious use of archival sources of French history, colorful and emotion-laden narratives, and the writing of history to advance political causes. In painting the dominance of David's classicism was abruptly challenged in 1819 by the young Géricault's realistic and somberly emotional *The Raft of the Medusa*, exhibited that year. Architecture, however, remained loyal to the neoclassical formulas of the end of the eighteenth century.

Polignac. In August 1829 Charles X surprised everyone by suddenly bringing to power a group of men so reactionary that it seemed obvious he wanted to destroy the Charter. The head of this new government, Prince Jules de Polignac, thought he could compensate for his unpopularity by some military adventure that would play on nationalist feeling. He seized upon an insult to the French consul by the dey of Algiers as a pretext to dispatch an expedition for the ostensible purpose of putting an end to the Barbary pirates. Brilliantly executed, the operation resulted in the capture of Algiers on July 5, 1830. But paradoxically, this success contributed to the fall of the ministry and the throne, for it encouraged Charles X in his struggle against the opposition at a critical moment when his best troops were in North Africa.

The Revolution of 1830. In the later 1820s the prosperity of the decade's earlier years gave way to depression, unemployment, and widespread distress. A banking crisis brought on many bankruptcies among banking houses and in industry and commerce. Poor harvests from 1827 through 1829 created shortages that were soon reflected in soaring prices for bread and potatoes, the staples of most people's diets. An extraordinarily cold winter in 1829–30 added to the distress and suffering. People blamed the government for their troubles. The narrowly limited suffrage precluded any mass expression of grievances at the ballot box in these difficult years, but market riots and attacks on grain convoys were frequent. Those who could vote were hurt by the depression, too, and they expressed their dissatisfaction by electing a majority of opposition deputies in 1827.

The Bourbon monarchy had some mortal enemies—republicans and Bonapartists—but by themselves they were not a serious threat to the regime. More serious were the liberal monarchists, who held more than 40 percent of the seats in the Chamber of Deputies after 1827. They were alienated from the government, especially after the formation of the Polignac ministry, not only by economic grievances but also by fear of government encroachment on property rights, on freedom of the press and of teaching, and on civil equality. In 1830 their fears, grievances, and ambitions briefly but effectively focused on the constitutional issue of ministerial responsibility.

In the spring of that year the deputies respectfully petitioned the king for a change of ministers. Convinced that he must defend his constitutional prerogative, Charles parried by dissolving the Chamber. When a new election returned a hostile majority, he decided on a kind of coup d'état, invoking Article 14 of the Charter. The Four Ordinances published on July 26 established censorship of the press, changed the electoral law to favor conservative candidates, dissolved the newly elected Chamber, and ordered new elections.

Spurred on by journalists, the people of Paris rose in rebellion. In three days of street fighting—the "Three Glorious Days"—they took over the capital. The opposition deputies, who feared above all the establishment of a republic, persuaded the head of the younger branch of the Bourbon family, Louis Philippe, the duke of Orléans—reputed to be sympathetic to the opposition's political views—to head a provisional government as lieutenant general of the kingdom. Charles X fled to Rambouillet, a few miles west of Paris. There he abdicated in favor of his grandson, Henry, the duke of Bordeaux, and called on Orléans to perform the duties of regent. But this solution was ruled out by the revolution's leaders. Charles X left the country without offering any further resistance, and the Duke of Orléans was proclaimed king of the

French on August 9, 1830, in a purely civil ceremony devoid of all the symbols of divine-right monarchy.

III. THE JULY MONARCHY (AUGUST 1830–FEBRUARY 1848)

Louis Philippe. Philippe of Orléans, who became king at the age of fifty-seven under the name Louis Philippe I, was the eldest son of a cousin of Louis XVI who had acquired a sinister notoriety in the Revolution.[1] A member of the Jacobin Club like his father, he had served in the army and taken part in the battles of Valmy and Jemmapes. He followed his commander, Charles Dumouriez, in his vain attempt against the Convention and into exile. He then experienced difficult years when he had to work for a living. He later became reconciled with the elder branch of the Bourbons, and during the Restoration Louis XVIII restored his rank and property. But after 1815 the regime's enemies turned to him, and the prince, without openly compromising himself, did nothing to discourage the liberal opposition's interest in him.

Large and robust, with features that somewhat recalled those of Louis XIV, Louis Philippe in certain ways incarnated the virtues of the well-to-do notables who had brought him to power. He was an excellent husband and father, a businessman shrewd to the point of avarice, good-natured, benevolent, and courageous in the face of danger. But in politics he preferred cunning, and under a facade of calculated cheerfulness he hid a strong-willed desire to exercise personal government despite constitutional requirements.

Features of the Regime. The revolution had been carried out in defense of the Charter. The structure of the state therefore generally remained the same, with some modifications to satisfy public opinion:

- The voting age was lowered from thirty to twenty-five and the tax requirement from 300 to 200 francs. Eligibility requirements for officeholders were lowered from forty years and 1,000 francs to thirty years and 500 francs. These changes increased the electorate from about 90,000 to nearly 170,000, and the number of those eligible to hold office from about 10,000 to 25,000.

- Catholicism ceased to be the state religion and became, as under the Napoleonic concordat, that of "the majority of the French."

---

1. Louis Philippe of Orléans (1747–93) had, out of ambition and bitterness, stirred up the opposition of the nobility and the parlements. His agents were in no small way responsible for the popular violence of 1789. Although he was the richest landowner in the kingdom, he called himself "Citizen Equality." A member of the Convention, he had the grim courage or cowardice to vote for the death of Louis XVI. This did not prevent him from being guillotined in November 1793.

• The chambers had the right to propose laws.

But the very essence of the regime was radically changed: the principle of divine right or the historic right of the former monarchy, so firmly maintained by Louis XVIII, was replaced by the principle of national sovereignty, as in 1789, and of contract between king and nation. Consequently, the new king was called the king of the French, and the tricolor flag replaced the white fleur-de-lys as the national emblem. The king's name emphasized the break with the Bourbon past; he chose to be not Louis XIX or Charles XI, but Louis Philippe I. At the same time the political influence of the church was curtailed.

The Bourgeoisie in Power. The revolution of 1830 seemed to mean the defeat of the old privileged classes. Most of the nobles who had served Charles X refused to take the oath to the new king and lost their positions. The aristocracy of birth became less influential in the national government, and the aristocracy of money, whether based on land or on business, became more so. In the 1830s and 1840s the new notables were able to put the state's administrative machinery and resources to the service of their economic interests.

The National Guard, an armed militia of the well-to-do citizens in each town, maintained control over disappointed republicans and Bonapartists, and especially over disillusioned workers, who found their lot unaltered by the change in regime.

The Opposition. The condition of the working class, whose numbers grew as industry expanded, were as harsh as before, and socialist theories began to spread. In November 1831 social unrest broke into the open in Lyons, when silkworkers, the so-called *canuts*, united in an early extralegal union, and their sympathizers seized control of the city and held it for two weeks until they were overcome by a large force from the regular army.

In Paris the republicans, who were organized in secret societies, stirred serious riots against the regime. Hatred of Louis Philippe was spread by a flood of publications and insulting caricatures, and they inspired seven attempts on the king's life.

The Legitimists, supporters of the elder branch of the Bourbons, tried to stimulate an uprising in the Vendée in the spring of 1832. When it failed, they confined themselves to legal opposition, which was more annoying than dangerous.

The Bonapartist pretender, Louis Napoleon, made two attempts to raise the army against the Orléanist regime—at Strasbourg in 1836 and at Boulogne in 1840. The government unwisely encouraged the growth of the Napoleonic legend in 1840, when it organized elaborate ceremonies

[handwritten marginal note: Aristocracy of money had always been important]

to celebrate the return of Napoleon's body to Paris, in hopes of associating itself with the emperor's "glory."

The humiliated Catholics, spearheaded by the great writer Félicité de Lamennais, began a movement to ally the church with liberalism. In 1834 the Vatican put an end to that movement, but the church regained a degree of sympathy among the working classes by its increased commitment to works of social charity, exemplified by the establishment of the Society of St. Vincent de Paul in 1833 and the work of Sister Rosalie Rendu in the southeastern slums of Paris. On the other hand, as popular threats to order multiplied and revolutionary social and economic doctrines gained currency among the urban working class, the bourgeoisie increasingly saw the church as a bulwark against revolution, and the government itself increased its support of the church in the late 1830s and 1840s. The clergy, however, avoided close identification with the Orléanist regime and openly opposed the government's control of secondary education.

The Government. The revolutionary ferment that developed out of the explosion of July 1830 was intensified by its repercussions in neighboring Belgium and Italy. For a time the new regime seemed threatened. The king entrusted power to a prominent businessman and political figure, Casimir Périer, who succeeded in restoring order.

Périer's death in May 1832 left the field to the king. Patiently he played on the ambitious rivalries of the chief politicians, pitting one against the other in a series of brief ministries—ten in eighteen years. Finally he found in François Guizot a minister after his own heart, willing to leave the reality of power to him and assume responsibility for it himself.

Guizot ran the government from October 1840 to February 1848, despite growing hostility among the public. A tame majority was guaranteed him in the chambers by the small number of electors (then about 240,000), who were fairly easy to manipulate, and by the fact that more than a third of the deputies were also officeholders, and thus in government pay. To those who demanded an extension of suffrage, Guizot replied, "Get rich," meaning "Manage to pay 200 francs in direct taxes." In its broadest sense, this phrase characterized the mentality of a regime that seemed to be in the exclusive service of the upper middle class of businessmen and property owners.

By the end of 1846 the opposition began to demand reforms that would have prevented officeholders from being elected deputies and lowered tax eligibility for voting. The obstinate refusal of the king and Guizot led to the revolution of February 1848.

Foreign Policy. What today appears to be Louis Philippe's great achieve-

ment, his resolutely peaceful foreign policy, was one of the major grievances of a public aroused by a romantic nationalism that was stimulated
by the growth of the Napoleonic legend.

To begin with, Louis Philippe had to maneuver between the sovereigns of the Continent, who considered him a usurper, and the most
fanatic of the victors of July, who spoke of planting the tricolor flag on
the Rhine and tearing up the shameful treaties of 1815. Their indignation exploded when the king refused to support the revolutions that
broke out in northern Italy and Poland.

The Belgian revolution of 1830 demonstrated his reluctance to
become involved in foreign revolutions, for he refused to permit the
Duke of Nemours, his second son, to accept the throne of independent
Belgium. And he lent himself to a solution favorable to England's interests. It was at this time that the expression "Entente Cordiale" gained
currency. Louis Philippe would have liked to transform it into a true
alliance, but the British declined. Their interests conflicted with those
of France on several points, such as Spain, the distant Pacific Ocean,
and particularly the eastern Mediterranean. There a bitter conflict arose
in 1840 over claims by the Egyptian pasha, Mehemet Ali, who was
supported by France. The British foreign minister, Lord Palmerston, in
concert with Russia, Austria, and Prussia—and conspicuously exclud-
ing France—demanded that Mehemet Ali abandon his claims. The exasperated French public and even the ministry, then headed by
Adolphe Thiers, contemplated war, but Louis Philippe knew that
France was unprepared for a war against a European coalition and that
war might lead to the overthrow of the monarchy, as it had done in
1792. He dismissed the bellicose minister and negotiated a settlement.

The Conquest of Algeria. The conquest of Algeria gave partial satisfaction
to popular dreams of military glory, provided an outlet for the army's
need for action, and laid the cornerstone of a new French colonial empire. Louis Philippe dared not abandon Algiers, which the troops of
Charles X had recently captured, for this conquest sustained national
pride. But he first hoped to limit the occupation to the immediate environs of four coastal cities. Arab tribes, urged on by a leader of great
courage, Emir Abd-el-Kader, harassed the French positions. To ensure
the security of the first settlers, the French gradually extended their
occupation. In 1840 the government, smarting under the humiliation of
the Mehemet Ali affair, decided on the total conquest of Algeria. Command of the operation was entrusted to the resolute general Thomas
Bugeaud, and he was assured of the men and matériel required to complete the assignment. By the end of 1847 Abd-el-Kader was a French
prisoner, the conquest complete, and more than 100,000 Europeans,
including 40,000 French, were settled in Algeria.

Under the leadership of François Guizot, France established a foothold on the west coast of Africa and acquired islands in the Pacific that had potential value as bases for trade with the Far East.

Industry and Transportation. Industrial growth, slowed by the depression of the late 1820s, resumed in the mid-1830s and accelerated to unprecedented levels in the 1840s. In 1846 the index of industrial production stood 50 percent higher than in 1831. Between 1842 and 1847 production of coal rose 43 percent, of pig iron 30 percent; the number of coke-fired blast furnaces more than doubled, as did the number of steam engines in use. The principal stimulus in the 1840s was the rising demand for rails and rolling stock for railroads. The Railway Law of 1842 authorized the construction of a national railway network and provided for joint financing by the state and private enterprise. In the next five years 2 billion francs were poured into railroad construction and equipment. Established industrial firms expanded and new enterprises were formed to supply the new demands.

Improvements in the royal highways begun in the 1830s, the establishment in 1837 of systematic tax support for the maintenance of local roads, the construction of canals, and especially the construction of railroads—about 1,500 miles were in use by 1848—opened the way to the formation of a national market. The railroads offered cheaper as well as faster and more dependable passenger transportation, and the rapidly growing number of passengers in the early years—more than 12 million in 1847—gave a hint of hitherto undreamed of geographic mobility to come. The establishment of electrical telegraph connections between Paris and provincial cities, begun in 1845, combined with the capability of moving troops rapidly by rail, multiplied the central government's powers of coercion throughout the country and gave centralization a new effectiveness.

Population. The pattern of French population growth drastically altered in the late 1840s. For a century or more, growth had been evenly distributed throughout most of France, and the rural population had increased steadily. Now these trends were reversed. Between 1846 and 1851 twenty-five departments lost population, and for the first time since census taking began rural population declined, beginning a trend that has continued to the present. The population now shifted to the most industrialized and commercially developed departments.

This demographic revolution reflected the beginning of a fundamental change in the structure of the economy. Under the July Monarchy the rural population reached its highest recorded density, and it was larger than agriculture could then support. Only the combination of agriculture and domestic industry, especially the production of woolen and linen cloth, enabled it to survive. This industrial base was undermined by the new mechanized, low-cost cotton industry. Rural areas could no longer feed as many mouths as in the past, and thousands left to seek their livelihoods in industrially and commercially expanding cities and towns.

Education. The breaking of ancient working and living patterns was facilitated by the expansion of primary education. The Guizot School Law of 1833 required every commune to have a primary school for boys, free to those too poor to pay tuition. For the first time every male child in France could have a primary education and learn to read and speak standard French, an indispensable tool for a mobile population in a modernizing economy.

The Beginnings of Socialism. Urbanization and industrialization, which concentrated poverty and social disorganization and made them more visible to the educated classes, stimulated an unmatched outpouring of ideas for radical reform of the economy and society. The utopian socialists Charles Fourier, Louis Blanc, and Etienne Cabet condemned capitalist, competitive society and called for the formation of producer cooperatives by associations of workers, who would share in ownership and profits. Popular novelists—George Sand, Eugène Sue, Victor Hugo—made a wider public aware of the new social problems, and in 1841 parliament passed the first social legislation—a law limiting the workday of children.

The Arts. Romanticism continued to shape literary production, especially in the 1830s. The novels of Stendhal, Honoré de Balzac, and Hugo are monuments of French Romantic literature. Sentimental lyric poetry remained the accepted form, but in the 1840s the young Charles Baudelaire was writing the poems that were published in 1857 as *Les Fleurs du Mal* (Flowers of Evil), which challenged all accepted standards of form and subject matter and turned French poetry in new directions.

In painting Eugène Delacroix continued the Romantic tradition. In lithographs and paintings Honoré Daumier depicted, with some venom, scenes of middle-class life, and more sympathetically the life of the poor. In Paris in the 1840s the young Gustave Courbet was starting his career, which turned French painting decisively from Romanticism to a new realism.

The first performance of Hector Berlioz's romantic *Symphonie fantastique*, in December 1830, was a revolutionary event of that year. Although he was little appreciated by his contemporaries in his own country, Berlioz was France's only great Romantic composer.

SUGGESTIONS FOR FURTHER READING

Artz, Frederick B. *France under the Bourbon Restoration*. Cambridge, 1931.

Beach, Vincent W. *Charles X of France*. Boulder, Colo., 1971.

Bertier de Sauvigny, G. de. *The Bourbon Restoration*. Philadelphia, 1966.

Dunham, Arthur L. *The Industrial Revolution in France, 1815–1848*. New York, 1955.

Howarth, T. E. B. *Citizen-King: The Life of Louis-Philippe, King of the French*. London, 1961.

Johnson, Christopher H. *Utopian Communism in France: Cabet and the Icarians, 1839–1851*. Ithaca, N.Y., 1974.

Johnson, Douglas W. J. *Guizot: Aspects of French History, 1787–1874*. London, 1963.

Leys, Mary D. R. *Between Two Empires: A History of French Politicians and People between 1814 and 1848*. New York, 1955.

Merriman, John M., ed. *1830 in France*. New York, 1975.

Pinkney, David H. *The French Revolution of 1830*. Princeton, 1972.

Rémond, René. *The Right Wing in France from 1815 to De Gaulle*. Philadelphia, 1966.

Bertier de Sauvigny, G. de. *Nouvelle Histoire de Paris: La Restauration, 1815–1830*. Paris, 1977.

Jardin, André, and A. J. Tudesq. *La France des Notables (1815–1848)*. 2 vols. Paris, 1973.

Vigier, Philippe. *La Monarchie de Juillet*. 5th ed. Paris, 1976.

20
The Second Republic

The Second Republic began in an atmosphere of romantic euphoria. Those who remembered 1793 marveled at a regime that renounced proscriptions, confiscations, and wars. Accumulated frustrations were released in a great carnival of processions, speeches, and publications. Less than three years later disillusionment replaced hope, and the majority of the nation thankfully placed their fate in the hands of the "man of destiny," haloed by memories of the Napoleonic adventure.

The February Revolution. Louis Philippe's and Guizot's stubbornness in rejecting any electoral reform drove the opposition to carry their appeal to the public in a series of public meetings camouflaged as banquets. This procedure, borrowed from England, was devised to get around the law against political gatherings.

The "banquet campaign" began in Paris in July 1847 and then spread to most provincial towns. This agitation was intensified by an economic depression that had been raging since 1846, creating unemployment and lowering wages, and by the revolutionary ferment that was developing elsewhere, particularly in Germany and Italy.

A banquet was scheduled to be held in Paris on February 22, 1848. The government prohibited it. That was the spark that ignited the explosion. The organizers were willing to yield, but their more determined supporters launched violent demonstrations. Louis Philippe tried to calm the rioting by dismissing Guizot. During the evening of February 23, however, demonstrators clashed with soldiers guarding the Ministry of Foreign Affairs, and sixteen people were killed. The rioters carried the bodies through the streets, calling the people to arms. During the night and the next morning, barricades went up in the eastern sections of Paris. Marshal Bugeaud, who was responsible for keeping public order, found himself immobilized by the wavering of the king, who continued to seek a political solution. The soldiers began to fraternize with the insurgents, who also had the support of numerous members of the National Guard. Discouraged, Louis Philippe abdicated in favor of his grandson, Philippe, the count of Paris,[1] and fled in disguise.

The Duchess of Orléans went before the Chamber of Deputies with her son in order to have him recognized as king. When the rioters invaded the Palais Bourbon, the duchess and most of the deputies fled. Two republican deputies, Alphonse de Lamartine and Alexandre Ledru-Rollin, announced the formation of a provisional government, and its members left to assemble at the city hall.

It has been said that never was a revolution more inevitable and more accidental. The Orléanist regime, taken by surprise, collapsed almost without a struggle. Most sectors of the nation, whose aspirations it had ignored, could not bring themselves to care much.

The Provisional Government. Circumstances brought to power a disparate, improvised group of eleven men, most of them journalists. The best known was the poet Lamartine, whose Romantic eloquence set the regime's style. Louis Blanc, a socialist theorist, became the workers' advocate. Both the government and its supporters were divided between the partisans of a political revolution and the radical advocates of social and economic revolution, inspired by ideas picked up from the socialist writers of the 1830s and 1840s.

There was great haste to proclaim the Republic, and in subsequent days to yield to demonstrators' demands and pass a host of measures that showed the idealistic character of the new regime: abolition of the death penalty in political cases; abolition of slavery in the colonies; complete freedom of the press, assembly, and association; the right to work; and a number of others. Most important, the government decided to convene a Constituent Assembly elected by universal manhood suffrage.

---

1. Ferdinand, the duke of Orléans, Louis Philippe's eldest son, had been killed in an accident in 1842.

The Beginnings of Disillusionment. The new republic was accepted by the nation with sentimental demonstrations of goodwill and brotherhood. The clergy, who had been attacked and vilified in the Revolution of 1830, participated in this one, and religion was honored.

But the disorders had sharply worsened the economic crisis. The government decreed the forced acceptance of paper money and imposed a 45 percent surtax on every franc levied in taxes. The property owners began to grow uneasy. Rising unemployment made bands of disaffected workers available to agitators. To remedy this situation—and to guarantee the newly proclaimed right to work—"National Workshops" were organized in Paris. Unemployed workers, organized into battalions, were employed pell-mell in the rather pointless job of ground leveling for a wage of two francs a day.

Advocates of a socialist and popular republic attempted to delay elections on the grounds that the masses first needed to be educated. The results of the election, which took place on April 23–24, justified their apprehensions, for the great majority of Frenchmen, especially those in rural areas, demonstrated their preference for the existing social order. The socialist republicans won fewer than 100 seats, as against more than 500 for the moderate republicans and about 200 for the monarchists.

The Assembly met on May 4 and named an executive commission of five members, including Lamartine and Ledru-Rollin. The extremist clubs, disappointed by the elections, attempted the violent overthrow of the Assembly on May 15, but the middle-class National Guard quickly restored order. The government arrested the principal radical leaders, effectively decapitating the extreme left of the republican movement.

The June Days. The frightened majority pressured the government into dismantling the National Workshops, which were drawing hordes of unemployed to Paris. Unemployed bachelors between seventeen and twenty-five were ordered to enlist in the army, while others were to be moved to the provinces to labor on various public works.

The workers then rose in protest with shouts of "We're staying! Bread or lead!" When the government refused to give in, desperate workers raised barricades and seized control of the eastern half of the city. The Assembly delegated full power to General Louis Cavaignac, the minister of war. Under his command regular army troops, the Garde Mobile, and National Guards from Paris and the provinces—many rushed to the scene by the new railroads—attacked the insurgents, who defended themselves with grim despair. Losses were terrible on both sides, and repression was pitiless. Cavaignac, now chief of the executive power, demanded and got laws that limited freedom of the press and freedom of assembly.

Those four days of civil war had serious consequences, for they marked the beginning of the workers' hatred of the bourgeoisie, and of the terror felt by the bourgeoisie, whether liberal or conservative, at the mention of socialism. The fraternal glow of 1848 was replaced by class struggle.

The Constitution. From June to November 1848 the Assembly discussed and finally approved a new constitution, based on the principles of popular sovereignty and the separation of powers. Its preamble, an expression of the loftiest idealism, reminded citizens that they had duties as well as rights, and that society owed fraternal assistance to needy citizens—but the right to work was dropped. It was not to appear in a French constitution until 1946.

The legislative power consisted of a one-chamber assembly of 750 deputies elected by universal manhood suffrage for three-year terms. The executive power was held by a president of the Republic, elected directly by the people for a four-year term. He named the ministers, who were responsible only to him. He was not eligible for reelection to a consecutive term. No provision was made for the possibility that the president and the Assembly might come into conflict. The president could not dissolve the Assembly, nor could the Assembly dismiss the president.

The Election of the President (December 10, 1848). It was decided to proceed immediately with the election of the president of the Republic and postpone the Assembly election until later. General Cavaignac, the candidate of the moderate republicans, had the support of the bureaucracy. Against him stood Alexandre Ledru-Rollin, Lamartine, and Prince Louis Napoleon Bonaparte, nephew of the great emperor (see p. 236). Bonaparte had been elected to the Assembly in September 1848, and he had seemed too insignificant to be dangerous. But he had the advantage of his name and had managed to secure the support of the politically active Catholics. Nevertheless, the results of the election were still amazing: Bonaparte won 5,434,000 votes (75 percent) and Cavaignac 1,448,000. The others divided the remaining 5 percent. Almost all the men Louis Napoleon chose as ministers belonged to the monarchist right, and to please the Catholics he sent French troops to Rome to force republican revolutionaries there to restore the temporal power of the pope (see p. 279). The discouraged republicans decided to step down immediately and make way for the Legislative Assembly provided for by the new constitution.

The Legislative Assembly. The elections of May 13, 1849, gave an overwhelming victory to the conservative parties, which formed an alliance with the Bonapartists and ran as the "Party of Order." Together they won an absolute majority, with 450 deputies. The left republicans (the Montagnards) received almost 2 million popular votes, far more than in 1848, and held 180 seats. The moderate republicans had fewer than 80. The majority agreed with the president on a reactionary policy, but it quarreled with him on the form the reaction should take. The majority wanted to restore the monarchy. Louis Napoleon hoped to consolidate his personal power and reestablish the empire.

The Reaction. A popular demonstration in June 1849 against the expedition to Rome furnished the president with an excuse to move against the Montagnards. "It's time for the good to take heart and the wicked to tremble," proclaimed Louis Napoleon. Rigorous measures were taken against newspapers and republican associations, and thirty Montagnard deputies were arrested.

Count Frédéric de Falloux, a Catholic Legitimist, proposed a law to relax state controls over education, as Catholics demanded. The moment was favorable because the middle-class Voltairians were alarmed by the specter of socialism and looked to religious education to restrain the people. Yet the Napoleonic university retained its monopoly over higher education and the granting of degrees at all levels. Under the circumstances, the Falloux Law, a truly liberal measure that enlarged the area of free choice in education, looked like an instrument of social reaction. The republicans, who feared Catholic teachers' influence on the young, never forgave the Catholics.

The Assembly eventually decided to "purge universal suffrage." The law of May 31, 1850, set a condition on the right to vote which practically eliminated the entire floating working-class population: three years' residence in the same commune.

Foreign Policy. The republicans had bitterly criticized Louis Philippe's pacifism. Once in power, they proved even more cautious than he. It is true that domestic difficulties made caution necessary. Confronted by the great upheavals of 1848–49 in Germany, Italy, and the Austrian Empire, France followed a policy of almost total noninvolvement.

The only foreign intervention was in large part a response to domestic considerations. The pope had had to flee Rome on November 24, 1848, and the Italian republicans had established the Roman Republic. French Catholics demanded that Louis Napoleon restore the pope to his states as the price of their votes in the presidential election. As president he was all the more willing to do so in order to thwart the Austrians, the usual watchdogs of Italy. A small expeditionary force under the command of General Nicolas Oudinot encountered unexpected resistance when it first tried to enter the city on April 30, 1849. Paris dispatched reinforcements, and Oudinot mounted a full-scale siege. The city finally fell on July 3, and Pius XI reentered Rome and reestablished his temporal power under the protection of a permanent French garrison. The republicans were indignant that the only action by an army of the French Republic was to reestablish a clerical and reactionary regime.

The Constitutional Conflict. All of the monarchists hoped for a restoration of the monarchy, but they could not agree as to who should occupy the throne. The Legitimists wanted the grandson of Charles X, the Count of Chambord; the Orléanists favored the Count of Paris, grandson of Louis Philippe. This conflict, in which the clash of principles was expressed as a dynastic quarrel, paralyzed the royalists.

Louis Napoleon, for his part, took advantage of his official travels across France to turn public opinion in his favor. "The name of Napoleon," he said, "is a program in itself. At home it means order, authority, religion, and the well-being of the people; abroad, national dignity." In July 1851 he asked the National Assembly to revise the constitution to permit his reelection at the expiration of his four-year term. But the proposal failed to win the 75 percent of the votes necessary to revise the constitution.

The Coup d'Etat. Louis Napoleon decided to resort to force. Duke Charles de Morny, his half brother, drew up the plans, and loyal and bold men were placed in key posts. On the night of December 1–2, 1851, the army occupied strategic positions in the capital, and the police arrested everyone who might have led a resistance. The texts of two decrees were posted. The first dissolved the Assembly and abrogated the electoral law of May 31, 1850. The second called upon the people to vote on the following proposition: "The French people wish to continue Louis Napoleon in authority and delegate to him the powers necessary to draft a constitution on the principles proposed in his declaration of December 2."

In Paris about 300 deputies met at the city hall of the Tenth Arrondissement and voted to depose the president, but they were arrested and carted off to prison. On December 3 some militants, urged on by republican deputies, erected a few barricades in the east end of Paris, but the workers in general were not disposed to oppose Louis Napoleon, who had just ousted conservative ministers and deputies and restored universal manhood suffrage. The barricades were more thinly manned than those of June 1848, but this time the workers at least enjoyed the sympathy of the bourgeoisie, who opposed Louis Napoleon. The new government feared that the two factions might join in open insurrection. On December 4 Morny flooded the city with troops, and that afternoon one unit fired repeatedly on an inoffensive crowd strolling on the Boulevard Bonne-Nouvelle. Nearly 400 victims fell. This ruthless display broke any inclination toward violent resistance the bourgeoisie may have had, and during the night the workers' barricades were destroyed and order imposed on the capital. The bloodshed, however, left an indelible stain on the beginning of Louis Napoleon's rule.

Outside Paris the coup d'état set off the largest provincial uprising of the century. In the south and southeast nearly 70,000 men—peasants and a scattering of townspeople—took up arms against Louis Napoleon's new government, and more than a third of them clashed violently with the military and the police. The government, proclaiming that order and property were threatened by a peasant revolt, imposed martial law on thirty-two departments and sent in mobile columns of troops, which easily dispersed the ill-equipped and ill-organized insurgents. More than 26,000 people were arrested and judged by special courts whose verdicts could not be appealed. They sentenced 10,000 to deportation and nearly as many to exile or enforced residence. This was the last great peasant revolt in France. In an increasingly urbanized society, large-scale collective violence was henceforth confined to the cities.

The mass of the population accepted the coup as an accomplished fact. A plebiscite held on December 21, 1851, produced 7,145,000 yes votes and 646,000 noes. But a million and a half voters abstained, and in Paris the noes and abstentions combined outnumbered the yeses.

The short life of the Second Republic ended many fond hopes for a more egalitarian and fraternal society. Before the June Days and the coup d'état, many people believed that the gulf between rich and poor could be narrowed and bridged by peaceful means, that class distinctions could be submerged in growing affluence. After the June Days and the peasant uprising the thoroughly frightened propertied classes saw their salvation only in repression, and they looked to the administration, the army, and the church to provide it. The working class, disillusioned by the realities of parliamentary democracy, looked increasingly to revolution for redress of their grievances.

SUGGESTIONS FOR FURTHER READING

De Luna, Frederick A. *The French Republic under Cavaignac, 1848*. Princeton, N.J., 1969.

Duveau, Georges. *1848: The Making of a Revolution*. New York, 1967.

Jennings, Lawrence C. *France and Europe in 1848: A Study in French Foreign Policy in Time of Crisis*. Oxford, 1973.

McKay, Donald C. *The National Workshops: A Study in the French Revolution of 1848*. Cambridge, Mass., 1933.

Margadant, Ted W. *French Peasants in Revolt: The Insurrection of 1851*. Princeton, N.J., 1979.

Marx, Karl. *The Eighteenth Brumaire of Louis Bonaparte*. New York, 1963.

Price, Roger. *The Second French Republic: A Social History*. Ithaca, N.Y., 1972.

Simpson, Frederick A. *The Rise of Louis-Napoleon*. London, 1925, 1950.

Agulhon, Maurice. *1848 ou l'apprentissage de la République (1848–1852)*. Paris, 1973.

Girard, Louis. *La IIe République*. Paris, 1968.

21
The Second Empire: Domestic Affairs

The reestablishment of the imperial monarchy testifies to the deep impression left by Napoleon I in the national consciousness. After a return to an authoritarian regime, his nephew moved by stages toward a liberal and parliamentary form of monarchy. The success of this delicate operation constitutes a unique case in the history of modern dictatorships. His greatest achievement, however, lay in breaking down the obstacles that still impeded the modernization of the French economy and in bringing the country the benefits of a remarkable prosperity.

I. POLITICAL DEVELOPMENTS

The Reestablishment of the Empire. The constitution that was announced at the time of the coup d'état was promulgated in January 1852. Modeled on that of the Year VIII (1799), it gave virtually all power to a president of the Republic, who was elected for ten years by universal manhood suffrage. Three assemblies assisted him. A Senate composed of 150 dignitaries named by the president was responsible for ensuring respect for the constitution, which it could amend by *senatus consultum*, or senate decree. The Legislature, elected for six years, approved—and on occasion rejected—laws and taxes proposed by the president, but its debates were not public. The Council of State, named by the president, drafted proposed legislation.

The prince-president moved from the presidential palace, the Elysée, to the royal palace of the Tuileries and surrounded himself with a veritable court. In September 1852 he toured the country, and everywhere he was greeted with cries of "Long live the emperor!" The Senate soon voted to reestablish the imperial rank for Louis Napoleon, subject to popular approval. A plebiscite held on November 20 resulted in a vote of 7,839,000 in favor and 253,000 against. On December 2, 1852, the anniversary of the Battle of Austerlitz, the first Napoleon's greatest victory—and of the coup d'état—Louis Napoleon proclaimed the reestablishment of the Empire and assumed the title of Napoleon III.

The Emperor. Napoleon III seems to be a unique and somewhat enigmatic personality. Some of his characteristics are worth remembering:

- Habitual duplicity, the reflex of an old conspirator and prisoner; he had spent six years, 1840–46, as a political prisoner.

- Invariable coolness in the face of danger and trouble.

- A quite average intelligence. "The emperor is a greatly misunderstood incompetent," said Thiers. On the other hand, he had a cosmopolitan outlook, spoke German, English, and Italian perfectly, and showed a keen interest in economic and social questions and in ancient history.

- A fertile imagination that delighted in grandiose and contradictory schemes.

- A character that was both indecisive and stubborn. Sometimes he appeared to drift with the tide of events; sometimes he followed his plans with the obstinacy of a sleepwalker, gently brushing aside all objections.

- Indolence combined with boredom with administrative details, which led him to leave his subordinates free to implement his decisions as they pleased and to shape policies to their own liking.

In January 1853 Napoleon III married a Spanish noblewoman, Eugénie de Montijo, who had charmed him with her dazzling beauty. She gave court life a liveliness and brilliance that enhanced the regime's prestige. After the birth of their son, the Prince Imperial, on March 16, 1856, and the deterioration of the emperor's health, she concerned herself with policy making. The extent of her influence remains uncertain, but her support of conservative and clerical causes alienated many potential supporters of the regime. She never won popular affection, and on balance she was a liability to the emperor.

The Authoritarian Empire. Until 1860 the imperial dictatorship functioned without opposition. The press was bridled by a system of warnings, and a newspaper that was placed on notice twice could be suspended or closed. In elections the system of official candidacies placed all the administration's resources at the disposal of the man chosen by the ministry, while the opposition candidate was denied all means of publicity. Napoleon III did succeed in incorporating universal manhood suffrage, long cherished by republicans and feared by conservatives, in an authoritarian system of government—his one original contribution to political science and practice.

Napoleon III won over the clergy by material favors. Religious congregations and Catholic education were permitted to expand. The emperor also worked to reconcile the commercial middle class and the working class by giving a strong stimulus to economic life.

The royalist opposition was deprived of its troops when the clergy rallied to the Empire. All it could do was remain aloof from court and public functions and carry on a discreet opposition in salons and in the French Academy.

More dangerous was the republican opposition, which simmered in workshops and secret societies and was encouraged from abroad by the writings of such famous exiles as Victor Hugo. Fanatics attempted three times to kill the emperor. The most shocking attempt was the work of an Italian patriot, Felice Orsini, who wanted to punish the man he considered responsible for the crushing of the Roman Republic and to provoke French intervention in Italy. On January 4, 1858, three bombs were thrown at the emperor and empress when they arrived at the Opera, killing eight and wounding 148 among the densely packed crowd of bystanders.

The Move toward Liberalism. Napoleon III's intervention on behalf of Italian independence in 1859 led him to shift his regime in a liberal direction. The Italian venture alienated some Catholics because it jeopardized the temporal power of the pope, which was considered indispensable to papal independence. It also alienated business circles, for to ensure England's neutrality, the emperor firmly committed himself to a free-trade policy, which caused problems for many industries that had to face foreign competition. Only the republicans applauded the effort to liberate their Italian brothers. It was therefore natural that the emperor moved closer to them to compensate for the disaffection of the conservatives.

This change took place without any systematic plan, successive modifications alternating with moments of hesitation and retreat. The first concessions, granting greater freedom of expression and increasing the Legislature's power, and those that followed in 1862, 1867, and 1869, strengthened the liberal republicans. In the legislative elections of 1863 they won 2 million votes and in 1869 3.3 million. But by then they were no longer united: in opposition to a minority of intransigent republicans there appeared a "third party" that favored an accommodation with the imperial regime provided that it moved toward a liberal parliamentary system. Its leader, Emile Ollivier, was called upon to form a ministry in January 1870. He persuaded Napoleon III to promulgate a *senatus consultum* that summarized and coordinated all the changes that had been made over the past ten years. This form of new constitution established a regime similar to that of the Charter of 1814, with the addition of universal manhood suffrage. The Senate retained the power to interpret the constitution and shared the legislative power, just as the old Chamber of Peers had done. The elected chamber could choose its president and propose laws. The ministers were still responsible solely to the sovereign, and he retained the right to appeal directly to the people through plebiscites.

These provisions were submitted to a plebiscite. The result was a triumph for Napoleon III: 7,538,000 voted in favor of the changes, 1,572,000 against. The Empire appeared to be stronger than ever.

Social Policy. The workers had been disappointed in the Republic and had not been sorry to learn of the coup d'état, for the name of Napoleon was popular. In his youth Louis Napoleon had been interested in social ideas, and he showed a sincere desire to improve the workers' conditions. During his imprisonment he had written a pamphlet, *The Extinction of Pauperism*, which revealed his familiarity with works of utopian socialists and his sympathy with them.

His good intentions were first demonstrated almost exclusively by the founding of agencies for charitable works. Only after 1860 did he try to rally the more educated workers to him and away from the middle-class republican party. A law of 1864 permitted strikes provided that neither force nor violence was used, and in succeeding years there were many strikes. In 1866 he granted toleration, though not legal recognition, to craft guilds, the forerunners of trade unions.

Delegations of French workers were authorized and even given subventions to make contact with British trade unions. Out of these meetings came the First Workers' International in 1864. At first Napoleon III tolerated it, and it soon gathered an impressive number of members. Headquartered in Paris, it originally eschewed political activity, but in the late 1860s, under the leadership of a new generation of militants, it committed itself to preparing for political and social revolution. In 1867

the imperial government began systematic harassment of the organization and its leaders, but it survived as a small, determined nucleus of
revolutionary workers.

The Empire never succeeded in winning over the working class, but
on the other hand, the activists were few and confined to the larger
cities. The great mass of workers remained not only unorganized but
politically quiescent.

II. ECONOMIC ACTIVITY

The Ideas of Napoleon III. The emperor's economic ideas were influenced
by the socialist school of Saint-Simon. He rejected the liberal dogma
that government should not intervene in economic life; he held, on the
contrary, that the state had the right and the duty to promote and direct
it. He therefore surrounded himself with advisers imbued with the
same spirit, among them Michel Chevalier, a former Saint-Simonian.
As in most authoritarian regimes, material achievements were expected
to serve as diversion and compensation for lost liberties. Besides, economic progress would serve the emperor's humanitarian goals.

The emperor's plans were given a boost by a fortunate coincidence:
between 1852 and 1872 the economy of Western Europe experienced
rapid expansion and prosperity. He came to power on the rising productivity curve that began in the 1840s and was only briefly interrupted
by the events of 1846–48. The government of the Second Empire seized
and exploited this circumstance and promoted the changes necessary to
sustain and accelerate the industrial takeoff and to adapt the economy to
the rhythm of the new capitalist-industrialist order.

The Capital Market. The savings put aside by the French had to be
mobilized to serve the new enterprises. To this end the Commercial
Code of 1807 was changed to facilitate the formation of limited-liability
joint-stock companies. In addition the formation of large banking establishments was encouraged—Crédit Foncier, Crédit Mobilier, Crédit
Lyonnais, Société Générale. With their many branches and the promise
of profits they offered, they drained off idle capital and lent it to establish
or to modernize industrial, commercial, and agricultural enterprises both
in France and abroad. Paris became a great market for capital, and its
stock exchange was a scene of feverish activity.

Communications. The development of railways, the mainspring of modern economies, had been delayed in France by widespread skepticism,
a lack of readily available capital, and a policy dispute between believers
in private enterprise and advocates of public ownership. But neither the
state nor private entrepreneurs alone could marshal the vast initial capi-

tal required, and a compromise was reached in 1842. The state undertook to purchase land for the right of way and to prepare the roadbed. Private companies would be granted concessions to operate the railroads, and they would lay the rails and provide the rolling stock and other equipment. The law prescribed a national network radiating from Paris to the borders and one line connecting the Atlantic and Mediterranean coasts in the south. Construction had only started when it was slowed by the financial crisis that began in 1846 and then by the revolution of 1848. After Louis Napoleon won control of the government in 1851, he authorized many new lines, and private capital eagerly invested in them. The government encouraged the merger of companies operating contiguous lines, and by 1857 all were fused into five networks radiating from Paris and one in the south, each operated by a single large company. To ensure construction of secondary lines, in 1858 the state guaranteed interest payments on private companies' investments in them. By the end of the Empire more than 10,000 miles of rail lines were in operation.

The creation of a comprehensive rail network had far-reaching economic and social consequences. The most distant corners of France were brought within a day's journey of Paris. The cost of passenger travel was cut in half, and in the last years of the Empire the railroads were carrying more than 100 million passengers annually. The ancient isolation of rural life was breaking down. Rail companies moved freight for rates only a third the rates for haulage by road. In the late 1860s they were carrying more than twice the quantity of freight moved by road. Secondary roads, however, took on new importance as feeders to railroads, and the government concentrated its road-building and improvement efforts on them. Road traffic continued to increase despite the competition of the railways. So did traffic on canals and rivers; their low costs for heavy, nonperishable freight permitted competition with the railroads.

With the railways and improved roads, a national market emerged. Local food shortages disappeared. Cash crops for distant markets began to replace the ancient subsistence agriculture. Local fairs were doomed. The sharp reductions in transportation costs encouraged the growth of large industrial and commercial enterprises serving regional and national markets. The hub of the rail network, Paris grew in importance as a distribution and financial center.

Government-sponsored mergers in the field of ocean shipping led to the creation of two large maritime transportation companies—the Messageries Maritimes, with links to North Africa and the Orient, and the Compagnie Générale Transatlantique, with routes to America. Using iron ships powered by steam engines and backed by the worldwide policy of the Empire, these companies broke the British monopolies on those routes. A major event in this competition was the construction of the Suez Canal, completed by Ferdinand de Lesseps with French capital and the diplomatic support of Napoleon III, despite British opposition. The tonnage of the French merchant fleet remained small, however, and less than a fifth of it was steam-powered. Most French overseas trade moved in foreign ships.

Industry and Commerce. Napoleon III boldly broke with the protectionism of earlier regimes. Secret negotiations between his adviser Michel Chevalier and Richard Cobden, the English apostle of free trade, resulted in a trade agreement signed on January 23, 1860. All prohibitions were lifted and replaced by very moderate tariffs. Similar treaties were subsequently concluded with eleven other countries.

The abrupt reversal of commercial policy raised an outcry of protest from industrialists, but it had the salutary effect of forcing them to modernize their plants in order to meet competition from abroad. Improved efficiency enabled them not only to hold domestic markets but also to double the value of their exports.

Industrial production expanded dramatically during the Empire, especially in iron and steel, where production tripled, and in machinery, where it quadrupled. Both of these industries benefited from advances in technology and from the soaring demands of the railroads. The magnitude of the demand for their products and the heavy capital investment required favored large enterprises, and the first French companies with many thousands of workers appeared. In such older industries as woolen textiles, change was less marked. Domestic industry, though in retreat, continued to provide employment for thousands of workers, and the small artisan shop with a handful of workers remained common.

In retail trade the first large department stores were established and introduced revolutionary merchandising techniques—fixed prices, small profit margins on a large volume of sales, carefully trained sales staffs, advertising, and catalog sales to a national—even international—market. The pioneering store was the Bon Marché, which opened in Paris in 1852. Most retail commerce, however, was still carried on in small shops operated by their owners.

Public Works. Financed by special funds that eluded parliamentary control, large public works stimulated all sectors of the national economy through the investment of capital, the materials used, the wages paid, and the new and improved transportation provided. In addition to the work undertaken on the railways and roads, the other great accomplishments were the draining of the Dombes, Sologne, and Cotentin swamps, the planting of great pine forests in the Landes region, and the rebuilding of the central quarters of a number of cities, including Lyons, Marseilles, Toulouse, and Paris.

The Transformation of Paris. Most of the major cities benefited from public renovation and beautification projects, but nothing equals the work accomplished in the capital. In 1850 Paris was being stifled by an urban framework no longer suited to a large and rapidly growing population. For the modernization work he had in mind, Napoleon III chose a man of vigor and determination, Baron Eugène Haussmann, whom he named prefect of the Seine.

Administrative reorganization facilitated the material changes. A decree of 1860 annexed the surrounding communes—Auteuil, Passy, Monceau, Montmartre, Belleville, Bercy, Vaugirard, and others—to the city of Paris, and the whole was divided into twenty arrondissements or districts.

Haussmann's work can be summarized as follows:

- Sanitation: demolition of unhealthful neighborhoods, improvement of the water supply, construction of a network of underground sewers, and creation of a central marketplace.

- Improved traffic flow: opening of new streets, clearing of the areas around railway stations and crossroads, installation of gas lamps throughout the city, the replacement of paving stones with asphalt, and introduction of bus service. As a side benefit, the wide new boulevards would facilitate the work of putting down popular uprisings, if any should occur.

- Beautification: opening of vistas, construction of new monuments such as Garnier's Opera House, the joining of the Tuileries with the Louvre, and the creation of the wooded parks at Boulogne and Vincennes and smaller parks within the city, following London's example.

Haussmann may be criticized for his unorthodox financial methods, his creation of opportunities for land speculation, his destruction of much of the city's architectural heritage, and the monotonous effect of his overuse of straight lines in laying out new streets. To his credit (and the emperor's), he made Paris the most beautiful city in the world, and gave it streets that admirably served its needs for nearly a century.

Population and Society. The population of France increased only modestly during the Second Empire. At 36 million in 1872, after the loss of Alsace and Lorraine, it was scarcely above the level of 1851. Other European countries were growing much more rapidly. Germany's population reached 41 million in 1870, exceeding the French population for the first time—an ominous development in an age of mass conscript armies.

The rural exodus begun in the 1840s continued. Urban population increased by 23 percent, and the larger cities especially attracted the shifting population. Paris and its immediate suburbs added more than half a million inhabitants. Marseilles grew from 195,000 to 301,000, Lyons from 177,000 to 323,000, and the industrial cities of St. Etienne, Lille, and Roubaix approximately doubled their populations.

Overall the French people benefited from the Empire's growing productivity and prosperity. The average French citizen was better nourished in 1870 than at mid-century. Diseases of malnutrition declined. The army's conscription records showed that men were growing taller and had fewer disabling physical defects. Higher agricultural prices, rising farm wages, and the rural exodus ended widespread rural pauperism, and wandering bands of vagabonds ceased to be a problem. Nonetheless, for most peasants life remained hard, typified by long hours of labor, primitive housing, repetitious diet, and crude manners and speech. Industrial workers, divided between unskilled factory workers and skilled artisans, did not yet form a homogeneous class. Artisans shared in the growing productivity of the times—real wages rose by 20 percent in the 1850s and 1860s—but factory workers generally did not. Thousands of them in the burgeoning factory towns lived in conditions more miserable than those of the rural poor.

More children were attending primary school than ever before. In 1866, 68 percent of those between the ages of five and fourteen were in school, up from 51 percent in 1851. The proportion of illiterates among conscripts dropped from 35 percent in 1850 to 20 percent in 1868. Minister of Education Victor Duruy made pioneering efforts to provide public secondary education for girls, but they met with much hostility from the church and the public, and the classes attracted few students.

Increased primary schooling did little to facilitate upward social mobility. Secondary and higher education, the gateway to the professions and higher government posts, remained a privilege of the well-to-do. The new business aristocracy recruited from within its own ranks.

Arts and Literature. The Second Empire, a time of censorship, police surveillance, and material preoccupations, was not a great age of French science, philosophy, or political thought. Popular literature and art were derivative and conformist, but a few bold writers and painters were pioneering new forms, techniques, and tastes. Gustave Flaubert and Emile Zola produced the first great realistic novels in French literature. Jean-François Millet and Gustave Courbet, leaders of the new realism in art, rejected the historical and mythological subject matter of academic painting and painted scenes from the daily life of ordinary French men and women. The Salon des Refusés, founded by Napoleon III himself in 1863, provided a public forum where young revolutionary painters experimenting with new techniques, refused showings at the Academy's exhibitions, could display their works. Edouard Manet exhibited his *Dejeuner sur l'Herbe*, called "the first modern painting," in the Salon des Refusés in 1863, and the Impressionists exhibited there their early, revolutionary visions of light and reality.

In architecture the official neo-baroque style found its most opulent expression in Charles Garnier's new opera house in Paris. Eugène Viollet-le-Duc, with the emperor's encouragement, revived interest in medieval architecture and directed the restoration of Notre Dame of Paris, the walled city of Carcassonne, and the castle of Pierrefonds. The most original architects were those who adapted industrial materials—especially iron and glass—to architectural uses, as in the innovative pavilions of the Paris Central markets, designed by Victor Baltard; the new Salle du Travail and the stacks of the Bibliothèque Nationale, by Henri Labrouste; and the railway station train sheds.

SUGGESTIONS FOR FURTHER READING

Bury, J. P. T. *Napoleon III and the Second Empire*. London, 1964.

Campbell, Stuart L. *The Second Empire Revisited: A Study in French Historiography*. New Brunswick, N.J., 1978.

Miller, Michael B. *The Bon Marche: Bourgeois Culture and the Department Store, 1869–1920*. Princeton, 1981.

Payne, Howard C. *The Police State of Louis-Napoleon Bonaparte, 1851–1860*. Seattle, 1966.

Pinkney, David H. *Napoleon III and the Rebuilding of Paris*. Princeton, N.J., 1958, 1972.

Thompson, James M. *Louis-Napoleon and the Second Empire*. Oxford, 1964.

Williams, Roger L. *The World of Napoleon III, 1851–1870*. New York, 1965.

Zeldin, Theodore. *The Political System of Napoleon III*. London, 1958.

Bellesort, André. *La Société française sous Napoléon III*. Paris, 1932.

Duveau, Georges. *La Vie ouvrière sous le Second Empire*. Paris, 1946.

Plessis, Alain. *De la fête impériale au mur des fédérés (1852–1871)*. Paris, 1973.

22

The Second Empire: Foreign Policy

The foreign policy of Napoleon III was as unhappy and unsuccessful as his internal government was skillful and beneficial. It exhausted itself in the pursuit of grandiose and contradictory objectives. Conducted in secret, with hesitation and stunning surprises, it aroused the distrust and hostility of other countries, and with the best of intentions it eventually led France into a disaster comparable to that caused by the megalomania of Napoleon I.

I. THE SUCCESSES

Objectives and Methods. The foreign policy of Napoleon III was inspired by objectives that were difficult to reconcile. The spiritual heir of Napoleon I, he felt obliged to pursue a policy of power and influence that appealed to the nationalism and military chauvinism of the French while making them forget the shackles of dictatorship. France's great mission could be to destroy the treaties of 1815 and ensure the triumph of the principle of nationality—in other words, the self-determination of peoples who against their will were subject to foreign domination or were artificially divided by outworn dynastic interests.

In addition, a policy of colonial and maritime expansion would serve the nation's economic interests. The parallel exportation of French culture would be served by active protection of religious missions throughout the world, which would also win the imperial government the gratitude of French Catholics.

Napoleon III undoubtedly hoped to realize these grandiose schemes peacefully, and he appealed as often as possible for international congresses. But if a resort to arms proved necessary, he was determined to avoid at any cost the mistake that had precipitated the downfall of Napoleon I: he would not make war on England.

The emperor liked to keep his dealings with foreign powers secret from his ministers, and he followed so many interconnecting and contradictory schemes that he eventually became entrapped in them and brought about his own downfall.

Overseas Enterprises. Some of the Second Empire's undertakings smacked of classic colonialism, such as the military and administrative bases established in Senegal, Cochin China, New Caledonia, and Somaliland (Djibouti).

The conquest of Algeria was completed by the difficult pacification of the mountain regions of Kabylia. Here Napoleon displayed remarkable foresight: he planned to grant Algeria autonomous status in the form of an "Arab Kingdom," which he would rule.

The protection of Christian missionaries was the reason given for a joint Franco-British expedition to China in 1860. Peking was captured, and in retaliation for China's resistance the fabulous summer palace of the Chinese emperors was pillaged and burned.

That same year, 1860, an expeditionary force was sent to Syria to save the Maronite Christians, who were threatened with genocide. Napoleon III also revived the right to protect the shrines of the Holy Land which France had held since the time of Francis I (see p. 102). Elsewhere in the Near East, penetration took the very modern form of economic and cultural infiltration, notably at Constantinople and in Egypt.

More will be said later about his most extraordinary overseas adventure, the takeover of Mexico.

The Crimean War. The political situation after 1850 encouraged Tsar Nicholas I to pursue a constant goal of Russian policy, the partition or domination of the Turkish Empire, "the sick man of Europe." A quarrel over protection of the shrines of Palestine gave him the opportunity to press for Russia's right to protect all of the sultan's Orthodox subjects. When the sultan refused, Nicholas' army invaded the Romanian provinces, and Turkey declared war. England, determined to block the Russians from acquiring Constantinople and control of the straits that connect the Black Sea with the Mediterranean, sought the help of France. Napoleon III, who dreamed of major changes in Europe, was eager to ensure England's goodwill. Thus, although French interests were not directly involved, France allied itself with England, completing the reversal of the ancient hostility between the two countries begun by Louis Philippe. They declared war on Russia on March 25, 1854.

Following some unsuccessful skirmishes in Romania and the Baltic Sea, the western Allies decided to attack Sevastopol, in the Crimea, the major Russian naval base on the Black Sea. A Franco-British expeditionary force landed north of the base, and after the bloody battle of the Alma on September 20, 1854, cleared the approaches to the town. But then the indecision of the Allied commanders enabled the Russians to organize a formidable system of trenches and earthen redoubts. The siege of Sevastopol dragged on throughout the winter, resulting in enormous losses from illness among the Allied forces.

Unlike the British, the French could replace their losses through conscription; eventually the French outnumbered their ally three to one, and the supreme command passed to the French general Amable Pélissier. After slowly eroding the enemy's defenses, he launched a general assault on September 8, 1855. The capture of the bastion at Malakoff by General Patrice de MacMahon forced the Russians to abandon the devastated town.

The Congress of Paris. Several months of diplomatic maneuvering preceded the restoration of peace. Nicholas I died on March 1, 1855. His son, Alexander II, under pressure from Austria, at last accepted the preliminaries of peace on February 4, 1856.

The powers met in an international congress in Paris, in symbolic recognition that the city was once again the capital of Europe. Napoleon III staged the congress, with a great display of pomp, between February 26 and April 6, 1856. The independence and integrity of the Ottoman Empire were again guaranteed by the great powers. Russia lost almost all the territory it had gained since the beginning of the century in its effort to control the Turkish straits. England consolidated its position in the eastern Mediterranean. As for Napoleon III, he was satisfied to assume the prestigious role of arbiter of European politics and to begin the dismantling of the order established in 1815 by the Congress of Vienna.

He took advantage of the authority thus acquired to intervene actively in the Balkans. With his support the principalities of Wallachia and Moldavia united to form the new independent kingdom of Romania in 1859.

The Italian War. After the failure of the revolutions of 1848, the hopes of Italian patriots for an independent and united national Italian state were focused on the kingdom of Piedmont-Sardinia. King Victor Emmanuel and his minister Camillo Cavour were prepared to resume the struggle to liberate Italy from the Austrian yoke, but they could do nothing without foreign help. Napoleon III was quite ready to give it, for as a young man he had taken part in the uprising in Romagna in 1831, and he retained a romantic attachment to the Italian national cause. But the difficulties of the undertaking made him hesitate for a long time.

In July 1858 he suddenly made his decision. Cavour was invited to confer with him in the greatest of secrecy at Plombières in eastern France, where the emperor was taking the waters. Out of their discussions came a verbal agreement on a plan of action. A defensive military alliance would be concluded between France and Piedmont, Cavour would provoke Austria into declaring war, Napoleon would come to his aid, and after the victory a totally free Italy would be reorganized as a federation headed by the pope. As the price of its aid, France would receive Nice and Savoy.

The first part of this plan was carried out to the letter. Irritated by Piedmont's systematic provocations, Austria declared war at the end of April 1859. Immediately a powerful French army moved to link up with the Piedmontese army in northern Italy. Defeated at Magenta on June 4 and at Solferino on June 24, the Austrians retreated beyond the Mincio River. Then, to everyone's surprise, Napoleon decided to end the war. He met with Emperor Francis Joseph at Villafranca and agreed to sign an armistice that would lay the bases for an arrangement quite different from the one that had been envisaged at Plombières. Austria would retain Venetia and the rulers of central Italy would be restored. Not having fulfilled its promise to liberate Italy "as far as the Adriatic," France did not claim Savoy.

What were the reasons for this sudden change of heart? For one thing, the French army had suffered appalling losses and seemed to be incapable of a long siege war. For another, Germany was stirring, and Prussia threatened to move its army to the Rhine. Finally, the revolutionary movement that was sweeping central Italy threatened the pope's temporal power, which Napoleon III could not sacrifice without alienating French Catholics. Little concerned with these problems, the Italian patriots felt betrayed. Cavour indignantly submitted his resignation.

The Creation of the Kingdom of Italy. The Villafranca agreement, confirmed by the Treaty of Zurich on November 11, 1859, provided for the restoration of the rulers of central Italy—Parma, Modena, Tuscany, and papal Romagna. But their revolutionary governments invoked the principle of self-determination and demanded their union with Piedmont. Napoleon III eventually agreed, but as compensation asked for Savoy and Nice, as the Plombières agreement had stipulated. Cavour, who returned to power in January 1860, accepted the deal on March 24. Plebiscites on both sides ratified these decisions.

Flushed with this success, Napoleon III was able to induce the French to accept—and to defend against Europe's hostility—the bold actions of the creators of modern Italy: Garibaldi's landing in Sicily, the overthrow of the Bourbon monarchy in Naples, the march of the Piedmontese across the Papal States, and the proclamation in March 1861 of the kingdom of Italy, incorporating not only the former kingdom of the Two Sicilies but also the provinces of the Marches and Umbria, taken from the Holy See.

II. THE FAILURES

The Roman Question. In the eyes of the Italians, the new kingdom could have no capital but Rome. But Pope Pius IX rejected all suggestions that he voluntarily abandon the last remnant of the Papal States. Pressured by indignant French Catholics, Napoleon III dared neither to abandon him nor openly to oppose the aspirations of the Italians. On September 15, 1864, he signed an ambiguous agreement with the government of Victor Emmanuel. The French troops that had been stationed in Rome since 1849 would be withdrawn at the end of 1866, but in return the Italian government promised not to move against the papal city; as a gesture of its good faith, it would establish itself at Florence.

The indignation that this agreement aroused in Italy drove Napoleon to attempt the impossible in order to satisfy at least the Italian claims on Venetia. The Austro-Prussian War, which broke out in 1866, provided him the opportunity. He encouraged Italy to ally with Prussia and, as the price of his own neutrality, secured the promise of Venetia from Austria. The Italians were beaten on land and sea, but the diversion they provided helped the Prussians to triumph in Germany (see p. 301). By the Treaty of Vienna, signed on October 30, 1866, Francis Joseph ceded Venetia to Napoleon III, who immediately turned it over to the Italians. Their pride wounded, they gave him little thanks.

Scarcely had the French evacuated Rome, in accordance with the agreement of September 1864, than Garibaldi gathered a new volunteer army and prepared to march on Rome. Since the Italian government made no move to stop him, Napoleon hastily dispatched a French brigade, which halted the Garibaldians at the Battle of Mentana in November 1867. The French then resumed their positions in Rome. On the very eve of the Franco-Prussian War, Napoleon III renounced an alliance with Italy rather than abandon the pope, and only the fall of the imperial regime in France permitted the completion of the unification of Italy.

On several occasions Napoleon III had seriously compromised his country's interests and his regime's stability to help the Italians achieve national unification, but his waverings brought him only rancor and bitterness in Italy. His policy had, moreover, led to the creation of a united and possibly hostile nation of 27 million people on France's southeastern border.

The Mexican Adventure. The emperor's Italian policy also helped to lead him into the most disastrous undertaking of his reign. The idea of intervening in Mexico no doubt fulfilled a number of very different desires: to defend Latin Catholicism against the Protestant "giant of the north," to support a conservative monarchical party against a popular reform government, to secure a base for France's economic and cultural expansion in Latin America. But Napoleon undoubtedly also saw in it an opportunity to become reconciled with Austria and to provide some consolation to angered French Catholics.

The affair began in 1862 as a simple military show of force, in collaboration with England and Spain, to compel the reform government of President Benito Juárez to recognize Mexico's debts to foreign creditors. Then, when the two allies withdrew, the French contingents pushed inland from Vera Cruz. A humiliating defeat before the town of Puebla only drove Napoleon (as in the case of the defeat outside Rome in 1849) to double the stakes. Reinforcements were sent, bringing the expeditionary force to 30,000 men. Under General Elie Forey, they seized Puebla, and on June 7, 1863, they entered Mexico City. Preoccupied by the Civil War, the United States could only watch. Prompted by their French protectors, an assembly of the conservative elite offered the crown of Mexico to the Austrian archduke Maximilian, brother of the emperor Francis Joseph.

Maximilian, who arrived in Mexico in June 1864, never succeeded in crushing Juárez' forces or in reconciling all the conservative factions. His authority also suffered from the intrigues of the commander of the French troops, General Achille Bazaine. The end of the American Civil War in 1865 enabled the United States government to invoke the principle laid down by the Monroe Doctrine in 1823—no foreign intervention in the western hemisphere—and to demand the withdrawal of French forces. Weakened at home, trapped by his European commitments, and especially fearful of the next moves of a resurgent Prussia, Napoleon III was forced to yield. In February 1867 the last French soldiers left Mexico, and shortly afterward the unfortunate Maximilian fell before a Mexican firing squad.

The affair brought France nothing but losses in men and money and the hostility of the United States; Napoleon's personal prestige was badly shaken.

The Polish Question. After 1857 Napoleon III managed to restore friendly relations with Tsar Alexander II. They were compromised by the attitude he took in 1863, when the Poles once more rose against Russian rule. French public opinion was enthusiastically on the side of the rebels. Napoleon III made considerable efforts to organize an international congress to discuss the issue, but England and Austria declined to cooperate. The sole result was to destroy any sympathy the tsar had for France and to drive him to align himself closely with Prussia, which had hastened to help put down the Polish insurrection.

Affairs in Germany. In the face of Bismarck's efforts to unify Germany to Prussia's advantage, Napoleon III was paralyzed by ambivalence. On the one hand, logic did not permit him to treat the Germans' aspirations any differently than those he had championed in Italy. On the other, he was not blind to the danger that a united Germany represented to French predominance in Europe. Hence the hesitations and mistakes that finally brought the regime and France to the debacle of 1870.

The first move in the great political game begun by Bismarck was the conquest of the Danish duchies of Schleswig and Holstein in 1864. England was ready to intervene in force, but Napoleon refused to participate in any such action.

The next year, before beginning the struggle with Austria, Bismarck visited the emperor to sound out his attitude on German unification. The chancellor was surprised to discover that Napoleon was particularly preoccupied at the moment with assuring the king of Italy of possession of Venetia. As for the benefits France might expect as a price for its neutrality, Napoleon intended to be recompensed once the belligerents, exhausted by lengthy conflict, approached him to request his mediation. Reassured, Bismarck moved to a showdown with Austria. He found an opportunity in 1866. Napoleon's plan to assume —and profit from—the role of mediator was dashed by the speed with which the Prussian army triumphed over the Austrians at Sadowa on July 3, 1866. Some of Napoleon III's advisers wanted an immediate military show of force on the Rhine, but the emperor chose the path of negotiation. Bismarck wanted no interference, and he distracted the French with deceptive plans for mediation while he drew up his terms of peace with Austria, embodied in the Peace of Prague on August 23, 1866. Although Bismarck's judicious moderation allowed Austria to escape rather lightly, the creation of a North German Confederation under the aegis of Prussia marked a great step toward German unification.

In France Napoleon III was sharply criticized for the inertia he had shown. To redeem himself, after a fashion, he made a desperate effort to secure territorial compensation for France. One after another he proposed annexation of the German territories on the west bank of the Rhine, Belgium, and Luxembourg. The Prussian minister disdainfully rejected these "requests for tips" and skillfully used them to turn England against Napoleon and persuade the states of southern Germany to sign secret treaties of military alliance with Prussia.

These states, however, clung to their independence. To overcome this regional resistance by a more powerful wave of German nationalism, Bismarck looked to a war against France. His diplomacy had succeeded perfectly in isolating and unnerving France, but a plausible reason still had to be found. In due time the ineptness of imperial diplomacy provided it.

The Origins of the War. After a revolution, the Spanish throne became vacant in 1868. Bismarck maneuvered to have Prince Leopold von Hohenzollern, cousin of King William I of Prussia, chosen to mount it. The news, published on July 2, 1870, aroused deep disquiet in France. Were the Hohenzollerns not attempting to revive the old policy of encirclement once achieved by the Hapsburgs? Communicating directly with Berlin, Napoleon demanded the withdrawal of the "Hohenzollern candidacy." The old king William "advised" his cousin to withdraw. He did so on July 12, to the great disappointment of Bismarck.

This splendid diplomatic victory was transformed into a disaster by the rashness of the foreign minister, the duke of Gramont, and the empress. They persuaded the emperor, then weakened by illness, to send the French ambassador to Ems, where King William was then vacationing, to request a guarantee that such a candidacy would never be proposed again. Surprised by this improper request, the king gave a formal but courteous refusal. Before releasing the king's report of the episode—the famous Ems telegram—Bismarck skillfully edited it in such a way as to arouse the indignation of both Germans and French. The "Gallic bull" charged the "red rag," as Bismarck commented. The war party won out over the pacifism of Napoleon III. Prime Minister Emile Ollivier appeared before the Legislature to declare that he accepted "with a light heart" a war that was necessary for the honor of the country. Swept away by a tide of chauvinism, the people of Paris hailed the decision. The declaration of war was delivered to Prussia on July 19, 1870.

The Defeat. Prussia's mobilization plans, which made maximum use of railways, had been prepared far in advance. Bismarck dispatched to the front more than 500,000 men, well equipped, well trained, and commanded by officers spoiling for a fight. Mobilized in great disorder, the

French army could send fewer than 300,000 men to meet them when hostilities began. The French generals, who had gained their experience mostly in the Algerian wars, imagined that they could replace science and discipline with courage and improvisation.

After preliminary skirmishing on the borders, the German armies ensured the conquest of Alsace by their victory at Froeschwiller on August 6, and that of Lorraine at the Battle of Forbach on the same day. The French Army of Lorraine, commanded by the incompetent Achille Bazaine, allowed itself to be shut up in Metz, where it languished for more than a month before it surrendered on October 27. The Army of Alsace, led by Marshal MacMahon, withdrew to Châlons, where reinforcements reached it, along with the emperor himself and his young son. From there it marched eastward to relieve the siege of Metz, but its slow and bungling movement allowed the German armies to surround it at Sedan, in the Meuse Valley. To avoid a massacre, Napoleon III surrendered on September 2. He and nearly 100,000 men were taken prisoner.

The Fall of the Empire. At the news of the disaster, the regime collapsed. As in 1848, all it took was the invasion of the Palais Bourbon by demonstrators and leadership from Paris' republican deputies. They marched the crowd to the city hall and proclaimed a republic and the establishment of a provisional government. The spokesmen of the regime—assemblies, high officials, military men—put up not the slightest resistance. The empress regent fled to England, where Napoleon III rejoined her after peace was established in 1871. He died at Chislehurst on January 9, 1873.

SUGGESTIONS FOR FURTHER READING

Barker, Nancy Nichols. *Distaff Diplomacy: The Empress Eugénie and the Foreign Policy of the Second Empire.* Austin, Tex., 1967.

Cameron, Rondo E. *France and the Economic Development of Europe, 1800–1914: Conquests of Peace and Seeds of War.* Chicago, 1966.

Case, Lynn M. *French Opinion on War and Diplomacy during the Second Empire.* Philadelphia, 1954.

——— and Warren Spencer. *The United States and France: Civil War Diplomacy.* Philadelphia, 1970.

Hanna, Alfred J., and Kathryn A. Hanna. *Napoleon III and Mexico: American Triumph over Monarchy.* Chapel Hill, N.C., 1971.

Howard, Michael. *The Franco-Prussian War: The German Invasion of France, 1870–1871*. New York, 1967.

Pottinger, E. Ann. *Napoleon III and the German Crisis, 1865–1866*. Cambridge, Mass., 1966.

23
The Third Republic: From Conservatives to Radicals

The regime of the Third Republic grew out of a compromise imposed by circumstances. But in the long run it proved to be the most flexible and durable of all those that France had known since 1789. Despite the ferocity and occasionally the baseness of the party struggles at home, the country grew accustomed to the practice of parliamentary democracy, developed its economic potential, created a colonial empire, and by shrewd diplomacy forged the alliances that enabled it to resist German might in 1914.

I. A DIFFICULT BIRTH

National Defense. The provisional government that seized power on September 4, 1870, as the Government of National Defense, at first attempted to negotiate with Bismarck, but the victor's demands persuaded it to continue the fight. By the end of September, Paris was surrounded and besieged by the Germans. Léon Gambetta, the most persistent advocate of resistance, managed to leave the capital in a balloon and established his headquarters at Tours, where he undertook to mobilize the nation's resources. Encouraged by a great surge of patriotism, he raised and organized a total of almost 600,000 men. Divided into three main armies—the armies of the Loire, the North, and the East—they exhausted themselves in operations designed to lift the siege of Paris.

Meanwhile, the armed forces bottled up in the capital, assisted by the National Guard, tried to pierce the enemy's lines, and failed. By mid-January 1871 the situation in Paris had become unbearable. Food supplies were running short, the winter was unusually cold and fuel scarce, and the Germans began artillery bombardment of the city. The members of the government who had remained in Paris feared that continued resistance—probably futile in any case—might strengthen the hands of radicals in Paris and lead to a popular revolt. Despite Gambetta's fiery exhortations, they surrendered and signed a general armistice on January 28.

The Peace. Three weeks were allotted for the election of a National Assembly with authority to make peace. It met at Bordeaux on February 12 and elected Thiers head of the executive power. He met with Bismarck at Versailles and negotiated the preliminaries of peace.

The conditions, accepted by the Assembly on February 26 and confirmed by the Treaty of Frankfurt on May 10, were harsh: the cession of Alsace and northern Lorraine, including Metz (some 5,400 square miles and 1.6 million people), partial military occupation until payment of a war indemnity of 5 billion francs within three years, and most-favored-nation tariff status for Germany.

The wealth accumulated by the nation during the Second Empire permitted the enormous indemnity to be paid off speedily and the material destruction repaired. But the trauma of the defeat could not be erased so easily, nor the burning desire to take vengeance and recover the provinces torn from the country against the wishes of their population. All this would remain a permanent source of tension in Franco-German relations.

The National Assembly. Elections were held on February 8, 1871, in very exceptional circumstances. Lacking directives from a central government or well-organized parties, the voters in the provinces generally turned to prominent local men, who traditionally were monarchists and peace advocates. The republicans, mobilized by Gambetta, offered them only the prospect of continuing a hopeless war. Thus in the 630-member National Assembly that met at Bordeaux on February 12 there were more than 400 monarchists and only a few more than 200 republicans. The Third Republic began its existence with a National Assembly dominated by men who rejected republican government.

Thiers. The royalists did not want to see the monarchy blamed for sacrifices made necessary by the mistakes of the previous regime, as had been the case in 1815. Moreover, they needed time to come to an agreement concerning the man who would be the future monarch. The Assembly therefore chose a "chief of the executive power of the French Republic . . . until the institutions of France have been established." The man chosen was Adolphe Thiers, Louis Philippe's former minister, who had earned a high reputation for courageously denouncing the mistakes that led to the catastrophe. This little old man of sixty-eight thirsted for power and knew how to exercise it. He made good use of his experience in all branches of government, his sound historical knowledge, his tireless energy, and his clear and simple eloquence.

The Paris Commune. Thiers was immediately confronted by a tragic crisis—the insurrection of Paris against the National Assembly. Parisians had emerged from the five-month siege in a dangerously unhealthy physical and psychological condition. The Assembly's first decisions—to abolish the salaries paid to the National Guard, to end the moratorium that had suspended the payment of rents and debts of all kinds during the siege, to establish the seat of the Assembly at Versailles instead of Paris—intensified their anger.

The explosion took place on March 18, when Thiers ordered the seizure of 200 cannon that the Paris National Guard had assembled at Montmartre and Belleville to keep them from falling into Prussian hands. An excited mob rallied some of the Versailles soldiers to their side, killed two generals, and stopped the operation by armed force. Obsessed by memories of the Revolution of 1848, Thiers withdrew to Versailles with all officials and loyal troops. Their retreat left the field free for a "Central Committee of the National Guard," which had been formed the preceding week. It organized the election of a "General Council of the Commune" and invited the other cities of France to form similar municipal governments. There were in fact several attempts of this kind, notably at Lyons, Toulouse, Narbonne, and particularly Marseilles, where a virtual street battle occurred, but they were brief episodes. Paris was isolated in its revolt.

In Paris the Commune split into conflicting groups—political revolutionaries in the Jacobin tradition, federalists, and social revolutionaries of various ideological persuasions. Divided among themselves and preoccupied with the struggle against the forces of Versailles, they had little opportunity to apply their ideas on political, social, or economic reorganization.

While Thiers, aided by Marshal MacMahon, rebuilt an army with the prisoners returned by the Prussians, the Communards took the offensive against Versailles. Their undisciplined ranks were routed by the regular troops and their leaders executed on the spot in reprisal for the murders committed on March 18. From then on the civil war was marked by pitiless cruelty.

Early in May the government troops methodically captured the outlying forts of Paris. On May 21 they unexpectedly broke through the perimeter wall and seized the western quarters of the capital, but they needed another week of bitter street fighting to break the fierce resistance of the Communards, who systematically set fire to the areas they were forced to abandon. In this way such venerable monuments as the Tuileries, the city hall, and the Palace of Justice were destroyed. Four hundred eighty hostages were killed, among them the archbishop of Paris, Georges Darboy. For their part, the troops ignored MacMahon's orders and gave no quarter. In all, this "Bloody Week" may have cost 20,000 lives among the rebels. In its wake military courts sentenced another 250 to death (though only twenty-six were actually executed) and 13,000 to prison, deportation, or enforced residence.

The Socialist International, which had played only a small and moderate role in the affair, was blamed for all its crimes. This blunder enabled Karl Marx to invent the legend that the Paris Commune, which in fact espoused many differing ideologies, was the first communist revolution. For the moment the French republican leaders vigorously repudiated all ties with socialism, for the memories of the June Days of 1848 combined with the experience of 1871 to create a mortal fear of social revolution.

The Thiers Government. By the Rivet Law of August 31, 1871, the Assembly consolidated and defined Thiers's authority by giving him the title of president of the Republic with the powers held by a prime minister in a parliamentary regime.

Through the cooperation of Thiers and the Assembly's conservative majority, order was restored in the country, its finances reestablished, a new army was raised, and some powers were restored to the departmental general councils and municipal councils. The chief accomplishment of this government was to secure the total liberation of the country by the end of September 1873, eighteen months before the date designated in the Treaty of Frankfurt. This result was achieved by early payment of the enormous war indemnity of 5 billion francs. Two large loans supplied the means. The second loan drive, launched in July 1873, strikingly demonstrated the patriotism and wealth of the nation and the renewed confidence in France abroad: 3 billion francs were sought and 43 billion were offered, 26 billion of it from other countries!

The Failure of the Monarchical Restoration. The National Assembly had a mandate only to make peace, but after that task was completed, its monarchist majority decided to keep it in session to give France a monarchical constitution. In February 1871 Thiers pledged that he would raise no barrier to the eventual restoration of the monarchy, which the majority of the Assembly desired. But near the end of 1872 he came out publicly for a conservative republic. Shortly afterward, on May 24, 1873, the Assembly forced him to resign and replaced him with Marshal MacMahon. This brave soldier, who was a convinced Legitimist, was supposed to be a figurehead president while the real power was exercised by the premier, Duke Albert de Broglie, a prominent Orléanist member of parliament.

The main obstacle to the restoration sought by Broglie and the majority remained the division of the royalists into two factions—the Legitimists, who supported the Count of Chambord (Henry V to the faithful), and the Orléanists, who supported the grandson of Louis Philippe, the Count of Paris. The two parties held different concepts of royal power: the Legitimists were devoted to dynastic rights, symbolized by the white flag, and the Orléanists accepted the principle of popular sovereignty, symbolized by the tricolor flag. A reconciliation between the two pretenders, which had been long and vainly sought, was achieved in August 1873 by a move of the Count of Paris. He went to pay homage to his cousin at his residence in Frohsdorf, in Austria; in return the Count of Chambord, who had no children, recognized him as his heir.

The Assembly and the government prepared to receive Henry V, but he would return only with the white flag, symbol of "his principle," as he solemnly let it be known. The majority of the nation—particularly the army, for which MacMahon spoke—would not agree to give up the tricolor flag. Confused and more divided than ever, the monarchists resigned themselves to solving the problem by waiting, as Broglie proposed. By a law of November 20, 1873, they extended MacMahon's mandate for seven years.

The Constitutional Laws. The law that instituted the "Septennate" also created a parliamentary commission responsible for drafting constitutional laws. Its halfhearted labors bogged down in Byzantine discussions, while the Assembly seemed to be struck impotent by the fragmentation of the former majority. The republican opposition used this argument to demand the election of a new assembly. Certain moderate monarchists came to think it would be better to create a republican regime themselves, one that would closely resemble the parliamentary monarchy of their dreams. At the same time the republicans were alarmed by the rapid rise of the Bonapartist party, and it seemed to them urgent to erect a barrier of established institutions, even if those institutions fell short of their ideal. From the conjunction of these two compromises emerged the constitutional laws of 1875, which established the Third Republic. The extreme reluctance of the conservative Assembly to accept the inevitable was shown once more on January 30, 1875, in the famous vote on the Wallon Amendment, in which the Republic was accepted in principle by a one-vote majority.

If this kind of constitution resembles no other in form, its ambiguities permitted it to develop without a revolutionary break. The president of the Republic, head of the executive power, was elected for seven years by the two chambers meeting as the National Assembly. He named the ministers and officials, but he was not responsible to the Assembly, for all his acts had to be countersigned by a minister; *he* was responsible to the Assembly. On the other hand, the president had the right to dissolve the Chamber of Deputies with the consent of the Senate.

This upper house, with 300 members, was intended to preserve the conservative spirit of the National Assembly within the Republic. The Assembly in fact initially designated seventy-five senators for life. The others had to be forty years old and were elected by departmental electoral colleges composed of deputies, councillors general, councillors of arrondissements, and one delegate from each municipality. The Senate would thus represent rural France and the influential local citizens. Its stability would be assured, for only one-third of the Senate seats would be up for election every three years.

As for the Chamber of Deputies, which was elected by universal manhood suffrage, its composition was to be specified by an organic law that was ultimately approved. One man was to be elected from each district of 100,000 people or fraction of 100,000.

The National Assembly at last dissolved on December 31, 1875.

The Crisis of May 16, 1877. The elections of January 1876 brought a strong republican majority of 340 in the 553-member Chamber of Deputies. In the Senate their conservative opponents miscalculated and found themselves much less numerous than they had expected. Initially MacMahon chose republican moderates as his ministers, Armand Dufaure and then Jules Simon. But he felt that Simon lacked the pugnacity to oppose the leftists' anticlerical campaign. When he expressed his misgivings, Simon resigned on May 16, 1877, although he had the confidence of the Chamber. The Chamber responded a month later with a motion of no confidence in Broglie, whom MacMahon had recalled to power. The president then used his constitutional right to dissolve the Chamber.

The electoral campaign that followed was hard fought, with conservatives on one side and republicans on the other, each side forming a bloc and using all available means of propaganda. "When France makes her sovereign voice heard, it will be give in or get out," proclaimed Gambetta, the great spokesman for the left.

And indeed, when the republicans won, retaining a comfortable majority of seats, the president gave in to the rule of the majority and recalled Dufaure. After this unhappy experience with the right of dissolution, no other president of the Third Republic ever dared to make use of it. Thus this crisis helped to shift the Third Republic toward government by assembly—in other words, a system in which governments would be only committees that exercised powers delegated to them by a majority in the Chamber.

The senatorial elections of January 1879 cost the conservatives their last bastion; the republicans now gained a majority in the Senate. The discouraged MacMahon resigned. Meeting together on January 30, 1879, the two chambers immediately elected an old republican of 1848, Jules Grévy, to take his place. The Third Republic was at last firmly established and led by dedicated republicans. As if to seal the final demise of the monarchy and the *ancien régime*, the chambers voted to make the anniversary of the fall of the Bastille, July 14, the national holiday.

II. POLITICAL DEVELOPMENTS

The Functioning of the Regime. The president of the Republic—and there would be seven between 1879 and 1914 (see Table 3)—in principle had only a secondary role in the political life of the country, since the composition of the government and the conduct of affairs were entrusted to the premier, himself necessarily only a delegate of the majority of the moment. But behind the scenes the president acted as arbiter and adviser, particularly in matters of foreign policy. In effect he represented an element of continuity and experience, all the more influential because responsible ministers changed more frequently.

Governments did in fact succeed each other rapidly, with forty-six between 1879 and 1914 and another forty-five between 1914 and 1940, the longest of them lasting no more than three years, the shortest only a few days. This instability, which undermined the influence of the regime, stemmed from the fact that in the Chamber of Deputies there were no solidly organized national parties that alternated in power, as in Great Britain and the United States, but rather a multitude of "parliamentary groups" with changing and misleading labels. Each too small to form a homogeneous ministry, they were obliged to form coalitions that the least incident might destroy. Yet the system was less inauspicious than might be supposed. The "ministerial crisis" even appears to have been essential to the proper functioning of the system, for it permitted the administration to meet situations and problems as they arose, in each instance appealing to the most appropriate coalition without causing too much disruption. In any case, the continuity of government was ensured by the stability of the administration; the more often the ministers changed, the freer it was to pursue its plans.

Table 3. Presidents of the Third Republic, 1871 – 1940

TERM	PRESIDENT	REASON FOR LEAVING OFFICE
February 17, 1871 May 24, 1873	Adolphe Thiers	Forced to resign
May 24, 1873 January 30, 1879	Patrice de MacMahon	Voluntarily resigned
January 30, 1879 December 28, 1885 December 2, 1887	Jules Grévy (Reelected)	Forced to resign
December 3, 1887 June 24, 1894	Sadi Carnot	Assassinated
June 27, 1894 January 16, 1895	Jean Casimir-Périer	Voluntarily resigned
January 17, 1895 February 5, 1899	Félix Faure	Died suddenly
February 18, 1899 February 18, 1906	Emile Loubet	Completed term
February 18, 1906 February 18, 1913	Armand Fallières	Completed term
February 18, 1913 February 17, 1920	Raymond Poincaré	Completed term
February 17, 1920 September 21, 1920	Paul Deschanel	Resigned/mental illness
September 23, 1920 June 3, 1924	Alexandre Millerand	Forced to resign
June 13, 1924 June 13, 1931	Gaston Doumergue	Completed term
June 13, 1931 May 6, 1932	Paul Doumer	Assassinated
May 10, 1932 May 2, 1939 July 11, 1940	Albert Lebrun (Reelected)	Resigned

In the final analysis the development of the regime was seen most clearly in the gradual rise to power of the "new social strata" that sprang from the middle and petty bourgeoisie and the lower classes, who replaced the upper bourgeoisie of the first generation of republicans.

The Opportunists. Having captured the field in 1879, the republicans divided into Radicals and Opportunists. The Radicals wanted to shelve the compromises that had given birth to the Republic and introduce such fundamental changes as the elimination of the Senate, the separation of church and state, an income tax, and voting for deputies by departmental lists instead of for single deputies. The Opportunists wanted to reassure the bourgeoisie, who were enamored of order and economic development. While reforms were accepted in principle, they were to be effected cautiously, "at the opportune moment."

Men of the latter persuasion dominated the government for the next twenty years. The most prominent of them, Jules Ferry, conducted a relentless war against the Catholic church, striving particularly to end its control over the education of the young. Since mid-century, when the church had won a freer hand in education, enrollments in church primary and secondary schools had increased more rapidly than those in lay schools. The church had been hostile to the Republic since the revolution of 1789, and the new republican leaders feared that Catholic schools would raise up a generation of antirepublicans. As good positivists, moreover, they were convinced that universal secular education was essential to scientific and moral progress. In 1881 and 1882, following Ferry's initiative, the Assembly made primary education compulsory and free for all French children aged seven through thirteen, and banned all religious education from the state schools. At the same time the first steps were taken to remove members of Catholic orders from teaching posts in the public schools. In 1879 the state reestablished its monopoly over higher education and the granting of degrees, ceded by the conservative National Assembly in 1875, and in succeeding years poured millions of francs into the upgrading of the public universities.

The Opportunist governments approved laws guaranteeing freedom of assembly, freedom of the press, and, by the Waldeck-Rousseau Law of 1884, freedom to organize unions. They made the Senate more democratic by eliminating life senators and giving communes a number of elector-delegates proportional to their populations.

In economic and financial matters the Opportunists behaved like prudent managers, keeping careful watch to see that the budget was balanced and that the gold reserves in the vaults of the Bank of France were replenished. The general and prolonged depression of the Western economy between 1873 and 1895 turned them back to a protectionist tariff policy, which the peasantry was loudest in demanding, abandoning the free-trade policies of Napoleon III.

Boulangism. The regime was seriously threatened in 1887–89 by a coalition of malcontents who gathered under the banner of General Georges Boulanger, a man whose ambition was matched only by his mediocrity. He had won popularity as minister of war in 1887 by a display of chauvinistic nationalism, and he found zealous admirers among Radicals as well as Bonapartists and even royalists, all united in dissatisfaction with the Opportunist Republic. Unemployed workers in industrial cities and Paris, thrown out of work by the economic depression in the mid-1880s, provided mass support, and the Boulangists made use of new techniques of cheap printing and photography to appeal to this sector of the electorate. The party's only program was dissolution (of the Chamber of Deputies) and revision (of the constitution). Clumsily the government increased the general's freedom of action by forcing him into retirement. He undertook to run for each Chamber seat that fell vacant, hoping to turn a succession of victories into a plebiscite in his favor. A triumphant electoral victory in Paris on January 27, 1889, seemed to put power in his hands, but he pulled back from the use of force that his followers expected. The government had time to recover. Boulanger, threatened with arrest, ignominiously fled to Belgium, and his party collapsed. Still, the political situation in the country was permanently affected. The Boulanger Affair brought into the political arena a new authoritarian, superpatriotic, demagogic right, which appealed especially to the growing mass of disaffected voters in the cities.

The Panama Scandal. Three years later the regime was shaken again, this time by the political and financial Panama scandal. The company founded by Ferdinand de Lesseps to build a new interocean canal went bankrupt, dragging down in its wake thousands of small investors who had subscribed to its loans. This debacle was followed by a flood of revelations about bribes paid to politicians. Many leading Radicals were compromised, Georges Clemenceau among them. The backlash reinforced the position of the moderate republicans. The moderates watched with misgivings the rise of socialist parties inspired by a Marxist, Jules Guesde, the anarchist Mikhail Bakunin, and a great orator, Jean Jaurès. In the elections of 1893 they won thirty-seven seats.

The Ralliement. Some moderate republicans believed the moment had come to stop the war against Catholicism. Pope Leo XIII had asked French Catholics freely to accept the republican regime. This so-called *Ralliement* policy was beginning to produce better relations when an explosive scandal reawakened old passions.

The Dreyfus Affair. In 1894 a Jewish officer, Captain Alfred Dreyfus, was convicted by a military court of communicating military secrets to Germany and condemned to military disgrace and deportation for life. First his family and friends, then journalists and an increasing number of politicians denounced the case as a monstrous judicial blunder. They accused high-ranking military officers, and the right and the clergy in general, of stifling truth and justice. With equal vehemence the rightists accused the Jews and Freemasons of plotting against the army. The country was torn into two violently hostile camps: Dreyfusards, or revisionists, who found their support chiefly among anticlerical republicans, Protestants, Jews, and intellectuals, and anti-Dreyfusards, who were old enemies of the Republic—monarchists, Bonapartists, Catholics, superpatriots, and anti-Semites.

Nationalist and antirepublican agitation took on such a menacing tone in 1899 that the parties of the left and center united to form a "Ministry of Republican Defense," headed by René Waldeck-Rousseau. The highest court had already ordered a new trial for Dreyfus, and when the second court-martial pronounced him guilty "with extenuating circumstances," Waldeck-Rousseau promptly pardoned him. In 1906 the Court of Cassation, France's highest appeals court, reversed the military verdict and pronounced Dreyfus innocent.

The Radical Republic. The Dreyfus Affair ended the rule of the Opportunists and the middle bourgeoisie's dominance of the government. Into their place moved the Radical republicans, who represented especially the petty bourgeoisie of shopkeepers, clerks, schoolmasters, and lesser civil servants. The Radicals, supported by the Socialists, controlled the Government of Republican Defense, which survived with only one change of premier until 1905, and they remained an influential government party through most of the remaining decades of the Third Republic.

In 1899, in the aftermath of the Dreyfus Affair, they undertook to republicanize the army and to reduce the power and influence of the Catholic church. Officers compromised in the affair were removed or reassigned, and control of promotions was shifted from the officer corps to the Ministry of War.

The chambers attacked religious congregations first through a general law on associations, passed on July 1, 1901, which required every religious order to obtain authorization from both chambers to remain in France. When the elections of May 1902 reinforced the left bloc, the government's parliamentary coalition, a new ministry headed by Emile Combes pursued the anticlerical policy to the point of persecution. Few authorizations were granted. One hundred thirty-five orders were dissolved; their property was seized, 10,000 of their schools were closed, and priests and nuns still teaching in state schools were expelled. In 1904 a new law banned teaching by members of any religious order, authorized or unauthorized, in church or state schools. Church schools lost a third to a fourth of their enrollments but did not succumb to the anticlerical attack.

Combes broke diplomatic relations with the Holy See, and in 1905 he was preparing to abolish the Concordat of 1801 when he resigned in the wake of a parliamentary incident that weakened his position.

His successor, Maurice Rouvier, proceeded to terminate the Concordat, but attempted to give the Law of Separation a truly moderate character. The law granted the church complete independence from state control as well as from state support but permitted it to retain its property. The intransigence of Pope Pius X prevented the French episcopate from benefiting from the law's well-intended provisions. The Law of Separation provided that church properties, including churches and other buildings, were to be returned to the "religious associations"; the pope forbade acceptance under these terms, and the properties passed to the state or the communes.

The separation brought hardship to the church and the clergy in the next decade, but it also brought some benefits, including the establishment of a basis for an eventually more peaceful coexistence between Catholics and unbelievers.

The Socialists obeyed the directives of the Second Workers' International and withdrew from the left bloc at the end of 1905. In the Chamber of Deputies the socialist factions united under the label SFIO (Section Française de l'Internationale Ouvrière, or French Section of the Workers' International), and under the leadership of the great orator Jean Jaurès intended to keep their opposition within the legal parliamentary and electoral framework. But in the labor world the CGT (Confédération Générale du Travail, or General Confederation of Labor), formed in 1902, was dominated by violent syndicalist ideology that rejected political action in favor of "direct action," including ultimately a general strike to overthrow the government and the capitalist system. Between 1906 and 1911 the country saw a series of massive strikes that affected even public services. The Radical ministry of Georges Clemenceau (1906–09) resisted them with a brutal efficiency that widened the breach between Radicals and Socialists.

After 1911 the growing tension on the international scene gave new influence to republican moderates, who worked for the resolution of religious quarrels and reconciliation with the right in a program of national defense. Raymond Poincaré, who became premier in January 1912 and president in February 1913, personified this policy. It was expressed in the law of August 3, 1913, which extended the length of military service from two to three years. The Socialists had vigorously opposed the extension, however, and in the elections of May 1914, campaigning as the peace party, they won twenty-nine new seats and emerged as the second largest party in the Chamber, with 103 deputies. An independent socialist, René Viviani, was the head of the government when World War I erupted.

III. ECONOMY AND SOCIETY

Population. With a population of 39.6 million on the eve of World War I, France had fallen in a century from the most populous of the great European powers west of Russia to the least populous. Natural increase had almost ceased, and the population would have begun to decline but for immigration and, after 1890, a diminishing death rate. The birth rate was the lowest in Europe and much below Germany's, whose population in 1914 exceeded 64 million.

The rural exodus had continued and accelerated under the Republic. In the four decades after 1870 the total population had increased by only 8 percent, but the urban population had more than doubled. In fourteen cities the population exceeded 100,000, and the population of Greater Paris had reached 4 million. One French citizen in ten lived in the capital or its suburbs in 1914.

Industry and Agriculture. Industrial production continued to grow at a steady but unspectacular rate of about 2 percent annually, slower then in Germany or the United States. In the final decade before the war the rate rose above 5 percent, reflecting especially expansion in the heavy metal industries and in the new chemical and automobile industries. In 1914 France ranked fourth among the industrial powers of the world.

French agriculture suffered two blows under the early Third Republic. First was an infestation of phylloxera, voracious plant lice that destroyed a third of France's vineyards before they were stopped in the 1880s by the grafting of immune American vines on the French stock. The second blow was the competition of the grains and meat of North and South America and Australia. Drastic reductions in freight costs, brought about by the introduction of iron- and steel-hulled steamships and the extension of railroads into the interiors of these continents, enabled them to undersell European producers in their own markets. French agricultural interests demanded and obtained tariff protection against this competition. The peasantry weathered the crisis —on the eve of the war more than 40 percent of the active population still worked the land—but at a cost of a technologically backward agriculture and high food costs to consumers.

Transportation. In 1879 the government launched a vast program of canal and local road construction and improvement and the construction of secondary railway lines to link virtually every commune with the national network. By 1914 France had 31,000 miles of operating rail lines, more than double the mileage of 1874. Freight traffic increased fourfold and passenger traffic fivefold in those decades. The roads and rail lines bound the country more closely together politically and culturally as well as economically, and gave ordinary citizens unprecedented mobility. Twenty-one percent of all French citizens recorded in the census of 1911 were born outside the departments where they were counted. In 1861 only 11 percent had left their native departments.

At the turn of the century automobiles were only a Parisian curiosity. By 1914 more than 100,000 were in use, and more than half of them were owned in rural areas.

Standards and Life Styles. France of the Third Republic, dominated by business and propertied interests, lagged behind its industrialized neighbors in social legislation to protect the safety and welfare of workers. The distribution of income among the rich and the poor was grossly inequitable. Nonetheless, the population in general did share in the growing productivity of the economy. Real wages in industry rose by 40 to 50 percent. Agricultural incomes moved upward after 1900, although there were great variations from region to region. People lived better. They ate less bread and more meat and wore more attractive clothing. They had more leisure. The usual twelve-hour day of the Second Empire had generally given way to the ten-hour day, and a 1905 law restricted the miners' workday to eight hours.

The effects of free and compulsory primary education were seen in the rapid drop in illiteracy. In 1903 the number of illiterates among army conscripts dropped below 5 percent for the first time. Virtually everyone could now use the French language and read city newspapers, national magazines, and popular books, cheaply printed on the new rotary presses, distributed by railroads, and sold at low cost in railway station bookstalls throughout the country. This development, combined with growing geographic mobility and the influence of universal military conscription, was ending rural isolation and integrating the peasantry into the national community.

New or expanding occupations, such as schoolteaching and the lower civil service posts, offered opportunities for limited upward mobility, but the social structure remained generally rigid. Secondary education and the baccalaureate, still closed to all but the well-to-do and a few exceptionally gifted boys from poor families, remained a barrier to almost all movement from the lower levels of society into the ruling elite.

Women. The French woman's approved role at the turn of the century was that of the minimally educated housewife who stayed at home, managed the household, and raised children. In reality, 37 percent of adult women before 1914 were gainfully employed, a higher proportion than in any other European country. Most of them held routine and inferior jobs and were paid less than men. After 1881 they could attend public lycées established especially for women, but in 1913 only one-fifth of the public lycée and college students were women. Of the 42,000 university students in 1913, only 4,250 were women. The right to vote and to hold public office was denied them, but feminist organizations, which concentrated on pressing for women's suffrage, won few followers among French women.

Literature, Arts, and Sciences. The first four decades of the Third Republic were one of the great ages of French literature, art, and science. In poetry the names of Arthur Rimbaud, Paul Verlaine, and Stéphane Mallarmé, in fiction Emile Zola, Guy de Maupassant, Anatole France, Romain Rolland, and Marcel Proust, in criticism Hippolyte Taine, the brothers Edmond and Jules Goncourt, and Ernest Renan are a galaxy that can scarcely be matched. Auguste Rodin won a reputation as one of the great sculptors of modern times. In the 1870s and 1880s the Impressionist painters Claude Monet, Edgar Degas, Pierre Renoir, Camille Pissarro, and others revolutionized painting, and although they were scorned at first, they revolutionized taste as well. In the next generation Paul Cézanne, Henri Matisse, then Pablo Picasso, Georges Braque, and many more continued the great artistic tradition that made Paris the art capital of the world. The work of the chemist Louis Pasteur and the physicists Pierre and Marie Curie reaffirmed the eminence of French science.

IV. FOREIGN POLICY

Colonial Expansion. The policy of vigorous colonial expansion, begun in 1800 by Jules Ferry and then pursued by all succeeding governments, had three objectives:

- To reinforce the prestige of the republican regime.

- To ensure the French economy sources of raw materials and markets.

- To help France recover its position as a great world power and to reverse the humiliation of 1870–71.

The public generally remained hostile to such undertakings, however, and complained that the resources that should have been devoted to national development and to the reconquest of the lost provinces were being squandered. It is true that Bismarck encouraged the French along the path of colonialism precisely to distract them from the idea of revenge.

France extended its hold over North Africa eastward by imposing a protectorate over Tunisia in 1881, southward by plunging deep into the Sahara Desert, and westward by establishing a protectorate over Morocco in 1912. Morocco had been the stake in an active international competition.

French penetration into black Africa, starting from existing settlements on the coasts, was achieved by treaties with tribal chiefs and some brief military actions against the more powerful rulers. That effort culminated in the creation of two large colonies—French West Africa and French Equatorial Africa. They were linked up with the French Sahara in 1901 by military expeditions sent out from Algeria, the Congo, and Senegal.

The conquest of Madagascar, begun before 1870, was completed, with some difficulty, by General Joseph Gallieni. In Indochina the government of Napoleon III had acquired Cochin China and established a protectorate over Cambodia. Jules Ferry undertook to extend French domination to Annam and Tonkin, thereby provoking a short war with China, the suzerain of those states. By the Treaty of Tientsin in 1885 the empress of China recognized a French protectorate over them. From the Red River Valley a railway opened up a zone of French influence in the Chinese province of Yunan.

In all, the new French colonial empire created by the Third Republic expanded to include about 3.8 million square miles and 50 million subjects, ten times more than in 1871.

The Period of Isolation (1871–90). For a time the defeat of 1870–71 and the uncertainties of the domestic situation condemned France to a secondary role in international politics. Only in 1880, in the wake of Ferry's colonial undertakings, did French foreign policy regain some vitality as it clashed with the rival ambitions of England and Italy. These quarrels were a source of great satisfaction to Bismarck, who always feared the formation of some coalition against German preeminence on the Continent.

One hot spot was Egypt, where France had earlier acquired a kind of financial and cultural protectorate. The British, maneuvering with skill and decisiveness, took control of the Suez Canal Company and then imposed British political domination over the Nile Valley. The French, who had been shuffled aside, took every opportunity to cause them trouble.

As for Italy, the establishment of a French protectorate over Tunisia had frustrated its own ambitions in that country, where a large colony of Italian nationals already lived. This disappointment led Italy to join Germany and Austria in the Triple Alliance in 1882. Thus protected, the Italian premier, Francesco Crispi, increased his provocations, but the tension between France and Italy was limited to a customs and financial war, more damaging to Italy than to France.

The Period of Alliances (1890–1914). Bismarck's retirement in 1890 led to great confusion among European alliances. Russia, no longer bound to Germany and in veiled conflict with England in Asia, encouraged suggestions of an alliance from the French, who were eager to end their diplomatic isolation. A series of increasingly precise agreements between 1891 and 1901 established a political and military alliance between the two powers. It was financial as well, for French funds in an amount approaching 10 billion francs were to develop Russia's railways and industrial plant and armed forces.

The Russian alliance tended to poison Franco-British relations, because it encouraged French leaders to confront the British more or less openly in the Far East and particularly in Africa. In 1898 tension reached a critical point with the Fashoda incident. A French expedition commanded by Captain Jean-Baptiste Marchand had crossed the African continent from the west coast and reached the upper Nile, a British preserve. Under the threat of war, the French government, then in the midst of the Dreyfus Affair, had to yield and recall Marchand.

But after this storm the air gradually cleared as the two powers realized they needed each other to resist the increasingly disquieting policies of William II's Germany. A state visit by King Edward VII to Paris in May 1903 signaled the rebirth of the Entente Cordiale. An agreement on April 8, 1904, amicably settled all the colonial differences between the two countries. It was not a formal alliance, but in the following years the chiefs of staff had secret contacts to plan joint operations against Germany.

The architect of this rapprochement on the French side was Théophile Delcassé, foreign minister in five successive ministries between June 1898 and June 1905. He also managed to mend fences with Italy. In a secret agreement in December 1900 the two powers gave each other a free hand in Morocco and Tripolitania respectively. And when the Triple Alliance of 1882 was renewed in 1902, Italy assured France that it was not aimed against the French.

The Drift to War. In 1905 the German chancellor Bernhard von Bülow seized the opportunity provided by a weakened Russia, defeated by Japan and paralyzed by revolutionary upheaval. Kaiser William II landed at Tangier, Morocco, and made a defiant speech in which he declared that he intended to defend Morocco's independence against France. Despite Delcassé, the French government adopted a conciliatory attitude and agreed to an international conference. Thanks to England's firm support, the Algeciras Conference went in favor of France, and the Franco-British entente emerged strengthened, just the opposite of what Bülow had intended. Moreover, the crisis was the starting point for a rapprochement between England and Russia, which culminated in 1907 in an agreement similar to the one signed by France and England in 1904. A Triple Entente of England, Russia, and France now arose in opposition to the Triple Alliance of the Central Powers. It was less solidly built but covered much more territory and population.

In the first of the series of Balkan crises that led to World War I, a conflict between Russia and Austria over Bosnia in 1908–9, France gave its ally only lukewarm support, and Russia had to beat a humiliating retreat.

Russia gave tit for tat in 1911, when France again confronted Germany. To show its opposition to French expansion into Morocco, Germany sent a cruiser to the port of Agadir. Russia offered no help to France, and only the loyal support of England permitted a compromise to be reached. As the price of Germany's disclaimer of interest in Morocco, France ceded it a slice of the Congo.

Russia's sullen attitude in this crisis made French leaders fear that the Franco-Russian alliance had been seriously weakened. In October 1912 Poincaré felt compelled to offer formal assurances that France would support Russia in the event of a German attack, even if the war started over a Balkan conflict. At the same time additional agreements were concluded between the chiefs of the general staffs. Thus the machinery that was to draw France into World War I was in place.

SUGGESTIONS FOR FURTHER READING

Brogan, Denis W. *France under the Republic (1870–1939)*. New York, 1940.

Chapman, Guy. *The Dreyfus Case*. London, 1955.

Edwards, Stewart. *The Paris Commune, 1871*. London, 1971.

Evenson, Norma. *Paris: A Century of Change, 1878–1978*. New Haven, Conn., 1979.

Horne, Alistair. *The Fall of Paris: The Siege and the Commune, 1870–71*. New York, 1966.

Kennan, George F. *The Decline of Bismarck's European Order: Franco-Russian Relations, 1875–1890*. Princeton, N.J., 1979.

Lorwin, Val R. *The French Labor Movement.* Cambridge, Mass., 1954.

McManners, John. *Church and State in France, 1870–1914.* London, 1972.

Moody, Joseph N. *French Education since Napoleon.* Syracuse, N.Y., 1978.

Seager, Frederick H. *The Boulanger Affair: Political Crossroads of France, 1886–1889.* Ithaca, N.Y., 1969.

Shattuck, Roger. *The Banquet Years: The Arts in France, 1885–1918.* New York, 1958.

Thomson, David. *Democracy in France since 1870.* 5th ed. New York, 1969.

Weber, Eugen. *Peasants into Frenchmen: The Modernization of Rural France, 1870–1914.* Stanford, Calif., 1976.

Williamson, Samuel R., Jr. *The Politics of Grand Strategy: Britain and France Prepare for War (1904–1914).* Cambridge, Mass., 1969.

Zeldin, Theodore. *France, 1848–1945.* Vol. 1, *Ambition, Love, and Politics.* Vol. 2, *Intellect, Taste, and Anxiety.* Oxford, 1973, 1975.

Ganiage, Jacques. *L'Expansion coloniale de la France sous la Troisième République.* Paris, 1968.

Mayeur, Jean-Marie. *Les Débuts de la Troisième République (1871–1898).* Paris, 1973.

Rebérioux, Madeleine. *La République radicale? (1898–1914).* Paris, 1973.

24
World War I

U nlike the Empire in 1870, the Third Republic did not confront its old enemy alone in 1914, but with two powerful allies and the moral advantage of being the victim rather than the aggressor. For four years the nation endured unprecedented suffering with a resolution and courage that astounded friend and foe. Victory, barely won at last with the help of the United States, enabled France to recover the eastern provinces lost in 1871, but it left the country bled white.

The Declaration of War. The assassination of the heir to the Austrian throne by a Serbian terrorist on June 28, 1914, was like a time bomb: more than a month went by before the inevitable crisis erupted, but then events moved swiftly.

On July 23 Austria, encouraged by Germany, addressed an unacceptable ultimatum to Serbia. Poincaré and René Viviani, premier and foreign minister, were then on an official visit in St. Petersburg. After assuring the Russians that France would fulfill the terms of their alliance, they left immediately for Paris.

On July 28 England's mediation efforts failed. Austria declared war on Serbia.

On July 29 the tsar ordered partial mobilization. Germany warned that it would take steps if more were done.

On July 30 Russia ordered general mobilization.

On July 31 Germany sent an ultimatum to the tsar demanding an end to Russian mobilization and asked the French government whether France would remain neutral; if so, it would have to turn over the bases of Toul and Verdun as guarantees.

On August 1, although England's support was still in doubt, France rejected this demand and ordered general mobilization. Germany declared war on Russia.

On August 2, contrary to German expectations, France failed to initiate hostilities and even ordered its troops to withdraw 10 kilometers (6.2 miles) from the border. Belgium rejected a German ultimatum demanding free passage for its troops.

On August 3, on the false pretext that French aircraft had flown over Nuremberg, Germany at last declared war on France. German troops invaded Belgium.

On August 4 England, which had held back until Belgium was invaded, entered the war.

The Sacred Union. At the order to mobilize, the nation responded with resolution and even enthusiasm. It was the moment of revenge that had been foretold for forty years, the struggle for the recovery of the provinces taken in 1871, the crusade for freedom and right against an unjust aggressor. The Socialists reconsidered their pacifism and the syndicalists their antimilitarism. The murder of Jaurès, the Socialist leader, by a young nationalist on July 31 did not deter the Socialist deputies from joining in the vote of confidence in the government, and two Socialists took their seats with representatives of all the other parties in the ministry of "sacred union" formed by René Viviani on August 26.

War Plans. The German war plan, called the Schlieffen Plan, was based on the assumption that the Russian armies, given their slowness to mobilize, would be unable to move in force for at least six weeks. This delay would enable Germany to concentrate its forces quickly on the western front and secure a lightning victory over France. Then they could be sent eastward against the Russians.

The French army was to be eliminated by a vast flanking movement across Belgium and northern France that would encircle the French forces massed on the eastern and northern borders. The French general staff knew of this plan, but they underestimated its scope.

The Battle of the Borders. In the first weeks of combat the Schlieffen Plan worked perfectly. The ten days between August 6 and 16 were enough to break the heroic resistance of the small Belgian army. The left wing of the French armies, counterattacking on the Sambre River around Charleroi, was in turn severely beaten on August 21–24 and forced to retreat before it could link up with the small British Expeditionary Force, which was being mauled in the Mons region. Over the next days the German enveloping maneuver was carried out by forced marches across the plains of northern France, and the right wing of the German army approached Paris. The government joined 500,000 panicky Parisians in flight from the capital and established itself at Bordeaux, while General Joseph Gallieni stayed to defend the city.

The Miracle of the Marne. The general retreat of the French armies, instead of becoming a rout, took place in well-controlled order. The commander in chief, Joseph Joffre, was able to regroup and augment his forces, while the enemy forces were weakened by the very rapidity of their advance and the decision to divert two army corps from the French front to the east, where Russia had launched an offensive sooner than the German high command had expected.

On September 4 the army of General Alexander von Kluck, the right and advance wing of the German force, began to cross the Marne east of Paris. At the urging of Gallieni, Joffre ordered his troops to halt and stand. Fighting extended over a vast front from September 5 to 10 before the Germans retreated.

The Trench War. The victors were too exhausted to exploit their successes, and the Germans in Champagne were able to establish positions that were solid enough to halt any frontal attack. Attempting to outflank this line in the northwest, the Allies launched a series of attacks between September 2 and November 13. Each engagement extended the line of trenches. By the end of this "race to the sea," a continuous and stable front 434 miles long had been established between the North Sea and the Swiss border. Each side dug two or three lines of trenches defended by networks of barbed wire and continually reinforced by concrete or earthworks.

In 1915 the Germans turned their main effort against the Russians. Joffre launched a series of major offensives on the western front to relieve the pressures on the Russians. But the breakthrough that the high command kept seeking proved impracticable with the armament then available. To justify these unsuccessful and murderous attacks, the high command maintained that victory could be won by "nibbling attacks," the methodical erosion of the enemy's war potential. They forgot that in this game the attacker would inevitably lose more men than

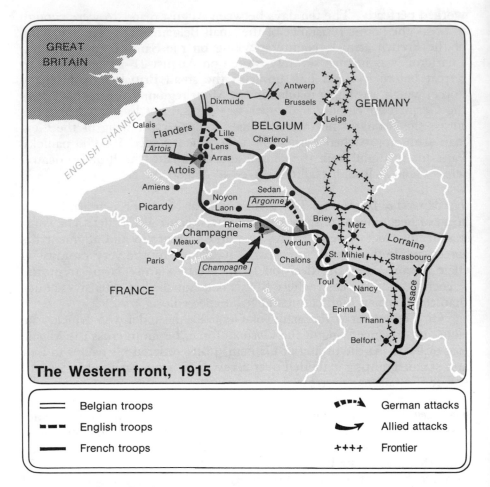

The Western front, 1915

═══	Belgian troops	◢▰▰▰◣	German attacks
▬ ▬ ▬	English troops	↘	Allied attacks
▬▬▬	French troops	++++	Frontier

the attacked. Indeed, in 1915 alone the terrible cost to France rose to 400,000 dead or captured and nearly 600,000 wounded or too sick to fight.

Verdun. The strategy of a "war of attrition" was adopted by the Germans in 1916. They attacked a point in the French lines that was both difficult to defend and essential to retain, the salient of Verdun. The battle raged from February to June 1916, with an unprecedented use of artillery of all calibers. General Philippe Pétain managed to organize the French defenses so that the German advance was contained and Verdun saved. In the eyes of the world this enormously costly victory was to symbolize the courage and staying power of the French *poilu.*

The losses suffered at Verdun did not prevent Joffre from mounting his own offensive on the Somme front, along with the British, who now had more men in the field. But there again, after some initial successes in July 1916, the Allied advance bogged down in the relentless horror of a war of attrition. The total losses were 615,000 French and British, 650,000 Germans.

Less costly in human life but no less disappointing were the diversionary operations against Germany's allies. The operation in the Dardanelles, urged primarily by the British, ended in a complete fiasco. The landing of a French force at Salonika, which was intended to save Serbia, came too late.

The Nation at War. At the end of 1914, despite all predictions, it was clear that the war would be long. The country's economy had to be reorganized and adapted to wartime needs. This was a difficult task, because the most industrialized regions were in enemy hands. The state's arsenals were inadequate, and an appeal was made to private industry. Since war contractors had financial aid from the state and a guaranteed market for their products, even if they were defective, a class of war profiteers arose. Businessmen who knew how to take advantage of various shortages also grew rich. Another group that profited from the war was made up of "specially assigned" skilled workers who were demobilized for employment in war industries at high wages. The peasants did not share in these special privileges, nor did the middle-class professionals. The latter, along with those who lived on fixed incomes, suffered more than any other group from the high cost of living, brought on by inflated paper money and the disappearance of some goods. The inequitable distribution of sacrifices caused tensions and bitterness. Imbued with the doctrines of economic liberalism, the government drew back from rationing or official price ceilings. Nor did it dare to introduce an income tax, which would have recovered at least some of the war profiteers' profits.

Because the Allies still controlled the seas, the French—at least in unoccupied areas—did not suffer the privations borne by the German population during the same period, despite the losses inflicted by enemy submarines.

In short, the country settled into the war without subjecting itself to the discipline of total economic mobilization.

The same ambiguity and half-measures prevailed in the political sphere. During the first months of the war, when the government was at Bordeaux and Parliament was in recess, Commander in Chief Joffre had virtually dictatorial power. His general headquarters at Chantilly was a kind of shadow government. But beginning in 1915 the ministers and legislators returned to Paris and expected to regain control over life on the home front and even over the armies.

Though the principle of national union remained intact, four successive governments rose and fell between 1914 and 1917, headed in turn by René Viviani (August 1914–October 1915), Aristide Briand (October 1915–March 1917), Alexandre Ribot (March 1917–September 1917), and Paul Painlevé (September 1917–November 1917).

The Crisis of 1917. This return to governmental instability was only one sign among many of the malaise in which the nation was sinking in 1917. The increasingly sharp criticism of the way the war was being conducted eventually forced Briand to relieve Joffre of his command in December 1916. His young and dapper successor, General Robert Nivelle, was sure that he could achieve the long-sought breakthrough of the enemy front by a miracle method he had devised, in conjunction with simultaneous offensives on all other fronts. But the revolution that broke out in Russia in March 1917 meant that no further effort could be expected from that quarter. On the other hand, the United States' entry into the war on April 2 promised to make a decisive difference—if France could hold out until the Americans arrived. Despite all warnings, Nivelle would not give up "his offensive," which had been in preparation for months. Launched on April 12, it broke apart against the Siegfried Line.

This time the high command's criminal incompetence had gone too far. In late April some units refused to move up to the front, and disobedience quickly spread to more than half the combat divisions. On May 15 Nivelle was replaced by Pétain, the victor of Verdun, who was known to be sparing of human lives and concerned for his men's welfare. He restored discipline, but for the remainder of the year there could be no question of launching large-scale operations.

In the last months of 1917 setbacks piled up for France's allies: the murderous failure of a major English offensive in Flanders, the disaster of Caporetto in Italy, the collapse of the Russian republican army of Aleksandr Kerensky, followed by the Bolsheviks' seizure of power.

This military situation could only reinforce the weariness brought on by three years of sacrifice and privation. Scarcely a family in France had not suffered the loss of a husband, a father, a son, a cousin, or an uncle. Prices of food were high and rising. Some essential foods and coal were in short supply, and consumers stood in long lines to obtain them. Parisians lived under the threat of artillery and aerial bombardment. The idea of ending the useless slaughter by a compromise peace was encouraged from abroad by President Woodrow Wilson at the end of 1916, by the offers of a separate peace made by the emperor Charles I of Austria early in 1917, and finally by the Russian Revolution.

Pacifist sentiments—they were called "defeatist" then—found increasing favor among Socialists and syndicalists. In May and June 1917 a wave of strikes broke out in the metals industry as union militants called for an end to a war that benefited no one but the capitalists. When the government refused Socialist leaders permission to attend an international Socialist Congress called in Stockholm to seek an end to the war, the Socialist party withdrew from the "sacred union." A former premier, Joseph Caillaux, called openly for negotiations. A few known or suspected cases of treason gave birth to dangerous rumors.

Clemenceau. In the midst of this crisis, on November 14, 1917, President Poincaré summoned a man he detested, the Radical senator Georges Clemenceau, to head the government. This vigorous old man of seventy-six thus reached the summit of a political career that had begun in 1871. As chairman of the Senate Commission of the Armies he had acquired great popularity among the ordinary soldiers, whom he often visited in their trenches. Nicknamed "The Tiger" for the ferocity of his arguments, he knew how to communicate his burning patriotism and implacable fortitude to everyone, whether civilian or soldier.

He demanded and secured dictatorial powers from the Chamber of Deputies. His ministers, chosen without concern for party, only carried out his decisions. Defeatists and pacifists were prosecuted without mercy, and two former ministers, Jean Malvy and Caillaux, were tried for treason. The country felt that it was at last in firm hands.

Victory. The restoration of morale and discipline in the army and on the home front came none too soon. With Russia out of the war, Germany could transfer most of its forces to the western front. In the spring of 1918 it had 192 infantry divisions available there, compared to 172 for the Allies—enough, it was believed, to win the war before the effect of American intervention could be felt. Moreover, the chief of the general staff, Erich von Ludendorff, had developed methods that would permit a breakthrough in the Allied front.

From March to July 1918 Ludendorff launched four powerful offensives at various points, and each time drove deep pockets into the Allied front. During the third attack the Germans again reached the Marne. Ludendorff's initial victories revealed the lack of coordination between the French and British armies, and the Allied governments finally agreed to establish a single supreme command. It was given to General Ferdinand Foch at a conference at Doullens on March 25. His command included the American Expeditionary Force, which was growing daily.

The turning point of the war came on July 18, 1918. On that day the German advance was stopped short by a powerful counterattack, with mass tank and air support, near Château-Thierry, in Champagne. All the ground that had been lost earlier that year was quickly recaptured. In a series of attacks the whole length of the front during August and

September, Foch prevented Ludendorff from recovering and forced him to retreat from trench to trench. The German army still held together, but its allies collapsed. Bulgaria asked for an armistice on September 29, Turkey on October 21, Austria-Hungary on November 3. A spectacular offensive by a French expeditionary force at Salonika, under General Louis Franchet d'Esperey, contributed to these successes.

Disturbed at the symptoms of disintegration in its armies, the German high command pressed the civilian authorities to end hostilities, and on October 3 a newly formed German government asked President Wilson for an immediate armistice. On November 7 a German delegation crossed the lines to negotiate with Foch. The armistice was signed on the night of November 10–11 at Rethondes, in the forest of Compiègne. Some people in France thought this agreement was premature, since it kept the war from being carried to enemy soil and left the reputation of the German army intact. But the conditions imposed by Foch put Germany at the mercy of the victors.

The Treaty of Versailles. The terms of the peace were worked out at conferences in Paris between January and June 1919. Clemenceau, given a free hand by the Chamber of Deputies, more than once found himself in opposition to the British prime minister, David Lloyd George, and President Wilson. They readily agreed to the return of Alsace-Lorraine to France, but the English-speaking allies refused to set France's eastern border at the Rhine, which Foch and the majority of the French considered necessary for their future security. Clemenceau had to be satisfied with a guarantee of their aid in the event of unprovoked German aggression and a few security provisions, including a limit of 100,000 men in the future German army; a fifteen-year occupation of the west bank of the Rhine, with a gradual evacuation conditional on fulfillment of the treaty; and permanent demilitarization of the region and of a zone thirty-one miles (fifty kilometers) wide on the east bank. The territory of the Saar, which France claimed because it had been French in 1814, would be administered by the League of Nations for fifteen years; at the end of that time a plebiscite would determine its final disposition.

France's allies acknowledged in principle that Germany should help to repair the destruction and losses it had inflicted on the invaded areas, but it was impossible to reach an agreement on the sum of these reparations and the mode of payment. These problems, which were indeed complex, were referred to a "Reparations Commission," which was to submit its report before May 1921. Meanwhile, Germany would have to make payments amounting to 25 billion gold francs.

The peace treaty was signed with great solemnity on June 28, 1919, in the great Hall of Mirrors at the palace of Versailles.

SUGGESTIONS FOR FURTHER READING

Farrar, Marjorie M. *Conflict and Compromise: The Strategy, Politics, and Diplomacy of the French Blockade, 1914–1918*. The Hague, 1974.

Ferro, Marc. *The Great War, 1914–1918*. London, 1973.

Horne, Alistair. *The Price of Glory: Verdun, 1916*. New York, 1962.

King, Jere C. *Generals and Politicians: Conflict between France's High Command, Parliament, and Government, 1914–1918*. Berkeley, Calif., 1951.

Néré, J. *The Foreign Policy of France from 1914 to 1945*. London, 1975.

Bonnard, Philippe. *La Fin d'un monde (1914–1929)*. Paris, 1973.

Ducasse, André, Jacques Meyer, and Gabriel Perreux. *Vie et mort des français, 1914–1918: Simple histoire de la Grande Guerre*. Paris, 1962.

Pedroncini, Guy. *Les Mutineries de 1917*. Paris, 1967.

SUGGESTIONS FOR FURTHER READING

25
The Third Republic between Two Wars

The euphoria of victory soon gave way to disillusionment. Weakened by its immense effort, France regained neither the place it had occupied in the world before 1914 nor its economic and social stability. The spread of foreign ideologies widened internal divisions, while French security was threatened by Hitler's Germany. The fragility and impotence of its governments, pawns in the game of politics, revealed the decay of the parliamentary system.

I. THE POSTWAR PERIOD, 1920–24

The Problems of Peace. France emerged from the war victorious but severely drained of its human resources. The loss of life amounted to 1.3 million killed or missing, the largest share of active men among all major belligerents. More than 1.1 million were permanently disabled. And in a kind of reverse selection, these losses struck the men who were most physically and mentally fit. The birth rate dropped precipitously after the outbreak of the war and recovered only in 1919, leaving another gaping hole in the French population. (See graphs, pp. 336–37.) Material losses were immense. In the combat zones, pounded by artillery fire, some 11,000 square miles, including entire villages and towns,

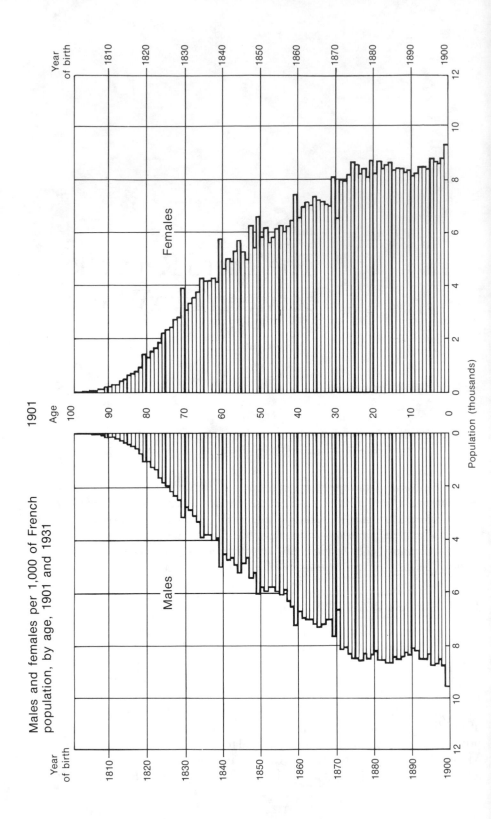

Males and females per 1,000 of French population, by age, 1901 and 1931

1901

Males

Females

Year of birth

Age

Population (thousands)

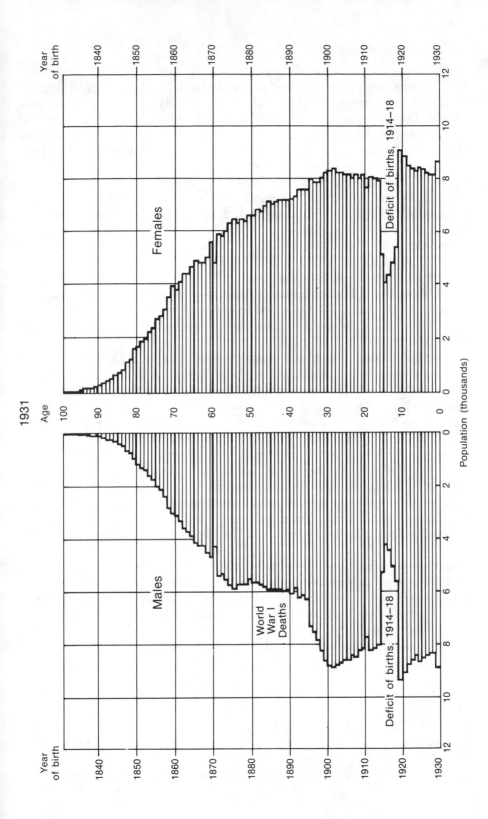

1931

Year of birth

Females

Deficit of births, 1914–18

Males

World War I Deaths

Deficit of births, 1914–18

Age

Year of birth

Population (thousands)

had become deserts of ruins or unusable land. In the occupied departments the retreating enemy had systematically destroyed industrial plants, flooded mines, carried off livestock, and destroyed transportation networks. In unoccupied areas industrial plants and railroads had deteriorated under constant use without adequate maintenance and replacements. To meet current war costs, which rose to more than 150 billion francs, the government had been obliged to liquidate a large share of French investments abroad and the country's gold reserve, and to contract immense debts both in France and among its allies. Where would the money come from to cover both the debts and the costs of reconstruction? "Germany will pay." This simplistic solution of course collided with the ill will of the defeated Germans and with their real inability to assume such a burden.

The two great interlocking problems—security and reparations—jeopardized France's relations not only with Germany but also with its two major allies, whose aid remained as necessary in peace as it had been in war.

In this regard disillusion came swiftly. The United States Senate refused to ratify the agreements made by President Wilson, so the guarantee accepted by Clemenceau in exchange for giving up the Rhineland disappeared. The security that might have been guaranteed by the League of Nations, Wilson's great dream, was equally ineffective, for the British and Americans denied it any real power to enforce its decisions. As for reparations, the British and Americans wanted to lighten the load as much as possible so as to facilitate Germany's economic recovery. When the French used the same argument to secure a reduction in the debts they had themselves contracted in the common cause, they encountered a categorical refusal. This attitude on the part of their allies nurtured a lasting resentment among the French people.

The National Bloc. The "Horizon-Blue Chamber" that emerged from the legislative elections of November 1919 demonstrated that the wartime nationalism had survived. The National Bloc, a coalition of rightist and center parties with a few Radicals, campaigned against the Bolshevik threat and won a crushing majority.

The rule of the National Bloc began with a kind of patricide, for when the senators and deputies met in February 1919 to elect a new president, they rejected Clemenceau, the "Father of Victory." After this humiliating defeat, Clemenceau retired from public life. His successor as premier, Alexandre Millerand, another Socialist turned conservative, was himself excluded from parliamentary life when he was elected president in September 1920, to replace Paul Deschanel, the weak character who had been chosen over Clemenceau, when Deschanel proved to be mentally ill and unable to perform his duties.

Two men in particular now dominated the political scene—Raymond Poincaré and Aristide Briand. In the eyes of the average French citizen, Poincaré, an indefatigable and methodical worker, embodied the virtues of economic and moral integrity and the will to apply the Versailles Treaty in all its rigor. Briand, subtle and indolent, was a fascinating speaker who leaned toward compromise solutions and retained a propensity for humanitarianism from his Socialist past.

The Birth of the Communist Party. The Socialists had willingly excluded themselves from the National Bloc, and their influence soon suffered from an internal schism. At the Congress of Tours, in December 1920, the debate on policy toward Lenin's Third International ended in a party split between the new pro-Soviet and revolutionary French Communist party and the SFIO the old Workers' International, which remained committed to the democratic, reformist, and patriotic ideals of Jaurès.

A parallel break in the labor movement took place in July 1921, between the CGT (Confédération Générale du Travail, or General Confederation of Labor), which echoed the reformist spirit of the SFIO, and the CFTU (Confédération Générale du Travail Unitaire, or General Confederation of United Labor), the transmission belt of the Communist party within the workers' movement. Alongside the two large labor federations was the CFTC (Confédération Française des Travailleurs Chretiens, or French Confederation of Christian Workers), founded in 1919. Much later it was to acquire considerable influence.

Reparations. Briand, head of government from January 1921 to January 1922, attempted to forge alliances in Eastern Europe to replace the prewar alliance with Russia. On the one hand, he helped Poland to strengthen itself against the Soviets and to expand into Silesia. On the other, he encouraged the formation of the Little Entente of Czechoslovakia, Romania, and Yugoslavia. Still, the problem of reparations became his chief preoccupation, as the string of international conferences in 1921 eroded the French position.

The discouraged Briand gave way to Poincaré, who at first negotiated stubbornly in defense of French claims. Eventually convinced that the Germans were playing games with Allied goodwill, he decided to resort to force. In January 1923 French and Belgian troops seized control of the mines and factories of the Ruhr, the principal center of German industrial might. At first the Germans countered this move with passive resistance and stay-away strikes, but the threat of a complete economic collapse eventually forced them to yield. New negotiations between Germany and the Allies began in January 1924. The result was the Dawes Plan, a reparations settlement that partially satisfied French demands.

Economic Recovery. French industry benefited from concentration, adoption of mass-production methods, and pent-up demand, and by 1924 it had pushed its production above prewar levels. Expansion continued through the 1920s, and in 1930 the index of industrial production stood 40 percent above the 1913 level. Growth was particularly striking in iron and steel and in new branches of industry—automobiles, rubber, petrochemicals, and electrical equipment. With this growth came a trend toward larger, more efficient industrial enterprises and greater dependence on mechanical power. In 1930 the number of companies with more than 500 workers was double the number in 1900.

The energy to power industry came principally from coal, and coal production rose 30 percent above prewar levels. Production of electricity increased from 3.5 billion kilowatt hours in 1920 to 15 billion in 1930, more than half from water power, which the government was developing as a partial substitute for diminishing domestic mineral sources of energy. In 1924 it established the Compagnie Française des Pétroles to ensure a dependable source of oil to meet the growing needs of industry and automobiles.

Inflation. Reconstruction was almost 80 percent completed by 1924. Greatly increased tax receipts encouraged hopes for a return to a balanced budget, but those hopes depended on Germany's fulfillment of its obligation to pay reparations.

Behind the brilliant facade of reconstruction and economic recovery, two disturbing symptoms belied the illusions of those who believed it possible to relive the good old days of the prewar Belle Epoque. In 1919 the foreign-exchange value of the franc, which had been kept at the prewar level by fiat during the war years, began to fluctuate downward (see Table 4). Prices at home soared. The consumer price index had doubled during the war, and it doubled again between 1918 and 1929. Wages generally kept pace with this increase in the long run, but everyone who lived on a fixed income was hard hit.

Table 4. Value of the franc in U.S. currency and retail price index, 1914−24

DATE	EXCHANGE RATE IN U.S. CURRENCY	RETAIL PRICE INDEX (1914 = 100)
August 1914	$0.20	100
February 1919	0.173	279
November 1919	0.09	302
November 1920	0.059	452
November 1923	0.05	375
November 1924	0.045	428

Employers. With postwar industrial expansion a new type of big businessman appeared, in control of huge enterprises. Their conspicuous influence on public policy and the advertising of their firms' products made the names of such men as Citroën, Renault, and Coty household words.

As a group employers were more conspicuous politically than ever before. During the war the government had encouraged those in key industries to join in national organizations to facilitate the state's direction of the war economy. In 1919 twenty-one of these organizations formed the Confédération Générale de la Production Française (General Confederation of French Production). It became the spokesman for big business and a powerful pressure group in its dealings with the government. Its militant antiunion stand contributed to increased polarization of organized labor and organized business.

Labor. The structure of the industrial labor force was powerfully altered by the introduction of mass-production methods. The typical new industrial worker was an assembly-line worker who repetitiously performed one simple operation that required little skill or training. These workers were readily replaceable and therefore had little economic power in their dealings with employers. Demand for skilled workers declined, and they sought to defend their interests through their unions.

Real wages in 1919 were 15 to 20 percent below the level of 1914. In 1918 the CGT abandoned its prewar revolutionary position to adopt a militant reform program, and workers by the hundreds of thousands joined it and the CFTC in the hope of winning higher wages. In 1919 the CGT launched a series of strikes that culminated in a general strike in May 1920. The organized employers, supported by the government, were ready to combat it, and the strike failed. The only important gain of a year of labor strife was the eight-hour day, established by law in April 1919. Disillusioned workers left the unions as quickly as they had flocked to them. The economic recovery eventually did lift real wages above the prewar level, but not until 1930.

Agriculture. Agriculture recovered more slowly than industry, reaching prewar levels of production only at the end of the 1920s. It continued to be technologically backward and labor-intensive. Thirty-three percent of the employed population still worked in agriculture in 1929, and the yields per acre were well below those of neighboring countries.

Women's Changing Role. The demands of war and labor shortages had brought more women into the work force than ever before—even bourgeois women, who earlier had rarely ventured into the labor market. Women took on greater responsibilities, had more money to spend, and acquired new independence, advances they were reluctant to surrender in peacetime. Moreover, the devastation of a generation of young men left thousands of women widowed, charged with the care of disabled husbands or sons, or with reduced chances of marriage, and they were obliged to make their own ways in the world. Women continued to work in industry and increasingly in offices. In 1921 they made up 40 percent of the labor force, and 42 percent of adult women were gainfully employed. More of them went into the professions. One-third of the university students in 1939 were women, up from one-tenth in 1913. Léon Blum's ministry in 1936 included three women secretaries of state, the first women cabinet members in French history.

Women rebelled against restrictive social conventions, and in cities short-haired women in short skirts smoking in public became a common sight. But the Republic continued to deny the vote to its female citizens. In 1919 and on a number of occasions thereafter the Senate voted down bills passed by the Chamber of Deputies which would have given women the same voting rights as men.

The Arts. Artistic and literary life enjoyed a strong revival. The ferment of the times was expressed by the surrealist movement, an antirational revolt against modern art as represented by Pablo Picasso, Georges Rouault, and others of the School of Paris, and an attack on bourgeois cultural values. Jean Arp (a Swiss), Max Ernst (a German), both Parisians by adoption, and André Breton were leading members of this movement. In literature there was a parallel rejection of traditional rationalism, as, for example, in the works of Marcel Proust and André Gide, the two French literary giants of the 1920s. The cinema emerged as a new art form as well as a purveyor of mass entertainment. In music American jazz won wide popularity. The International Exposition of the Decorative Arts, held in Paris in 1925, helped to shape and popularize a distinctive decorative style that eventually took its name from the exposition —Art Deco. Many examples of it survive in movie houses and hotels built in the 1920s and 1930s.

Religious Peace. The governments that emerged from the National Bloc majority sought to avoid a revival of the conflicts that had poisoned relations between state and church before the war. Briand reestablished diplomatic relations with the Vatican. Lengthy negotiations resulted in 1924 in a settlement of the vexing problem of the title to church property, unresolved since the separation of church and state in 1905.

II. THE RETURN TO THE POLITICS OF PARTIES

The favor that Briand and Poincaré showed the church angered the Radicals and helped to drive them into an alliance with the Socialists in the elections of May 1924. The issues of the high cost of living and finances were no less important. The Left Cartel won a majority in the Chamber of Deputies. Its first act was to force the resignation of President Millerand, who opposed the leftist program, but it could not prevent his replacement by one of the most moderate Radicals, Gaston Doumergue. The Socialists had no desire to enter the government that was now formed by Edouard Herriot, leader of the Radical party, but they did support him with their votes.

The militant anticlericalism of the Cartel aroused the indignation and concern of Catholics. But more dangerous to the Herriot government was the worry of people who had money, a lot or a little, but refused to subscribe to the loans that the Treasury had to float to meet its obligations. The franc plummeted; in March it traded below 3.5 cents. On April 10, 1925, the Senate, abandoning its usual role, overthrew Herriot.

A period of extreme instability followed; in sixteen months six ministries fell, one after the other, as the franc continued its slide. By July 1925 it had fallen below 2 cents.

Poincaré and Financial Stabilization. In July 1926 Doumergue at last called on Poincaré to form a broad-based coalition ministry. Representatives of all major parties except the Socialists participated. The support of British and American financiers was won by the Mellon-Béranger agreement of September 1926, which settled the difficult problem of French war debts to the United States. Confidence returned and the value of the franc rose so rapidly that the French export trade was hampered.

The legislative elections of April 1928 were a victory for the parties of the right and center, which had supported Poincaré. Poincaré could then proceed to restore order in the monetary system. A law of June 25, 1928, ended the compulsory acceptance of paper money, in effect since August 1914, and again made the franc convertible to gold, but at a rate that represented no more than a fifth of the value of the "Germinal franc" (named for the seventh month in the Republican calendar), which had been unchanged since March 1803. The new gold content of the franc made the dollar equivalent to 25 francs, 52 centimes (that is, the franc was worth 4 cents). Such a devaluation, the first of a long series, enabled the Treasury to pay off part of the debts it had contracted in Germinal francs in heavily depreciated francs. But it effectively wiped out four-fifths of the holdings of all those who, often out of patriotic enthusiasm, had lent their gold and their savings to the state. Public credit and even the French way of thinking were permanently affected. Particularly hard hit were the frugal bourgeoisie, who had been the backbone of the Republic. Now, disillusioned and poorer, they were ready to listen to the Republic's enemies, who promised to protect middle-class interests against big business, big labor, and governments that were subservient to them.

In the short run, however, this monetary stabilization was salutary. During the great world economic crisis that raged after 1929 the franc stood as a hard currency. Foreign capital poured into France, and the government could borrow on the money market on terms unknown since 1914.

Briand and Foreign Policy. Throughout the governmental confusion between April 1925 and March 1932, and even under Poincaré, the Ministry of Foreign Affairs was headed by Aristide Briand. His policy of conciliation was carried out largely through the League of Nations. His principal aim was to gain from Germany voluntary recognition of its new western boundaries and from England a pledge to defend them. This was the object of the Locarno Pact of October 16, 1925. A year later Germany was admitted to the League of Nations. Briand worked to secure the entry of the United States into the vast system of collective security that he envisioned. His efforts achieved only a *pro forma* success—the Kellogg-Briand Pact, a general renunciation of war, solemnly signed in Paris by the representatives of fifteen powers on August 27, 1928. But it was only a noble declaration of intent, with no practical effect— which explains why all the nations of the world (with five exceptions) could eventually approve it.

At a conference held at The Hague in August 1929, the German foreign minister, Gustav Stresemann, took advantage of this atmosphere of conciliation to secure the early evacuation of the Rhineland and a new system of reparations payments, the Young Plan, which included both a substantial reduction of the total German debt and the elimination of foreign controls over Germany's finances.

Briand took increasing delight in his role as the "Apostle of Peace," but he was also accused of weakness and naiveté by a segment of the French public. He proved to be a herald of the future in September 1929, when he launched the idea of a European federation, but his plan was not taken seriously in his time.

The Rightist Government. Financial stabilization restored the Radicals' freedom to maneuver, and they used it to rejoin the opposition in September 1928. Poincaré then reshuffled his government, eliminating the representatives of leftist parties. When his failing health forced him to retire in July 1929, the center-right coalition continued to dominate the nine governments that succeeded one another until the elections of June 1932. The most prominent statesman of this period was André Tardieu, a brilliant and abrasive man who did not conceal his technocrat's distaste for the impotence into which the game of party politics had plunged the parliamentary regime. He tried to draw politics out of its traditional rut by giving priority to economic development and social reform. Thus he established a modest system of social insurance and family allotments, and seized the opportunity provided by the healthy financial situation to launch a vast program to modernize highways, railways, electrification, laboratories, hospitals, and schools.

At the same time construction was begun on the Maginot Line, a series of underground fortifications that would (everyone thought) make the eastern border impregnable.

The Colonial Empire. Public euphoria was also sustained by France's achievements in the colonies, which were honored by the Colonial Exposition held in Paris in 1931, the last great celebration of colonial imperialism before its collapse. The war had further expanded the French empire. France had not only recovered the territories in Equatorial Africa ceded to Germany in 1911 but also acquired some of the former German colonies—Cameroon and Togo—and a temporary mandate over Syria and Lebanon, fragments of the old Ottoman Empire. Nationalist feeling among the subject populations had not yet awakened enough to disturb the colonizers. Nationalism in the colonies was still limited to a few small groups led by intellectuals who for the most part had studied in the mother country. The support they found in the Communist party was not of the kind to arouse much sympathy for them. The most serious incident of armed resistance, that of Abd-el-Krim in Morocco in 1925–26, seemed almost like an epilogue to the French wars of conquest.

III. THE DECAY OF THE REGIME

The Return of the Radicals. In the elections of May 1932 the parties of the left won a majority. Since the Socialists were still loath to take part in a bourgeois government, it was the Radicals that led the shaky governments over the next two years. These weak governments were overwhelmed by a combination of foreign dangers and domestic difficulties, most of which were unavoidable.

First, there were financial difficulties. The world economic crisis halted Germany's reparations payments. After a year-long moratorium imposed by the American president Herbert Hoover, the Lausanne

Conference in July 1932 freed Germany from all its obligations in return for a minimal payment of 3 billion Reichsmarks. That pledge was almost immediately repudiated by Adolf Hitler, who became the German chancellor in 1933. Instead of the 62 billion francs that France had first claimed, between 1920 and 1931 it received little more than 8 billion in specie and 4 billion in kind. The loss of this income contributed to budget deficits beginning in 1932. And the French economy, which at first had been spared the dislocations of the world depression, now began to feel its impact: exports fell, industrial activity slackened, unemployment rose, the future seemed uncertain, and capital fled.

Second, foreign dangers appeared. Hitler came to power early in 1933, and in October of that year Germany dramatically left the League of Nations, underlining the failure of Briand's dreams. Would fascism, already well established in Italy, now triumph elsewhere in Europe? In a different way the Soviet threat increased, for under Stalin's fist the chaos in Russia had bred an awesome economic and military power whose subversive agents were everywhere. Whether they were more afraid of communism or fascism, French citizens tended to see themselves in terms of their foreign sympathies, and political passions became increasingly explosive.

Third, political factions were organizing. The discrediting of parliamentary politics and the Fascist and Nazi examples encouraged the growth of organizations made up of men determined to take to the streets to impose their ideas. In addition to the royalist Ligue d'Action Française (League of French Action), which was greatly weakened when Pope Pius XI spoke out against it in 1926, there were the Ligue des Jeunesses Patriotes (League of Patriotic Youth), founded by the Parisian deputy Pierre Taittinger, and, most important, the Croix-de-Feu (Cross of Fire), a veterans' organization led by Lieutenant Colonel François de la Rocque, which claimed 260,000 members in 1935.

The Crisis of February 6, 1934. A political and financial scandal gave these organizations an opportunity for a massive demonstration against the regime. At the end of December 1933 the press exposed the enormous swindles of Serge Stavisky, a Russian-born Jewish adventurer. Some politicians were compromised along with him. Throughout January the affair grew by dramatic leaps. Stavisky died in suspicious circumstances; so did a magistrate who was investigating him. Even the premier, Camille Chautemps, was indirectly implicated, and he resigned. His chosen successor, the Radical Edouard Daladier, presented his cabinet to the Chamber of Deputies on February 6. The fascist leagues and veterans' associations mobilized their members and, in the tradition of nineteenth-century Paris revolutionaries, marched on the Palais Bourbon, the seat of the Chamber of Deputies. Their uncoordinated movements ran head on into the police, who opened fire, killing fifteen and wounding more than a thousand. The demonstrators were stopped short of the palace.

Sharply attacked, Daladier resigned, and the former president Gaston Doumergue was called from retirement to form a ministry of national union along with Herriot and Tardieu. Doumergue was given freedom to act through decree-laws, and he drew up a constitutional amendment that would have strengthened the executive branch. But the Radicals absolutely refused to accept it, and Doumergue was forced to resign. From 1934 to 1936 politics returned to a succession of revolving-door ministries, most of them based on coalitions of centrists and Radicals.

Threats from Abroad. These two years, which were marked at home by economic depression and ill-timed efforts at deflation or wage reductions, also saw a heightening of international tension. Italy began a war of conquest in Ethiopia in October 1935. It demonstrated the impotence of the League of Nations and wrecked the efforts of French foreign minister Pierre Laval to secure an alliance with Mussolini, who threw himself into the arms of Hitler.

To counter the German danger, France's leaders sought to revive the old Russian alliance. A Franco-Soviet treaty was signed in May 1935 and ratified by the Chamber of Deputies on February 27, 1936. Hitler declared that this act nullified the Locarno Pact and marched his troops into the demilitarized Rhineland. The French army, a defensive force since 1918, was not prepared for the swift offensive action that the situation demanded. The government, now headed by the Radical Albert Sarraut, merely issued verbal protests against this flagrant violation of the Versailles Treaty, and England, even less prepared, opposed any military action. Thus the last opportunity to block Hitler's projected moves was missed.

The Popular Front. Under the threat of fascism, represented at home by the right-wing leagues and abroad by Hitler and Mussolini, the forces of the left closed ranks. The Soviet Union ordered the French Communists to join this effort at unity, and even set the example by its alliance with the bourgeois French state. The syndicalists went even farther along this route; the Socialist CGT and its Communist counterpart, the CGTU, merged in March 1936. The tactical alliance forged by political parties of the left and center took the name of Popular Front and announced a program to "bar the way to fascism" and ensure "bread, peace, and freedom." In the legislative elections of May 1936 the Popular Front won 378 seats, against 241 for the parties to its right. The Socialists emerged with the largest representation in the chamber—146

seats. The losers were the moderate center parties, the principal win-
ners the extremes of right and left. The Radicals lost 600,000 votes and
43 seats. The Communists doubled their popular vote and raised their
representation from 10 deputies to 72. Deputies of the extreme right
increased from 80 to 120.

The Communists declined to participate in the government but
promised to support it. The Radicals, however, joined the ministry
formed by the leader of the Socialist party, Léon Blum. He was a
sensitive and generous intellectual but too scrupulously honest and too
far from demagoguery to captivate and lead the masses or to violate
legality. As a Socialist and a Jew (he was France's first Jewish premier),
he was subject to violent attacks from the extreme right.

The Blum Government. When Blum took office on June 6, he had to deal
with a critical social situation. In the flush of their electoral victory,
workers, led by union militants in the Paris region, took control of their
workplaces and occupied them around the clock. Their purpose was to
make certain that the new government fulfilled the Popular Front's
promises of reforms. The strikes spread throughout the country and
grew into the nation's greatest social upheaval since 1848. Blum brought
together representatives of the CGT and of employers at the Hôtel
Matignon, the premier's residence, and under his mediation they signed
the Matignon Agreement, which provided for immediate wage increases
of 10 to 15 percent and guaranteed workers the right to collective bargaining. A few days later Parliament approved laws instituting the forty-hour
week and annual two-week vacations with pay. The sit-down strikes then
ended, and strikers returned to their jobs.

The strike crisis resolved, the Blum government turned to the Popular Front program. A National Grain Office was created to stabilize
grain prices and ensure a fair return to producers. The Bank of France,
accused of using its powers to dictate financial policy to previous governments, was brought under stricter government control. Part of the
aircraft industry was nationalized. Preparations were begun for a public
works program that would help to cut unemployment. The fascist
leagues were dissolved. Compulsory education was extended to age
fourteen, and an effort was launched to democratize public secondary
education. The newly created Secretariat for Sports and Leisure promoted a wide range of individual sports and other leisure activities.

This reforming zeal, however, soon became mired in insoluble difficulties. The expected economic recovery did not take place. The
forty-hour week, for which French industry was not technically prepared—and with which its owners were not in sympathy—disrupted
production. The wage increase was wiped out by rising consumer
prices, and strikes and other protests resumed, further decreasing production. Unemployment remained high. The balance of foreign trade

showed a growing deficit, and the flight of capital abroad accelerated. Though in June 1936 Blum pledged "neither devaluation nor deflation," in September he had to devalue the franc. This action, almost universally unpopular in France, did not turn the economy around, and the difficulties persisted. In February 1937, to appease his supporters among the Radicals and to calm public anxiety, Blum announced a pause in the Popular Front's program.

Events abroad added to his problems. The civil war in Spain, which began in July 1936, stirred up passions and threatened to split the government coalition. Blum and the Socialists wanted to aid the Spanish Republic, but the Radicals insisted that France avoid involvement in the war. The Communists bitterly criticized Blum when he went along with Britain and adopted a policy of nonintervention. Pressed on all sides, Blum asked Parliament for a temporary grant of full powers to deal with the growing economic crisis. When the Senate refused, he resigned on June 22, 1937.

The Last Governments. The ministries that succeeded Blum's were led by the Radicals Camille Chautemps and Edouard Daladier, first within the framework of the Popular Front—that is, with the participation of the Socialists and the support of the Communists—and then, in the face of mounting danger abroad, with the support of the center and right replacing that of the extreme left. The practice of government by decree-laws, which people had grown used to by then, underscored the decay of the parliamentary system.

In November 1938, when the conservative finance minister, Paul Reynaud, decreed the end of the forty-hour week, raised taxes, and dismissed hundreds of civil servants, the CGT called a one-day general strike in protest. The government took a hard line, and most workers lacked the confidence to respond to the strike call. The strike was a complete failure and a serious rebuff to the Communist party, which had organized it. This was the end of the Popular Front. The hopes for social reform that it represented were not revived for many years.

Reynaud's policies and the determined way he applied them reassured the rich and the business community. The franc stabilized, and industrial production, stimulated by mounting expenditures on armaments, began to recover.

The Economy in the 1930s. The disarray of politics in the 1930s was matched by the malaise of the economy. Industrial production dropped by one-third in the depression years, and though it turned upward in 1938, it still remained below the levels of 1928–30. Industrialists in the 1930s, not so boldly innovative as they had been in the preceding decade, clung to established methods and practices at the price of growing technological backwardness. Unemployment, though much less severe in France than in other industrialized countries, continued to be a chronic, intractable problem.

French agriculture was hard hit by the collapse of agricultural prices in the Great Depression, and farm income sank. The government's response was to protect established interests by tariffs and price supports, and French agriculture continued to be small-scale, high-cost, and inefficient. The number of peasants who abandoned the land for the cities reached a new high in the 1920s and continued at a somewhat lower rate through the 1930s, but at the end of the decade a third of the working population still worked the land.

Demographic Stagnation. Although mortality rates continued to drop—infant mortality by 30 percent in the decades between the wars—the population was stagnant. In 1935 the annual number of births dropped below the number of deaths and remained there into the 1940s. The nation seemed to face depopulation. The government's efforts in the 1920s to raise the number of births by legislating against birth control and abortion seemingly had little effect. The number of births steadily declined, and the average number of children per family remained below two. The payment of family allowances to all families with children, begun in 1939, came too late to influence the birth rate before the war. In 1939 the nation's population was 41.3 million, up only 2 million since 1920. In the same period Germany's population had risen by 10 million.

Social Reform. The net social gains of the 1920s and 1930s were few. In 1939 the eight-hour day and paid vacations remained, but the forty-hour week was a casualty of the Reynaud decree-laws of 1938. A comprehensive social security system such as other industrialized nations had adopted, a goal of organized labor since 1918, remained a distant hope.

A bright spot in the gloomy picture was the ending of tuition charges in public secondary schools in 1933. Stiff new examinations, however, and the subsidiary costs of keeping a child in school prevented any rapid democratization of secondary education. Enrollments rose by 20 percent in the five years after tuition charges were dropped, but they still represented only a small fraction of the children of secondary school age.

Arts. The arts reflected the somber mood of the 1930s. André Malraux explored the human condition and celebrated heroic action in his novels. Louis Ferdinand Céline, in *Voyage au but de la nuit* (1932), expressed a dark pessimism and disgust for human beings. Picasso's painting of aerial bombardment of a Spanish village, *Guernica* (1937), was both a timely political protest and an expression of eternal human tragedy. In the cinema Jean Renoir's masterpiece, *La Grande Illusion*, was a gentle appeal for an end to war.

The decades between the wars saw the emergence of the pivotal figure of twentieth-century architecture, Charles-Edouard Jeanneret-Gris, known as Le Corbusier. He was a theorist and polemicist as well as a practicing architect and urban planner in Paris. More than any other single person, he turned contemporary architects toward functionalism, design based on simple geometric forms, and the conviction that architecture can improve the human condition.

Toward War. After Blum's resignation in June 1937 the Radical government, and particularly the foreign minister, Georges Bonnet, practiced a policy of appeasement toward Germany and Italy. Germany's annexation of Austria, achieved without resistance in March 1938, brought only a mild protest from France.

The crisis over Czechoslovakia, which Hitler provoked soon afterward, was different, for France was committed by treaty to defend that country. But unilateral intervention seemed unthinkable. England still refused to fight. The USSR declared that it was ready to march, but on condition that Poland and Romania give Soviet armies the right of transit, which both countries categorically refused. All that France could do was support the efforts of the two British leaders, Neville Chamberlain and Viscount Halifax, who sought a negotiated solution. On the brink of war, Hitler, Chamberlain, Daladier, and Mussolini met in Munich on September 20, 1938, and reached an agreement that averted war at the cost of giving Hitler everything he had demanded and consenting to the dismemberment of Czechoslovakia. French public opinion was divided between relief among the large majority and indignation among the more farsighted.

The annexation of what remained of Czechoslovakia in March 1939 —in violation of the Munich agreement—changed British policy. The British government finally grasped Hitler's real intentions, and it hastened to offer guarantees to the small and middle-sized countries of Eastern Europe threatened by Germany, including Poland, which had long been bound to France by a defensive alliance. When it became evident that the next German objective would be Danzig, England and France tried to bring the Soviet Union into the anti-Hitler coalition. Their efforts failed in early August, as much because of mutual suspicion as because of Poland's absolute refusal to permit Russian troops on its soil. On August 23 the Soviet Union and Germany signed a nonaggression pact, by which the USSR specifically agreed not to aid the Poles or the Western powers in case of war. To the conciliatory remarks that Hitler issued as late as August 25, Daladier replied that this time France would fulfill its commitments.

On September 1, the same day that German troops invaded Poland, the French government ordered general mobilization. It took place in an atmosphere of gloomy resignation, in contrast to the tempered enthusiasm of August 1914. The next day the Chamber of Deputies accepted the inevitable and voted war credits without discussion. On the evening of September 3, war was formally declared.

SUGGESTIONS FOR FURTHER READING

Bankwitz, Philip C. F. *Maxime Weygand and Civil-Military Relations in Modern France*. Cambridge, Mass., 1967.

Colton, Joel. *Léon Blum: Humanist in Politics*. New York, 1966.

Hughes, Judith. *To the Maginot Line: The Politics of French Military Preparations in the 1920s*. Cambridge, Mass., 1931.

Kemp, Tom. *The French Economy, 1913–1939: The History of a Decline*. London, 1972.

Schucker, Stephen A. *The End of French Predominance in Europe: The Financial Crisis of 1924 and the Adoption of the Dawes Plan*. Chapel Hill, N.C., 1976.

Talbott, John E. *The Politics of Educational Reform in France, 1918–1940*. Princeton, N.J., 1969.

Werth, Alexander. *The Twilight of France, 1933–1940*. New York, 1942.

Wohl, Robert. *French Communism in the Making, 1914–1924*. Stanford, Calif., 1966.

Chastenet, Jacques. *Histoire de la Troisième République*, vols. 5–7. Paris, 1960–63.

Duroselle, Jean-Baptist. *Le Décadence, 1932–1939*. Paris, 1979.

Fohlen, Claude. *La France entre deux guerres*. Paris, 1966.

26
World War II

In the war forced upon the world by Hitler, France suffered an unprecedented military disaster that brought it under German military occupation for four years. The regime of the Third Republic, which was held responsible for the disaster, was replaced by the authoritarian government of Marshal Pétain, established at Vichy. At first welcomed with relief, Pétain's government was brought into disrepute by its efforts to appease the occupier. In contrast, the resistance movement, launched from abroad by General de Gaulle and little noticed at the outset, eventually won the nation's admiration and wide support.

I. THE DEFEAT

The Phony War. By the end of September 1939 Poland was overrun and ceased to exist as a state, and its territory was divided between Germany and the Soviet Union. French assistance was limited to a symbolic offensive in the Saar, which was halted on October 1. Daladier at least firmly rejected Hitler's proposal, made on October 6, for a peace based on acceptance of the accomplished facts.

Actually Hitler would have preferred to launch an immediate attack in the west, and only very unfavorable weather conditions that autumn and an unusually severe winter forced him to postpone his offensive. The Allies played a defensive waiting game, building up their arms supplies while they weakened the enemy by an economic blockade.

Six months of almost total inaction followed. This period of the so-called phony war corroded the nation's morale. Once it became obvious that an invasion was not imminent, people tended to indulge in their pleasures and private interests, whether they were in uniform or not. Defeatism was fostered both by the Communists, whom the German-Soviet alliance had suddenly returned to their pre-1936 antimilitarism, and by those who secretly longed to be done with a war that seemed to have neither an end nor an aim.

The stout resistance by the Finns, who were attacked by the Russians on November 30, gave rise to plans for allied intervention across the Scandinavian states, but the difficulties proved insurmountable. Blamed for its inertia, the Daladier ministry was forced to resign on March 20, 1940.

Paul Reynaud, who replaced him, joined England in a plan to deprive the Germans of access to Swedish iron ore (essential to the German war industry), which was transported through the port of Narvik and the coastal waters of neutral Norway. But Hitler acted first; on April 7–9 he invaded Denmark and Norway. The French and the British nonetheless succeeded in seizing the ore port of Narvik on May 27. But the fate of the war was already being decided elsewhere.

Blitzkrieg (May–June). The German offensive, long in preparation, was unleashed on the morning of May 10 with a massive attack on Belgium and Holland. The battle began under the worst conditions for the French and British. More than half the available French divisions were immobilized in the east on the Maginot Line. Instead of extending the line along the Franco-Belgian border, the government had based its initial defenses on the Albert Canal, which in northern Belgium linked up with the natural barriers of the Scheldt and Meuse rivers. The Belgian army alone was quite unable to defend them, and the French command wanted to move its forces into Belgium in advance of a German attack; but the Belgian government, at the urging of King Leopold III, refused until the last moment to reverse the policy of strict neutrality it had adopted in 1936. When Germany attacked, the French supreme commander, Maurice Gamelin, decided to move his best divisions, including his strategic reserves, into Belgium as swiftly as possible in order to join with what remained of the Belgian and Dutch troops and give battle outside his nation's territory. This maneuver neatly served Hitler's strategy of striking at the weakest point of the hinge between the end of the Maginot Line and the mobile northern wing of the Allied forces, at a point where the mountainous and wooded Ardennes plateau, cut by deep valleys, made an attack by armored divisions seem improbable. Once the breakthrough had been achieved, Germany would drive toward the northwest and envelop the Allied forces that had advanced into Belgium. It was a kind of modified Schlieffen Plan, rolling up and enveloping the French front in the north and in Belgium instead of on the eastern front, as was intended in 1914. The campaign unfolded as planned. On May 15 German armored columns broke through the French line at Sedan, and the break was soon beyond repair. Five days later the Germans reached the sea near Abbeville, cutting off forty-five French and British divisions to the north. One hundred thirty thousand French and 200,000 British escaped the trap in small boats from Dunkirk, but they left behind them all their heavy equipment, a loss that could not be replaced for months. Gamelin, overwhelmed by the swiftly moving events, was relieved of his command on May 19 and replaced by General Maxime Weygand, Marshal Foch's chief of staff in 1918. At the same time Marshal Pétain entered the government as vice premier. By appealing to these old heroes of World War I—Weygand was seventy-three, Pétain eighty-four—Reynaud sought to restore public confidence.

His military initiative immobilized by the immense flood of refugees blocking the roads, and lacking a strategic reserve, Weygand could not mount a counterattack in time to drive back the enemy. He nonetheless managed to establish a last line of resistance that stretched almost continuously from the mouth of the Somme to the Vosges. But he had only 60 divisions to oppose Germany's 138. On June 5 the Germans attacked across the Somme and the Aisne, sending columns in the directions of Rouen, Paris, and Dijon. After that it was only a matter of isolated French units fleeing from the enemy amid millions of panic-striken refugees. To make things worse, Italy entered the war on June 10 in order to share in the division of spoils.

The Armistice. The ministers, who left Paris precipitously on June 10, assembled in Bordeaux on the fifteenth. Meanwhile, the chaotic discussions that took place between the army commanders and the British leaders suggested a daring solution to Reynaud: stop the futile struggle in France by a simple military surrender, move to North Africa with everything they could carry, and continue the fight from there, using the resources of the colonial empire and the still intact French navy. Weygand and Pétain, however, were categorically opposed to this idea. Weygand was not about to make the army bear the shame and responsibility of the defeat alone, and Pétain believed it was the government's duty to stay with the French people to help them through the ordeal. Both were convinced that Great Britain would not hold out long and that it would try to negotiate peace at France's expense.

On the evening of June 16 Reynaud turned over power to Pétain, who immediately began discussions on an armistice. Hitler wanted at any price to prevent the French fleet from going to reinforce the British fleet, and it also suited his plans to maintain a semblance of independent government in France that would assume administrative responsibilities and keep order for him. He therefore proved relatively accommodating. Still, he gave himself the pleasure of celebrating his victory by a symbolic gesture: the armistice was signed on June 22 at Rethondes, the very spot where the Germany of William II surrendered on November 11, 1918. An effective halt to hostilities did not come until June 25, after an armistice with Italy was signed at Rome.

France was divided into two parts, an occupied zone that included the entire north of the country and the Atlantic coast, which remained under German military authority, and a so-called free zone, where the French government retained all the attributes of sovereignty, including control of an army of 100,000 men. Except for some units intended for the defense of the colonial empire, the French fleet was to be assembled and disarmed in its regular home ports; Germany pledged not to touch it. In accordance with usual wartime practice, the costs of the army of occupation would be borne by the vanquished, and the prisoners of war—1.5 million of them—would not be freed until a peace treaty had been concluded.

II. THE GOVERNMENT OF MARSHAL PÉTAIN

The End of the Third Republic. From Bordeaux, in the Occupied Zone, Pétain and his government moved to Vichy, a spa where large hotels could house government offices.

An overwhelming majority of the French welcomed the armistice with relief. Their gratitude extended to the old marshal, who had put his reputation and safety on the line to preserve the country from extreme misfortune. He was persuaded that he had been called upon to undertake the task of national renewal. The first step along this road was to liquidate the regime that had led the country into disaster.

This political operation was carried out by Senator Pierre Laval, to whom Pétain gave a free hand. Between July 4 and 10, Laval, masterfully alternating persuasion and threats, managed to win over the senators and deputies gathered at Vichy, as well as the president, the weak-willed Albert Lebrun. On July 10 the two chambers, legally convened as the National Assembly, accepted the following text by a vote of 569 to 80, with 17 abstentions: "The National Assembly grants full power to the government of the Republic, under the authority and signature of Marshal Pétain, to promulgate by one or several decrees a new constitution

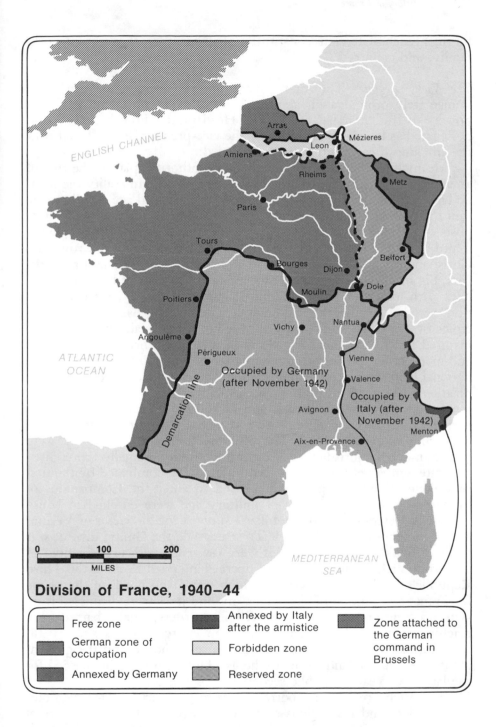

Arras

Leon

Mézieres

Amiens

Rheims

Metz

ENGLISH CHANNEL

Paris

Tours

Belfort

Bourges

Dijon

Poitiers

Moulin

Dole

Angoulême

Vichy

Nantua

ATLANTIC
OCEAN

Périgueux

Vienne

Occupied by Germany
(after November 1942)

Valence

Occupied by
Italy (after
November 1942)

Avignon

Menton

Aix-en-Provence

MEDITERRANEAN
SEA

0   100   200

MILES

Division of France, 1940–44

Free zone

Annexed by Italy
after the armistice

Zone attached to
the German
command in
Brussels

German zone of
occupation

Forbidden zone

Annexed by Germany

Reserved zone

for the French State. This constitution shall guarantee the rights of work, family, and country."

The Vichy Regime. The first "constitutional decrees," which were immediately promulgated, abolished the office of president, gave full powers to the "Marshal of France, Head of the French State," and designated as his eventual successor the vice-premier, Pierre Laval. But the announced constitution was postponed.

Meanwhile, the old marshal, the sole authority, played the role of an absolute monarch, surrounded by a kind of cult. In reality the mental lapses and indecisiveness that came with advanced age usually made him the puppet of his entourage and ministers. In high administrative posts and among the ranks of his loyal admirers appeared the people the Third Republic had fought, disturbed, or disappointed: old royalists, Christians of both Catholic and Protestant persuasions, military officers, big businessmen, and antiparliamentary fascists of both right and left. With its motto "Work, Family, Country," the "National Revolution" set itself against the parliamentary democracy based on the principles of 1789. The new order that it hoped to establish was at first inspired less by National Socialism than by the Christian corporative and moral order of the Portuguese regime of Antonio Salazar. Thus the national labor unions were abolished and replaced by corporative organizations that included representatives of workers and employers chosen by the government. Strikes and lockouts were banned. A peasant corporation supervised agriculture and, in the government's words, "all conditions of peasant life." The other sectors of the economy were placed under the jurisdiction of committees that nominally represented the state, employers, and labor, but in fact were dominated by the first two alone. Young people were pressed to enter the Companions of France movement, and those of military age were enrolled in youth camps. A Veterans' Legion mobilized support for the victor of Verdun among veterans of World War I. To strengthen the family, divorce was made difficult, and large families were rewarded with tax benefits.

From Vichy issued a series of decrees intended to undo the Third Republic's public school system, which was given much of the blame for France's decline and fall. Freemasons and Jews were dismissed from state teaching posts. Members of religious orders, legally barred from teaching since 1904, though tolerated in church schools since 1918, were formally authorized to teach in church schools, and the government gave financial aid to such schools. Tuition was again charged for the last three years in public secondary schools.

The Vichy regime also borrowed from totalitarian states such odious practices and institutions as arbitrary arrest and detection, brutal police interrogations, special tribunals, persecution of Jews, and a militia in the service of "public order," which sadly resembled the sinister S.S. of Nazi Germany.

The Occupied Zone. In violation of the armistice, the Germans simply annexed the three departments of Alsace-Lorraine to the Reich. Young men of military age there were forcibly inducted into the Wehrmacht, and the Germanization of administration and property was actively pushed. The departments of Nord and Pas-de-Calais were attached to the military command at Brussels. The rest of Occupied France was subject to a military commander (*Militärbefehlshaber*) resident in Paris, assisted (and watched) by security forces (*Abwehr*) and propaganda services (*Propagandastaffel*), and by Ambassador Otto Abetz, representing the foreign minister. The French officials who remained in office were closely subordinated to them, and all acts of the Vichy government— appointments and various decrees—were subject to their approval. Out of ideology or self-interest, some misguided Frenchmen became parties to this oppression through the fascist-inspired press and other organizations. Among them were Marcel Déat, a former Socialist minister, and Jacques Doriot, a dissident Communist who founded the PPF (Parti Populaire Français, or French Popular Party). They vehemently denounced the Vichy government for its reluctance to give full support to the German cause.

The German authorities used the terms of the armistice agreement and others that they added unilaterally to exploit France's resources methodically and brutally. The total of these expropriations has been estimated at 50 percent of national income. Particularly in the cities the French became familiar with rationing, hunger, cold, and fear—of the German secret police (the *Gestapo*) and the increasingly intense British and American bombardments.

The Beginnings of Collaboration. The policy shifts of the Vichy government and its leaders were determined by its relations with Germany. At the beginning two opinions clashed over the way the armistice should be applied. Some, like General Weygand, minister of national defense, wanted honest compliance with the armistice terms but no additional cooperation with the temporarily victorious adversary. Others, led by Pierre Laval, believed that the best way to safeguard France's future was to join freely in the German war effort, in the hope of better treatment when peace came. As for Marshal Pétain, he was chiefly moved by the desire to protect the French from the terrible fate of the Poles and to relieve the sufferings of the population and prisoners of war. He believed that this goal was most likely to be achieved—and a regenerated conservative France established—by collaboration with Germany.

Laval supported his pro-German policy by an argument drawn from a tragic event: on July 3, 1940, a large part of the French fleet, anchored in the harbor of Mers el-Kébir in Algeria, was attacked and destroyed by the British, who were afraid that the ships might be used against them. The shock of this attack, which killed 1,300 French sailors, stirred French indignation and turned Admiral François Darlan, the principal creator and chief of French naval forces, into an implacable enemy of England.

Laval eliminated Weygand's opposition on September 6 by sending him to Algeria as its civil and military governor. A trip made by Hitler to confer with Spain's dictator, Francisco Franco, on the Spanish border provided Laval with the opportunity to press his policy. A meeting between Pétain and Hitler at the railway station at Montoire on October 24, 1940, heralded a new policy of collaboration between Germany and France. But the concessions that Pétain hoped to secure by this gesture, which deeply shocked the public, did not materialize. Disappointed, the marshal joined a kind of anti-Laval conspiracy among the ministers, and Laval was suddenly dismissed on December 13, to the outrage of the Germans.

Darlan. Laval's replacement as foreign minister, Pierre Etienne Flandin, an intelligent and courageous right-wing member of Parliament, espoused Weygand's policies, but he was given no time to pursue them. On February 9, 1941, he was dismissed on orders from the Germans. The government passed into the hands of Admiral François Darlan, who was simultaneously vice-premier, foreign minister, minister of the interior, and minister of the navy. For the fourteen months he was in power, this able, ambitious, and opportunistic sailor tacked with the winds of circumstances. In May 1941 he went so far along the path of collaboration as to grant the Germans use of French military bases in Syria from which to support a revolt against the pro-British government of Iraq. When the Germans grew uneasy over Weygand's efforts to build a new army in North Africa, Darlan had him recalled to France. But when German reverses in Russia and Libya early in 1942 suggested the possibility of an Axis defeat, Darlan became less accommodating.

In April 1942 Hitler demanded that Laval be returned to power. Despite his repugnance for Laval, Pétain gave in, and by a special constitutional decree even gave him control over domestic and foreign policy. Thereafter the "National Revolution" was set aside, and a large number of the Vichy regime's original supporters withdrew from it.

Life in Occupied France. During the occupation the French people lived in an economy of growing scarcity. The Germans drained off much of the national product. Imports were few. Both industrial and agricultural production were well below even the depressed levels of the 1930s.

Rationing and wage and price controls failed to halt inflation; retail prices more than doubled between 1940 and 1944. Wages did not keep pace. For most urban residents the occupation meant a monotonous and skimpy diet, standing in long lines to buy food, riding overcrowded public transportation, and trying to keep warm in underheated rooms.

The End of the Vichy Regime. When the British and Americans landed in North Africa, on November 8, 1942, the French overseas forces rallied to them. Weygand and many others pleaded with Pétain to go there to resume the struggle. He refused to do so, still convinced that his presence in France was more useful. The Germans, for their part, considered the armistice agreement of June 1940 annulled and invaded the Free Zone, where they disarmed the small French armistice army. As the Toulon fleet was about to be captured, it was scuttled by its own crews.

The Vichy government lost its last cards along with its fleet and colonies. From then on, as far as the Germans were concerned, it was no more than a docile and contemptible tool within a totally occupied France. Laval governed virtually alone, pursuing his collaboration policy with energy and courage worthy of a better cause. His main discussions with the Germans were concerned with the requisitioning of French manpower for German industries. In exchange for more than 600,000 French workers sent to Germany through the STO (Service du Travail Obligatoire, or Compulsory Labor Service), he secured the return of some 100,000 war prisoners.

Once the Germans were embroiled in an exhausting war in Russia, they ruthlessly exploited their power over French productive capacity. In 1942 they took more than half of French aircraft, automobile, and machinery production. They also drew heavily on French agriculture, even though production had fallen until it hardly met domestic needs. In 1944, for example, one-fourth of French meat production went to Germany. A rigged exchange rate between the German mark and the French franc enabled Germans to buy in France at half the market price.

III. RESISTANCE AND LIBERATION

De Gaulle and Free France. Four days before the armistice, a French voice on the BBC called on Frenchmen to continue the struggle despite the defeat. It was the voice of General Charles de Gaulle, a theorist of mobile warfare whom Paul Reynaud had brought into his cabinet on June 5, and who stayed in London after the armistice. At first his appeal brought no response. The general appeared to be a mercenary in the service of the British—the people who were responsible for the massacre at Mers el-Kébir. But Prime Minister Winston Churchill recognized him as the leader of all Frenchmen who wanted to go on fighting, and he promised material support for Free French armed forces. Their numbers, few at first, grew gradually until there were enough to form distinct French combat units within the British forces. It was hoped that De Gaulle could rally France's overseas territories, but North Africa was kept firmly leashed to Vichy by General Weygand. An attempt by the Free French to seize Dakar, in French West Africa, failed miserably in September 1940. They did, however, manage to establish themselves in French Equatorial Africa.

In the spring of 1941, Darlan turned over the French air bases in Syria to the Germans. De Gaulle pressured the British to attack Syria with the help of a Free French division, hoping then to assume control over it. But the French army in Syria, under General Henri Dentz, remained loyal to Pétain. After its surrender, most of his officers and soldiers, indignant at having been attacked by Frenchmen, refused to join De Gaulle, and Syria passed under British control.

This disappointment undoubtedly persuaded the British and Americans to keep De Gaulle and the Free French totally in the dark about their large-scale operation in North Africa in November 1942. To win over the French forces there, which so far had been loyal to Pétain, they counted on General Henri Giraud, an able soldier who was very popular in the army and was looked up to for his sensational escape from a German prison camp. He was spirited out of France by the Americans and taken to Algeria, but it was soon apparent that the Vichy commanders and governors in Africa were not willing to follow his lead and shift their allegiance. As luck would have it, however, Admiral Darlan was in Algeria at the critical moment. Claiming that he had secretly been given a free hand by Marshal Pétain, he halted French resistance to the American invasion, ostensibly on orders from Vichy. The British and Americans recognized him as the head of the French government in Algeria. His rule was cut short when he was assassinated by a young Gaullist on December 23. Giraud then assumed the role for which he had first been intended.

De Gaulle did not enjoy being shoved into the background. He managed to convince Roosevelt and Churchill of the need to unify the French war effort. At the end of May 1943 he went to Algeria to preside over the French Committee of National Liberation as co-chairman with Giraud. The other positions on the committee were divided between Gaullists and Giraudists. Giraud had no political sense, and he was soon relegated to purely military functions. De Gaulle, now master of the situation, eliminated from the committee those who had in any way served Pétain's regime and added representatives of the resistance movement within France. With some former members of Parliament from the Third Republic, he established a Consultative Assembly, which made a study of the future political organization of liberated France. Finally, on May 26, 1944, the Committee of Liberation proclaimed itself the Provisional Government of the French Republic.

Meanwhile, Giraud was able to enlist enough men to form two armored and five infantry divisions, equipped by the Americans. They soon proved their worth. They took a very active part in the Italian campaign in the summer of 1943, under General Alphonse Juin, and not long afterward, under Generals Jean Leclerc and Jean de Lattre de Tassigny, helped to liberate France.

The Resistance. The spirit of resistance developed earlier and stronger in the Occupied Zone, which was subject to German extortions, but the Unoccupied Zone offered more possibilities for organized movements. The distribution of clandestine pamphlets and periodicals, the organization of relay stations to help escaped prisoners of war cross the line between Occupied and Unoccupied France and across the Spanish border, the collection and transmission of intelligence—these were their main activities. The numbers and effectiveness of the resisters grew remarkably after June 1941, when the Communists found themselves once more in the camp of Germany's enemies as a result of Hitler's aggression against the USSR. Acts of sabotage and assassination of occupation troops led to brutal reprisals and the shooting of hostages. Hatred of the Germans grew.

These activities intensified in 1942 and led to the formation of the *maquis,* small bands of partisans who hid out in the forests and mountains. At first they were composed of young men who wanted to evade the obligatory service in Germany and were often commanded by former officers of the armistice army. The total occupation of France, and with it the collapse of the Vichy regime's illusions, now assured the resistance the help or at least tolerance of most of the population.

A representative of General de Gaulle, Jean Moulin, parachuted into France in January 1942 and made contact with the various independent movements. In May 1943 their leaders met secretly in Paris to form the CNR (Conseil National de la Résistance, or National Council of the Resistance). Improved liaison between London and the resistance in France permitted the systematic parachuting of arms beginning in November 1943. Finally, in February 1944, all the armed organizations were united in principle in the organization known as the FFI (Forces Françaises de l'Intérieur, or French Forces of the Interior). The Communists, however, anticipated an eventual seizure of power and tried to infiltrate these groups, and even to retain their own means of action, such as their armed bands of FTP (Francs-Tireurs Partisans, or Partisan Sharpshooters).

The resistance in France was nominally a patriotic, nonpartisan movement directed against the German occupation. In fact, most of its members came from the prewar political left, and it developed into a leftist-oriented political movement committed not only to the liberation of France but also to its reorganization along lines advocated by the prewar left. The Charter of Resistance, drawn up by the National Resistance Council and accepted by all resistance groups, called for a planned economy, the nationalization of big industries and banks, a guaranteed right to work, labor participation in management, and a comprehensive social security system. The leadership of the new leftist France, according to resistance plans, would come out of the resistance movement itself, replacing the discredited elites of the Third Republic and Vichy.

De Gaulle and his associates in the resistance outside France came from the traditional government and military elites of prewar France, politically oriented to the right. The political differences between them and the resistance inside France were fundamental. While the country remained occupied, these differences were submerged in a common patriotism; but once France was liberated, they could lead to serious conflict, even to civil war.

The Liberation. When the Allies landed in Normandy on June 6, 1944, all the forces of the FFI, alerted by London, went into action. Despite the useless losses resulting from lack of arms and many mistakes, they contributed to victory by disrupting enemy communications and transportation. The American command was so impressed that it abandoned its original plan to place the liberated provinces under Allied military administration, which would have dealt directly with existing local authorities, without taking the provisional government in Algiers into account.

The rapid and complete collapse of the Vichy government contributed to the same end. On August 20 Marshal Pétain was forcibly removed by the Germans and taken first to Belfort, then on September 9 to Sigmaringen, in Germany. With several other figures of the Vichy regime, Laval went there to join him. Everywhere in France prefects and mayors more or less spontaneously turned over power to the liberation committees that sprang up and to commissioners of the Republic sent by the provisional government in Algiers.

Pressed by the Communists, the Paris Liberation Committee called on the people to rise against the German occupiers on August 19. The decision was premature, for the Allied armies were still far off, and the German military commander, General Dietrich von Choltitz, still had enough troops to crush the FFI. Fortunately, he realized the ultimate futility of the struggle and had the courage to disobey Hitler, who had ordered him to destroy the capital by dynamite and fire. Warned of the critical situation, General Dwight D. Eisenhower authorized the French Second Armored Division, commanded by General Leclerc, to advance directly on Paris. Its first units entered the city on the evening of August 24, and the next day it liberated the city. While Von Choltitz signed the surrender of his garrison, Paris welcomed the liberators in a delirium of joy. De Gaulle, arriving in the capital on August 25, paid a symbolic call on the National Council of Resistance, now installed in the city hall. The next day, accompanied by members of the council, all significantly a pace or two behind him, he marched triumphantly down the Avenue des Champs Elysées.

When the Allied armies landed in Provence on August 15–16, the French contingent—260,000 men in seven divisions moved up from Italy—was as large as the American. General de Lattre de Tassigny, who commanded that first French army, was thus able to determine his own operations. His advance was rapid, and by September 12 his forces in Burgundy linked up with the armies moving down from the north.

The resistance movement both within and outside France had proved its value to the country. Through the resistance the nation participated in its own liberation—an important psychological benefit to a people shaken by the collapse of 1940. It ensured a reasonably orderly transfer of power to a new government and administration, avoided an Allied military government, and forestalled an Allied deal with Vichy or a Communist seizure of power.

The End of the War. By November only the north of Alsace and part of Lorraine remained to be liberated, but a million Frenchmen were still prisoners of war in Germany, along with 600,000 requisitioned workers and almost 200,000 prisoners in concentration camps. To free them France had to continue and accelerate its military effort. Military strength was also needed to ensure that France's interests were taken into account by its allies when peace was concluded, for the "Big Three"—Churchill, Roosevelt, and Stalin—treated France as a minor consideration. (De Gaulle was not invited to the Yalta Conference in February 1945.) More than 100,000 FFI volunteers soon swelled the ranks of French units from England and Africa. Under Generals Leclerc, de Lattre, and André Béthouart, these armies liberated the rest of France and penetrated deep into southern Germany. This enabled De Gaulle to secure the presence of a French representative at the signing of the surrender on May 7, 1945, and later the formation of French occupation zones in Germany and Austria.

The Summing Up. The loss of life in France attributable to the war reached 600,000, far less than during World War I. Another difference was that two-thirds of the dead were civilians—deportees, executed, and bombing victims. On the other hand, the material destruction was certainly greater. This time it extended over the entire country as British and American bombers concentrated on ports, railway stations, rail lines, and bridges. In addition, more than a million buildings were destroyed or damaged.

Finally, to meet German demands, the amount of paper money in circulation had had to be increased, from 142 billion francs on August 31, 1939, to 632 billion in October 1944. At the official exchange rate the franc was in 1944 worth 2 cents in U.S. currency; on the black market it brought less than half a cent. The torrential monetary inflation made recovery even more difficult. As for the psychological damage, its importance can be guessed, but its depth cannot be measured.

SUGGESTIONS FOR FURTHER READING

Aron, Robert. *France Reborn: The History of the Liberation.* New York, 1964.

Bloch, Marc. *Strange Defeat.* New York, 1949, 1967.

Chapman, Guy. *Why France Fell: The Defeat of the French Army in 1940.* New York, 1969.

De Gaulle, Charles. *The Complete War Memoirs.* New York, 1964.

Funk, Arthur L. *Charles de Gaulle: The Crucial Years, 1943–1944.* Norman, Okla., 1959.

Horne, Alistair. *To Lose a Battle: France, 1940.* Boston, 1969.

Kedward, H. R. *Resistance in Vichy France.* Oxford, 1978.

Lacouture, Jean. *De Gaulle.* London, 1970.

Paxton, Robert O. *Vichy France: Old Guard and New Order.* New York, 1972.

———— and Michael Marrus. *Vichy and the Jews.* New York, 1981.

Sweets, John F. *The Politics of Resistance in France, 1940–1944: A History of the Mouvements Unis de la Résistance.* DeKalb, Ill., 1976.

Werth, Alexander. *France, 1940–1955.* New York, 1956.

Azéma, Jean-Pierre. *De Munich à la Libération, 1938–1944.* Paris, 1979.

Michel, Henri. *Histoire de la Résistance en France.* Paris, 1960.

————. *Histoire de la France libre.* Paris, 1972.

27
The Fourth Republic

The first misfortune of the Fourth Republic was that it did not immediately succeed the Third. If it had, concern would undoubtedly have been shown to establish the strong and stable executive power that had been all too clearly needed in previous years. But in the interim there had been the authoritarian, monarchical Vichy government. In reaction, a parliamentary form of government was created in which ministries were at the mercy of partisan wrangling. The second fundamental weakness of the constitution was that it was accepted by only a minority of the French. This weak regime had to face the perils of the postwar international turmoil and the crisis of decolonization, and was not up to the effort. It fell after only twelve years.

The Government of General de Gaulle. Everything pointed to General de Gaulle as the man to preside over France's recovery. He had given proof of his vision and his strength of character, the people had acclaimed him, all the resistance organizations had joined him, and finally, he was himself convinced that he had been called for this mission. When he formed his government early in September 1944, he included representatives of both the external and the internal resistance, two Communists among them. Not without some difficulty he managed to restore the authority of the state, end the anarchical power of the local liberation committees, and dissolve the popular militias dominated by Communists.

Summary executions (at least 10,000 and perhaps many more), personal vengeance, and arbitrary arrests were replaced by the methodical severity of courts of justice set up to judge those who had collaborated with the enemy. They handed down 35,000 verdicts, including 2,800 death sentences (767 of which were carried out). The most important cases were judged by a high court. Marshal Pétain, who had surrendered voluntarily, was condemned to death after a trial that aroused much passion, but De Gaulle commuted the sentence to life imprisonment. Laval was executed. A vast purge drove thousands of civil servants and officers from their posts and replaced them by people who could claim to be resistance fighters.

While actively pressing the war effort, De Gaulle's provisional government instituted a series of reforms that permanently changed the life of the nation: the nationalization of coal mines, airlines, the Renault automobile works, electric and gas companies, major insurance companies, and several large banks; the revival of free labor unions; the establishment of industrial committees in enterprises with more than 100 workers; the generalization and consolidation of social security; and the creation of a planning commission to modernize and guide the economy.

The Beginning of Political Reconstruction. The provisional government hastened to declare all the Vichy legislation null and void. Although it might have been logical simply to return to the institutions of the Third Republic, as some proposed, De Gaulle and the political forces that sprang from the resistance, and undoubtedly the majority of the French as well, wanted to start afresh.

Overruling the Consultative Assembly, De Gaulle decided to hold a referendum on France's future government, a procedure that was eminently suspect in the eyes of old republicans. No less repugnant to them was De Gaulle's decision to grant the vote to women.

When general elections were held on October 21, 1945, French men and women elected deputies and answered two questions: First, should the elected assembly draw up a new constitution? Ninety-six percent of the voters said yes. Second, should the assembly's powers be limited to a period of seven months and the draft constitution be submitted to a referendum? Sixty-two percent voted yes. The elections themselves, based on a system of proportional representation, revealed a sharp change in traditional alignments. The Communists, with 26 percent of the vote and 158 deputies, emerged as the largest party in France. Immediately behind them came the MRP (Mouvement Républicain

Populaire, or Popular Republican Movement), a new group grown out of a small prewar liberal Catholic party, with 23.3 percent of the vote and 152 deputies. The Socialists retained virtually the same share of the vote they had won in 1936, 23.4 percent. The Radicals, with 10.5 percent, and the other moderates, with 15.6 percent, were overwhelmed.

The three major parties readily agreed on November 13 to confirm General de Gaulle as head of government. But the bargaining over cabinet posts irritated the general, and his annoyance burst into the open when the Assembly sought to impose stricter control over his actions. Unwilling to make the compromises required by parliamentary governments, he suddenly resigned on January 20, 1946.

The Constitution of the Fourth Republic. The Assembly replaced De Gaulle with the presiding officer it had chosen a few weeks earlier, the Socialist Félix Gouin. The draft constitution that it adopted in April gave full power to a unicameral assembly and established a president of the Republic who would be only a figurehead. The plan, strongly supported by the Communists and publicly denounced by De Gaulle, was rejected by 53 percent of the voters in a referendum on May 5. The discredited Constituent Assembly had to dissolve, and another assembly was elected on June 2. This time the MRP, with 22.6 percent of the vote, clearly outdistanced the Communist Party, with 20.8 percent, and the Socialists, who won only 16.1 percent. The leadership of the government fell to the head of the MRP, Georges Bidault.

The first draft constitution was modified so that the all-powerful National Assembly, as it was now called, would be balanced by a second assembly (no longer called the Senate but the Council of the Republic), with 320 members chosen for six years by a complicated system of two-stage elections. This council would only deliver opinions, which the Assembly need not follow, and participate (as the old Senate had done) in the election of the president. He was elected for seven years and held most of the prerogatives given him in 1875, but not that of dissolving the Assembly. This right now belonged to the cabinet but was hedged with so many conditions that it was used only once in a dozen years.

This poor compromise was accepted on October 13 by 53 percent of the voters but by only a third of those who were eligible to vote. Out of weariness or perplexity, 32.4 percent of the voters stayed home. To these congenital weaknesses of the constitution practice soon added others that led the regime back to the rutted ways of the Third Republic. In particular, various procedures were used to evade the requirement of an absolute majority of votes to install a premier as well as to topple him. The requirement itself was eventually eliminated. Ministerial instability became even more common than under the Third Republic;

twenty-four governments rose and fell between December 1946 and May 1958. The absurd ritual of ministerial crises, which sometimes lasted several weeks, reinforced the impression that government was a kind of "shadow play," as De Gaulle styled it.

Party Politics. In the first National Assembly, elected on November 10, 1946, the Communist party again held the most seats, closely followed by the MRP. Wedged in between them, the smaller Socialist party was in a position to mediate. Thus from its ranks came the first president of the Fourth Republic, Vincent Auriol, a hearty and cautious southerner, and the first premier, Paul Ramadier. In January 1947 Ramadier formed his first government on the basis of "tripartism," which had been the rule since the end of 1945—a formula for representation from the three large parties, the MRP, the Socialists, and the Communists.

Early in May 1947 the Communists voted against the government in a debate on economic and social policy. Ramadier immediately expelled their representatives from his cabinet.

Driven into the opposition, the Communists, who controlled the CGT, unleashed a series of major strikes and paralyzed all public services. Socialist unionists protested against this political use of the right to strike and withdrew from the CGT to form a rival organization, the CGT-FO (Force Ouvrière, or Workers' Force).

At the same time another opposition arose on the right when General de Gaulle emerged from retirement to make a series of major political speeches. At Strasbourg on April 7, 1947, he launched the RPF (Rassemblement du Peuple Français, or Rally of the French People), intended to be a popular coalition to put an end to sterile political quarrels and reform the "ill-made" constitution. In the municipal elections of October, candidates who belonged to this organization won 40 percent of the vote. Thus faced with massive opposition from left and right, the governments of the Fourth Republic sought support from a "third force," a heterogeneous coalition of the MRP, Socialists, Radicals, and Anti-Gaullist conservatives. The premiers who succeeded Ramadier were chosen from these diverse parties.

The legislative elections of June 1951 further complicated the game. The RPF won 117 seats, largely at the expense of the MRP, which had 88, but four other parties—Communists, Socialists, Radicals, Independent Peasants—received about as many. In this "hexagonal chamber," government coalitions, which were more necessary and fragile than ever, usually brought to power men of the center right or the Radical party; beginning in March 1952, the Socialists joined the opposition. As for the RPF deputies, they eventually entered the "system" that their leader had condemned and voted with the government. Disappointed and angry, De Gaulle disavowed them and called a halt to his RPF

experiment. The deputies who had been elected under this label thereafter called themselves Social Republicans.

The banner of antiparliamentarism was then raised by a movement
launched by Pierre Poujade, basically a tax rebellion, which united
small shopkeepers and craftsmen whose way of life was threatened by
changes in the economy.

Two statesmen emerged from this legislature with lasting influence:
Antoine Pinay in 1952, the first premier of the Fourth Republic from
the right, the perfect incarnation of the average Frenchman enamored of
both order and freedom, the restorer and prudent manager of public
finance; and Pierre Mendès France, leader of the revived Radical Socialist party, a passionate and courageous intellectual who as premier in
1954–55 imposed a very personal style of government.

In December 1955 Premier Edgar Faure, for the only time in the
life of the Fourth Republic, exercised the power to dissolve the National Assembly. The third and last assembly of the regime was elected
in January 1956. The surprise of this election was the strength of the
Poujadist movement, which won fifty-two seats and 12.5 percent of the
vote, at the expense of the MRP, which received a weak 10.6 percent,
and of the Social Republicans, with 4 percent. The Republican Front,
a coalition of noncommunist leftist parties, seemed to have a slight advantage, for the president of the Republic, René Coty,[1] chose Guy
Mollet, secretary general of the Socialist party, to head the government.
His ministry, which was preoccupied by the Algerian problem, was the
longest-lived of the Fourth Republic—sixteen months, from January
1956 to May 1957. Then a drift to the right successively brought to power
two Radicals and a member of the MRP, Pierre Pflimlin, who was to
preside over the liquidation of the regime in May 1958.

The Demographic Revolution. In 1946 the number of live births in France,
which had been about 600,000 a year in the 1930s, scarcely more than
the number of deaths, suddenly jumped to 840,000. Not until 1975 did
births again fall below 800,000 yearly. The death rate dropped dramatically—from 15.6 per 1,000 inhabitants in 1935–37 to 13.1 in 1946–50
and 10.5 in the 1970s. Infant mortality plummeted, from 45.4 per 1,000
inhabitants in 1935–37 to less than 5 per 1,000 in the 1970s. France,
which had faced imminent depopulation in the 1930s, was growing
more rapidly than at any other time in the century and a half in which
population data had been recorded (see Table 5).

The causes of this demographic revolution are not clear, but among

---

1. His election on December 23, 1953, exemplified the incoherence of partisan divisions: he won
only after seven days and thirteen ballots. Wise, modest, and conciliatory, he was to win the
affection of the French.

the contributory factors were government encouragement of childbearing through family allowances, economic security resulting from high employment, and the institution in 1945 and 1946 of a comprehensive social security system that ensured expert medical care to all. The influence of universal medical care and of improved living standards was also evident in the increase in life expectancy—for men from 56 years in the 1930s to 69 years in 1974, and for women from 62 to 77 years. The exodus from rural to urban areas, which had slowed during the depression years of the 1930s and which the Vichy government had tried to reverse, vigorously resumed after the liberation. In 1946, 46.8 percent of the population were officially classified as rural; in 1962, 39.5 percent; and in 1975, only 27 percent. France was rapidly ceasing to be "a nation of peasants" and becoming a nation of city dwellers. In 1975 three French people in five lived in cities of 20,000 or more. The number of communes with populations in excess of 100,000 rose from 27 in 1936 to 42 in 1962, and to 48 in 1975.

Table 5. Population of France, 1936 – 79 (in millions)

YEAR	POPULATION
1936	41.9
1946	40.5
1951	42.0
1961	45.9
1971	51.0
1979	53.4

Economic Revolution. Little in France's situation in 1945 suggested that the country was about to enter upon a second industrial revolution that would shatter as many established habits and expectations as the first had done a century earlier. After the liberation the transportation system was in ruins, the northern and eastern industrial regions were devastated and looted, surviving plants were old and outworn, channels of finance were disrupted, the currency was in disarray, the old leadership—both political and business—discredited, and the political future uncertain. But even before the adoption of the new constitution, as we have seen, the provisional government created a planning commission, and under the leadership of Jean Monnet it prepared a plan for the reequipment, modernization, and revival of French industry and agriculture. The government of the Fourth Republic adopted the plan. Its application was facilitated by American financial and technical aid extended under the Marshall Plan and by a new spirit of enterprise and cooperation between government and business. By 1948 the index of industrial production reached the prewar level, and in the next ten years it rose at the extraordinary rate of 7 percent a year. In the Fourth Republic's short life, industrial productivity more than doubled.

In rural France governmental policy and a new enterprising generation combined to accomplish a revolution in both agricultural production and peasant life. Encouraged by government credit policies and educational and technological extension services, farmers adopted new techniques, mechanized operations, consolidated fields, formed cooperatives to market their products, and organized to press their interests with the government. The "Tractor Revolution" multiplied the number of tractors in use on French farms from 56,000 in 1946 to half a million in 1958 and to more than a million in 1966. By the mid-1960s grain yields per acre were double the prewar levels. The index of agricultural production, 61 in 1945, stood at 130 in 1961.

This expanding production was coming from fewer farms and fewer hands. The number of individual farms dropped from 2.4 million in 1942 to 1.9 million in 1953 and to 1.3 million in 1975. In the 1930s a third of the work force was employed in agriculture. By 1960 that proportion had dropped to one-fifth. In 1975 it was less than one-tenth.

The population generally shared the economy's growing productivity, though not equitably. The purchasing power of weekly wages in 1958 was 50 percent higher than it had been in 1949. By the late 1950s people were beginning to spend a smaller proportion of their growing incomes on necessities—food, clothing, and shelter—and more on culture and leisure, a trend that continued in the next two decades. Beginning in the 1950s, growing affluence and the baby boom were reflected in the rise in secondary school enrollments, from around 500,000 to nearly 1,300,000 in 1959–60, more than half of them women.

The Arts. The upheaval of war and the shattering of old values stimulated a "literature of engagement," of commitment to political action, represented especially by Albert Camus, Jean-Paul Sartre, and Simone de Beauvoir. Political engagement led many writers, artists, and scholars at least to flirt with communism, among them the poet Louis Aragon, the physicist Frédéric Joliot-Curie, and Pablo Picasso. After 1947 the hardening of the party line alienated most of them.

American influence, excluded during the occupation, revived as French intellectuals and writers discovered the novels of William Faulkner and Ernest Hemingway, new American films, and American writings in the social sciences.

The dislocations of the war and the isolation of the occupation years deprived Paris of its century-old position as the capital of modern art; primacy had passed to New York. In contrast with the preceding century, the postwar decades in Paris produced few great artists and no universally influential forms or styles.

European Policy. In the first years of the Fourth Republic, domestic policy was dominated largely by economic problems but also by the tense international situation—the "cold war" between the United States and its allies on the one hand and the Soviet bloc on the other. France, which was rebuilding its economy with Marshall Plan aid, could only align itself with the United States. In April 1949 it signed the North Atlantic Pact, a defensive alliance of West European states, Canada, and the United States. Fearful of becoming simply an American protectorate, France hoped to maintain some independence within the framework of a united Europe. The Council of Europe, established in May 1949 in cooperation with England, did no more than establish—in Strasbourg—a phantom assembly without power. Far more effective and daring was the effort begun in May 1950 by the French foreign minister, Robert Schuman, to carry out Jean Monnet's idea of a European Coal and Steel Community (ECSC), which laid the foundations for Franco-German reconciliation, the cornerstone of any European structure. Although England refused to join the organization, it operated well.

An unfortunate development, however, hindered European cooperation. The United States was drawn into war with North Korea in June 1950. Concerned with what it saw as worldwide Communist aggression against the "free world," it pressed its European allies to stockpile arms and sought to rearm West Germany. To avoid creating an independent German army, the French government proposed the creation of a European Defense Community (EDC), so that German contingents could be integrated with a European army. After difficult negotiations, France, Germany, and Italy signed a treaty to put the proposal into effect. But its ratification by the French National Assembly was opposed by both the Communists and the Gaullists, while the other parties (except the MRP) were divided. Eventually, on August 20, 1954, under Premier Mendès France, the EDC was killed by a procedural vote. This experience was remembered when the Common Market was created. For that undertaking the government began by having the Assembly adopt the principles worked out in preliminary negotiations. Only then did it sign the Treaty of Rome, on March 23, 1957, creating the European Economic Community (EEC).

Colonial Policy in Black Africa. The Constitution of 1946 proclaimed that "France and its overseas territories form a union based on equality of rights and duties, without distinction of race or religion." By virtue of this clause, the National Assembly and the Council of the Republic included deputies from the former colonies, while in each colony a territorial assembly exercised extensive powers in local budgetary and administrative matters. Thus political elites were formed, and they soon wanted to take the governments of their respective countries into their own hands. A "framework law" approved in 1957 providing for a governor appointed by Paris but aided by ministers elected by the territorial assemblies, whose powers were also increased, gave them some satisfaction.

The Indochina War. During World War II Indochina fell under the control of the Japanese, who encouraged anti-French nationalist movements. After the collapse of Japan, General Leclerc, sent by De Gaulle, reoccupied Cochin China and negotiated with Ho Chi Minh, leader of the Viet Minh, the principal nationalist movement, which was under Communist influence. Ho agreed to negotiate out of fear of the Chinese, who wanted to expand into Tonkin. He even traveled to France but failed to obtain the concessions he sought.

War became inevitable by the end of 1946, following tragic incidents provoked or aggravated by the inept local French authorities—the brutal bombardment of Haiphong and the massacre of Frenchmen in Hanoi in reprisal. The Viet Minh was effectively supported by the USSR and Communist China. The French military effort was difficult to sustain because of distance and lack of understanding and support from the French public, and it exhausted itself without result. Meanwhile, the successive governments in Paris, from which Britain and the United States more or less dissociated themselves, did not know how to extricate France from the quagmire honorably. Only the psychological shock of the disaster at Dien Bien Phu in May 1954, when an important French position was surrounded and overrun by the Viet Minh, changed the situation. The major powers were holding a conference in Geneva to discuss Asian affairs. There, through their mediation, Mendès France negotiated an agreement that enabled France to withdraw from Indochina and turn responsibility for helping South Vietnam to escape Communist domination over to the United States.

In this war, which lasted more than six years, France lost 92,000 dead and 3 trillion francs to no avail. Domestically the conflict had contributed to divided parties and a discredited regime.

North Africa. The French were all but unanimous in believing that Algeria—a French possession for more than a century, the home of a million Europeans, and administratively merged with France—was and should remain an integral part of the nation's territory. At most they conceded that they might have to grant Algeria a certain degree of administrative autonomy and hasten the civil equality promised to the Moslem population in March 1944. To this end an "organic statute" adopted on September 1, 1947, instituted an Algerian assembly composed of equal numbers of Frenchmen and Moslems and endowed with budgetary powers.

The situations of Tunisia and Morocco were different. There the protectorate system would normally have led to independence. But the security of French Algeria seemed to demand continued control over the countries that bordered it. It was therefore not until March 1956, after a series of confused developments and under the inevitable pressure of events and world opinion, that Morocco and Tunisia finally regained total independence.

Meanwhile, the Algerian nationalists had grown in strength. On November 1, 1954, they began an open rebellion in the mountainous province of Constantine. When rigorous repression did not succeed in restoring order, the French proclaimed a state of emergency in March 1955, placing the country under martial law. Whatever their composition and secret desire for peace, the governments in Paris were under double pressure—from the French in Algeria, who demanded protection, and from army officers, who were determined to make up for the humiliations they had suffered in Indochina. Socialist Guy Mollet nonetheless promised complete political equality for all inhabitants of Algeria and agreed in principle to negotiate with the leading rebel organization, the FLN (Front de Libération Nationale, or National Liberation Front)—but only after a cease-fire, a condition unacceptable to the FLN. Since the impasse was total, the war settled into a test of strength marked by atrocities on both sides, as is usual in civil wars.

The Suez Affair. The active propaganda that Arab countries were conducting against France and the support they were giving the rebels in Algeria drove Guy Mollet to strike at the man who appeared to lead the campaign, the Egyptian dictator Gamal Abdel Nasser. His decision on July 26, 1956, to nationalize the Suez Canal affected England's interests as much as those of France. Together they planned to intervene in force, in cooperation with Israel. The operation began on October 31 with an Israeli offensive against Egypt. On November 5 French and British paratroops landed at the canal. The enterprise was badly conducted, and it had attained only a few of its objectives when it was halted on November 6 under the combined threats of the United States and the USSR and the censure of the United Nations. Though Nasser had been defeated militarily, he won his point, while French influence in Egypt and the entire Near East suffered nearly total eclipse.

The Final Crisis of May 1958. As hopes faded in Algeria for a peace imposed by military means, the *pieds noirs* ("black feet"—Europeans who had settled in the country) and the military feared that France would seek a political solution out of sheer exhaustion—in other words, negotiations with the FLN that would result in independence. They believed that only a strong government could put the situation right. But how might the pitiful regime of the Fourth Republic be changed? In France itself many politicians, notably the president, René Coty, concluded that the constitution had to be revised.

A ministerial crisis that began on April 15, 1958, strikingly revealed the regime's impotence. Almost a month of futile discussions were necessary to select the man who would form the new government—Pierre Pflimlin. On May 13, the very day that he appeared before the Assembly for approval, a group of "activist" conspirators in Algeria took advantage of a large demonstration to seize the seat of government in Algiers and to form a "Committee of Public Safety." The army did not react. On the contrary, General Raoul Salan, commander of the French forces in Algeria, supported the Committee of Public Safety and issued an appeal to General de Gaulle. De Gaulle, in a brief communiqué to the press on May 15, declared, "I am ready to assume the powers of the Republic." Then he retired to his home at Colombey, in Lorraine, to await the collapse of the regime. The Assembly approved Pflimlin's ministry and voted a state of emergency. The government hastily agreed to constitutional revision in principle, but it was no longer sure of obedience by the security forces—police, gendarmes, and mobile riot squads (the CRS or Compagnie de Securité Républicaine). Rumors of preparations for a military putsch in France bred panic. On May 24 a Committee of Public Safety took power in Corsica. General de Gaulle broke his silence on May 27 to declare, "I have begun the regular process necessary for the establishment of a republican government capable of ensuring the unity and independence of the country." At the same time he condemned all illegal action. If he indeed sought power, he wanted to be invested with it legally, within the framework of existing institutions.

The next few days saw his scenario unfold as he conducted conversations with the politicians—their numbers grew daily—who discovered in him the only alternative to either a popular front or a military dictatorship.

On May 28 the Pflimlin government resigned, and the leftist parties organized a great "antifascist" demonstration.

On May 29 President Coty announced that he had called upon "the most illustrious of Frenchmen" to form a government and declared that he would himself resign if Parliament did not agree.

On May 31 the governing committee of the Socialist party, which as late as May 27 had declared itself unanimously opposed to De Gaulle, yielded to the pleas of Guy Mollet, who the day before had gone to Colombey to see the general. By a vote of 77 to 74, the committee accepted in principle the premiership of De Gaulle.

On June 1 the Assembly voted 329 to 224 to accept the government formed by De Gaulle. It included a good number of leaders of the major parties, from the right to the Socialists and some personal followers who were not members of Parliament.

On June 2 the Assembly granted De Gaulle's government full powers for six months and entrusted him (under certain conditions) with the task of drafting a new constitution.

The Fourth Republic was not yet officially buried, but it was already dead.

SUGGESTIONS FOR FURTHER READING

Fall, Bernard B. *Street without Joy: Indochina at War, 1946–1954*. 4th ed. Harrisburg, Pa., 1964.

Hoffmann, Stanley. *Decline or Renewal? France since the 1930s*. New York, 1974.

Horne, Alistair. *A Savage War of Peace: Algeria, 1954–1962*. New York, 1968.

Luethy, Herbert. *France against Herself*. New York, 1955.

Mortimer, Edward. *France and the Africans, 1944–1960*. New York, 1969.

Talbott, John E. *The War without a Name: France in Algeria, 1954–1962*. New York, 1978.

Williams, Philip M. *Crisis and Compromise: Politics in the Fourth Republic*. 3d ed. Hamden, Conn., 1964.

Wright, Gordon. *The Reshaping of French Democracy*. New York, 1948.

Chastenet, Jacques. *De Pétain à De Gaulle*. Paris, 1970.

Grossner, Alfred. *La IVe République et sa politique extérieure*. Paris, 1961.

28
The Fifth Republic

Returning to power after twelve years in retirement, General de Gaulle realized his ambition of giving the country institutions more in harmony with his ideas. Under his firm hand the crises associated with decolonization were overcome, and France recovered a stability, prestige, and prosperity that it had not known for a long time. But once the danger was past, the aloof power of the aging monarch became less tolerable. The student revolt of May 1968 revealed the depth of popular discontent. The astonishing recovery that De Gaulle then achieved was his last triumph; less than a year later he was forced to retire. After him Georges Pompidou and Valéry Giscard d'Estaing, each in his own way, sought to continue the best aspects of his legacy. In 1981 the French people ended the right's control of the Fifth Republic by electing a Socialist president, François Mitterrand, and a Socialist majority in the National Assembly.

I. THE RETURN TO ORDER

The Birth of the Fifth Republic. From Algiers to Paris, those who called upon or accepted General de Gaulle saw a strong government as the only means left of solving the Algerian problem. For him, however, the crisis was only an opportunity to gain power in order to rebuild the state along the lines he envisioned. Once that was done, he could think about the Algerian problem—and many others. On a brief visit to Algeria on June 4–7 he brought the army back in line and calmed tempers at least momentarily without dashing any hopes. Thus he won the time needed to prepare the new constitution.

The plan was drafted by a committee of experts led by Michel Debré and underwent a succession of reviews by the cabinet, a constitutional consultative committee, and the Council of State. Finally, in a ceremony, symbolically staged on September 4 (the anniversary of the proclamation of the Third Republic in 1870) on the Place de la République, General de Gaulle solemnly presented the text to the nation. The results of the referendum that was held on September 28 belied all predictions. Not since 1936 were there so few abstentions (only 15 percent), and the constitution was approved by 79.25 percent of those voting. To be sure—and no one failed to realize it—what was approved was less the document than the general.

The Constitution of 1958. The Constitution of the Fifth Republic attempted the difficult task of reconciling two principles: the separation of powers, with a strong independent executive, and the government's political responsibility to the Parliament. To do so it established a two-headed executive, consisting of a president and a premier. The president of the Republic was elected for seven years by an electoral college of some 80,000 officeholders—members of the two chambers and the general councils, and representatives of the municipalities. As guardian of the constitution and guarantor of the life of the state and national independence, he chooses the premier; on the premier's recommendation, he then names the other members of the government. In addition to the functions accorded the chief of state in the preceding constitution, he enjoys three prerogatives that emphasize his predominance:

- The right to dissolve the National Assembly.

- The right to appeal directly to the nation through a referendum.

- The right, in case of a crisis that threatens the institutions or security of the nation, to assume full powers (under Article 16).

The prime minister conducts policy and names all officials but is responsible to Parliament.

Parliament is composed of two houses—the National Assembly, elected by universal suffrage, and the Senate, elected as under the Third Republic (see p. 310). Laws must be passed by both houses, but in the event of a conflict, the final word belongs to the Assembly. Several new provisions limit the power of Parliament:

- Ministers may not be members of it.

- The duration of the two regular annual sessions is strictly limited.

- The constitution spells out the areas covered by laws; beyond those areas the government may act through decrees or regulations that have the force of law.

- The government may fix the agenda.

- A vote of censure adopted by an absolute majority is necessary to overthrow a government.

Alongside the two houses is a nine-member Constitutional Council, responsible for ensuring the proper functioning of institutions, and an Economic and Social Council, a purely consultative body.

The Functioning of the Regime. Elections for the first legislature of the new regime took place at the end of November 1958 according to a system imposed by De Gaulle: voting by single-member districts, in two rounds, with a majority needed to elect. The winner was the UNR (Union pour la Nouvelle République, or Union for the New Republic), a party formed several weeks earlier to support the general. With 26 percent of the final vote, it won 198 seats, while the Communists, victims of the method of balloting, won only 10 seats with 21 percent of the vote.

Not surprisingly, De Gaulle was elected president of the Republic by 78.5 percent of the votes in the elections at year's end. On January 8, 1959, René Coty formally turned over power to him, and on that same day the new president chose Michel Debré as premier.

The Senate was still to be elected. The solidly based influence of local elites brought it a larger proportion of politicians of the Fourth Republic hostile to De Gaulle. The Luxembourg Palace, home of the Senate, became the center of irritating but powerless grumbling against the government.

In the National Assembly there were always enough deputies of various persuasions to join with the solid UNR bloc to support the government against the Communist and Socialist left and a right-wing opposition, which repudiated De Gaulle's Algerian policy.

The divisive Algerian problem and the imperious personality of General de Gaulle—made Parliament's role even less important than the already restricted one allotted to it by the constitution. De Gaulle constantly went over its head to address the nation directly. Radio and television broadcasts, theatrical press conferences, and trips to the provinces were all splendid opportunities to exert that "magistracy of words" in which he displayed his talent for striking phrases. Then in February 1960, after army officers in Algiers staged another insurrection, the Debré government obtained special powers to legislate by decree in security matters for a year, and in April 1961 De Gaulle assumed full powers under Article 16 of the constitution.

Algerian Independence. Europeans in Algeria, the army, and most of the French in France agreed that the secession of Algeria was unacceptable. But no one in France, De Gaulle included, had a clear idea of the ultimate goal to aim for or the path to follow. And so the solution to the Algerian problem came only by halting steps on a long and painful road.

In October 1958 De Gaulle offered the rebels a cease-fire, to be followed by negotiations between France and representatives of the Algerian people. The leaders of the Algerian rebels, who had set themselves up as the Provisional Government of the Algerian Republic (the GPRA), refused the offer.

A second effort to open negotiations broke down in June 1960, when the Algerians refused to lay down their arms before negotiations began.

That summer and autumn French public opinion began to shift, especially among labor unions and intellectuals, who openly protested the cruelties of the French army in its repressive operations in Algeria. Sensing this change, De Gaulle ordered a referendum in France on the issue of Algerian self-determination. On January 8, 1961, 75.2 percent of those who voted (56 percent of those eligible) approved self-determination for Algeria in principle.

On April 11, 1961, De Gaulle publicly declared that France should consider granting full independence to its former colony. A few days later, on April 22, four retired generals—including two former commanders in chief of the French army in Algeria, Raoul Salan and Maurice Challe—seized control of Algiers with the support of several parachute battalions and imprisoned the government's representatives. Most army officers, however, remained neutral in the face of the enlisted men's hostility. On April 23 De Gaulle made a brief speech to the nation in which he scornfully denounced the "quartet of retired generals . . . supported by a group of fanatical officers" who were trying to lead France to disaster, and he ordered all soldiers to ignore the orders of "these heads of the mutiny." Two days later Challe and his supporters called off their coup. In France itself, however, a group of fanatical supporters of "French Algeria," the OAS (Organisation de l'Armée Secréte, or Secret Army Organization), began a campaign of terror against the people they held responsible for failure to support the army's efforts in Algeria. De Gaulle himself narrowly escaped an assassination attempt in September 1961.

All the same, secret negotiations with the GPRA were resumed. They continued, with frequent disagreements and interruptions, until March 1962, when the two parties signed the Evian Agreement. It recognized Algerian independence, provided for a cease-fire and for the formation of a provisional executive composed of Algerians and French to preside over the transition to independence, and established guarantees for French residents and the various French interests in Algeria.

In a referendum in France on April 8, 1962, 91 percent of the voters and 64.9 percent of those eligible approved the Evian Agreement. The OAS stepped up its terrorist activities in France and in Algeria. A massive flight of Europeans from Algeria began. The indifference that De Gaulle displayed toward this chaotic drama won him the enduring hatred of its victims.

On July 1, 1962, 99.7 percent of the voters in Algeria approved the Evian Agreement and Algerian independence. The last French troops left North Africa in June 1964.

The End of Decolonization. The constitution of 1958 established a "community" between France and its now fully autonomous former colonies, with its own executive council and a senate. Its president was by law the president of the French Republic. Those former colonies that wanted total independence would cease to belong to the community.

In August 1958 De Gaulle went in person to Madagascar and the other countries of French black Africa to present this partnership program. Except in Guinea, where the nationalist leader Sekou Touré openly declared his hostility, De Gaulle was given a warm and positive reception. In the referendum on the constitution in September 1958 all the colonies except Guinea gave an overwhelming yes vote, signifying their approval of the "community." Guinea voted 95 percent no, and Touré proclaimed its independence. France immediately terminated all administrative, economic, and technical assistance to the new state.

Elsewhere the leaders who were most eager to retain ties with France were pressured by young nationalists inspired by the examples of Vietnam and Algeria. De Gaulle understood the strength of nationalist feelings and convinced the French that those feelings must be satisfied if French interests were to be safeguarded. In May 1960 Parliament revised the constitution of 1958 to allow members of the community to become independent states while still remaining within the community. The remaining ties would take the form of bilateral agreements of cooperation. Almost all of the former colonies declared independence and signed such agreements during 1960 and 1961. Except for a few small and remote holdings, the second French colonial empire quietly ceased to exist.

II. THE HEIGHT OF THE REIGN

Constitutional Reform. The settlement of the Algerian problem, the successful completion of decolonization, economic recovery, and the declaration of a more proud and independent foreign policy all brought the moral authority of General de Gaulle to a peak.

Immediately after the triumphal referendum of April 8, 1962, on the Algerian settlement, he signaled his intention to exercise executive power still more fully by replacing Premier Debré with a nonparliamentarian, Georges Pompidou, his former chief of staff. On August 22 at Petit-Clamart he miraculously escaped a second assassination attempt by the OAS. The experience prompted him to hasten the reform he had been considering to complete his constitutional work—the election of the president of the Republic by universal suffrage. On September 12 the cabinet decided that this reform should be submitted to a referendum. Politicians immediately rose in an uproar and were supported by the Constitutional Council and the Council of State. The head of state, they said, was violating the constitution, which called for Parliament's approval of such a constitutional revision. The president of the Senate, Gaston Monnerville, even spoke of impeachment. In the National Assembly Paul Reynaud, last premier of the Third Republic, proposed a motion of censure, and it was carried. The ministry resigned, and De Gaulle dissolved the National Assembly. Thus the vote on the referendum would be followed by legislative elections.

The referendum, on October 28, 1962, approved De Gaulle's proposal by 62 percent of those voting but by only 46 percent of those eligible. This relatively poor showing encouraged the opposition to make a considerable effort in the elections but to no avail. After the two rounds of balloting on November 18 and 25, the UNR was returned with 233 deputies instead of 198, just short of a majority. With the support of independent republicans who called themselves Gaullists, the Pompidou ministry secured a majority that enabled it to govern without difficulty until the presidential election of December 1965.

The Presidential Election of 1965. The defeated parties looked hopefully to the presidential election scheduled for December 1965, and actively prepared for it by regrouping their forces. The Radicals, Socialists, and Communists supported the Socialist François Mitterrand in a campaign that made extensive use of television, for the first time in France. On the evening of the first round of voting, December 5, De Gaulle was incensed to learn that he had failed to secure a majority. He won 43.7 percent of the votes, with the rest going to five other candidates. The best placed of these candidates, François Mitterrand, got 32.2 percent. As the constitution provided, he and De Gaulle alone appeared on the second ballot.

But Mitterrand was unable to win the voters of the right and center who had first supported the other candidates. On December 19 he was clearly defeated by De Gaulle, who won 54.6 percent of the votes and now began a second seven-year term.

Foreign Policy. Foreign policy was General de Gaulle's "special preserve," and there he kept his own counsel and paid little attention to Parliament's. Restoring France's prestige, which had been so seriously compromised by the defeat of 1940 and then by the weaknesses of the Fourth Republic, giving it a role commensurate with its glorious past, and ensuring its independence vis-à-vis the two superpowers that together dominated the world—such seem to have been the aims of Gaullist policy. Because the strength behind that policy was not so great as its ambitions, it often relied on theatrical effects in the hope that if appearances were kept up, they would be accepted as reality.

Since France fell into the United States' zone of influence—a fact recognized by its Soviet rival—De Gaulle had to turn his policy of independence against American power. In March 1959 he withdrew the French Mediterranean fleet from the NATO command. Three months later he insisted that the United States remove its strategic bombers from France. In 1963 he withdrew French naval forces in the Atlantic and the English Channel from NATO. In 1966 he took all remaining French forces from its command and ordered the closing of all NATO bases on French soil. At that time the Strategic Headquarters of the Allied Powers in Europe (SHAPE) were transferred from France to Belgium. Despite obstacles raised by the Americans and against strong opposition within France itself, De Gaulle sought to provide France with an independent atomic strike force. The first French atomic bomb was detonated in the Sahara on February 13, 1960, and a vast and costly uranium-refining complex was established at Marcoule, in the Rhône Valley. In 1962 De Gaulle refused to take part in the Geneva disarmament conference, and in 1963 he declined to sign the U.S.-Soviet agreement suspending nuclear tests.

The general's European policy, too, was tinged with anti-Americanism. He wanted a "European Europe," not an "Atlantic" one. And so he sought to link himself more closely with Germany, thanks to the personal relations he had established with Chancellor Konrad Adenauer. To that end he vigorously pursued the development of the Common Market, obliging France's partners to resolve their differences on agricultural policy. For the same reasons he blocked Britain's entry into the Common Market; in his view, Britain would have been a Trojan horse for the United States.

The same tendencies appeared in relations with the rest of the world. If De Gaulle firmly supported the United States in such grave crises as the overnight construction of the Berlin Wall in 1961 and the U.S.–Soviet confrontation in October 1962 over the missiles installed in Cuba, he broke with the Western alliance by making overtures to the Soviet Union during his trip to Moscow in 1966, by establishing relations with Communist China in January 1964, by openly criticizing American military intervention in Vietnam, by condemning Israeli actions in 1967, and by encouraging French-Canadian separatism.

These striking displays of independence served the general's domestic policy by playing to the chauvinist feelings of Frenchmen of all parties, including the Communists, but they also alienated some of his early supporters, particularly among the MRP and Socialists, who could not forgive his denial of and contempt for the ideal of a politically integrated Europe.

Economic Progress. At the end of December 1958 De Gaulle put into effect a series of vigorous recovery measures drafted by the minister of finance, Antoine Pinay. He reduced the budget deficit by cutting subsidies to the nationalized railroad and coal companies, agriculture, and consumers; increased direct taxes; devalued the franc again (by 17.55 percent) and created a "heavy franc," equivalent to 100 old francs (worth 20.3 U.S. cents); ended some currency-exchange controls; and liberalized foreign trade.

These measures, bolstered by the return of political stability and the early benefits of the Common Market, at first brought spectacular results. From 1959 to 1963 the annual growth rate of the gross national product outstripped that of all European countries, the United States, and Canada. Foreign debt, which amounted to $1.7 billion in 1958, was completely paid off by the end of 1962. This growth, however, was accompanied by a dangerous inflation, so that in 1963 some stabilization measures—limited price and credit controls, tariff cuts, and reduction of state spending—were taken. They braked the inflation but also slowed economic growth and brought back an unfavorable balance of trade.

The rapid economic changes also brought social problems. Farmers, unable to keep up with the rapid strides of modernization, more than once unleashed violent demonstrations. Industrial workers had better protection in the form of a guaranteed minimum wage tied to the cost of living, but it seemed to them that the gap between the lowest and highest wages was growing. Particularly after 1963, unemployment began to reappear. The unrest rooted in these problems was one factor in the explosion of the spring of 1968.

A Consumer Society. The economy's soaring productivity in the late 1950s and 1960s increased disposable income and at the same time flooded the market with consumer goods. The combination brought on a revolution in French consumption habits, priorities, and expectations. By 1967, 65 percent of all households had automobiles, a luxury for the few in the 1930s and 1940s. Household appliances, formerly the exception, became the rule (see Table 6).

Table 6. Appliances per 100 French households, 1954 – 77

	1954	1960	1977
Refrigerator	7.5	26.3	92.9
Washing machine	8.4	24.6	75.0
Vacuum cleaner	14.0	8.8	56.3[a]
Radio	71.7	83.0	86.0[a]
Television	1.0	13.6	87.0
Record player	—	—	46.0[a]

[a]1972

Vacations with pay were lengthened from two weeks to three weeks in 1966 and to four weeks in 1969. The percentage of family budgets spent on culture and leisure rose by nearly 15 percent between 1958 and 1974.

Housing. As a result of the low levels of construction in the twenties, thirties, and forties and then of the postwar increase in population, France suffered from a severe housing shortage after the war. In the 1950s and 1960s government subsidies and the lifting of rent controls sparked a building boom that in three decades radically changed the appearance of French cities and their environs, and provided improved, if not ideal, housing for the burgeoning population. In the 1950s, 1,840,700 housing units were completed; in the 1960s, 3,733,200; and from 1970 through 1978, 4,338,100 more.

Beginning in 1959 the government was increasingly active in establishing metropolitan and regional plans and requiring local authorities and builders to conform to them. As part of the master plan for the Paris region, adopted in 1965, five entirely new towns, each with a projected population of 200,000 to 300,000, were built in the environs of Paris. Some older suburbs were rebuilt and expanded, the most conspicuous being La Défense, an office and apartment complex a few miles to the west of Paris, intended as a business and financial center that would relieve crowding in central Paris.

Education. The left's old dream of democratization of secondary education became a reality under the conservative Fifth Republic. Enrollments in secondary schools, public and private, rose from 1.2 million in 1958–59 to 4.9 million in 1977–78. The school-leaving age was raised from 14 to 16 years in 1959. The curriculum was made more uniform, especially in the initial grades, but in the *lycées* a wide range of specialized occupational training programs were offered as alternatives to the traditional academic curriculum. The number of students who graduated from a *lycée* rose from 41,433 in 1955 to 153,685 in 1975, but in the latter year 291,300 students earned diplomas or certificates in nontraditional programs.

Higher education, which before World War II had been the preserve of a tiny elite preparing for professional and academic careers, was inundated by students. In 1938–39 university enrollments stood at 79,-000, in 1958–59 at 192,000. In 1967–68, the year of the student revolt, there were 478,000 on the university rolls. Ten years later, despite the disillusionments of the late 1960s and 1970s, enrollments had climbed to 824,000. The new students came largely from the increasingly affluent middle class. Relatively few sons and daughters of working-class and peasant families attended the universities.

The sexual composition of higher education enrollments did change. In 1938 fewer than one-third of university students were women, in 1975 more than half. In the 1970s women broke the last barrier to the upper reaches of the education system when several young women were admitted into the Ecole Polytechnique, the most prestigious of the *grands écoles* that are the principal entry into the country's directing elite.

Campus Unrest. The swelling of university enrollments produced an excess of educated men and women. The majority of students had shunned the sciences and economics to follow the traditional literary curriculum, and now they had trouble finding jobs appropriate to their training. The consequent disillusionment was a contributing factor in the student revolt of 1968 and continuing student malaise in the 1970s.

The raising of the school-leaving age and the steep climb in secondary and higher education enrollments prolonged the school years of most French young people and created a large new group in French society—adolescents. Hitherto most French young people, the children of peasant and working-class families, left school at thirteen or fourteen and moved directly from childhood to adulthood. Under the Fifth Republic, students—and their contemporaries who congregated near the universities—became a distinct interim group, with their own distinctive dress, hair styles, language, music, and codes of behavior. In the 1960s they were in rebellion against the conventions of adult society, and the conflict between generations placed a new strain on traditional family solidarity and discipline.

III. THE DECLINE

The Crisis of 1968. The legislative elections of March 1967 reduced the Gaullist majority by forty seats and strengthened various parties of the left-wing opposition, which together won 48.9 percent of the vote. At the beginning of the session Premier Pompidou cut their attacks short by securing Parliament's approval to economic and social affairs by decree.

During the following months many signs pointed to the development of a malaise that was as widespread as its causes were varied and vague. Still, no one foresaw the extraordinary crisis that nearly wrecked the regime.

Its spark was student agitation that began at the University of Paris at Nanterre at the end of March 1968. On May 3 violence erupted at the Sorbonne in Paris. The contagion was spread by dramatic accounts of brutal police repression by radio commentators at the scene. Over the next few days the movement encompassed a good part of the academic community, including professors. Labor unions and some of the leftist parties were at first bewildered by this vast human outpouring, tinged with romanticism and anarchism, in which delirious words were more important than action. After May 13 the agitation spread to the working class. Wildcat strikes paralyzed the country. General de Gaulle cut short his official trip to Romania to make a televised address to the nation on May 24. Unlike all his earlier speeches in times of crisis, it had no effect. Georges Pompidou called a meeting of labor and employer representatives, and the so-called Grenelle agreement, signed on May 27, brought wage earners considerable benefits.

It was rejected by the workers, however, and the general strike continued. The CGT and the Communist party talked excitedly of a left-wing government headed by Mitterrand and Mendès France. The government's supporters were plunged into disarray when they learned on the morning of May 29 that De Gaulle had left the Elysée Palace for his residence at Colombey. Did this mean a power vacuum? In reality he went to Germany to make sure of the loyalty of the army commanders stationed there. Returning to Paris on May 20, he gave a short (three minutes) speech in which he denounced the Communist threat to the Republic and announced his decision to remain at his post, to retain his ministers, and to dissolve the Assembly. He called on his supporters to demonstrate their support. More than 500,000 people paraded down the Champs Elysées that evening, hailing the chief of state.

The situation changed completely. The parties of the left, which invoked democracy against personal government, could not refuse to accept the verdict of universal suffrage. Union organizations, hostile to the extreme left, got their members back to work. The rioting students, who came under increasing criticism, were finally dispersed. Perhaps the most extraordinary fact about these wild days was that while the clashes caused thousands of injuries, there were only two deaths.

The End of the Reign. The elections of June 23 and 30, 1968, showed the public's revulsion against the anarchy that the parties of the left seemed to favor. The UNR, the Gaullist party, which had now become the UDR (Union pour la Défense de la République, or Union for the Defense of the Republic), won 294 seats, giving it an absolute majority in the new Assembly, while votes for the left fell to 41 percent, and the number of Communist deputies fell from 73 to 34.

General de Gaulle demonstrated his willingness to make changes by replacing Georges Pompidou with Maurice Couve de Murville, who had faithfully served him as foreign minister since 1958. Edgar Faure, minister of national education, undertook to restructure the entire organization of higher education. Most important, the general sought to satisfy the desire of local and professional interests for a greater voice in the state's decision-making process.

De Gaulle submitted to a referendum a project for reform of the Senate and of the regional administration. The issues thus posed were not institutionally of the first importance, although De Gaulle thought the measures essential to the resolution of the nation's difficulties. Certainly he wanted a referendum as a means of forcing the French to take a clear stand on his role as the country's leader; the legislative elections of the preceding June were not enough. On April 10 he announced that he would resign if a majority repudiated the project. This was a dangerous gamble, for if the majority favored regional reform, they could not understand why the reform had to extend to the Senate, as the general demanded, apparently out of anger against that body. Moreover, his familiar threat of "chaos or me" had lost its credibility when Georges Pompidou let it be known that he was ready to succeed De Gaulle if necessary. In the referendum of April 27, 1969, the vote went 53.2 percent against De Gaulle. The next morning he issued a haughty two-line communiqué: "I am ceasing to exercise my functions as president of the republic. This decision takes effect today at noon."

Retiring to Colombey, he refrained from any public appearance, any public statement, and almost any human contact apart from his family. He occupied himself with editing his speeches and writing his memoirs. The nation and even the world mourned at his sudden death on November 9, 1970.

IV. AFTER DE GAULLE

The Pompidou Presidency. In the presidential election after De Gaulle's resignation, Georges Pompidou, the single candidate of the UDR and the right, faced four candidates of the divided left and one from the center, Alain Poher, president of the Senate, who had become known and respected in his role as interim head of state. The split in the left-wing vote made Poher the best-placed candidate to oppose Pompidou in the second round of voting. The disgruntled leftist voters abstained in large numbers (35.5 of the registered voters), and Pompidou was elected by a comfortable 57.5 percent majority of those voting.

This solid and skillful man from Auvergne had a reassuring presence and jovial manner. In all areas he subtly combined firmness and flexibilty, loyalty to Gaullism and accessibility to other political groups. The premier he selected, Jacques Chaban-Delmas, brought a new style to relations between the government and Parliament, which played a larger role in important decisions. The "new society" that he sought to create was to be based on cooperation and an appeal to responsibility. In this spirit Chaban-Delmas secured the adoption of a series of useful social reforms. For his part, Pompidou retained the major points of Gaullist foreign policy—independence vis-à-vis the superpowers, cooperation with the African countries—but gave them a less provocative, more amiable quality. His main innovation was to end France's opposition to Great Britain's entry into the Common Market. The decision certainly was not relished by the public, since in the referendum on the subject held on April 23, 1972, the favorable vote represented only 36.1 percent of the registered voters, compared to 17.2 percent negative. The others (46.7 percent) abstained or cast blank or invalid ballots.

This limited success strengthened the opposition's disenchantment with Chaban-Delmas' government. To the right and left of the majority there were increased signs of displeasure with the "UDR state," which was accused of using its power to benefit the "moneyed interests." President Pompidou decided to take action and replaced Chaban-Delmas with Pierre Messmer, a faithful, discreet, and incorruptible Gaullist. With him Pompidou won the legislative elections of March 1973. The majority parties narrowly beat a left-wing coalition, with 46.9 percent of the vote against 45.5 percent. But thanks to the system of majority voting, they won 278 deputies out of 490. The UDR could thus continue to govern.

The End of Pompidou. Contrary to expectations, the legislative elections were not followed by any changes either in the makeup of the government or in its policy. The president's only important initiative, a constitutional reform that would have reduced the presidential term from seven years to five, failed to secure the necessary three-fifths majority in the assemblies. Pompidou was forced to abandon it.

Early in 1974 the government seemed bewildered by the effects of the world economic recession—skyrocketing oil prices, industrial stagnation, inflation, rising unemployment. Public concern was heightened by persistent rumors about the president's health. These reports proved grimly accurate when he died suddenly on April 2, 1974. His death forced the parties to face a presidential election with no time to prepare either candidates or programs.

Presidential Election, 1974. No fewer than a dozen candidates ran in the elections of May 1974. This time the left seemed more united, thanks to the personality and leadership of the Socialist François Mitterrand, who arranged an alliance with the Communists and some Radicals under the banner of a "Common Program" of government, launched with consider-able fanfare. On the right, the UDR was divided. A majority supported Jacques Chaban-Delmas, while a small faction led by Jacques Chirac supported the candidate of the Independent Republicans, Valéry Giscard d'Estaing, who had served six years as De Gaulle's finance minister and now promised "change within continuity." He also had the support of the reform-minded centrists who had opposed the preceding govern-ment.

The first round gave a large advantage to Mitterrand, who won 43.4 percent of the votes, compared to Giscard d'Estaing's 33 percent. But in the second round Giscard d'Estaing attracted the votes of the right and center that had gone to other candidates. The duel between these two exceptionally able men excited French voters, and never before was the percentage of abstentions so low. Giscard d'Estaing won by a margin of less than 1 percent of the vote.

Valéry Giscard d'Estaing. Giscard d'Estaing's government was essentially a continuation of the Gaullist-Pompidolian regime. In foreign affairs it followed the same basic policies: support of the Common Market, close cooperation with West Germany, friendly relations with the United States but resistance to American pressures to support its anticommu-nist policies, and continued development of an independent nuclear strike force. Economic and cultural ties with former French colonies in Africa were assiduously nurtured. One change, motivated by concern over oil supplies, was the increasing favor shown to Arab oil-producing countries and growing coolness toward Israel.

The Economy. France was hard hit by OPEC's repeated escalations of oil prices in 1974 and after, and by the resulting dislocations in the world economy. The spectacular increase in France's gross national product in the 1950s and 1960s had been fueled largely by oil. In 1973 67 percent of the nation's energy requirements were filled by oil, almost all of it imported. The fivefold price increase created a drain on French foreign exchange and put a damper on the economy. In 1975 the index of industrial production declined for the first time since 1945, and unemployment rose to 900,000, 45 percent higher than in 1974. The retail price index was up 13 percent over the preceding year's level.

The Barre Plan. In 1976 Giscard d'Estaing named a new premier, Raymond Barre, an academic economist with no political affiliation, and charged him with revitalizing the economy. The guiding principles of Barre's plan were increased freedom for the private sector and government action to direct industry into the most advantageous areas. Price and wage controls were gradually removed. Subsidies to ailing companies were stopped. Industries no longer competitive in world markets, such as textiles and steel, had to retrench. High-technology industries in which France had competitive advantage, such as aerospace, electronics, telecommunications, and biotechnology, were encouraged by government subsidies and other support. To reduce dependence on foreign oil, the government speeded the construction of nuclear power plants, from which the country was then drawing less than 1 percent of its energy, and set a goal of obtaining 20 percent of its needs from that source by 1985.

The application of the Barre Plan involved many painful adjustments. Unemployment generally continued to increase.

Parliamentary Elections, 1978. The continuing economic troubles seemed to offer the leftist opposition parties their first real chance since the establishment of the Fifth Republic to win a majority in the National Assembly and challenge the Gaullist presidential regime. The Socialists and Communists were still tenuously linked on a common electoral program at the beginning of 1978, but the union broke up before the election. In the first round the four leading parties—Gaullists, Giscardians and their allies, Socialists, and Communists—ran about even, each winning around 21 percent of the vote.

In the second round the two leftist parties supported the same candidates, but the government parties won 50.5 percent of the votes and a comfortable majority of seats—154 Gaullists and 123 Giscardians.

Giscardian Twilight. After the election Giscard d'Estaing could pursue his policies with renewed assurance of public and parliamentary support. In foreign affairs he continued to follow an independent policy, reminding the United States in 1980 that "the Atlantic alliance is an alliance of *free* peoples." The government declined to join in American-proposed sanctions against the Soviet Union for its intervention in Afghanistan, maintained amicable relations with the Palestine Liberation Organization, and on occasion dispatched troops to Africa to support regimes friendly to French interests. At home the emergence of a "New Right," including neo-Nazi groups, posed problems. The government and the president himself were discredited by their tepid reaction to a wave of anti-Semitic violence in 1980, by scandals involving two former ministers, and by Giscard d'Estaing's haughty and evasive response to charges of personal financial irregularities.

The economy continued to be the central concern of most French citizens. By the time elections came round again, in 1981, the Barre Plan had produced mixed results. Dependence on foreign oil was down. Economic growth remained sluggish, though in 1980 it was above the European average. But the number of unemployed remained high—1.7 million in 1981, 7.6 percent of the work force. Inflation continued at an annual rate of about 12 percent.

Beginning in 1975 the annual number of live births dropped below 800,000 for the first time since World War II, and the birth rate fell below the level of 1935–37. Concern for the future of the family raised by the falling birth rate was heightened by a decline in the annual number of marriages and a 40 percent increase in the annual number of divorces between 1970 and 1977. Juvenile delinquency became a troublesome problem. The number of youths tried and convicted by the courts, which ranged from 17,000 to 24,000 annually in the mid-1960s, exceeded 33,000 in 1975 and 1976. The number of girls among these delinquents more than doubled.

V. TURN TO THE LEFT

Presidential Elections, 1981. Giscard d'Estaing's term expired in 1981, and he announced that he would seek reelection. This time he had rivals within his own conservative constituency. The most serious of them was Jacques Chirac, head of the Gaullist Rally for the Republic (Ralliement pour la République), Giscard's premier in 1974–76, and since 1977 mayor of Paris. On the left the Communists and Socialists were still divided. Mitterrand entered the race as the Socialist candidate, and Georges Marchais, head of the Communist party, was his party's candidate. Half a dozen other candidates, including two independent Gaullists and an ecologist, ran in the first round.

On the first ballot Giscard d'Estaing won 28 percent of the votes, Mitterrand 26 percent, Chirac 18 percent, and Marchais 15 percent, the Communist party's poorest showing since 1945. Before the second round the Central Committee of the Communist party asked Marchais's supporters to vote for Mitterrand on the second ballot. Chirac issued a lukewarm endorsement of Giscard d'Estaing. In the final vote Mitterrand received 51.7 percent of the vote, and on May 21, 1981, he took office as the first Socialist president of the Fifth Republic.

Parliamentary Elections, 1981. One of Mitterrand's first acts as president was to dissolve the National Assembly and call new elections. Conservatives, shaken by the outcome of the presidential election, hoped to put a brake on the new Socialist president by winning control of the Assembly, but they trailed on the first ballot and were swamped on the second. The Socialists won 269 seats, a majority of the 491-seat Assembly. The Gaullist representation dropped from 153 to 83 seats, and the Giscardians from 116 to 61. The government's majority, including the Communists (who lost almost half their seats) and the Radicals, numbered 333, more than 68 percent of the chamber. The combined right controlled only 155 seats.

Mitterrand. President Mitterrand named as his premier Pierre Mauroy, Socialist mayor of Lille. The ministry included four Communists in minor posts, the first Communist ministers since 1947.

The new government moved quickly to replace Barre's economic program of austerity and reliance on private initiative with expansionist and interventionist policies. It raised minimum wages and social security payments, reduced the length of the work-week, added a fifth week to paid vacations, levied a tax on fortunes of the rich, and nationalized five groups of industries and the remaining private banks. It greatly increased expenditures on industrial research and took measures to channel investment into high technology industries with promise of substantial growth. The preceding government's ambitious nuclear power program was continued with little change.

In its most revolutionary act the new regime reversed the nation's centuries-old process of political centralization. The office of prefect, created by Napoleon in 1801, on the model of the intendents of the monarchy, and scarcely changed in the subsequent 180 years, was abolished, and the ministry planned to transfer most of the prefect's powers to locally-elected assemblies and officials.

Mitterrand's government proved more eager than its predecessors to preserve NATO and to ensure continued American military presence in Europe. It condemned the Soviet invasion of Afghanistan and warned that France would not condone direct Soviet intervention in Poland. Established defense policies, including De Gaulle's independent nuclear striking force, were continued without significant change.

As France moves into the middle 1980s it approaches the thousandth anniversary of the establishment in 987 of its first and greatest ruling house—the Capetians—and the two hundredth anniversary of the outbreak of the French Revolution in 1789. The supremacy that the nation achieved under the Capetian Bourbons in the seventeenth century is now long passed and its revolutionary example long supplanted by those of more recent revolutions in Russia and China. But France's view of herself and of her place in the world is still shaped by that long and impressive past as well as by present economic and political realities. Moreover, though the France of Mitterrand does not equal the France of Louis XIV, it does rank among the half-dozen top industrial powers of the world, shares with West Germany the leadership of the powerful European Economic Community, and speaks with an influential voice in world affairs. For the present the responsibility for maintaining that position and preparing France for the twenty-first century rests with the Socialists, nominally in the nation's revolutionary tradition. The history recorded in this volume suggests, however, that they will not quickly change the face and form of France and that before long power will swing back to their opponents on the right with their somewhat different view of the appropriate means to keep France secure at home and respected in the world.

SUGGESTIONS FOR FURTHER READING

Ardagh, John. *The New French Revolution.* 2d ed. Harmondsworth, Eng., 1973.

————. *France in the 1980s.* Harmondsworth, Eng., 1982.

Brown, Bernard E. *Protest in Paris.* Morristown, N.J., 1974.

De Gaulle, Charles. *Memoirs of Hope: Renewal and Endeavor.* New York, 1971.

Flower, J. E., ed. *France Today: Introductory Studies.* 2d ed. London, 1973.

Frears, J. R. *France in the Giscard Presidency.* London, 1981.

Grosser, Alfred. *French Foreign Policy under De Gaulle.* Boston, 1967.

Kriegel, Annie. *The French Communists: Profile of a People.* Chicago, 1972.

Pickles, Dorothy. *The Fifth French Republic.* London, 1966.

Seale, Patrick, and Maureen McConville. *Red Flag/Black Flag: Revolution 1968.* New York, 1968.

Servan-Schreiber, Jean-Jacques. *The American Challenge.* New York, 1968.

Singer, Barnett. *Modern France: Mind, Politics, Society.* Seattle, 1981.

Wright, Gordon. *Rural Revolution in France.* Stanford, Calif., 1964.

Wylie, Lawrence. *Village in the Vaucluse*. 3d ed. Cambridge, Mass., 1974.

Debbasch, Charles. *La France de Pompidou*. Paris, 1974.

Touchard, Jean. *Gaullisme, 1940–1969*. Paris, 1978.

Viansson-Ponté, Pierre. *Histoire de la République Gaullienne*. 2 vols. Paris, 1970, 1971.

Some Histories of France

Cobban, Alfred. *A History of Modern France*. 3 vols. Harmondsworth, Eng., 1965.

Duby, Georges, and Robert Mandrou. *A History of French Civilization from the Year 1000 to the Present*. New York, 1964.

Gagnon, Paul A. *France since 1789*. Rev. ed. New York, 1972.

Guerard, Albert. *France: A Modern History*. Rev. ed. Ann Arbor, 1969.

Knapton, Ernest John. *France: An Interpretive History*. New York, 1971.

Wright, Gordon. *France in Modern Times*. 3d ed. New York, 1981.

Duby, Georges. *Histoire de la France rurale*. 3 vols. Paris, 1975–76.

Lavisse, Ernest, ed. *Histoire de France depuis les origines jusqu'à la Révolution*. 18 vols. Paris, 1906–11.

_____. *Histoire de France contemporaine depuis la Révolution jusqu'à la paix de 1919*. Paris, 1920–22.

Index